Selective Remembrances

Selective Remembrances

Archaeology in the Construction, Commemoration, and Consecration of National Pasts

EDITED BY PHILIP L. KOHL,
MARA KOZELSKY, AND
NACHMAN BEN-YEHUDA

The University of Chicago Press   Chicago and London

PHILIP L. KOHL is professor of anthropology and the Kathryn W. Davis Professor of Slavic Studies at Wellesley College and the author of *Central Asia: Paleolithic Beginnings to the Iron Age* and *The Making of Bronze Age Eurasia*. **MARA KOZELSKY** is assistant professor of history at the University of South Alabama. **NACHMAN BEN-YEHUDA** is professor of sociology at the Hebrew University in Jerusalem and the author of *Deviance and Moral Boundaries: Witchcraft, the Occult, Science Fiction, Deviant Sciences and Scientists*, published by the University of Chicago Press, and *Sacrificing Truth: Archaeology and the Myth of Masada*.

The University of Chicago Press, Chicago 60637
The University of Chicago Press, Ltd., London

Printed in the United States of America

16 15 14 13 12 11 10 09 08 07 1 2 3 4 5

ISBN-13: 978-0-226-45058-2 (cloth)
ISBN-13: 978-0-226-45059-9 (paper)
ISBN-10: 0-226-45058-9 (cloth)
ISBN-10: 0-226-45059-7 (paper)

Library of Congress Cataloging-in-Publication Data

Selective remembrances : archaeology in the construction, commemoration, and consecration of national pasts / edited by Philip L. Kohl, Mara Kozelsky, and Nachman Ben-Yehuda.
p. cm.
Includes bibliographical references and index.
ISBN-13: 978-0-226-45058-2 (cloth : alk. paper)
ISBN-10: 0-226-45058-9 (cloth : alk. paper)
ISBN-13: 978-0-226-45059-9 (pbk : alk. paper)
ISBN-10: 0-226-45059-7 (pbk : alk. paper) 1. Archaeology—Political aspects—Case studies. 2. Archaeology and state—Case studies. 3. Nationalism—Case studies. 4. Historiography—Political aspects—Case studies. 5. Memory—Political aspects—Case studies. I. Kohl, Philip L., 1946– II. Kozelsky, Mara. III. Ben-Yehuda, Nachman.
CC135.S45 2008
930.1—dc22 2007017497

⊗ The paper used in this publication meets the minimum requirements of the American National Standard for Information Sciences—Permanence of Paper for Printed Library Materials, ANSI Z39.48–1992.

ZAAL KIKODZE

This volume is dedicated to the memory of Zaal Kikodze. His entire life was devoted to the promotion of intercultural understanding and the resolution of ethnic and national conflicts. Zaliko distinguished justifiable national pride from xenophobic chauvinism. He recognized our interdependence on one another and our participation in an intricately interconnected past and shared future.

Contents

Introduction

Selective Remembrances: Archaeology in the Construction, Commemoration, and Consecration of National Pasts

PHILIP L. KOHL, MARA KOZELSKY, AND NACHMAN BEN-YEHUDA

The thirteen case studies presented here illustrate how reconstructions of the remote past from early historical or archaeological sources may be manipulated to support and validate contemporary political purposes, including specific nationalist agendas. This collection has been a long time in the making. It was conceived, a decade ago, as a sequel to the volume edited by Philip L. Kohl and Clare Fawcett in 1995, *Nationalism, Politics, and the Practice of Archaeology*, which focused on the relationship between nationalism and archaeology in Europe and East Asia. The new collection was intended to extend the discussion by treating the Near East and South Asia. But in the years since 1995, numerous studies have examined the political context in which archaeology and the reconstruction of the remote past are practiced.[1] Consequently, this second volume departs substantially from the first: it builds upon a wide body of scholarship for a more mature treatment of a subject that in 1995 had only begun to be investigated. Moreover, in the intervening years, nationalism itself has taken on new forms, and in response earlier assumptions have had to be expanded, revised, or even rethought. Many of the current essays therefore focus on subtler types that occupy hard-to-see places: for example, the nationalisms of stateless nations, amateur archaeologists, and religious organizations. This volume seeks to elaborate Kohl and Fawcett's original study, then, by incorporating new insights into nationalism, as well as probing the role of identity politics in the discipline of archaeology. Because the new avenues of exploration have arisen not in isolation but with a heritage reflected in the first volume, it may help to take a look at the accumulated wisdom that sits at the core of this collection.

In many ways, this volume claims the same agenda as *Nationalism, Politics, and the Practice of Archaeology*. That book explored the complex relationship between archaeologists and the state. Principally, the essays demonstrated that archaeology is a politicized discipline, for the state needs the remote past to justify its authority and to exercise its rule. Several of the essays revealed that governments, which often are the source of funds for archaeological research, may set the agenda of study and, in extreme cases, coerce scientists (indirectly or overtly) to abandon methodological rigor and professional objectivity. "Archaeology," Kohl and Fawcett concluded, "thus appears as a discipline almost in wait of state interference."[2]

The same emphasis on official nationalism and archaeological research appears in this collection as well; it remains a pressing problem in need of additional study. In this context, Nachman Ben-Yehuda, in chapter 8, "Excavating Masada: The Politics-Archaeology Connection at Work," carefully describes the way official Zionist platforms of the Israeli state influenced the archaeological record. The Masada myth, which recounts how a sect of Jews sacrificed their lives in an unsuccessful rebellion against Roman conquerors in AD 73, provided a stirring story to legitimate and bolster Israeli statehood. The story gave Israelis a historical narrative and glorified the exercise of zealotry in the Israeli cause. Ben-Yehuda shows how the prominent Israeli archaeologist and politician Yigael Yadin distorted and continuously reinterpreted archaeological evidence to emphasize and confirm Flavius Josephus's problematic historical account. Although this present collection is distinguished by its geographical focus on the Middle East, including particularly Israel and Palestine, the broader and essentially universal relationship between the practice of archaeology and state politics remains a principal subject of scrutiny throughout the volume.

Post-Soviet and Soviet-bloc states, where the futures of archaeology and national identity are still adjusting to new and unstable conditions, also continue as a subject of investigation in this volume. In 1994

Michael Ignatieff published a book entitled *Blood and Belonging: Journeys into the New Nationalism*, which revealed a shift in nationalism and its politics that was only then becoming evident and which by now has significantly unfurled. The catch phrase "the new nationalism" was partially an implicit reference to the fall of the Soviet Union and the crises of identity that blew like a furious storm across the dissolute empire. As has been much acknowledged, the fall of the Soviet Union changed the world. The political geography of much of Eurasia has been remapped, and many areas and new states have become embroiled in armed conflicts that typically are concerned with competing national claims over land. On a metaphysical level, the dream of an international communist revolution has dissipated, and ethnically defined nations, not internationalism, provided the over-reaching narrative of the late twentieth century. Because this process continues to be important, a second major theme of the current volume is how the Soviet disintegration has influenced the study of the remote past.

The authors of chapters 1–3 examine the question of the relationship between archaeology and nationalism in post-Soviet contexts in new ways. For one thing, nationalism looks different today than it did twelve years ago. In this sense the term *new nationalism* might also be applied to our more sophisticated understanding of what nationalism really is. The scholarship on nations and nationalism has undergone a rapid growth, becoming ever more nuanced and complex. Scholars have investigated official nationalisms, unofficial nationalisms, and imagined communities. Nationalism has been explored from the perspective of imperial rulers, as well as their subaltern subjects.[3] The literature on identity has simply exploded in the past two decades. Undoubtedly the reason is that nationalism does not seem to be going away; if anything, as shown by the crises in post-Soviet states, it is becoming an even stronger force in world politics. So we could say that one goal of this volume is to keep the study of archaeology in sync with the growing theoretical literature on nationalism. It simply remains true that as long as the world is divided into neatly demarcated nation-states, those states will continue to justify their existence by invoking their pasts—real or imagined.

Additionally, the collection expands into areas of the world that the first volume did not consider. Whereas *Nationalism, Politics, and the Practice of Archaeology* analyzed trends primarily in western Europe, the former Soviet Union, and East Asia, this book moves beyond those areas to investigate the nationalism-archaeology relationship in eastern Europe, the Caucasus, the Middle East, and South and Southeast Asia. In addition to the once-Soviet-dominated regions of Romania, Ukraine,

Crimea, Daghestan, and Azerbaijan, studies are included that focus on Iraq, Turkey, Iran, India, Thailand, Israel, and Palestine. One consequence of this grouping is to demonstrate that geography and history influence the ways in which politics plays itself out in archaeology. Areas of the world that have been directly under Western colonial rule or in its shadow and in opposition to Western imperialism use the remote past quite differently from those that do not share such experiences. Although some essays explore the direct role of the state in the archaeological enterprise, most examine more subtle nationalist influences upon archaeology, whether from subaltern or religious perspectives. Both of these latter kinds of influence are in many ways more difficult to isolate and study because, unlike state initiatives in archaeology, subaltern and religious influences often are not as organized, nor as policy-driven.

Archaeology from the "Other Side"

In contrast to the emphasis on state and imperial uses of the remote past in *Nationalism, Politics, and the Practice of Archaeology*, the present volume also contains several essays that explore archaeological research from a subaltern perspective, in which colonial or near-colonial subjects have imbued archaeological research with agendas of liberation. With its emphasis on archaeologists in the service of the state, the 1995 volume concentrated on "the *abuses* of the relationship between nationalist politics and archaeology, with the *problems* that may emerge."[4] Many of the essays there demonstrated how archaeologists, especially in colonial environments, used artifacts from the past to support the aims of the imperial state. In this volume, several authors pick up the other side of the dialogue to show how imperial subjects used archaeology to buttress their own authorities, pasts, cultural traditions, and claims to the land. Yet each of these studies demonstrates that even when used to support liberationist agendas, nationalism can distort disciplinary standards. Archaeology can perpetuate the dangerous cycle of ethnic rivalries.

Nearly every post-Soviet essay can be described as "archaeology from the other side," in which new states are struggling with an uncertain future and an uncertain identity in the wake of the collapsed imperial power. The fall of the Soviet Union resulted in the sprouting of new avenues of study throughout its former republics. Previously, as Victor Shnirelman noted in the 1995 volume, the Soviets repressed archaeological investigations that had a nationalist or regional component and instead advocated either an "internationalist" or, particularly from the mid-1930s on, a Russian chauvinist archaeology. Now states of the former Soviet Union are struggling to express and define their newly conceived national identities. Current archaeological research reflects the murkiness of this strange moment.

The challenges facing archaeologists in this region of former Soviet domination is perhaps most evident in Gheorghe Alexandru Niculescu's treatment of the state-approved *History of the Romanians*—an official history that traces this twentieth-century nation to its presumed beginnings before or as a consequence of its incorporation into the Roman Empire. The Romanian nation-state as it is constituted today actually has a much shorter national history. Early Romanian nationalism emerged following 1848 but did not congeal into a state free of Russian and Hungarian influence until the 1880s. From then on, it had a turbulent history and a mixed historical record until it fell under the shadow of the Soviet Union after World War II. Finally, with the collapse of the Soviet Union, Romania has been struggling to reestablish itself. In short, modern Romania has existed as an independent state for approximately sixty years before Soviet domination and for only fifteen years after its collapse. The official history of Romania, however, uses archaeological evidence to build an ancient ethnic pedigree and thus is at odds with reality. As the editors of *The History of the Romanians* compiled their book, they showed little regard for authorial integrity or for evidence and archaeological rigor. They rejected, moreover, any data or archaeologist presenting a contrary picture. In the absence of a long-standing independent archaeological tradition, Niculescu argues, Romanian scholarship is especially vulnerable to the nationalist demands of the state.

Whereas Niculescu takes a top-down view of nationalism and archaeology, Murtazali Gadjiev looks at the problem of amateur scholars conducting research in the former Soviet Republic of Azerbaijan and the Autonomous Republic of Daghestan, Russia. Here, where more than thirty different ethnic or national groups have been dominated since the mid-nineteenth century, under first Russian and then Soviet rule, newly established freedoms of ethnic expression and, in Azerbaijan, of political independence have a bittersweet taste. The reason is that several of the more prominent ethnic groups vie for recognition and authority in their new states. In his essay critiquing the supposedly newly discovered *Albanian Book*, Gadjiev reveals how this forged "ancient" manuscript captured Daghestan's inflamed nationalist imaginations in the mid-1990s. In Daghestan, much as in Romania, archaeology has become the currency of national identities seeking to establish themselves in the absence of Soviet power. Nationalist politicians backed by amateur scholars quickly accepted the *Albanian Book* at face value. In addition to providing a linguistic "code" unlocking the ancient, hitherto unreadable, Caucasian Albanian language, the *Albanian Book* actually credited the Lezgis, one of southern Daghestan's and northern Azerbaijan's principal ethnic groups, as heirs to the ancient Caucasian Albanian state. The book also enabled leading Lezgi nationalists to associate their people, quite fancifully, with other, even earlier ancient civilizations, such as the Sumerians. Eventually serious scholars, like Gadjiev, exposed the *Albanian Book* as a forgery, though not before the movement for an independent Lezgistan had become separatist in the middle 1990s.

Gadjiev also recounts the recent remarkable discovery by the Georgian scholar Z. Alexidze that the Caucasian Albanian language is directly ancestral to Udin, a northeast Caucasian language spoken today by eight thousand or so people living in a few isolated mountain villages in northwestern Azerbaijan and eastern Georgia. This determination seemed almost too good to be true, in the sense that it should have dampened or defused any contemporary political exploitation of ancient Albanian history. The few surviving Udins have no serious political aspirations to reclaim the Albanian empire as their national heritage. They simply hope to express their linguistic and very mixed cultural heritage, including the preservation of its distant Christian roots. Nevertheless, this seemingly innocuous discovery can be exploited by nationalist politicians, as may be happening today in Azerbaijan, where some scholars apparently embrace this Caucasian Albanian heritage to justify Azeri claims to the disputed territory of Nagorno-Karabagh.[5]

Mara Kozelsky's essay on Crimea also takes a nonstatist approach to nationalism and archaeology by investigating the influence of the Russian Orthodox Church on the study of the past. Like Daghestan, where numerous ethnic groups compete for authority and political primacy within their autonomous republic in the newly delineated Russian Federation, Crimea is torn between a mixed population and a troubled past. It is a territory contested by Russia and Ukraine and is also conceived as a homeland of the formerly dispersed population of Crimean Tatars, who are now returning after years of exile that began with their forced deportation in 1944 during Stalinist times. Currently, the population is divided almost equally between Russians and Ukrainians, aside from this significant and today newly returned and vocal Tatar minority. Each group seeks to stake a claim to the land. With potentially explosive ethnic rivalries and the sudden absence of Soviet-style archaeology, control over the remote past has become very important and is up for grabs. Kozelsky shows that one of the key contributors to the new archaeology is the Russian Orthodox Church. These church archaeologists in Crimea are heirs to a rich historical tradition of scholarship well grounded in method and evidence. Yet, in an environment that is balancing precariously between equally unstable national groups—Russians, Ukrainians, and Crimean Tatars—church archaeology is inextricably imbricated in the nationalist process. It ultimately contributes to building a Russian identity in an area historically populated by Crimean Tatars and currently attached to Ukraine, by purporting to demonstrate that Russians first converted to Christianity on the Crimean peninsula.

Victor Shnirelman's chapter on Russian and Ukrainian archaeology can also be considered in the context of a response to the collapse of official Soviet-sponsored archaeology. In Russia and Ukraine, much as in Daghestan, amateur scholars have captured the public's attention with a dangerous brand of pseudoscience. Here obsession with ethnic origins has emerged in alarming ways, with many nationalists tracing Russian and Ukrainian roots to the linguistically constituted Aryan race, a mythical construct with a sorry and continuing history of misappropriation (cf. also the essays by Shaw on Turkey and by Ratnagar on India that also discuss past and current misuses of the Aryan construct). Influenced by neo-Nazism in the most extreme cases, pseudoscientific peddlers of the past manipulate or simply make up archaeological data that connects the Slavs to this master race. It is no small irony, as Shnirelman notes, that Russian and Ukrainian Slavs, once reviled by Nazi Aryanism, now appropriate that identity for themselves. Shnirelman's contribution reflects forcefully the incipient danger of an unregulated archaeology conducted under politically unstable conditions.

Whereas Kozelsky demonstrates the continuing strength of Russian Orthodoxy and its church archaeology, Shnirelman documents the rise of new cults in Russia. The invention of new neo-pagan traditions and beliefs is a fascinating phenomenon that occurs on a broad scale throughout the former Soviet Union. The popularity of neo-pagan movements today is probably associated in some way with the pervasive loss of belief in Marxist ideology. The potential dangers of such movements wax and wane with the stability of the Russian state. Neofascist groups remain prevalent throughout Russia, although, ironically, their strength is somewhat dissipated by the increasingly influential and officially sanctioned authority of Russian Orthodoxy. This trend may contain its own inherent dangers, but, at its best, it should serve to marginalize the neo-pagan movements. If this is true, the pilgrims to Arkaim and similar sites may over time increasingly resemble other "lunatic fringes" who regularly visit ancient monuments, such as the Druidic worshippers who go to Stonehenge during the summer solstice. It is still too early, however, to conclude that such marginalization will occur. Xenophobic neo-pagan cults cannot yet be dismissed as innocuous curiosities in today's Russia.

The essays dealing with post-Soviet identity reflect how difficult it is for new archaeological traditions to form in very uncertain political environments in the wake of a collapsed imperial power; other essays in this volume take a longer look at the history of anticolonial archaeological traditions that emerged in response to direct imperial rule or under the threat of its domination. Such anticolonial uses of archaeology are illustrated by the Thai and Iraqi cases explored by Rasmi Shoocongdej and Magnus T. Bernhardsson, respectively. In Thailand, as Shoocongdej illustrates in her essay, "The Impact of Colonialism and Nationalism in the Archaeology of Thailand" (chapter 13), archaeology developed on a unique path that was partly in response to Western imperial uses of the discipline. Primarily, Shoocongdej argues that the Thai state was caught between expanding French and English empires. It maintained its independence through the careful nurturing of national unity, which was in part based on a rigorous study and appreciation of the newly recognized Thai cultural and historical heritage. Archaeology played a crucial role in this endeavor by providing evidence for a long-standing Thai state. However, most significantly, she notes that the concerted effort to present a strong and fluid Thai identity in the face of Western imperial power came at the expense of denying Thailand's diverse ethnic and cultural pasts.

As in Thailand, archaeology in Iraq constituted an important barrier between the West and the newly self-conscious Iraqis when the discipline was bound up in the fight against British encroachment. In the 1930s, for example, Iraqi archaeologists struggled not only to prevent artifacts from being funneled to London, but also to support the authority of a new state emerging from first Ottoman and then British rule. As Bernhardsson lucidly shows, archaeology contributed crucially to the formation of a national heritage in those early days of the Iraqi state. Later under Saddam Hussein, however, some archaeologists not only continued to plumb the material evidence to extol the glories of ancient Mesopotamia, but also tried to link the dictator directly to former illustrious rulers, such as Nebuchadnezzar and Hammurabi. While Hussein exercised complete control and directed the construction of a secular Iraqi state, the inevitable connection between archaeology and nationalism was distorted, if not caricatured, by such coerced nationalist fervor. Now with the removal of Hussein's regime and the future of Iraq as uncertain as that of many of the post-Soviet states, Iraqi archaeologists have to participate once again in redefining their nation and national identity.

As usual, Turkey represents a special case grounded in its history as a collapsed multiethnic imperial power on the periphery of the West that felt compelled after World War I to redefine itself as a secular, ethnically homogeneous nation. Wendy Shaw's essay, "The Rise of the Hittite Sun: A Deconstruction of Western Civilization from the Margin" (chapter 5), sensitively shows how the rewriting of Turkish history, which was officially sponsored by Ataturk himself in the early 1930s, mirrored and inverted the theories of Western origins that were then popular, including notably the civilizing roles attributed to superior Aryans. She insists that such historical contextualization is essential to understand the otherwise inexplicable, indeed untenable, features of the so-called Turkish Historical Thesis, which was then being elaborated to subsume and identify all the past and present peoples of Anatolia as Turks. However flawed, the Turkish historical narrative refuted or stood in opposition to often equally problematic Western hegemonic scholarly discourses. The incredibly rich archaeological remains from Turkey were invoked continuously to support this rewriting of the past, and some prehistoric finds, such as the Hittite sun, initially symbolized the emergent secular state, though their significance today is continuously reinterpreted and contested as Turkey continues to redefine itself. A serious consequence of this rewriting of the Turkish past, however, should not be overlooked: its denial or minimization of the ethnic diversity of the peoples still living within Turkey's borders. The widespread application of the Turkish label led inevitably to the classification of more than 10 million Kurds, who aspired to greater cultural autonomy in eastern Anatolia, as "mountain Turks," an epithet that fortunately has finally been removed.

Iran, too, was not colonized in the modern era, although both Britain and Russia, in particular, interfered in its internal affairs during the nineteenth and early twentieth centuries, and in 1953 the United States effectively repositioned the last shah on his throne after the CIA helped overthrow the elected leader of Iran, M. Mossadegh, who fatefully had tried to nationalize the Iranian oil industry.[6] Before the modern era, however, powerful Iranian rulers had periodically established centralized imperial states and exercised regional hegemony throughout much of the Near East; it was a proud legacy that extended back at least to the time of the formation of the Achaemenid Empire in the sixth century BC. Kamyar Abdi's chapter (chapter 7) reviews this distinctive and still resonant cultural tradition and properly historicizes the use of the term *Persian Gulf* for the critical body of water that separates Arabian and Iranian lands and through which much of the world's oil today is exported. Western readers may be surprised at the sensitivity of this issue for Arabs and Iranians alike and at the stereotypical depictions of the Other that the debate over the name of this body of water elicits. Like other symbols of state, names are important and carry political connotations that some wish to affirm and others prefer to deny. As Abdi reminds us, such serious "name games" are not unique to the politically volatile Near East; they are typically played after real or threatened political upheavals, such as the one that led to the long and acrimonious debate over what to call the former Yugoslav Republic of Macedonia.[7] Certainly foreign archaeologists trying to work in the Middle East should be conscious of the seriousness of this issue and recognize that the term *Persian Gulf* has historical priority and is internationally approved by the United Nations. It may be harsh, however, to condemn as opportunistic all archaeologists working in Arab countries who opt for *Arabian Gulf* or even the seemingly innocuous and neutral *Persian/Arabian Gulf* or simply *the Gulf*. Unlike *Macedonia*, which refers to a land controlled by an internationally recognized state, the *Persian Gulf* refers to an international body of water that is not and cannot be owned by any state.

The most passionate case of nationalist archaeology "from the other side," however, might very well come from Palestine. In "An Archaeology of Palestine: Mourning a Dream" (chapter 11), Ghada Ziadeh-Seely levies a harsh critique of Israeli archaeological practices. She recounts the nearly insurmountable obstacles that Palestinian archaeology has encountered since it was officially formed in the mid-1970s with the critical assistance of Albert Glock at Birzeit University. Despite increasing recognition and legitimacy accorded to Palestinian archaeologists, Israeli officials prohibited them from gaining access to sites and discouraged the study of Palestine's Ottoman and Islamic heritage. After the first intifada of 1987, archaeology became one more of many focal points of the Israeli-Palestinian conflict. Official repression of Palestinian archaeology increased as ancient sites became crucial to each group's claim to the land. The pressures between politics and archaeology reached a peak with the assassination of Glock, a murder that remains unsolved today.[8] Ziadeh-Seely presents the poignant narrative of Palestinian archaeology under Israeli repression and speculates about the discipline's future. Right now, she argues, Palestinian archaeology is at a crucial juncture. With greater Palestinian appreciation for Palestine's past, and with international recognition of Palestinian rights, archaeology is poised to make crucial contributions to the region's identity. However, Ziadeh-Seely argues that like other traditions of national scholarship, Palestine's liberationist archaeology faces numerous problems, including the challenge to maintain standards of objective inquiry and scientific integrity and not just to invert the practices of their adversaries.

Religion (Sacred and "Civil"), Archaeology, and Nationalism

One of the most significant new trends in the scholarship on nationalism has been the increasing acceptance of the influence of religion upon identity formation.[9] Traditional narratives, characterized by Ernest Gellner's and Benedict Anderson's classic works, have associated the rise of nationalism with the rise of modernity and secularism. New nation-states, according to this formulation, replaced old regime empires. In the ancient regime, scholars theorized, states commandeered loyalty from their subjects based on a duality of authority consisting of the monarch and the church. As the ancient regimes collapsed and nation-states took their place, the new states grounded their legitimacy in civic or ethnic ties rather than in religion. Scholars have recycled this narrative in various ways.

Those theories and many others share the assumption that nationalism is secular. Some even construe oppositional relationships between nationalism and religion. When scholars have attempted to treat religion in the context of nationalism at all, they usually depict it as a shadow issue; the often obvious presence of religion in nationalist discourse is dismissed as manipulative rhetoric devoid of any real content. This dismissal occurs partly because, despite their great variety, these theorists approach the study of nationalism from Western perspectives. As Peter Van Der Veer argues in *Religious Nationalism: Hindus and Muslims in India,* the failure to take religious nationalism seriously in the past stemmed from "the simple reason that both nationalism and its theory depend on a Western discourse of modernity," which relies upon a bipolar opposition of the "'religious' to the 'secular.'"[10] This opposition today seems simply inaccurate and fails to characterize nationalism in either Western or non-Western contexts. Pope Benedict XVI formerly opposed Turkey's bid to enter the European Union and insisted, "Europe was founded not on a geography, but on a common faith. We have to redefine what Europe is."[11] Many stridently patriotic Evangelical Christian movements in the United States have adopted a Crusader-like image of Islam and seem intent on demonstrating the inevitability of Samuel Huntington's thesis of a clash of civilizations.

Religious nationalism everywhere is on the rise. Ever since the Iranian revolution of 1979 that ushered in the Islamic Republic of Iran, it has become increasingly apparent that religion is a guiding component in how people conceive of nations. Whether President George W. Bush invokes religious sentimentality to manipulate supporters or whether he really believes it is relatively unimportant. What is important is that this discourse makes a connection with millions of voters who find common identity in a religious basis. Likewise, a recent headline in the *New York Times* expresses a theme that has reoccurred throughout the war in Iraq: "Insurgent Leader in Iraq Vows to Wage Protracted Holy War." Both Iraqis and Americans who respond to these headlines believe that Iraqi identity is indissolubly linked to Islam. Religion is not the principal danger here; rather, it is nationalism. However, when national identity is construed on religious bases, it is perhaps even more impenetrable and incapable of self-criticism than when articulated on an ethnic or any other secular platform.

The indisputable evidence that religion remains at the forefront of nationalist self-conceptions in the United States, the Middle East, and elsewhere prompts a rethinking of the nearly indissoluble connection between nation and religion. Many scholars, including Peter Van Der Veer, mentioned above, are giving the role of religion in politics more credence. It is no less imperative, therefore, that the literature on nationalism and archaeology be reassessed with this factor in mind. Scholars have noted in passing that biblical scholars—scholars who used archaeology to support biblical narratives—contributed significantly to the early formation of the discipline.[12] Yet few studies have investigated the continuing relationship between religion, identity, and archaeology closely and critically. And scholars have not investigated the role of theology in the discipline of archaeology. It is important to ask, How have differing faith-based epistemologies created national archaeological traditions? Even today a cursory glance at archaeology in Israel, India, Russia, Ukraine, and many other places in the world will tell us that Western assumptions about progress of a "secular" archaeological science have real limitations and may not even apply to or be relevant in some national traditions of archaeological research.

Using archaeology to construct meaningful memories, which can then serve in various processes of nation-building and molding individual identities, is linked, as the chapters in this book show, to ideologies. However, ideologies are not disconnected from religion, and some of the chapters examine this process within the context of religion and nationalism and take into account state-religion relationships. Indeed, the entire area referred to as biblical archaeology illustrates this point quite vividly.

Some countries have separated state from religion based on either a constitution (e.g., the United States) or tradition (e.g., the United Kingdom); others have not. The type of connection(s) between nationalism and religion is different depending on whether a state is theoretically secular or explicitly religious. For example, neither Israel nor Iran has separated state from religion, and very strong theocratic elements play a role in the nationalism these two states present. In both countries, it is legal and legitimate to rely on and use religious symbolism and language in public state-sponsored national ceremonies and rhetoric. There is less explicit use of religious symbolism in countries where a separation between religion and state supposedly exists (e.g., Turkey).

The concept of civil religion is relevant here and can be applied most forcefully to states that have theoretically separated state from religion. This concept has best been characterized as "any set of beliefs and rituals, related to the past, present, and/or future of a people ('nation') which are understood in some transcendental fashion."[13] The concept simply means that religious (transcendental) connotations, symbols, or values are attached to state national rituals, symbols (e.g., Independence Day, Memorial Day), and rhetoric. The "In God We Trust" motto on U.S. dollar bills is a good illustration of the state appropriation of religious ideas. It is as if the monetary system, secular by nature, gets a sacred value. Whether the concept of civil religion is at all applicable to states that have not separated state from religion is an open and interesting question.

The idea that the state (which in many cases is perceived as a secular entity) wants, demands, and practices religious ideas, concepts, and language apparently to charge its supposedly secular conduct with transcendental symbolism and power means that religion has played an important and complicated role in legitimating nationalism, even secular nationalism. Sacredness, which is basically a religious idea, and the experience of the holy are not sentiments that states are willing to forget or ignore, and states have tried to harness this powerful realm in their attempts to create and sustain nationalism and make it sacred. In this respect, the idea of a civil religion continues one of the oldest cultural roles of religion: creating and sustaining social and cultural cohesion, integration, and solidarity.

Archaeology, a scientific discipline that typically is perceived as an essentially secular enterprise, can be interpreted as serving a critical role in such a civil religion, where a state uses the discipline not only to legitimate the type of nationalism the state wants to crystallize (e.g., in Saddam's Iraq) but also to make nationalism appear sacred. In this

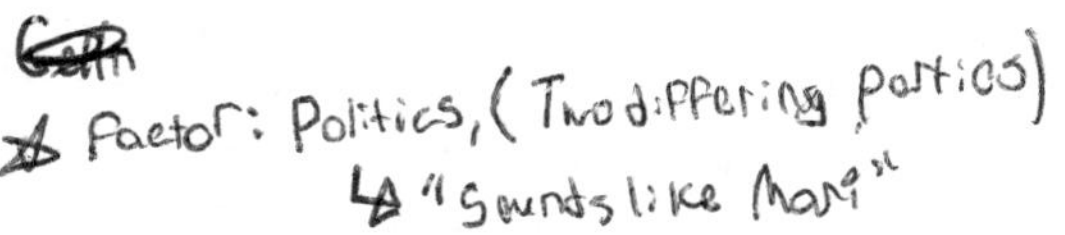

process archaeology may help to revive (or may create) the memory of ancient deities, languages, clothing, and artifacts and connect them directly to attempts to place contemporary expressions of nationalism in a context of a lengthy history that is informed and charged by the sacred. A time long past is thus connected to the present, bridging sometimes hundreds of years, in ways that appear to integrate what otherwise must have been very different cultures into one cultural context on national platforms that produce personal and national identities. Without archaeology and without acknowledging its service to a civil religion, such an effort either would not be possible or would be much more difficult.

The connection between nationalism, religion, and archaeology is featured in many chapters in this volume. Some of them take up this theme explicitly; others include it implicitly. Chapters on Israel, for example, inevitably deal with the influence of religious narratives on archaeological exploration. In contrast to Ben-Yehuda's work, which explores the role of a state-supported Zionist interpretation of the past, Michael Feige's essay (chapter 9) investigates how a fringe religious group influences archaeological study and interpretive outcomes. In particular, he explores Gush Emunim's stake in archaeological pursuits in Israel. "Gush Emunim," as Feige puts it, "is a fundamentalist religious group that believes that God gave the land of Israel to the Israelites and their descendants." Feige shows how the group appropriated the scientific discourse of archaeology to substantiate religious legends. Even after the state loosened its connection with archaeological support for Zionism, Gush Emunim perpetuated it. As amateur scholars and archaeologists, members conduct excavations on sites believed to have biblical significance and then use the sites as justification for Israeli settlements in the West Bank.

Similarly, Uzi Baram's "Appropriating the Past: Heritage, Tourism, and Archaeology in Israel" (chapter 10) examines this "second stage" of archaeology in Israel and argues that the state has loosened its interference in the reclamation of the past. Primarily, Baram argues, it has done so because the state is in a post-Zionist phase; Israel has achieved recognition and stability as a state and no longer needs the passionate legitimation of a strong Zionist movement. Moreover, the state has realized that archaeology has an economic role and has learned that a flexible "remote past" is one that will attract tourists. Ironically, however, even when archaeology has been liberated from the Zionist goals of the state, it is still inextricably bound up in religion. Tourist propaganda markets Jewish sites to Jews in the Diaspora and New Testament sites to Christians. Here, however, the relationship between archaeology, religion, and the past is influenced not only by the state, but by the tourist industry and consumers as well.

In other areas of the world, religious nationalism has an equally powerful, though at times not easily identifiable, role. If there is any area of the world where religious nationalism's use of the past is potentially even more politically explosive than in Israel and Palestine, it would be India, as exemplified by the rise of the Hindutva political movement. Shereen Ratnagar eloquently shows in chapter 12 how this movement has pursued its "politics of exclusion and of upper-caste dominance" by invoking a primordial past free of later alien intruders. Monuments built by the intruders, such as, famously, the Babur Mosque at Ayodhya, may be demolished on the pretext of obscuring or overlaying relics of this pristine past; major outbreaks of sectarian violence can result. Her focus in "The Aryan Homeland Debate in India" is on how a problematic linguistic construct, which was initially formulated under colonial rule in the nineteenth century and subsequently elaborated by generations of philologists, archaeologists, and physical anthropologists, has now been appropriated by scholars and politicians actively involved in the Hindutva movement to confirm a glorious Aryan past rooted in northern India that developed a unique indigenous civilization free of external interference. Ratnagar carefully reviews considerable linguistic and archaeological data that seriously question and even at times directly contradict this politically motivated, dangerously mythologized vision of ancient India.

Religious nationalism is not an isolated phenomenon, limited to a few seemingly odd or exceptionally religious areas like the Middle Eastern Holy Land or South Asia. Rather, as these essays demonstrate, the phenomenon is pervasive and repeatedly manifests itself in states that define themselves as secular. Will the Hittite sun or an Islamic minaret symbolize the capital of modern Turkey? The debate is current: the Islamist Welfare Party in Turkey rejects the use of the Hittite sun to represent the nation, for it speaks of a pre-Islamic past. Neo-pagan cults proliferate throughout the former Soviet Union; they may be dangerous in certain political contexts, but they should not be dismissed as crackpot expressions of social malaise or tricks imposed by hustling proselytizers of the past. Instead it must be recognized that an overarching and, for some, psychologically reassuring worldview has been abandoned and that people now try to find meaning in their lives by inventing new myths about themselves and their pasts. At the same time and for similar reasons, traditional religions reassert themselves. Russian Orthodoxy bears a continuing influence in archaeological scholarship in Russia and post-Soviet Ukraine today; Orthodox beliefs have significantly structured the pursuit of archaeological knowledge in Crimea, to the extent that archaeologists have formed a separate discipline called church archaeology that flourishes in the post-Soviet era. Here, as in Israel, religion and nationalism blend into an almost seamless discourse of identity that is hard to penetrate.

Just as Christianity has shaped archaeological study in parts of the world, so has Islam. Ziadeh-Seely notes that certain Islamic attitudes toward the distant past have in fact limited archaeological exploration. She writes: "To avoid embracing premonotheistic religions again, Islamic tradition encourages the detachment of Muslims from that distant past. The fear of reverting to idol worship is the likely reason for the Islamic discouragement of the faithful from admiring the material culture, particularly monuments that glorify individuals. This restriction extends even to the material remains of the Islamic era and includes the tombs of important early Islamic figures." She notes that in Palestine Islamic disdain for pre-Islamic history has led to a conceptualization of the past as an age of ignorance, *"Jahilliya,"* and therefore not worthy of study.

Nevertheless, in explicitly Islamic states, like today's Islamic Republic of Iran, the study of pre-Islamic national heritages flourishes along with the study of Islamic ones. The newly organized Iranian Cultural Heritage and Tourism Organization lovingly restores Sasanian, Parthian, and Achaemenid monuments as well as its revered Islamic sites; there is no contradiction now between the religious and the national or pre-Islamic heritages (fig. 1), although the period when the shah ruled is widely condemned, including his fascination with Iran's ancient past. Today both heritages are sources of justifiable pride and, as planned for the future in different political times, sources of substantial income from tourism.

Whether these authors take up religious nationalism as a deliberate theme or not, it is obvious that religion has contributed in crucial ways to the archaeological record. And while scholars have yet to theorize religious nationalism thoroughly, suffice it to say here that strong religious identities add a complicated layer to the study and uses of archaeology. As has become increasingly apparent, the Enlightenment vision of the Age of Reason, involving the separation of religion from rational thought and the absence of mystification from science, has not materialized. Most people (many archaeologists included) continue to view the world through a religious lens. Therefore, awareness of the role of nationalism in archaeology must be further elevated to thinking about *religious nationalism,* in which archaeological data is often manipulated in

Figure I.1. An Iranian advertisement for the Aria car from the *Iran Tribune*, a magazine formerly published in Teheran in English. The ad dates from about 1971. The locally produced Iranian automobile and the mythical horse-driven chariot both consciously evoke their glorious Aryan heritage, which, although claimed by many others, also continues to be a source of great pride for the Iranians. The unveiled and provocatively clad woman lounging over the hood of the car and tanning herself, however, is symbolic of all that was corrupt, commercial, decadent, and Western-influenced under the shah. Such an ad could not appear in today's Iran, even though the problematic association with the mythical Aryan past could be steadfastly maintained and extolled.

subconscious rather than conscious ways. When religion becomes part of the nationalist sentiment, the objective study of the past becomes much more challenging.

These comments are not intended to criticize the presence of religious interpretation and motivation in archaeological research, for many faith-inspired archaeologists have made substantial contributions to the field. Rather, we wish to promote greater reflection on the prevalence and consequences of religious nationalism in archaeological research. Like the study of nationalism and archaeology several years ago, religion has had a ubiquitous, yet undertheorized, presence in archaeological research. It is also important to note that, compared with official nationalism emanating from the state, which reflects a centralized ideology that is readily detectable in administrative agendas, policies, and so on, religious nationalism often operates in a more subtle and less easily situated fashion because it is often an inchoate, loosely organized phenomenon.

Memory and Commemoration: Linking the Past to the Present

The works presented here show conclusively that archaeology is a discipline that is highly susceptible to political pressures and influences (as demonstrated in the role of archaeologists in the Hindutva movement in India, for example). The key factor is that states need and use the remote past to justify their authority and exercise of rule. The "past," however, is quite complex.

A state must do everything possible to ensure that its citizens possess a consciousness of togetherness. States composed of multiple ethnic groups need to invest major efforts in doing so—or risk cultural and social disintegration. In the course of this task, states help bring into being, cultivate, and nurture personal and national identities that are construed to encompass common, significant, and shared elements. Such major cultural ingredients as a common language and a shared past and future have thus become major foci in attempts to create an impression and feeling of a unified and integrated culture. Evoking history and archaeology, or the past in general, constitutes a major cultural effort to create a consciousness of likeness among individuals. Attempts to integrate and even homogenize cultures are clearly aimed at creating and sustaining personal and collective identities, such as a Turkey composed exclusively of Turks or an Iraq conceived as Mesopotamian. Such identities are promoted by establishing boundaries that distinguish an "us" who share what is presented as a common past, and hence a common future as well, from "them," who do not. Consequently, the types of historical and archaeological sequences, events, facts, and interpretations that are selected, taught, and memorized in cultural transmissions are of crucial importance. These transmissions indeed serve as boundary markers and set the context in which personal and collective identities are established.

Fabricating and molding strong and unambiguous connections to a past (real, imaginary, or both) have—almost by definition—an ideological, moral, and political base. These activities define, for example, the true Romanians or identify modern Israelis with ancient Israelites. Without such a unifying base, creating boundaries will not be possible. When we examine archaeology (and history) in this context, we need to be aware that these disciplines have been involved in processes of socially constructing knowledge. As we try to understand how archaeologists (and historians) "make sense" of empirical knowledge, we need to pay careful attention to how they derive meaning from facts, how they interpret facts, and how they construct meaningful frames of explanation. Stuart L. Hills noted: "Increasingly in modern societies, scientists are contributing—sometimes unwittingly—to . . . ideological struggles. Interest groups use scientific research data as moral armaments to bolster their contention that there is only one possible view of the world—the real world. In so doing they mystify human behavior by imputing an inexorability and inevitability to those man-made social creations. . . . Scientists . . . have become our contemporary 'pawnbrokers of reality.'"[14]

It should thus come as no surprise that the creation of a consciousness of togetherness and shared identity, as well as that of collective memory, has become one of the hottest issues in the social sciences and humanities.[15] The reason is straightforward. Whatever past is out there somewhere—in texts, oral traditions, or archaeological sites—needs to be contextualized and interpreted. Freudian analytical theory argues that the most important key to deciphering human identity, personality, and the very essence of human consciousness is to be found in our individualistic, very early infancy/childhood years. A very similar idea seems to dominate our understanding about our cultural heritage. Times defined as "Golden Ages" are in strong demand, and if they cannot be found as such, they can be invented or manipulated creatively. Time and again analysts of cultures and societies are faced with myths of a glorious past, past traumas, or formative pasts that supposedly explain current events, cultures, and societies. More frequently than not, we encounter statements that imply that the key to understanding cultural identities (both of individuals and of collectives of individuals) is to be found in the past of these cultures. If one wants to unravel and decipher the riddle of cultures, one needs only to go back in time. Without the past, we are told, there is no present and no future. But what *is* the nature of the past? And how do we remember that past?

Basically, there seem to be two ways to answer the question of whether there was a "past." One of them assumes that there was such a past and we need to contrast its reality with its present construction. In other words, the assumption is that some events and processes did indeed take place, and the interesting and valid research pattern to follow is to examine how this past is interpreted, reconstructed, and presented in the present, and why it is dealt with thus. The other assumes that there was no "past," that the "past" has been constructed by manipulative and interested agents who create pasts to fit interests of the present (such as the quest for the mythical Aryan homeland in southern Russia, Ukraine, or northern India). It is possible, of course, to try to integrate these approaches, to use, for example, some old, weak, and flimsy evidence upon which a vigorous and compelling version of the past can be built. In the chapters of this book, as well as in Kohl and Fawcett's *Nationalism, Politics, and the Practice of Archaeology,* we can read how different agents in different nations selected different ways to relate to the past. We opt for the more realist position of assuming that some things happened in the past (and some things did not), though it has always been necessary to interpret or construct what happened. One should not abandon or compromise one's standards for reconstructing the past just to make it more politically palatable.

Recently a new subject for research on collective memory and commemoration has appeared: national/cultural trauma. A cultural trauma occurs "when members of a collective feel they have been subjected to a horrendous event that leaves inedible marks upon their group consciousness, marking their memories forever and changing their future identity in fundamental and irrevocable ways." Moreover, "trauma is not something naturally existing; it is something constructed by society."[16] While there are different approaches to analyzing cultural traumas, for such a real or constructed trauma to leave an effective impact, it must be remembered and commemorated. Tangible proofs for such a trauma—whether textual or physical/material or cultural—are always welcome and sought after by the moral entrepreneurs involved in the process of commemoration and remembering (e.g., in Romania and in Israel and Palestine).

This book presents superb, empirically detailed, and engaging historical narratives and evaluations. The chapters generally do not address directly the issue of the structuration of collective memory and the national identity that this memory is supposed to mold. However, we need to remember that collective memory is the social mechanism through which archaeology can, and does, help to construct national identities and shared feelings of a common cultural heritage geared to support nationalism.

The conceptual framework and terminologies used in the areas of social memory, commemoration, religious studies, and politics provide an external and powerful analytic framework that enables us to ask questions about this cross-cultural phenomenon in a global comparative perspective and suggest interpretive answers. The chapters of this book examine how such relatively new and complex nation-states as Iran, Iraq, Turkey, Russia, Ukraine, Azerbaijan, and the Autonomous Republic of Daghestan (or very new states such as Israel) try to link key elements in their present nationalisms to distant pasts—real or imaginary—by means of archaeological evidence. Using archaeology in this fashion enables states to develop nationalistic, unifying feelings; suspend disbelief; and legitimate and forge distinctive national identities. State-sponsored nationalistic-oriented events and processes are typically and intimately linked to religion, either directly or by a civil-religion connection, to create an ambience and semblance of sacredness in what otherwise could have been emotionless secular events and processes.

Archaeologists and the New Nationalism

Michael Ignatieff, mentioned at the beginning of this introduction, was not the first to announce a new nationalism. That term had been invoked by Theodore Roosevelt based on Herbert Croly's *The Promise of American Life*. In Roosevelt's usage, it advertised government-sponsored democratic programs designed to foster individualism and to counteract dehumanizing capitalist expansion. New nationalism resurfaced with an entirely different meaning after World War II, when scholars were prompted to rethink the optimism that had guided nationalism in the nineteenth century and the creation of states after World War I. Louis Snyder, for example, captured a common sentiment in 1968 with the release of his book *The New Nationalism*. Nationalism after World War II, he noted, looked dramatically different from its early modern and nineteenth-century antecedents, not to mention Theodore Roosevelt's program. Based in the liberating rhetoric that characterized the Glorious Revolution (1688), the American Revolution (1776), and the French

Revolution (1789), nationalism began in Western Europe as a movement for popular sovereignty; it cast off divine-right monarchy and hierarchical privilege. Opposition to monarchical rule and the press for popular representation later guided the unification of Italy, the unification of Germany, and the nationalist movements in eastern Europe.

The bloodbath of World War II exposed, however, the most dangerous consequences of nationalism and, in Snyder's words, "tamed" the movement. It ceased to be an attractive organizing force for most intellectuals in the West and instead heralded deadly ethnic rivalries and violent upheaval.[17] Similarly, Snyder's eminent predecessor Hans Kohn described the transformation of the nationalist ideal in World War II Germany as moving from a basis in human equality to "an exclusive, self-centered, closed society."[18] Snyder's and Kohn's observations continue to characterize our perceptions. Now in the West, we tend to regard newly emerging nationalist movements with suspicion. The wars that sprang up along the frayed borders of the Soviet Union and the disintegration of Yugoslavia seem to provide further salient evidence of nationalism's failure to bring peace and equality in its wake. And there is a political background for this perception, for as scholars in the West look upon national self-identification as anachronistic and dangerous, Europe unites into a supranational entity. The European Union marks a new stage of statehood and challenges the concept of nation. Thus, even as nationalism emerges in new places, it seems already archaic and outmoded in others.

Nationalism clearly is not yet finished in certain parts of the world. When the old empires broke up, national consciousness shifted to the once subject nations of the Middle East, Asia, and Africa. People are still emerging from the ruins of empires, still shaking the dust from their garments, and they remind us that striving to interpret the past has immediate utility. Often the formation of states is not slow, nor a final step in a gradual "progressive realization." Rather, as Aviel Roshwald has pointed out, states can emerge seemingly spontaneously "under extraordinary and short lived circumstances." He goes on to say that "if not grasped immediately, the opportunity to establish a separate polity may not recur for generations."[19] As is evident in Iraq and other rapidly formed states, the context of this newfound independence is often highly unstable. Old elites continually attempt to regain power; internal conflicts ensue over core political values; and government and society grapple over resources.[20] In light of these issues, archaeological and historical narratives have unavoidable, if not necessarily legitimate, roles in sorting out new identities, and sometimes they are put to use under urgent conditions.

Few people, if pressed, remain unsympathetic with the identity quest of newly recreated nations such as Afghanistan, whose best chance at achieving stability out of political and economic chaos may very well require a reusable inclusive past. For states or republics that have had official independent statehood for only short interludes at best before 1990, such as Romania and Ukraine, it is no wonder that the past is of monumental importance as they chart their future. Even in the European Union, which appears to have moved beyond national identities, historians and archaeologists are caught up, consciously or subconsciously, in the business of identity formation.[21] The past has purpose.

In 1983 Ernest Gellner asked the question, "Will nationalism continue to be a major force or a general political imperative in an age of advanced, perhaps even in some sense completed industrialism?"[22] Whether or not one rejects the connection between modernization and nationalism that is at the heart of Gellner's work, the issue of nationalism's future is one that occupies nearly everyone engaged in understanding the world today. Essentially, Gellner arrives at the lukewarm conclusion that although "the age of nationalism" will not come to an end, "the sharpness of nationalist conflict may be expected to diminish."[23] Twenty-five years later, the sharpness of conflict has not dulled. Nationalism appears to be formative and deadly, anachronistic, and possibly even—in certain cases—auspicious. In this continuum, archaeologists and historians have roles to play and choices to make. As critically self-aware intellectuals and researchers, we can confront the omnipresent danger of the political abuse of the remote past. We can also consciously construct the world around us to reflect the diversity that composes nation-states.

Politically responsible archaeologists and historians perform an essentially negative, though indispensable, role by pointing out that many accounts of the nationalists—religious or secular—are ambiguous, untenable, or dangerous and by showing how such accounts distort a record that can be alternatively and often more plausibly interpreted. This admittedly negative task is extremely important and should be performed whenever and wherever necessary. Archaeologists and historians working abroad, in particular, have the additional responsibility of being aware of the political contexts and consequences of their and their colleagues' works. Without such sensitive political awareness, the responsible scholar's own works can be easily misused or politically manipulated for dubious purposes.

Despite dismissals to the contrary,[24] we continue to believe that certain universal values and standards of evidence must be recognized and maintained. However much we may sympathize with an oppressed subaltern's interpretation of the past, we should maintain our disciplinary standards and resist dangerous revisionist or mythologized interpretations of the past based upon flimsy or unsupportable evidence. This point is eloquently made by Ghada Ziadeh-Seely when she decries the ultranationalist phase currently rampant in Palestinian archaeology; she notes that it makes no sense to criticize the practices of Israeli archaeology and then proceed to adopt its methods and its selective uses of the past. In other words, any interpretation of the past must be resisted or critically scrutinized if it excludes and impinges upon another's interests in the same or an overlapping past; when, in short, dangerous and morally questionable real-life consequences stem from such contestations.

Finally, there is also a positive political approach to interpreting archaeological evidence: namely, to demonstrate the continuous intercourse between cultures and peoples and the diffusion of ideas and technologies from one culture and people to another throughout prehistoric times and to insist that no single group was responsible for the constantly growing and shared history of cultural development. Such insistence on interconnections and borrowings does not contradict the archaeological record, as much as it accurately and demonstrably reflects it. The past, like the present, is a product of and belongs to all of us; consequently, it should be universally shared and appreciated.

Notes

Initially, Dr. Nandini Rao worked with P. L. Kohl in the solicitation of essays for a volume exploring the relationship between archaeology and nationalism in the Near East and South Asia, which was tentatively entitled *Peddling the Past*, a phrase that she had coined. Unfortunately, this original effort to collect essays, undertaken in the mid- to late 1990s, foundered and eventually was abandoned. Only earlier versions of Magnus Bernhardsson's contribution on Iraq and Rasmi Shoocongdej's essay on Thailand date from this initial attempt to assemble a collection. Dr. Rao's efforts helped lay the groundwork for the current volume, however, and are gratefully acknowledged. We would also like to thank Christopher Yarsawich for his outstanding assistance in the initial editing of Russian-language reference lists (and their translations) for this volume. We thank Northeastern University as well, for the Faculty Undergraduate Research Initiative that enabled us to compensate Chris for his contribution.

1. I. Hodder's 1991 study *Archaeological Theory in Europe: The Last Three Decades* (London: Routledge) was an early work that took into account the nationalist biases in intellectual archaeological history, as well as the relationship

between institutions and the nation. Some of the major studies that have appeared since 1995 are J. Atkinson, I. Banks, and J. O'Sullivan, eds., *Nationalism and Archaeology: Scottish Archaeological Forum* (Glasgow: Cruithne Press, 1996); M. Diaz-Andreu and T. C. Champion, eds., *Nationalism and Archaeology in Europe* (London: UCL Press, 1996); R. Bernbeck and S. Pollock, "Ayodhya, Archaeology, and Identity," *Current Anthropology* 37S (1996): S138–142; P. Graves-Brown, S. Jones, and C. Gamble, eds., *Cultural Identity and Archaeology: The Construction of European Communities* (London: Routledge, 1996); P. L. Kohl, "Nationalism and Archaeology: On the Constructions of Nations and the Reconstructions of the Remote Past," *Annual Review of Anthropology* 27 (1998): 223–246; L. Meskell, ed., *Archaeology under Fire: Nationalism, Politics, and Heritage in the Eastern Mediterranean and Middle East* (New York: Routledge, 1998); N. Abu el-Haj, *Facts on the Ground: Archaeological Practice and Territorial Self-Fashioning in Israeli Society* (Chicago: University of Chicago Press, 2001); P. F. Biehl, A. Gramsch, and A. Marciniak, eds., *Archäologien Europas: Geschichte, Methoden und Theorien* (Münster: Waxmann, 2002); L. Meskell, "The Intersections of Identity and Politics in Archaeology," *Annual Review of Anthropology* 31 (2002): 279–301; S. K. Brown and Y. Hamilakis, eds., *The Usable Past: Greek Metahistories* (Lanham, MD: Lexington Books, 2003); Y. Rowan and U. Baram, eds., *Marketing Heritage: Archaeology and the Consumption of the Past* (Walnut Creek, CA: Altamira Press, 2004); T. Guha-Thakurta, *Monuments, Objects, Histories: Institutions of Art in Colonial and Post-Colonial India* (New York: Columbia University Press, 2004); S. Fine, *Art and Judaism in the Greco-Roman World: Toward a New Jewish Archaeology* (Cambridge: Cambridge University Press, 2005); A. C. Gunter and S. R. Hauser, eds., *Ernst Herzfeld and the Development of Near Eastern Studies, 1900–1950* (Leiden, Netherlands: Brill Academic Publishers, 2005); S. Pollock and R. Bernbeck, *Archaeologies of the Middle East: Critical Perspectives* (Malden, MA: Blackwell, 2005).

2. P. L. Kohl and C. Fawcett, eds., *Nationalism, Politics, and the Practice of Archaeology* (Cambridge: Cambridge University Press, 1995), 8.
3. A representative, but by no means exhaustive, sample of important works in the study of nationalism since 1995 includes B. S. Cohn, *Colonialism and Its Forms of Knowledge: The British in India* (Princeton, NJ: Princeton University Press, 1996); F. Cooper and A. Stoler, eds., *Tensions of Empire: Colonial Culture in a Bourgeois World* (Berkeley: University of California Press, 1997); R. Beiner, ed., *Theorizing Nationalism* (Albany: State University of New York Press, 1999); R. S. Wortman, *Scenarios of Power: Myth and Ceremony in the Russian Monarchy*, 2 vols. (Princeton, NJ: Princeton University Press, 1999); J. Levy, *The Multiculturalism of Fear* (New York: Oxford University Press, 2000); A. Motyl, ed., *The Encyclopedia of Nationalism*, 2 vols. (Newark, NJ: Rutgers University Press, 2000); B. K. Axel, *The Nation's Tortured Body: Violence, Representation, and the Formation of a Sikh Diaspora* (Durham, NC: Duke

University Press, 2001); M. N. Layoun, *Wedded to the Land? Gender, Boundaries, and Nationalism in Crisis* (Durham, NC: Duke University Press, 2001); G. Pandey, *Remembering Partition: Violence, Nationalism, and History in India* (Cambridge: Cambridge University Press, 2001); O. Zimmer, *A Contested Nation: History, Memory, and Nationalism in Switzerland, 1761–1891* (Cambridge: Cambridge University Press, 2003).

4. Kohl and Fawcett, *Nationalism, Politics, and the Practice of Archaeology*, 5.
5. Some recent postings on the Internet have attempted to demonstrate that this disputed territory was part of Caucasian Albania, and not, as Armenian nationalists claim, part of ancient Armenia. Most likely, the claims of both sides are overstated and anachronistic: ancient kingdoms were, as a rule, multiethnic; and border areas, such as probably represented by today's Nagorno-Karabagh, often were incorporated into different political states at different times.
6. This story is well known; for a recent account, see the study by S. Kinzer, *All the Shah's Men: An American Coup and the Roots of Middle East Terror* (Hoboken, NJ: Wiley, 2003).
7. See the article by K. Brown, "Contests of Heritage and the Politics of Preservation in the Former Yugoslav Republic of Macedonia," in Meskell, *Archaeology under Fire*, 68–86.
8. See the recent study by E. Fox, *Sacred Geography: A Tale of Murder and Archaeology in the Holy Land* (New York: Henry Holt, 2001).
9. An early title in this subject is M. Juergensmeyer, *The New Cold War? Religious Nationalism Confronts the Secular State* (Berkeley: University of California Press, 1993); see also, by the same author, *Terror in the Mind of God: The Global Rise of Religious Violence* (Berkeley: University of California Press, 2003). The works pertaining to religion and terrorism or violence in general are too numerous to list here. Other select titles include C. Selengut, *Sacred Fury: Understanding Religious Violence* (Walnut Creek, CA: Rowman and Littlefield, 2003); and J. H. Ellens, ed., *The Destructive Power of Religion: Violence in Judaism, Christianity, and Islam* (Westport, CT: Praeger, 2004).
10. Peter Van Der Veer, *Religious Nationalism: Hindus and Muslims in India* (Berkeley: University of California Press, 1994), ix–x. For another nuanced discussion of the importance of religion for national identity (as well as a critique of historians' tendency to limit discussions of nationalism to the modern period), see A. Hastings, *The Construction of Nationhood: Ethnicity, Religion, and Nationalism* (Cambridge: Cambridge University Press, 1997); and A. D. Smith, *Myths and Memories of the Nation* (Oxford: Oxford University Press, 1999).
11. Cited in R. Spencer, "Pope Benedict XVI: Enemy of Jihad," *FrontPage Magazine*, April 20, 2005, www.frontpagemag.com/Articles/ReadArticle.asp?ID=17772.
12. Cf., for example, N. A. Silberman, *Digging for God and Country: Exploration, Archaeology, and the Secret Struggle for the Holy Land, 1799–1917* (New York: Doubleday, 1990); and Abu el-Haj, *Facts on the Ground*.

13. As defined by P. Hammond on p. 171 in his 1976 article "The Sociology of American Civil Religion: A Bibliographical Essay," *Sociological Analysis* 37 (2): 169–182; cf. also M. B. McGuire, *Religion: The Social Context* (Belmont, CA: Wadsworth, 1981), particularly 151–158; and R. N. Bellah, "Civil Religion in America," *Daedalus* 96 (1967): 1–21.
14. S. L. Hills, *Demystifying Social Deviance* (New York: McGraw-Hill, 1980), 44.
15. The literature and research in different disciplines on collective memory, commemoration, and remembering, on the individual and collective levels, and on the past can easily fill a small library. For some basic illustrative references, see R. Wagner-Pacifici and B. Schwartz, "The Vietnam Veterans Memorial: Commemorating a Difficult Past," *American Journal of Sociology* 97 (2) (1991): 376–420; B. Zelizer, "Reading the Past against the Grain: The Shape of Memory Studies," *Review and Criticism* (June 1995): 214–239; J. K. Olick and J. Robbins, "Social Memory Studies: From 'Collective Memory' to the Historical Sociology of Mnemonic Practices," *Annual Review of Sociology* 24 (1998): 105–140; J. K. Olick, "Collective Memory: The Two Cultures," *Sociological Theory* 17 (3) (1999): 333–348; U. Link, "Collective Memory, Psychology of," in *International Encyclopedia of the Social and Behavioral Sciences*, ed. N. J. Smelser and P. B. Baltes (Amsterdam: Elsevier, 2001), 2219–2223; L. Hubert and P. Arabie, "Collective Memory, Psychology of," in Smelser and Baltes, *International Encyclopedia*, 2223–2267; B. Schwartz, "Commemorative Objects," in Smelser and Baltes, *International Encyclopedia*, 2267–2272; B. Schwartz and H. Schuman, "History, Commemoration, and Belief: Abraham Lincoln in American Memory, 1945–2001," *American Sociological Review* 70 (2005): 183–203.
16. J. C. Alexander, R. Eyerman, B. Giesen, N. J. Smelser, and P. Sztompka, eds., *Cultural Trauma and Collective Identity* (Berkeley: University of California Press, 2004), 1–2.
17. L. L. Snyder, *The New Nationalism* (Ithaca, NY: Cornell University Press, 1968), 6–8. Snyder's book was reprinted by Transaction Publishers in 2003 with a new preface by J. D. Montgomery.
18. H. Kohn, "Nationalism," in *Dictionary of the History of Ideas*, ed. P. P. Wiener (New York: Scribner, 1974), 3:325–329.
19. A. Roshwald, *Ethnic Nationalism and the Unraveling of Empires: Central Europe, Russia, and the Middle East, 1914–1923* (London: Routledge, 2001), 3.
20. Ibid., 4.
21. M. Pluciennik, "Archaeology, Archaeologists, and 'Europe,'" *Antiquity* 72, no. 278 (Dec. 1998): 816–825.
22. E. Gellner, *Nations and Nationalism* (Ithaca, NY: Cornell University Press, 1983) 112.
23. Ibid., 121.
24. For some, the appeal to universal values necessarily is a hidden form of undesirable cosmopolitanism or even imperialism since it is impossible to decide whose values are universal (cf. A. T. Smith, "The End of the Essential

Archaeological Subject," *Archaeological Dialogues* 11 [1] [2004]: 1–35, particularly his reply on p. 28). This debate should not devolve into a quibble over words, but the denial of universal values or the view of them as somehow always tainted strikes us as the equivalent of questioning the concept of universal human rights, a concept that, however imperfectly and sporadically, has effected and continues to effect positive changes in human consciousness and actions throughout the world.

1

Russia and Eastern Europe

ONE

Russian Response

Archaeology, Russian Nationalism, and the "Arctic Homeland"

VICTOR A. SHNIRELMAN

Nowadays when politicians and the general public discuss Russia's future, one cannot help but notice the prevalence of archaeological, ethnological, and linguistic data within this discourse. Numerous amateur authors (various politicians, journalists, writers, unsuccessful engineers, biophysicists, and other admirers of "meta-history") do not hesitate to refer to prehistoric data as though they were the experts themselves. What are they searching for in the darkness of the ancient and the very ancient past? Why are they not satisfied with more recent historical evidence? Why do obscure images of legendary ancestors prove more attractive and desirable than famous historical heroes and activists?

In seeking answers to such questions, one has to start with the so-called Russian issue, or the crisis in Russian national identity following the collapse of the Soviet Union. In the past several years, a variety of theories about Russian identity have proliferated to fill the gaping void left by the evaporation of Soviet imperial identity. Most are propagated by Russian nationalists who appropriate the research of professional scholars and pose as scholars themselves. Predominantly, the most radical nationalists attempt to trace Russian identity to a mythic "Arctic Homeland" populated by Aryans. In this chapter I examine the works of those specialists who have contributed to the development of contemporary Russian nationalists' views of the most remote past in general and the Slavs' origins in particular. Mostly, however, I focus on the crucial role and disturbing appearance of the "Aryan idea" in Russian and Ukrainian nationalist myths.

Although I investigate the works of professional academics, I am primarily interested in amateur scholars, for their work constitutes the main source of the general public's knowledge of both the most remote past and the origins of the Slavs, especially of the Russians and the Ukrainians. Indeed, in contrast to scholarly literature, which is published in a small number of copies and is often very complicated, folk history reaches a much broader audience and is represented by fascinating popular series such as The True History of the Russian People. Moreover, it is this literature that provides to Russian and Ukrainian identity both a deep history and ancestors who, with a frightening rapidity, turn out to be "Aryans." Most professional scholars are unsympathetic toward this activity, treat it as a "distortion of academic knowledge," and either ignore the development or, in rare cases, demonstrate their irritation. By contrast, I regard myths of the most remote past as a very interesting and important field of research that illuminates crucial problems of concern for the general public and demonstrates an interesting shift in perceptions of Russian identity. An analysis of these myths clearly demonstrates contemporary radical Russian nationalists' fascination with the "Arctic homeland."

The Russians in Trouble

In order to understand "the Russian issue," one has to remember that the Russians still perceive themselves to be an imperial people: they dominated numerically in a huge multiethnic state, occupied almost all the key political positions, and, apart from the Mongolian interlude, have never been under any alien power. Russians suffered social and economic oppression but not ethnic or religious pressures. During perestroika many Russians advocated democratic human values, and it is on these grounds that they supported republican movements for sovereignty. In fact, the anti-Communist movements of the late 1980s, like the anti-monarchic movements of 1917, were directed against highly centralized political power, which had profited from a form of internal colonialism, that is, the appropriation of valuable resources from the periphery. In this respect, all these movements resembled contemporary movements for regional autonomy in some Western countries.

Yet, leaders of nationalist movements in the national federal and autonomous republics had their own view of current developments. Their goal was not democracy as such, but national liberation. It is at this point that their interests differed drastically from those of ethnic Russians. Nationalist and ethno-nationalist values and goals proved to be more sensitive and sounded more reasonable to the great bulk of non-Russians than the more abstract general democratic ideas.

After the disintegration of the Soviet Union in December 1991, ethno-nationalist values gained a victory in all non-Russian republics, not only in the newly established states but, to a certain extent, within the Russian Federation as well. As a result, more than 17 percent of ethnic Russians (25.3 million of 145.2 million) suddenly found themselves outside the Russian Federation and had to adapt to a new social and national environment. They were affected by this identity crisis as well because formerly most of them had been loyal mainly to the Soviet Union, rather than to the Russian Federation—let alone non-Russian republics (Laitin 1998).

The "Russian issue" developed as Russian identity suffered under the state-sponsored building of the "new Soviet people." In the Soviet era, traditional Russian folk culture was badly damaged by modernization, the merger of small villages in rural areas, and the mobilization of youth for participation in huge labor projects. The Russian Orthodox faith, which formerly functioned as a crucial basis of the Russian identity, was marginalized under the Soviet atheist regime; and by the end of the Soviet period, it was not perceived as an important aspect of Russian identity. It was even less productive to talk of any specific racial markers, because by the late twentieth century, the "Russian physical type" had become highly heterogeneous as a result of continuous colonization accompanied by numerous interethnic marriages, Christianization, and integration of the non-Russians into the Russian community. Finally, the collapse of the Soviet Union clearly demonstrated that the territory that Russians used to identify as their Motherland was a much more illusory category than they had thought. Of course, there were other concepts, such as the "Russian spirit" and the "Russian soul," but one could interpret them in various different ways, and the most thoughtful of the Russian nationalists were aware that it was hopeless to shape an identity on such a shaky basis.

A scholar from the provincial Russian city of Tambov resorted to metaphor to describe these problems: "In the totalitarian state . . . despite the seemingly 'privileged' place of Russia and the Russian nation [i.e., ethnic group], the Russian culture proved to be divorced from its ethnic and historical roots" (Malygina 1995: 39).[1] A radical St. Petersburg newspaper, *Za russkoe delo*, articulated this idea more sharply: "The Russian people were deprived of the nation status by their identification with, first, the 'Soviet people', then the 'Russian-speakers' and, finally, the 'Russian citizens' [*Rossiiane*]." An author of this article, a deputy of the Russian Parliament, complained that, first, "the Russian people have already forgotten their glorious past"; second, some antinational agents imposed a slave [*rabskuiu*] identity on them; and third, Russia would soon disappear as a nation-state (Chetvertkov 1996; cf. also Demin 1998: 25; Moleva 2000: 7; for this attitude and its basis in details, see Arutiunian 1992; Shnirelman and Komarova 1997). After the disintegration of the Soviet Union, ethnic Russians felt themselves orphans (Malygina 1995: 40). New borders transformed them into a northern people. Indeed, two-thirds of the state's territory was situated in the permafrost zone, which greatly affected Russia's new identity. At the same time, Russians became less sympathetic toward the political demands of the national republics and ethnic minorities attempting to upgrade their political status. The Russians treated this development as an inadmissible separatism threatening the disintegration of the Russian Federation itself.

The Russians were also psychologically injured by the loss of their "elder brother" image, which also had shaped their identity in earlier days. Under the late Soviet regime, the Russians were considered the civilizers, the bearers of the higher culture, obliged to generously share their material and intellectual resources with all the "backward" non-Russians. This myth was intentionally cultivated by Soviet authorities, especially from late Stalin times (i.e., the late 1930s) onward. Moreover, the Russians were depicted as a Messianic people, fated to lead humanity to a new, just civilization. The idea had practical political implications, rather than only intellectual ones, since at least some Soviet leaders were dreaming of the territorial enlargement of the country (see Chuev 1991: 14–17, 78, 100, 102–104). A struggle for unification of so-called divided peoples (such as the Ukrainians, the Byelorussians, and the like) under the Soviet umbrella was continuously emphasized by Soviet rhetoric as an excuse for expansionism. In the fall of 1991, the dissolution of the Soviet Union meant new nation-states for some peoples, many of whose lands had been unified with Russian help, while the Russians themselves suffered heavy losses, being divided by the new national borders. Needless to say, Russians in "the nearest abroad" took this new situation as an abominable injustice and blamed authorities of the Russian Federation for treason.

Early Indo-Europeans and Russian Nationalism

It is within this context that Russian nationalist myths began to proliferate. The Russian nationalists were very sensitive to all these developments and understandably anxious about the adverse economic, social, and cultural trends under the late Soviet regime. Yet, from the 1970s the radical Russian nationalist ideologists viewed all the Russian misfortunes as being caused by "Zionists," the West, and ethnic minorities (*inorodtsy*), as though these groups had attempted to undermine essential Russian values and strove for a territorial partition of Russia (Dunlop 1983; Yanov 1987). To meet the challenge of constructing a new identity, Russian nationalists attempt to impose an imperial identity upon ethnic Russians. First, they claim that the Russian people cannot revive without the help of a new imperial way of thinking, viewing empire as a symbol of restoration of the Russian state. They also depict ethnic Russians as an oppressed nation in their own state, arguing that "one should not continuously forget about the freedom of one's own nation while remembering the freedom of other nations" (Smolin 1999: 12).

Some of these ideologists turn to primordial myths of the most distant past to legitimate ethnic Russian interests and to prevent further disintegration of the state. They accuse Russian scholars of an "intentional falsification of history" in order to stir up fraternal peoples against each other. Thus, they claim that the "issue of the ancient past is a crucial issue of political strategy" (Krylov 1993: 2; see also Gusev 1996). They depict all Eurasia as a primordial homeland of the Slav-Russes, a people who, they claim, lived for thousands of years and made up the foundation of future human civilization. They push their theories of Russian identity back to the most remote past, representing prehistoric ancestors as prosperous and generous people, brave warriors and tireless conquerors, noble civilizers and builders of all the main ancient civilizations. Various authors locate the homeland of these ancestors either in the Eurasian steppes or in Asia Minor, and there are some who manage to derive them from the legendary Atlantis. Needless to say, they are amateur authors, whose activity began in popular journals and edited collections of science fiction (Shnirelman 1995; Shnirelman and Komarova 1997). Their fascinating fantasies are published in large printings and attract much bigger audiences than does academic literature. Moreover, all of these revisionist concepts have been viewed by less knowledgeable readers as an advancement of science and as concepts previously hidden by highly politicized Soviet academics for ideological reasons.

Many of the ideas in question were based less on academic knowledge and more on the forged *Book of Vles* compiled by Russian émigrés in the early 1950s (see Tvorogov 1990; Alekseev 1995; Shnirelman 1998a: 4–6). The *Book of Vles* told the story of pastoral ancestors who traveled extensively across the Eurasian steppes through the centuries, maintained their spiritual heritage, and defended their values in an endless struggle against treacherous enemies. Within this mythology an image of Slavic ancestors merged with the earliest Indo-Europeans, and the latter were called Aryans. The term that had been so discredited by the Nazis was thus restored. Furthermore, as the 1990s began, the myth in question was enriched with a new theme, that of the northern (Arctic) homeland, and the racial arguments acquired a seemingly sound footing. This chapter focuses on how, by whom, and why this myth was developed, and how it meets the needs of contemporary ethnic Russians' "national idea."

In order to legitimate these mythological views of the past, Russian nationalists refer to contemporary academic understandings of the earliest Indo-European developments. Over recent decades, three popular hypotheses about the Indo-European homeland and the proto-Indo-European expansion have emerged, based on linguistic and archaeological arguments. In the 1950s, the most popular idea was that of the Balkan, or Danubian, homeland developed by the linguist B. V. Gornung (1964) and continuously advocated by the prominent Soviet historian I. M. Diakonoff (1982; 1985; also see Trubachev 1991: 34–35, 65; 1997). In the 1960s–1970s, many Soviet archaeologists believed that the basic zone of settlement of the early Indo-Europeans was the steppe and forest-steppe of western Eurasia, from which location particular groups moved to other adjacent regions during the Bronze Age. Maria Gimbutas (1977; 1985) and her students advocated this hypothesis in the West. In the 1970s, two Soviet linguists, V. V. Ivanov and T. V. Gamkrelidze, challenged this view, claiming that the original homeland of the Indo-Europeans was in Asia Minor, not far from the region of the formation of the first civilizations of the Old World (Gamkrelidze and Ivanov 1984).

Among current myth-builders there is a diversity of theories about ancient Russian ethnic origins. Some refer to a Pontic-Caspian steppe homeland, others follow Ivanov and Gamkrelidze, and still others return to the idea of a Balkan homeland.[2] All of these homeland theories, however, are riddled with apparent anthropological and archaeological contradictions. Scholars distinguish between a western region of sedentary farmers (from the Balkans to the Dnieper River) and an eastern one of less-settled pastoralists as two completely different linguistic and cultural worlds. Thus, if they identified Indo-Europeans with the steppe cultures, they had to describe western farmers, including the Tripolye culture, as a quite different entity (part of so-called Old Europe, after Gimbutas).[3] Yet, if they pointed to the Balkan homeland, they faced the difficult problem of identifying linguistically and culturally the Chalcolithic and Bronze Age inhabitants of the steppe belt. The proponents of the Asia Minor homeland depicted an even more complex pattern; they constructed numerous early Indo-European migrations, including shifts both in culture and in ways of life. Discussions of the Indo-European homeland are still under way (Mallory 1989, 1997). The Russian nationalist authors are not greatly concerned with all this complexity. More often than not, they see no substantial difference between the Balkan cultures, including the Tripolye culture, and the steppe cultures. As previously mentioned, all Russian nationalists, regardless of their approach, identify Indo-Europeans with the Slav-Russes. As a rule, they also neglect all linguistic groups that are not Russian, including not only non-Indo-European groups but also non-Slavic Indo-European and even Slavic ones. Yet they make exceptions for the "black and yellow races" and for the Semites, who play a very special role in all these constructions (see, e.g., Krylov 1993; Gusev 1996; for analysis, see Shnirelman 1998b, 2001a).

From the late 1970s to the early 1980s, the imagined early migrations and deeds of the blond, blue-eyed Aryan civilizers, and especially the "Slav-Scythians," were very attractive for Russian writers (see, e.g., Zhukova 1981: 288; 1982; Nikitin 1985: 95–113; for an analysis, see Kaganskaya 1986; Shnirelman and Komarova 1997). One of them represented Achilles as a "Ross," a "Tauro-Scythian," and an heir of the great steppe tradition that spread high culture from Europe to China and India and, in particular, brought metallurgy to Greece. This author informed his readers that not only the Pelasgians (Russian nationalists believe that the Etruscan-Pelasgians were Slavs), but also the early inhabitants of Palestine, shared the same "ethnic roots" with the Slavs (Nikitin 1985; 1995: 289). This trend was combined with anti-Western and anti-American attitudes (see, e.g., Kobzev 1971; Medvedev 1983).

The groundwork for the current nationalist concept of an Arctic homeland for the Slavs was laid by the creative efforts of several scholars, pseudoscholars, and writers, including most notably the novelist Vladimir A. Chivilikhin (1928–1984; see his best-selling novel *Pamiat'* of 1982); Boris A. Rybakov (1908–2001), the former director of the Institute of Archaeology of the Soviet Academy of Sciences (for a selection of relevant articles, see Rybakov 1961, 1981, 1985, 1987, 1994, 1997a, 1997b); and the Soviet linguist Oleg N. Trubachev (1930–2002), who argued that the Slavs and the Indo-Aryans were closely related and established contacts with each other in the northern Pontic region (Trubachev 1976; 1977; 1979; 1984a; 1984b; 1991: 46–47, 68; 1992). For example, Rybakov did all he could to push Slavic roots far back into the Bronze Age, depicting their continuous development in eastern Europe during the course of several millennia and endowing the Slavs with a valor that could compete with the glory of the classical Greeks. Although he himself repeatedly fought against pseudohistories, his ideas today are popular among Russophile amateur historians (see, e.g., Gudz'-Markov 1997; Demin 1998: 112–135; Shambarov 1999: 147–196; Asov 1999).

Arctic Dreams

An Indologist, Natalia R. Guseva, was the key Soviet and post-Soviet advocate of the myth of the Arctic homeland. Her first idea was to discover and explain parallels in the spiritual worlds of the early Indo-Aryans and the early Slavs (Guseva 1977: 26). Although her book on Hinduism provided an extensive historiographic essay, she made no attempt to analyze various academic concepts that offered conflicting interpretations of the early Indo-European past and linguistic patterns in the Pontic region. For her, it was important to claim, rather than to prove, that before their migrations out of the steppe zone, the Indo-Aryans lived side-by-side with "proto-Slavs" from as early as the third millennium BC. Naturally, she referred extensively to O. N. Trubachev's ideas that maintained that the Slavs and the Indo-Europeans were closely related and lived alongside each other in the northern Pontic lands. She went much further, however, to extend the Slavic past far back into prehistory. And she put forward a hypothesis that some Indo-Aryan groups took part in the formation of a Slavic entity (Guseva 1977: 29–32; Akhudzha and Guseva 1982: 52). To put it another way, she "confirmed" the "Slavic Aryanism" by academic means. After that, one should not be surprised to hear her claim that Slavic ancestors proved to be steppe pastoralists. The correspondence between her view and the *Book of Vles* is obvious.

In the 1990s Guseva went even further and expressed affinity for the occult ideas of Helen P. Blavatsky (1831–1891), the views from which authors of the very early twentieth century, as well as Nazi ideologists (Herman Wirth, Alfred Rosenberg, and Julius Evola), derived the "light-bearing" Aryans from the northern Polar zone (Williams 1991: 140–144; Godwin 1993: 56–61). Yet, shyly refraining from mentioning Blavatsky's name, Guseva referred extensively to the obsolete teachings of Bal Gangadhar Tilak (1856–1920), a well-known leader of the Indian nationalist movement of the early twentieth century (see Godwin 1993: 11–13); he studied old Vedic literature and came to the conclusion that its cosmological ideas were formed in the Arctic regions (Guseva 1991a; 1991b; 1994a; 1995: 20–29; 2002: 4–6; 2003). As early as 1822, the French philosopher and esotericist Fabre d'Olivet introduced to European tradition a legend, rooted in the Vedic texts, of the Aryan or "Borean race" as having arrived from the North. He was the first to represent this as an arrival of the Hyperboreans from the imaginary Polar continent of Arctida, or Arctogäa (Godwin 1993: 44, 186–187; Stefanov 1995). Guseva either refuted or disregarded contemporary linguistic ideas about the genetic relationships among various Indo-European languages, as well as the probable territorial localizations of proto-Indo-Europeans and proto-Indo-Iranians. Instead, she herself compared accidental sets of Russian and Sanskrit words and argued that they were strikingly similar (Akhudzha and Guseva 1982: 51–53; Guseva 1992: 10–11; 1994b; 1994d: 38–40). It goes without saying that her approach ignored all the basic methods of modern linguistics.

Guseva's conclusions about a Polar civilization where the Aryans and the Slavs lived side-by-side and from which they later migrated together southward were fantastic as well (Guseva 1991b: 28; 1992: 10; 1994a; 1994d: 20–21, 32; 1995: 22–23, 30; 1997c: 31–32; 1998a). There are no archaeological confirmations of her claims (for the academic criticism of the "Polar hypothesis" and its mythological basis, see Bongard-Levin and Grantovsky 1983: 7–9; Kuklina 1985: 162–175, 180–185). In contrast, there is substantial archaeological data in favor of newcomers from the south settling northern regions in various periods (Shnirelman 1999a; cf. Ashikhmina 1997) and in favor of placing the location of the Indo-Iranian "homeland" probably somewhere between the southern Urals, northern Kazakhstan, and the forest-steppe zone of southern Siberia (Kuklina 1985: 185; Kuz'mina 1994; Matveev 1998). No less dubious is Guseva's persistent reasoning that the Scythians, though direct Aryan descendants, were so similar to the Slavs that the "classical Greek historians and geographers were unable to distinguish them" (Guseva 1991b: 27; 1994d: 12–13). It is well established that the Scythians were Iranian-speakers; that, in contrast to the Slavs, they were nomadic pastoralists; and that they were quite different culturally (Bongard-Levin and Grantovsky 1983: 22–25). Guseva uses all these tricks for one reason: to disprove the popular (in her own view) idea that "the Slavs came onto the surface of the Earth only during the first century AD" (Guseva 1995: 41). Yet, when specialists of Slavic ethnogenesis mention this date, what they refer to is the beginning of the disintegration of a common Slavic language. The separation of the Slavic linguistic communities from some more inclusive entity, perhaps the Baltic-Slavic one, obviously took place much earlier.

In the 1990s Guseva did her best to recruit specialists and to demonstrate that well-known scholars shared the idea of the Arctic homeland. Yet her attempts had very poor results. In 1994 she published a small collection of essays supported financially by the artist Ilya Glazunov. It was issued by the Vitiaz' Publishing House, which specialized in chauvinist literature under the direction of a well-known anti-Semite, Viktor I. Korchagin. Besides Guseva herself, the project involved her student S. V. Zharnikova; a leader of one of the Moscow neo-pagan groups, F. Razorenov; and two professional archaeologists: the aforementioned Rybakov and N. L. Chlenova, a specialist in south Siberia (Guseva 1994c). In 1998 Guseva managed to republish this collection in a volume put out by the Institute of Ethnology and Anthropology of the Russian Academy of Sciences (Guseva 1998a). Since no other Russian specialists were tempted by this dubious project, Guseva filled the vexing gap with extracts from Tilak's book *The Arctic Home in the Vedas*. In 2002 she managed to publish this obsolete book in Moscow with her own generous introduction (Tilak 2002).

At the same time, radical Russian nationalists combined Guseva's concept with Trubachev's ideas (Zhukov 1979; Skurlatov 1987: 214; Avdeev 1994: 49; Yeliseev 1994; Torop 1996: 36). Today Guseva has a number of amateur followers who reproduce her fantasies of a mild climate in the Arctic in the very late Pleistocene and early Holocene eras, of the proto-Indo-European ("Aryan") community formation there, and of the southward migration of its daughter branches under conditions of climatic deterioration, that is, as the Arctic region grew cold (see, e.g., Belov 1992: 11, 47; Asov 1994; 1998a: 174–183; 1999; Antonenko 1994: 19, 24–25, 31–37, 78; Konstantinovsky 1994; Kritov 1995; Demin 1996b, 1997a, 1997d, 1999b, 2000b; Alekseenko 1997a, 1997b; Kandyba 1997; Demin 1998: 34; Rechkin 1998: 15; Globa 1999; *Giperboreiskaia vera* 1999; Shambarov 1999; Kalashnikov 2000: 6; Larionov 2000: 22–23; Guk 2000: 144–147; Morozov 2000; Novgorodov 2000). The most prominent of them was Guseva's student S. V. Zharnikova, an ethnographer from the provincial city of Vologda. From the late 1980s, Zharnikova continuously advocated the idea of close relations between Slavic languages and Sanskrit and claimed that the proto-Indo-European homeland was situated in the Russian North, that is, the northern part of European Russia (Zharnikova 1986, 1988, 1989, 1994: 66–73). Zharnikova was especially fascinated with the swastika and did her best to confirm that both Indo-Iranians and Slavs inherited this symbol from the Tripolye culture, if not from Upper Paleolithic ancestors (Zharnikova 1985). Her ideas as well as Tilak's hypothesis were picked up and disseminated by journalists through such respected media outlets as *Izvestiia* (Filippov 1996) and the all-Russian NTV channel (*News*, September 9, 1996). They made their way even to the Moscow academic journal *Etnograficheskoe obozrenie* (Zharnikova 2000).

Guseva's and Zharnikova's ideas were gratefully advertised by a Russian fascist newspaper, *Russky Revansh* (1996, no. 1, p. 8); a racist magazine, *Nasledie predkov* (1995, no. 1, p. 14); and a respectable Russian patriotic magazine, *Nash Sovremennik* (1996, no. 5, p. 224). At the same time, Guseva's article about the Arctic homeland was published by the journal *Rodina,* established by the government of the Russian Federation and the administration of the Russian president. In this article Guseva recognized that there were different hypotheses about the proto-Indo-European homeland. Yet she claimed that her theory was well established and shared by most scholars (Guseva 1997a). At the very end of 1997, *Rodina* introduced a new section titled "Homeland." It was headed by Sergei Antonenko, then a postgraduate student at the Institute of Russian History of the Russian Academy of Sciences. He was already known as an admirer of esotericism, the occult, and the Aryan myth. Under his initiative, articles with a spirit of the "northern Aryan Homeland" and related mysticism were published in this section (see, e.g., Troshin 1997; Sviatopolk-Chetvertynskii 1998). Since then *Rodina* has distanced itself from this ill-conceived theory.

Zharnikova was also supported by academician Rybakov, who wrote positive reviews of her articles about the Polar homeland of the Aryans and the Slavs. This was no accident; in the late 1990s when he had already retired as director of the Institute of Archaeology, Rybakov overcame his former caution and began to use the term *Aryan* openly. He described the Aryans' long migrations together with their herds and identified the Slavs with their supposed direct descendants (again all of this sounds very similar to the *Book of Vles*). Yet he placed the Aryan homeland in the Dnieper River valley, claiming that the *Rig Veda* was completed there and the Aryan migration to India started from there. For this reason, Rybakov advised Ukrainians to learn Sanskrit (Rybakov 1998). The Dnieper location of the Aryan homeland made Rybakov's views coincide more closely with the ideas of the Ukrainian archaeologist Yuri A. Shilov, who rushed to point out that similarity with great satisfaction (Shilov 2000b: 105).

The Ukrainian Challenge

The idea of the Aryan homeland is as attractive for radical Ukrainian nationalists as it is for their Russian counterparts. Certain Ukrainian archaeologists proved particularly helpful. Among them the late M. Chmykhov and Y. Shilov, who was his colleague, deserve our special attention. Chmykhov was original in that he searched for Slavic roots in the proto-Neolithic period, or long before the Tripolye culture had emerged. He viewed central Ukraine as the primordial homeland of both the Slavs and the Indo-Europeans in general. He claimed that central Ukraine served to incubate archaeological cultures, identifying them unequivocally with ethnic groups. Moreover, he put forward a bizarre hypothesis that Upper Paleolithic newcomers from Ukraine launched a "Neolithization" in the Near East and accomplished a Neolithic revolution there (Chmykhov 1990: 19, 32, 35, 51). He depicted the Slavs as the indigenous population of Ukraine, who lived in the Indo-European homeland for over ten thousand years. For Chmykhov, Slavs were the only Indo-European group who could claim an indigenous status in the absolute sense of the word (Chmykhov 1990: 354–355). In turn, Ukraine was presented as the leading center of world civilization and a civilizers' homeland. Following Chmykhov's logic, the reader would conclude that the civilizers were the Slavs, although Chmykhov himself avoided stating this conclusion directly (Chmykhov 1990: 81–103; 1992: 89, 95; 1996–1997). Such a dubious idea of "civilizers" is frightening because it is closely related to racist theories. Indeed, Chmykhov argued that "different racial groups" developed different economic systems in the Neolithic (Chmykhov 1990: 60).

Shilov, an admirer of "alternative science" (Shilov 1994a: 3), went even further and claimed that a civilization and an early state had formed in Ukraine already by the sixth to fifth millennia BC, that is, earlier than anywhere else in the world. He argued also that the "Tripolye culture bearers themselves called their country Aratta" and that the "Sumerian kings originated there" (Shilov 1992: 110; 1996b: 8–9). Shilov seems to be the only researcher who has advocated this theory, and he based his idea of Aratta on an obscure, unknown source. Nonetheless, he argued that Sumerian writing emerged in Ukraine, that the Sumerians themselves arrived from there, and that their priests brought a literary tradition to Mesopotamia across the Caucasus (Shilov 1992: 112–113; 1996b). Later on, Shilov retracted some of his ideas, recognizing that the Neolithic process of domestication and the emergence of productive economies reached Ukraine from Asia Minor through the Balkans. Yet he still insists that the priests from Asia Minor learned writing in the northern Pontic area, which they allegedly visited at the very end of the seventh millennium BC. He also believes that Ukraine served as the "basis of world civilization" and that the "earliest state of Aratta" emerged there (Shilov 1997a; 1997b).

Shilov did not entirely invent this theory but is a follower of the Moscow Assyriologist Anatoly G. Kifishin, whose ideas circulated among certain general audiences but never gained recognition in the academic community. This author believed for a long time that all the main achievements of civilization were brought to the Near East from Ukraine. Recently, he has tried to advertise his sensational "discovery" in the Azov Sea region, where he has managed to discover and to "decipher" some "proto-Sumerian inscriptions" at the cliffs of the well-known archaeological site Kamennaia Mogila, near the city of Melitopol'. He maintains that about 160 stone tablets and 130 engravings were found there that dated to the Ice Age. In his view, "king-gods" ruled the area and gave birth to the historical Sumerian dynasties (Kifishin 1996; Nechiporenko 1996). Although all those inscriptions exist only as inventions of the author's imagination, he regards them as a convincing argument in favor of the Sumerians' arrival from Ukrainian territory. Behind Kifishin's rhetoric, one cannot help hearing the voice of the Ukrainian émigré Lev Sylenko, a founder of the neo-pagan Ukrainian Native Faith, who represented the Sumerians as a daughter branch of the ancient Ukrainians (Sylenko 1979; for his ideas, see Shnirelman 1998a: 12–13; 1999b: 18–22; 2001b: 130–132).

Borrowing from Kifishin, and perhaps indirectly from Sylenko, Shilov argues that the "Aryan state" that emerged in Ukraine during the Tripolye era was egalitarian and was ruled by enlightened priest-warriors. That is why he introduces the phrase "epoch of the sacred democracy" (Shilov 1996a). He actively disseminated his ideas through popular mass media (see, e.g., Shilov 1993, 1994b, 1994c, 1997a, 1997b).

One of the reasons the remote past acquired such significance among these authors was that it provided an academic legitimation for an independent Ukrainian state. Chmykhov argued that Ukraine was a "natural-climatic-social-economic organism" that deserved to be a sovereign state (Chmykhov 1996–1997). The Ukrainian nationalist magazine *Indo-Evropa* published Chmykhov's article together with a critique written by D. Telegin, a well-known Ukrainian archaeologist. Telegin severely attacked Chmykhov, easily disproved all his arguments, and demonstrated that there were no relationships at all between the Slavs and the Tripolye archaeological culture. Yet he too was fascinated with Slavic prehistory and was searching for the Slavic roots among the Neolithic population of the Dnieper-Vistula region in the late fourth to third millennia BC (Telegin 1996–1997). Chmykhov's ideas reached a broad audience.

Despite their rejection by academic specialists, Chmykhov's and Shilov's ideas were included in a standard textbook in ethnography, which was approved by the Ministry of Education of Ukraine (Ponomariov 1994: 101–102). Shilov's book depicting Ukraine as the Aryan homeland and the cradle of the earliest state, Aratta (Shilov 1995), was praised by the new elite Ukrainian journal *Geneza*. A reviewer emphasized that in Shilov's view, Vedic literature had come into being along the Dnieper River banks. The reviewer further wrote that due to Shilov's studies, a long line of development became obvious linking the "Lower Dnieper Aryana, Cimmeria, Tauria, Scythia, Antes' state, Kievan Rus' and Zaporozhie." In other words, there are intellectuals in Ukraine willing to look for Ukrainian roots among the Vedic Aryans (Ponomariov 1995). The new Aryan idea is advocated also by the most militant Ukrainian nationalists, such as the Ukrainian National Assembly, including its paramilitary wing, the Ukrainian Self Defense (Dymerskaya-Tsigelman and Finberg 1999). Radical Russian nationalists as well took an interest in Shilov's book, noting that at least some specialists supported their favorite idea of Slavic-Aryan unity ("Prarodina" 1995). At the same time, even some Russian nationalists recognized Shilov's admiration for mysticism and the occult (Antonenko 1996: 160), a fondness that stands in contrast to his pretensions as an objective scholar.

By the mid-1990s, Shilov had broken with Ukrainian nationalists (for the dramatic circumstances involved, see Shilov 1994a: 8–9), moved to Moscow, and become good friends with certain Russian ultranationalists. In order to gain greater legitimacy for his ideas, however, he exploits his prior relationship with his late mentor V. N. Danilenko (1913–1982), the famous Ukrainian archaeologist. Shilov is attempting to transform his late professor into a cult figure, as though the latter anticipated a reemergence of the contemporary "Aryan myth." For example, Shilov published a manuscript by Danilenko with financial support from the nationalist Russian All-People Movement organization, where he was a head of the Center for Scientific-Cultural Studies. He argued in the introduction that the manuscript's publication was aimed at "strengthening the prestige of Slavic and other Indo-European peoples" (Danilenko 1997: 4).

What is this so-called prestige? First, the Tripolye culture-bearers are identified with the Indo-Europeans without any reserve, a contention that would surely surprise most contemporary scholars. Second, the "earliest prehistoric-communist Indo-European state of Aratta" is said to have flourished in Ukraine in the sixth to third millennia BC. This fantasy exceeds even the Nazi imagination: the Nazis did not fathom such a long Reich. Third, all the achievements of this civilization supposedly came about because of the wanderings of "Hyperborean priests"; and fourth, the Tripolye "Aryans" are supposed to have made an invaluable contribution to the development of Sumerian civilization, an idea that recalls the amateur concepts of certain Ukrainian émigrés like the neo-pagan Sylenko. The atmosphere of secrecy that Shilov cultivates around Danilenko's legacy is also interesting. He asserts that all his teacher's most valuable items and manuscripts were stolen. This is a common argument, typically advanced for any fake such as the *Book of Vles*. Indeed, both Shilov (1997b, 2000a, 2000b) and Chmykhov (1990: 338) referred to the latter as an authentic historical document.

Yet Shilov's ideas have come under attack by Guseva, who protests in general against pseudoscience and, as a professional Indologist, points out that the "Vedic culture" formed in India after the arrival of the Indo-Aryans. She rejects Shilov's fantasies of historical Aratta, of the wandering Brahmin priests in Ukraine, and of the would-be "Indo-Aryan culture" that flourished there in the Neolithic-Chalcolithic periods. She says, reasonably, that archaeological materials from the Kamennaia Mogila site have nothing to do with the Sumerians, and she rejects Kifishin's "discoveries" as unscientific (even such a prolific myth-builder as A. Asov does not believe Shilov's and Kifishin's reports; cf. Asov 1999: 12). While coming out against "Ukrainian national-chauvinists," Guseva now criticizes the idea of close relations between Slavs and the Aryans. Yet, she still sticks to the notion of an Arctic homeland and of the joint Slavic-Aryan movement southward. She maintains that this view is shared by "Russian scholars" and "Indian specialists in Sanskrit" (Guseva 1997c). In brief, in her critical stance she is within the scholarly tradition, whereas her own ideas about the Aryan homeland and Slavic-Aryan specific relationships are as fantastic as Shilov's "audacious surmises" about the "Ukrainian Aratta." The editorial board of the Russian neo-Nazi magazine *Nasledie predkov*, where the article by Guseva cited above was published, disregarded her evaluation of Shilov's works. Instead, in 1997 they published a review of the second edition of Shilov's book *Aryan Homeland*, which they described as "having opened a new chapter in world archaeology" (*Nasledie predkov*, 1997, no. 4, p. 47). However, not all Russian nationalists are willing to share with the Ukrainians the honor of being descendants of the glorious Aryans. The Russian nationalists who hate Ukrainian political independence try to isolate Ukrainians from Aryanism. While recognizing the relationship between the Ukrainian and Tripolye cultures, they maintain that Semites developed the latter (Kirillin 2000). Somewhat more "elegant" are the views of the young historian A. V. Gudz'-Markov, who opposes the eastern Mediterranean race of the Tripolye people to the "Indo-European race" (Gudz'-Markov 1997: 6).

Unfortunately, sometimes in order to attract attention to their discoveries and to receive support from the authorities and the general public, archaeologists themselves use dubious rhetoric and add fuel to the fire of pseudoscience. One example is the Chelyabinsk archaeologist G. B. Zdanovich, who discovered a unique Bronze Age site, Arkaim, in the Chelyabinsk region in the southern Urals. In one of his popular articles, he wrote, "We, Slavs, consider ourselves to be settlers from the outside, but that is wrong. Even in the Stone Age there were Indo-Europeans and Indo-Iranians here [in the southern Urals]; they entered into the tribes of the Kazakhs, the Bashkirs, and the Slavs—and this is the common thread that unites us all. We are all relatives, all our steppe peoples—Turks and Slavs" (Zdanovich 1989: 40). His incautious pronouncements—on the relationship between Arkaim and the swastika, on the sacredness of the site, on its connections with complex cosmology, and more—were picked up by Russian neo-pagans and occultists, making Arkaim the pride of radical Russian nationalists, a "symbol of Russian glory" (see Shnirelman 1999c, 2001c). Some of them call Russia "Arya-Rus" and argue, with a reference to the Andronovo archaeological culture, that the "white race" of the "Aryan-Russes" began their migrations throughout the Old World from the Urals (Demin 1998: 48, 70–71). In spring 2005 Arkaim was visited, first by the Russian vice premier Dmitry Medvedev and then by President Vladimir Putin. Zdanovich has used that unique chance to convince the Russian president that the people of Arkaim had already built up a civil society (Melikova 2005). After that, while giving a talk in the Institute of Archaeology of the Russian Academy of Sciences on June 3, 2005, Zdanovich claimed that Arkaim might be the "national idea of Russia" (Koreniako and Kuz'minykh 2007). To put it differently, the Aryan idea was suggested to democratic Russia as the national ideology. This was immediately picked up by the radical Moscow periodical *Zavtra*, where an author claimed that Putin had visited Arkaim in search of the lost Russian national idea (Yerofeeva 2005).

Early Slavic Pagan Writing and Its "Destroyers"

Patriotic authors are especially sensitive to the problem of pre-Christian Slavic writing and literature; they have no doubts about its development in proto-history and even prehistory. For evidence, they refer to quite obscure and difficult-to-understand notes of early medieval chronicles about some signs used by the Slavs. Yet those signs could hardly be called writing, or they had nothing to do with the Slavs at all. Otherwise, these pseudoscientists point to the inscriptions and marks found on early medieval or even earlier archaeological sites, which were certainly non-Slavic (Skurlatov and Niklaev 1976; Zhukov 1977; Nud'ga 1979; Skurlatova 1979: 56; Saratov 1988: 63, 71; Shcherbakov 1987: 198–199; 1991: 237; Vasilenko 1988: 161; Zhukova 1989; G. Beliakova 1991; Dmitruk 1993; Avdeev 1994: 163; N. Beliakova 1994; Platov 1995: 82–83; Torop 1995: 40–41; Moleva 1996, 2000; Trekhlebov 1998; Shambarov 1999: 135–136, 141–142; Asov 1999: 194; 2000).

In reality, the earliest written records in Rus' date to the very late tenth to very early eleventh centuries AD. Merchants who used various scripts—Greek, Cyrillic, and Runes (Medyntseva 1998: 190–192; Danilevsky 1998: 207–208)—left them. The earliest Russian written document was found in Novgorod on July 13, 2000. It was a liturgical text brought from the south by the first Christian priests, possibly the Kievans, just after the baptism of Rus'. Three wooden planks were discovered covered with wax and dated to the very beginning of the eleventh century. The admirers of the *Book of Vles* would be frustrated indeed; King David's psalms make up the contents of this outstanding document (Vaganov 2000). Russian scholars confirm that those texts were evidently compiled by a Russian and used for education after Christianity had arrived in Novgorod. Interestingly, birch bark came into use for records only after that sort of "book" became known (Yanin 2001; Zalizniak and Yanin 2001). In terms of historical records, the first chronicles in Rus' appeared not earlier than the middle of the eleventh century (Tvorogov 1996: 372–373; Khaburgaev 1994).

Nevertheless, Russian and Ukrainian nationalists continue searching for ancestors who invented the earliest writing system, which the Slavs then introduced to the rest of the world. Thus, for example, an enthusiastic Ukrainian librarian, Nikolai Z. Susloparov (1901–1974), who was neither trained as a linguist nor had any experience in deciphering ancient inscriptions, "discovered" the "Tripolye alphabet" and identified the Tripolye culture-bearers with the Pelasgians (Susloparov 1996–1997; Znoiko 1984: 267–285). Contemporary Russian and Ukrainian nationalists have no doubts about the reliability of Susloparov's reconstructions, and they recall his name with admiration (Belokon' 1982: 153; Shcherbakov 1988: 106–107; Znoiko 1989: 15; Beliakova 1991: 5; "Akumuliator" 1990; Ivanchenko 1996: 9; Dovgich 1996–1997: 9; Luchin 1997: 299; Danilenko

1997: 81; Shilov 1997b: 16). Unfortunately, sometimes even specialists are not sufficiently cautious and make statements that raise false hopes for discovering Old Slavic writing in pre-Christian times (see, e.g., Buganov, Zhukovskaia, and Rybakov 1977: 204; Trubachev 1992: 45; Bandrivs'kyi 1992: 9). For example, academician Rybakov himself did all he could to prove that chronicles were written in pre-Christian Kievan Rus' (Rybakov 1987: 354–381; Dediukhin 1990: 148). In this way, he used his academic authority to encourage development of the myth of an ancient Slavic pagan literary tradition. This myth has reached its apogee of popularity in today's Russia.

The search for pre-Christian Slavic writing was especially encouraged by the discovery of tablets with "Sumerian-like" cuneiform at the site of Tartaria (in Romania), as well as the investigation of enigmatic signs on the pottery of the Chalcolithic Vinça culture in the Balkans. Some amateur authors rushed to call these signs the earliest alphabet invented by the "Slavs-Etruscans" (Perlov 1977; Skurlatov 1977b: 193; Zhuravskii 1988; Milov 1993: 1; Grinevich 1991: 28; 1993: 247–250; 1994; Asov 1999: 11–12). Certain Russian émigré amateur historians cultivated a myth of the "great Slavic pre-Christian chronicle writing." Some of them were involved in the production and dissemination of the forged *Book of Vles* (see, e.g., Lesnoi 1966: li; Miroliubov 1981: 178). The excitement over "proto-Slavic writing" and the imagined rich, pre-Christian literary tradition, coupled with its seeming invisibility, has led to another myth that holds Christians responsible for brutally destroying this heritage (Miroliubov 1981: 177–178; 1983: 115–116; Alexeev 1986: 37–57; Zhukova 1989; Bezverkhy 1993: 49; Antonenko 1994: 55; Beliakova 1994; Gusev 1996: 5; Demin 1998: 5, 194; Moleva 2000: 11–13). Such a myth about decline is very characteristic of nationalist mythology in general (Smith 1984: 104). It is deeply embedded in the works of Russian patriotic writers.

This perspective also is maintained by a veteran of the Russian neopagan movement, a leader of both the Moscow Slavic Pagan Community and the National Club of the Old Russian Battle Wrestling, A. K. Belov (1992). He identifies the Rugs, Rosses, Rosomons, Etruscans, Ruyans, and Varangians with each other and maintains that all of them formed the foundation of a strong proto-Slavic superethnos. Moreover, in his view, Rus' emerged much earlier than the Slavs themselves. He also identifies the proto-Indo-Europeans with the Cro-Magnons, represents Sanskrit as a language of Neolithic Europe, traces the Slavic tribes directly from the Corded Ware and Battle Axe cultures, treats the Tripolye culture as part of the latter, and does not doubt that there was a "Tripolye state." He calls the Neolithic a "period of the uniform European Vedas," claims that the idea of the Trinity (or "Three Gods") was already known to Neolithic believers, and accuses Christianity of plagiarism and distortion of this great idea. He hopes to trace a long continuous development of the Russian ethnos from Paleolithic times onward and to champion paganism for its invaluable knowledge, more advanced than contemporary science. Indeed, if "Cro-Magnon culture" developed over several tens of thousands of years and contemporary civilization is much younger, then the former had to have more impressive achievements than the latter (Belov 1992: 38; 1995: 32; see also Serov 1992; Gusev 1996). Thus, one must castigate Christianity for brutally and thoughtlessly destroying this ancient tradition.

Within this same mythological tradition, certain authors make attempts to represent the "Russian-(Aryan)-Jewish confrontation" as an eternal struggle waged throughout world history and prehistory. Rooted in the *Protocols of the Elders of Zion*, this trend became popular especially after the Arab-Israeli war of 1967 (Korey 1995). Yet, whereas there was only a slight hint of such a struggle in Skurlatov's articles (Skurlatov 1977a: 328; 1977b), Anatoly Kifishin depicted almost a cosmic-scale war between the proto-Indo-Europeans and the proto-Semites across the wide territory between the Danube River and Asia Minor (Kifishin 1977: 181–182). Currently, an Omsk neo-pagan, V. M. Demin, a retired colonel, identifies the Sarmatians with the "Hurrians-Semites" who ruined "Scythia-Rus'" (Demin 1998: 141).

There were also attempts to separate the Phoenicians and Canaanites from the Semitic world or to isolate the Jews from the Semites in order to argue that initially Palestine was populated by non-Semitic inhabitants related to the proto-Slavs. For example, one author claimed that the Natufians were the "Aryans" of Jericho, that is, "remote Russian ancestors" (Moiseev 1995: 20). Another one maintained that Semitic-speaking Phoenicians were the offspring of marriages between local Canaanite women and newcomers, the Indo-European warriors (Skurlatova 1979: 56; Skurlatov 1987: 215). Still others argued that the indigenous inhabitants of the Levant were Pelasgians (an Indo-European group said to be related or even identical to the proto-Slavs), who embraced both Philistines and Canaanites (Znoiko 1984: 288; Shcherbakov 1987: 178; 1995: 13; Nikitin 1985; Demin 1998: 107–109). In fact, the Philistines may have spoken an Indo-European language, but they arrived in Palestine roughly simultaneously with the ancient Israelis.

Recently, a poetess from Pskov has not only "read" an Etruscan inscription in Russian but also identified the Russians with the Aryans as though they had lived in the Levant from time immemorial and had been the true inventors of Christianity (Moleva 1996; 2000: 16, 89–106). Thus, the idea is advanced that the Jews had nothing to do with the early inhabitants of the Levant, and their invasion into Palestine had to be treated as the first manifestation of their attempt to rule the world. Some Russian neo-pagans add more fuel to this dangerous fire: they point to the key Jewish role in the creation of Christianity and blame the Jews for the destruction of the "great Russian Pagan heritage." It is this version of the remote past that is absorbed into contemporary anti-Semitic literature (Shnirelman 1998b, 2001a), which is for sale in abundance in Moscow and St. Petersburg. Finally, some authors go even further to depict an old universal confrontation between the white and the black worlds. They identify the white civilization with the North and Hyperborea, and the black one with the South and Atlantis (*Giperboreiskaia vera* 1999: 52–67).

Archaeology and Russian Ethnic Nationalism

Zeev Sternhell is probably correct that it would be unjust to blame scholars for how their theories are interpreted and abused. Nonetheless, one should not ignore the negative consequences of some ideas' having been simplified and enjoying a wide circulation among the general public. For example, it is certain that social Darwinism played a crucial role in the development of modern ethnic nationalism and racism (Sternhell 1976: 322). As Eric Hobsbawm teaches us, the "historians [including archaeologists and linguists] are to nationalism what poppy-growers in Pakistan are to heroin-addicts: we supply the essential raw material for the market" (Hobsbawm 1992: 3). Most of all this concerns those specialists who intentionally build up an ideology for ethnic nationalism, some of whom are discussed above.

At the same time, neo-Nazi ideology is developed and disseminated mainly by skillful interpreters who manipulate academic ideas and transmit them to the general public as popular versions presented in simple and intelligible forms. More frequently than not, these people are writers, journalists, half-educated persons, and amateur authors who felt uncomfortable with their former professions (Sternhell 1976: 323–324). One should also appreciate the process used and even encouraged by nationalists who willingly create an atmosphere of intellectual populism. This process was well described by Savely Dudakov, who writes: "Now there is no difference between 'literature' and 'reality'; what was invented by a writer, might be presented as a 'document,' which, in its turn, might serve as a basis for a new fiction. Naturally, one asks neither for references, nor for explanations of these 'well-known facts'" (Dudakov 1993: 140). Such casual relationships to fact are evident in the emerging alternative histories and prehistories currently sweeping through Russia and other post-Soviet states (Shnirelman 1995, 1996b, 2001d, 2002, 2006).

To be fair, one should note that recently Guseva has been feeling unhappy with too-closely-drawn similarities between her Arctic theory and Nazi and neo-Nazi constructions of prehistory. That is why she specifies a great difference between her "Aryan ideas" and Nazi-influenced views. She distances herself from Antonenko's book about "Aryan Rus" and points out that there was neither "Aryan" nor "Vedic" Rus. She adds that the Aryans were by no means "noble"; they practiced human sacrifice (Guseva 1997c: 32; 1997d). She also emphasizes that ancient Indian civilization and the Aryan newcomers who arrived later on had nothing to do with the Slavs (Guseva 1997b, 1997c). But she still holds to the idea of the Arctic homeland and, with reference to the "wisdom of Old Indian literature," warns Russians against the "internal enemy" (Guseva 1997e). Yet, she does not specify who this enemy is. Instead, she argues that Nazi concepts were aimed against the Slavs (Guseva 1998b: 23). She fails to mention the Holocaust, which was the direct result of Nazi Aryan propaganda.

In the 1920s–1930s, German nationalism actively exploited G. Kossinna's archaeological theories to confirm German and "Indo-German" superiority. Likewise, contemporary radical Russian nationalists do their best to prove great Slavic prehistoric achievements through references to archaeology. In the 1990s, a young Moscow historian, A. V. Gudz'-Markov, published two thick popular volumes about the early Indo-Europeans and the origins of the Slavs. Like his many other counterparts, he argued that Slavs were much closer to the "earliest [i.e., core] part of the Indo-European tree" than all of the other Indo-European peoples, that they kept invaluable early habits and traditions, and that for those reasons they had a responsibility to "unbind the tragic knots of all the Indo-European communities on the Earth" (Gudz'-Markov 1995: 299). Gudz'-Markov ascribed all Near Eastern civilizations of the fifth to third millennia BC to the Indo-Europeans only. His treatment of the Indo-Europeans as a race is as close to the German scholarly tradition of the very early twentieth century as it is radically different from contemporary academic views. True, Gudz'-Markov recognized that throughout their evolution the Slavs assimilated a number of other different groups; yet he included in this list only the "Indo-Europeans," thus showing that the purity of the "race" was not sullied. He emphasized that the Slavs managed to settle over a huge territory because of their "flexibility and firm immunity in relationships with adjacent peoples" and also because they enjoyed an "unconscious confidence in their own superiority" (Gudz' 1995: 36; see also Gudz'-Markov 1997: 5–6).

Finally, contemporary Russian nationalists tirelessly glorify the prehistoric site of Arkaim (Chelyabinsk region, southern Urals), dated to the seventeenth to sixteenth centuries BC, as a capital of the "Russian-Aryan civilization" and as a "symbol of Russian glory," a starting point of the migration of the "proto-Slavic group of the Aryan people." From this perspective, the southern Urals are viewed as the second Aryan homeland, where the Aryans resided after their exodus from the Arctic. It was there that they established their major civilization, which served as the basis for the ethnogenesis of a number of Indo-European peoples, most particularly the Slavs. The admirers of this myth view the southern Urals as the center of the world (sometimes, a mythical Belovodye), as if the prophet Zoroaster had been born and lived there. An endless flow of pilgrims arrives in the southern Urals annually at a certain time of the year to catch the rays of energy emanating from the cosmos (Shnirelman 1999c, 2001c; Nikulina 2000: 172–179).

The "Aryan Arctic myth" inspires some of its fanatics to quite extravagant actions. At the end of 1997, mass media reported on a scientific expedition, "Hyperborea—97," that visited the Kola Peninsula to test a hypothesis of the "earliest civilization of white people." The Moscow magazine *Nauka i religiia* (*Science and Religion*) began to publish detailed information about the "sensational" discoveries in August 1997 when a team of four researchers managed to find a gigantic carved human figure with outstretched arms on the high cliff, ruins of a megalithic observatory, and even a wild vine. *"Hyperborea has been found!"* the magazine announced. Thus, the "Russian past is extended many thousand years back into prehistory" (Demin 1997e; 1997d: 481–489; also see Lazarev 1997; Asov 1998b). Moreover, there are also reports of some "ancient signs similar to Druidic writings," or "runes" (Lazarev 1997, 1998a, 1998c, 2000), of the "earliest ogham writing system" (Lazarev 1998a; Demin 2000b: 48–49),[4] of the ability of the early Arctic inhabitants to fly with the help of some mechanisms, and even of the existence of a weapon of mass destruction at that time (Valentinov 1998). A newspaper published by ecologists reported that researchers discovered an "Etruscan anchor" (Burleshin 2001).

All these fantasies have a common source—information from the late Moscow philosopher Valery N. Demin (1945–2006), who was encouraged by the Arkaim case to organize a search for the "Hyperborean civilization" itself (Demin 1997a; 1997d: 481–489; 1999b; 2000a). Yet, except for highly emotional reports, neither Demin nor his followers were able to publish any persuasive confirmations of their assumptions. There were neither professional illustrations, nor a well-established chronology, nor any description of a cultural setting (actually, no excavations were made at all). Only a few photographs were published (Demin 1997a, figs. 14, 15; 1999b; Lazarev 1997) that demonstrated that something resembling a stone terrace had stretched along a natural hill. Only people with a good imagination could view this as a "cultural hearth," an "early observatory," and a "sacred well" (Demin 1997a: 52–55; 1997d: 485–486; Lazarev 1997). A gigantic figure that was observed by the "researchers" is obviously a natural formation (Kochemasov 1998). Nothing persuasive was added by the "archaeologist" who took part in the new field season of July 1998 (Lazarev 1998c). The so-called pyramid, which Demin was so proud of finding, is obviously a natural cliff without any traces of human activity (Demin 1999b: 143, 168). Journalist Y. S. Lazarev, who publishes widely about a "megalithic fortress," a prayer pole, and sacred sites, cannot but recognize that all of them were natural objects, although he says they might have been worshipped in the past (Lazarev 1998b, 1999a, 1999b). Incisions on the cliffs, which Lazarev advertises as the "alphabetic signs" of Paleolithic writing (Lazarev 1998a), prove to be recent artificial cuts left by geologists.

While talking about new "discoveries," Demin manifested his fascination with a would-be figure made up of stone blocks at the bottom of the Seid Lake. He was unable to provide a rational explanation for the nature and origin of this "construction," and therefore he developed fantasies about its intentional artificial flooding, as well as certain secrets hidden below the water, including a mysterious creature that lives there. Moreover, in Demin's presentation, the Sumerians turn out to be identical to either the Saami ancestors or the Indo-Aryans, and a surrounding landscape seems to be a stable basis of the "matriarchal nature of the Hyperborean sites" (Demin 1999a: 43–49). In brief, here we have a simple mystification, one of many that occur today. While ignoring all the achievements of professional northern archaeology, Demin pretended to be a pioneer and called for cooperation with archaeologists, ethnographers, linguists, and other specialists (Demin 1999a: 55). Yet the result of such cooperation would be that all of his "discoveries" would vanish into thin air. Therefore, when the Institute of Archaeology of the Russian Academy of Sciences proposed to provide him with professional archaeologists, he refused their help. For him, it was more convenient to employ amateur enthusiasts, and his team included a whole constellation of UFO enthusiasts, mediums, and occultists who managed to "discover" a UFO landing place, an aliens' base, and even a Big Foot. Specialists have already established that Demin and his partners took traces of recent routine geological activity for ruins of some ancient civilization. He was shocked and accused his critics of falsifications and failing to understand the "essence of the issue of matriarchate" (Demin 1999b: 167–169).

All of this is no accident. Although a leader of the northern project, Demin was not an archaeologist but a philosopher who defended his theses on Russian cosmism in 1997. In the Soviet period, he taught students atheism, struggled against the bourgeois philosophy, and, as a hobby, searched for the Big Foot and wrote science fiction stories. In the late 1980s, he transformed himself and began to promote ideas of the Russian cosmic movement and the occult (for the deep roots of this movement in Russia, see Rosenthal 1997). He also favored the contemporary neo-pagan myths of the earliest Slavs and the Northern Hyperborean civilization (see, e.g., Demin 1996a, 1996b, 1997b, 1997c, 1999a; Gromov 1996). In the early years of the 2000s, Demin published one book after another, in which he interpreted Russian folklore as well as folklore of many other peoples uncritically as authentic sources of historical knowledge. Thus, he assured his readers that the earliest civilization in the world, Hyperborea, the homeland of humanity, was a reality (Demin 1997d: 14–21; 1999b; 2000b; 2001). In his "Northern studies" Demin enjoyed the support of the National Committee of the North, as well as the administration of the Murmansk region, and his "discoveries" in the Kola Peninsula were advertised by the All-Russian TV channel ORT on November 22, 2002.

Like Kifishin, Demin was anxious about the earliest relationships between the Indo-Europeans and the Semites. He went so far as to interpret an innocent Russian folktale about a pockmarked hen as a recollection of the most ancient times when the Indo-Europeans were fighting to the death against the Semites. Yet, by contrast to Kifishin, he moved the battlefield to the Far North, where he said the "homeland of humankind" was situated. Furthermore, he maintained that the Indo-European migration southward was a result of the Indo-Europeans' defeat. To put it another way, a "Semitic assault" was dated to the Paleolithic era (Demin 1997d: 363–365; 1999b: 296–298). Demin was no less interested in the swastika, a figure that he viewed as the earliest symbol of the North and a confirmation of the "common Polar origins of the peoples of the world" (Demin 2000b: 412).

During recent years, hypotheses about the Arctic homeland have proliferated. Some amateur authors depict it as not only the earliest Indo-European center but also as a primordial realm of the Nostratic (Boreal) family of languages and even a nontropical homeland of humanity. One of them, a president of the Tomsk public organization Hyperborea—a Siberian Homeland, locates the homeland in the Taymyr Peninsula, believing that the earliest "proto-civilization" formed there (Novgorodov 2000). Demin generously included Novgorodov's article in his new book, demonstrating that he himself did not believe too much in his own "sensational discoveries" on the Kola Peninsula. Nonetheless, he was eager to extend the geography of his studies to include Greenland, Alaska, and northern Canada (Demin 2000b: 63).

Unlike Guseva, Demin openly recognized Blavatsky's great contribution to the development of the "Hyperborean idea" and emphasized proudly that a triumph of the latter was associated with the works of such traditionalists as Herman Wirth, Réne Guénon, and Julius Evola. Yet he still avoided discussing their relationships with the German Nazis. Instead, he pointed to the victory of the "theosophical concept of the development of a conscious life" and included extensive extracts from the fascist Evola's reasoning about the "noble Nordic tradition" in his book (Demin 2000b: 58–61, 287).

Inspired by the myth of Arkaim and Demin's achievements, the journalist A. Asov organized his own "scientific-archaeological survey" along the hilly flanks of Elbrus Mountain in the northern Caucasus, where he hoped to discover the new "early Slavic civilization." The name of the survey was telling: "The Caucasian Arkaim." After his first season in summer 2001, Asov quickly claimed that he had "discovered" the ruins of an "early temple" or "observatory," a "fortified site," and traces of iron smelting. Journalists were informed of the complete confirmation of his own hypothesis on the localization of the "legendary town of Kyiar," "the capital of the early Slavic state of Ruskolan'" (Grishchenko and Kolontaevskaia 2002; Serkov and Alekseev 2003; Malik 2004). An Internet site for Moscow tourists went even further. It announced the discovery of the "sacred Slavic town of Kyiar the Ancient," as well as the "temple of the Sun" ("Informatsionnyi paket" 2002).

The enthusiasts seemingly rushed to report all of those fascinating discoveries before they had actually been found. The tourist Web site announced the preparations for the new investigations in 2002 aimed at the "scientific confirmation of the Slavic town's location in the Caucasus." Additionally, "after the positive evaluation by the scientific commission, the Slavic people will obtain again their lost city—the source of the

Russian culture and Orthodox religion, where the pagan god-like heroes lived" ("Informatsionnyi paket" 2002). Who were these "wonderful scientists" who promised to make all these sensational discoveries? Asov apparently was assisted by Moscow tourists from the Nord-West Club, as well as those from the Piatigorsk Center of Youngsters' Tourism. Professional archaeologists were absent, and the tourists did not conduct any excavations. Judging by their reports, they were unable to distinguish traces of early human activity from natural objects. Instead, they took many pictures and conducted "astronomical studies" that fascinated no one but themselves, lay people, and some journalists. They also found several well-known medieval vaults that had been erected by evidently local non-Slavic inhabitants. The seasons of 2002–2003 added nothing new to what had been reported earlier. Yet, Asov collected data for his new book about the "Slavic state of Ruskolan'" (Asov 2002: 124–136; 2004: 112–124). In brief, we have here yet another mystification, another manifestation of what might be called the "Demin syndrome." In this case, there is an obvious reason for the mystification—an advertisement for northern Caucasian tourism!

The Aryan myth is aggressively carving its way into the midst of the highest Russian authorities and parliamentarians. Recently, a panegyric article about Aryans and the northern homeland was published in the elite magazine *President Parliament Government,* which is aimed at Russian parliamentarians and high officials. The author of the article, Pavel Globa, a founder of "Aryan astrology," does his best to convince his highranking readers that the "Hyperborean idea" is purely scientific. He refers to European folklore, Indian and Iranian Vedic literature (*Zend Avesta* and *Mahabharata*), Demin's pseudoscientific achievements (he calls them an "invaluable contribution to a revival of the Hyperborean idea"), and archaeological discoveries at Arkaim (interpreted as incredible evidence of the "true past of the Russian people"). He uses the same methodology that was extensively exploited by Nazi authors. Globa is aware of all these unpleasant associations and tries to avoid sharp criticism by claiming that the German Nazis distorted an innocent Aryan idea. He asserts that this idea per se is free from any negative connotations and that one should isolate it from its contemporary neo-Nazi advocates. Yet his article not only distorts or ignores all academic knowledge but also contains the same poisonous grains of racism obviously embedded in the Aryan idea. What besides racism is manifested by Globa's reasoning that the legendary king Yima took care to "purify the Aryan gene pool" (Globa 1999: 6:62–64)? Needless to say, more often than not these sorts of authors identify the "white race" with the Aryans and depict it as superior (see, e.g., Gusev 1996). Globa himself points to the essential psychological differences between the "Europeans, the descendants of the proto-Aryans, on the one hand, and the Asians, on the other hand, who are the bearers of the two forms of a collective psychology—a Solar one and a Lunar one." He says: "What is acceptable for a member of the white race . . . cannot be accepted by an 'Eastern kind' of person" (Globa 1999: 6:63).

In concert with him, V. M. Demin (the retired colonel) claims that the Russians and the Jews are incompatible and that the Jews prevent the Russians (the direct Aryan descendants, according to him) from conducting "Aryan studies." He believes that "Aryan studies would strengthen the Russian people." In the prehistoric past, he says, "our ancestors, the Aryans, were more advanced in their evolutionary development than many other ethnoi and affected the emergence of others who are currently considered civilized peoples" (Demin 1998: 6–7).

To Be Aryan

Why do contemporary Russian nationalists and racists have insatiable aspirations to locate the Indo-European ("Aryan") homeland in the Far North? Researchers have already argued that the Russian imagination holds a special fascination with the North, believing that it maintained a pure form of traditional Russian culture. Russian nationalists have long expected that the "rescue of Russia," in terms of both its culture and its natural environment, would come from the North and from Siberia, the only regions where Russian utopia seemed to come true (see Terebikhin 1993; Griffiths 1991; Slezkine 1994: 323–335). The new expectations emerged after the disintegration of the Soviet Union.

These fantasies, which are in high demand among Russian patriots, can be attributed to three different reasons. The first of them is symbolic. Russian nationalists hope that the current identity crisis might be overcome by linking Russians with a new "Hyperborean" or "Aryan" identity (in response to my newspaper article about the "Aryan idea," two young authors published their sharp criticism under the significant title "Who Are We If Not the Aryans?" See Larionov and Semenov 2001; also see Moleva 2000: 8, 98). One could discover here an archetype—an aspiration for an absolute principle: an absolute center of the world (i.e., the North Pole), as well as an absolute beginning in time (hence, the desire to identify one's ancestors with the Paleolithic primordial people). This image is obviously ambivalent. It includes, on the one hand, an idea of isolationism, which is inherent in Russian nationalism (the unique origin of the ancestors up to the cosmic aliens), and on the other hand, Russian Messianism (the Russians as the ancestors of all peoples or of only the "white race" and as the builders of culture and all the early civilizations). This identity contains attractive characteristics: the northern people are robust, courageous, reliable, truthful, and generous, have a deep knowledge of the world, and so on. The Arctic myth has racial connotations as well. Indeed, it claims that in the Ice Age the "white people" perfectly adapted themselves to changing natural conditions and thus became superior to "yellow" and "black" peoples. The result is that "the Russian, Slavic people enjoyed a great past, they were part of the great Aryan community, they are the heirs of that entity, and they will never be satisfied with the miserable role of a supplicant at the backyard of civilization" (Antonenko 1994: 83).

A second reason for the Aryan myth's popularity concerns the territorial integrity of the country, as if non-Russian minorities threaten this integrity. It also legitimates territorial expansion. Indeed, the myth of a homeland at the North Pole makes it senseless to talk of any territorial borders because it disconnects Russian identity from any well-bounded territory. Hence, any territorial expansion is possible. At the same time, radical Russian nationalists emphatically reject accusations of such expansion. Instead, they claim "in general that we have to know that we did not seize Russia from anybody, and always lived here," and that the Kuril Islands "are our primordial Russian Slavic territory." If somebody is surprised by such a claim, it is because "evil agents hide the remote past from us," says the editor-in-chief of the St. Petersburg neo-pagan chauvinist newspaper *Za russkoe delo*, Oleg M. Gusev (1994; also see Demin 1998: 10–11). By the "remote past" they mean all the Indo-European prehistory, which is treated as "Aryan" and ascribed to the "Slav-Russes." Following the same line and mentioning the early "Russian" raids into the Near East and western Europe, Demin concluded that the Russians "once again populated and domesticated the Eurasian North and Siberia. The Russians always and once again return to their ancestors' land" (Demin 1997d: 261). Finally, applying the same logic, Asov sees the Central Asian Seven Rivers (or Semirechie) region as the Indo-European homeland (and of course Slavs are included among the Indo-Europeans). To be precise, he clarifies that the Scythians, the Sarmatians, the Sakae, and the Massagetae were the direct ancestors of the Slavs. Thus, he extends the borders of the Old Slavic realm to both Central Asia and the northern Caucasus (Asov 1998a: 198, 207, 211). This approach restores the obsolete view of the Tomsk amateur archaeologist V. M. Florinsky, who, more than a century ago, wrote about the superiority of Slavic culture over Turkic, Finnish, and Mongolian cultures and maintained that the Aryan (i.e., Indo-European, in his view) homeland was situated in Turkestan. He listed the Central Asian nomadic pastoralists; the Iranian-speaking Sakae; and the Massagetae, who were close relatives to the Scythians and who lived in Turkestan during the Early Iron Age, as Old Slavs (Florinsky 1894; see also Shnirelman 1996a: 223–224). It is in this way that he attempted to represent Russian colonial expansion to Central Asia as a return to the homeland. As can be seen, contemporary Russian nationalists intentionally exploit the same arguments, and some of them express their admiration of Florinsky's constructions (see, e.g., Novgorodov 2000: 505; Demin 2003: 83–84, 88).

The third reason explaining the incredible attractiveness of the "Aryan heritage" is that it helps to identify an external enemy who might be blamed for all contemporary Russian misfortunes. From this perspective, the rehabilitation of the swastika is worth noting. In the view of many Russian nationalists, the swastika symbolizes an inherent attribute of Russian traditional culture. In fact, this rehabilitation is undertaken intentionally to revise the swastika's dreadful role in the history of the twentieth century as the symbol of the struggle for racial purity, with all its tragic results (Wistrich 1991: 75). It might be of interest to note that in Nazi propaganda the swastika was a symbol of aggression aimed not only against the Jews, but also against the Slavs. Contemporary Russian neo-Nazis nevertheless manifested their true perception of the swastika in the newspaper *Natsionalist*, an organ of the National Republican Party of Russia: the Aryan swastika is aimed against the Star of David (Bolotov 1993; cf. Mochalova 1996: 110; Kandyba 1997: 90–91). To conclude, one should recall that for Hitler himself, the swastika was a symbol "of the struggle for the victory of the Aryan man, and, by the same token . . . the idea of creative work, which as such always has been and always will be anti-Semitic" (Hitler 1971: 497; see also Quinn 1994: 4; Weissmann 1991: 135–137). Yet nowadays the swastika fascinates Russian skinheads, the major consumers of the Aryan ideology, which directs them against the Others, primarily immigrants.

Notes

1. Translations from non-English works are my own unless otherwise indicated.
2. Those who prefer the Pontic-Caspian homeland include V. Skurlatov, a former physicist, then Comsomol activist and employee of the Library of the Academy of Sciences of the USSR and now a nationalist politician, and the

journalist V. Torop. Those who follow Ivanov and Gamkrelidze include V. Shcherbakov, a former radio-physicist and today a science fiction writer and president of the Moscow Club of Secrets, and Y. Petukhov, formerly an engineer and today a science fiction writer and publisher. Finally, those who revert back to the idea of a Balkan homeland include the late V. Bezverkhy (1930–2000), a former professor of Marxism-Leninism, then a founder of the St. Petersburg neo-pagan Union of the Veneds, and G. Grinevich, a former geologist who became an activist of the nationalist Department of General History of the Russian Physics Society.

3. The Tripolye period dates to 4500–3300 BC and flourished in a territory that corresponds to present northeastern Romania, northern Moldova, and western Ukraine.
4. In fact, the Celtic ogham writing was used only in Ireland and minor parts of Scotland, Wales, and the Isle of Man and only between the fourth and mid-seventh centuries. See Friedrich 1966: 117–118.

References

Akhudzha, A., and N. R. Guseva. 1982. Tainye istoki vidimykh rek. *Tekhnika-Molodezhi* 8:50–53.

Akumuliator istorichnoï pamiati. 1990. *Literaturna Ukraïna*, March 1.

Alekseenko, S. A. 1997a. Ot Rusi k Slavianii. *Svet. Priroda i chelovek* 1:70–74.

Alekseenko, S. A. 1997b. India . . . bliz Plisetska. *Svet. Priroda i chelovek* 3:26–28.

Alekseev, A. A. 1995. Opiat' o "Vlesovoi knige." *Russkaia literatura* 2:248–254.

Alekseev, S. T. 1986. *Slovo*. Moscow: Sovremennik.

Antonenko, S. G. 1994. *Rus' ariiskaia (neprivychnaia pravda)*. Moscow: Pallada.

Antonenko, S. G. 1996. Nezhit': Razmyshleniia o sovremennom yazychestve. *Moskva* 9:157–165.

Arutiunian, Y. V., ed. 1992. *Russkije: Etno-sotsiologicheskije ocherki*. Moscow: Nauka.

Ashikhmina, L. 1997. Ancient migrations in the northern sub-Urals: Archaeology, linguistics, and folklore. In *Archaeology and Language*, vol. 1, *Theoretical and Methodological Orientations*, ed. R. Blench and M. Spriggs, 283–307. London: Routledge.

Asov, A. I. 1994. Vremena Sviatogora. *Nauka i religiia* 9:27–28.

Asov, A. I. 1998a. *Mify i legendy drevnikh slavian*. Moscow: Nauka i religiia.

Asov, A. I. 1998b. Sviatilishche Seid'-zor v gorakh Luiarva. *Nauka i religiia* 1:36.

Asov, A. I. 1999. *Atlanty, arii, slaviane*. Moscow: Aleteia.

Asov, A. I. 2000. *Slavianskie runy i "Boianov gimn."* Moscow: Veche.

Asov, A. I. 2002. *Sviashchennye prarodiny slavian*. Moscow: Veche.

Asov, A. I. 2004. *Ruskolan': Drevniaia Rus'*. Moscow: Veche.

Avdeev, V. B. 1994. *Preodolenie khristianstva*. Moscow: Kap'.

Bandrivs'kyi, M. S. 1992. *Svarozhi liki*. L'viv: Logos.

Beliakova, G. S. 1991. Puti—dorogi slavianskoi pis'mennosti. *Volkhv* 1:3–8.

Beliakova, N. Ye. 1994. Uroki drevnerusskogo: Vseiasvetnaia gramota: 1000 let zabveniia. *Za russkoe delo* 1 (2): 2–3; 1 (3): 3; 1 (4): 3; 1 (5): 2.

Belokon', I. 1982. Utro tvoreniia. *Moskva* 2:141–166.

Belov, A. 1992. *Slaviano-goritskaia bor'ba: Iznachalie.* Moscow: Zdorovie naroda.

Belov, A. 1995. Triglav. *Ataka* 72:31–33.

Bezverkhy, V. N. 1993. Filosofiia istorii. *Volkhv* 1 (7): 3–102.

Bolotov, S. S. 1993. Protiv svastiki—protiv kul'tury. *Natsionalist* 4:5.

Bongard-Levin, G. M., and E. A. Grantovsky. 1983. *Ot Skifii do Indii.* Moscow: Mysl'.

Buganov, V. I., L. P. Zhukovskaia, and B. A. Rybakov. 1977. Mnimaia "drevneishaia letopis'." *Voprosy istorii* 6:202–205.

Burleshin, M. 2001. Uzhas severnykh shirot. *Prirodno-resursnye vedomosti* 46 (Nov.): 3.

Chetvertkov, S. 1996. Razorvannyi narod—ne natsiia! *Za russkoe delo* 1 (33): 3.

Chivilikhin, V. A. 1982. *Pamiat'.* Moscow: Sovremennik.

Chmykhov, M. 1990. *Istoki yazychestva Rusi.* Kiev: Lybid'.

Chmykhov, M. 1992. Visim tysiacholit arkheologichnoi kosmologii v Ukraini. In *Kosmos drevn'oi Ukrainy,* ed. V. Dovgych, 66–99. Kyiv: Indo-Evropa.

Chmykhov, M. 1996–1997. Spokonvichni derzhavotvortsi. In *Onuky Dazhbozhi: Pokhodzhennia ukrains'kogo narodu,* vols. 1–2, ed. V. Dovgych, 10–11. Kyiv: Indo-Evropa, Taki spravy.

Chuev, F. 1991. *Sto sorok besed s Molotovym.* Moscow: Terra.

Danilenko, V. N. 1997. *Kosmogoniia pervobytnogo obshchestva.* Moscow: ROD.

Danilevsky, I. N. 1998. *Drevniaia Rus' glazami sovremennikov i potomkov (IX–XII vv.).* Moscow: Aspekt Press.

Dediukhin, B. 1990. Dorozhit' svoimi istoricheskimi korniami. *Volga* 7:143–152.

Demin, V. M. 1998. *Ot ariev k rusicham.* Omsk: N.p.

Demin, V. M. 2003. Ot ariev k rusicham (ot Drevnei Arii do Rossii). In *Drevniaia istoriia Russkogo naroda,* 3rd rev. ed. Moscow-Omsk: Russkaia Pravda.

Demin, V. N. 1996a. Gora Meru—proobraz Vselennoi. *Chudesa i prikliucheniia* 8:18–22.

Demin, V. N. 1996b. *Otkuda ty, russkoe plemia?* Moscow: Narodnyi fond "Rus' vozrozhdennaia."

Demin, V. N. 1997a. *Giperboreia—utro tsivilizatsii.* Moscow.

Demin, V. N. 1997b. Strana Lebediia—tysiacheletniaia dal' Rossii. *Nauka i religiia* 6:44–47.

Demin, V. N. 1997c. Strana Lebediia: Gde ona? *Chudesa i prikliucheniia* 7: 37–39.

Demin, V. N. 1997d. *Tainy russkogo naroda.* Moscow: Veche.

Demin, V. N. 1997e. Zdravstvui, Giperboreia! *Nauka i religiia* 11:14–15.

Demin, V. N. 1999a. Giperboreia—severnaia prarodina. In *Varvary,* ed. P. V. Tulaev, 7–56. Moscow: Metagalaktika.

Demin, V. N. 1999b. *Zagadki Russkogo Severa.* Moscow: Veche.

Demin, V. N. 2000a. Magicheskimi putiami Severa. *Nauka i religiia* 9:44–46.

Demin, V. N. 2000b. *Zagadki Urala i Sibiri: Ot bibleiskikh vremen do Yekateriny Velikoi.* Moscow: Veche.

Demin, V. N. 2001. *Giperboreia: Istoricheskie korni russkogo naroda.* Moscow: Grand.

Diakonoff, I. M. 1982. O prarodine nositelei indoevropeiskikh dialektov. *Vestnik Drevnei Istorii* 3:3–30.

Diakonoff, I. 1985. On the original home of the speakers of Indo-European. *Journal of Indo-European Studies* 13:92–174.

Dmitruk, M. 1993. Russkie—37 vekov nazad. *Nachalo* 36:10.

Dovgich, V. 1996–1997. Materik Indo-Evropa. In *Onuky Dazhbozhi: Pokhodzhennia ukrains'kogo narodu*, vols. 1–2, ed. V. Dovgych, 6–9. Kyiv: Indo-Evropa, Taki spravy.

Dudakov, S. Y. 1993. *Istoriia odnogo mifa: Ocherki russkoi literatury XIX–XX vv.* Moscow: Nauka.

Dunlop, J. B. 1983. *The Faces of Contemporary Russian Nationalism.* Princeton, NJ: Princeton University Press.

Dymerskaya-Tsigelman, L., and L. Finberg. 1999. *Antisemitism of the Ukrainian Radical Nationalists: Ideology and Policy.* Jerusalem: Hebrew University.

Filippov, V. 1996. Kuda ischezli drevliane i krivichi, ili pochemu vologodskii govor v perevode na sanskrit ne nuzhdaetsia. *Izvestiia*, Apr. 18.

Florinsky, V. M. 1894. *Pervobytnye slaviane po pamiatnikam ikh doistoricheskoi zhizni: Opyt slavianskoi arkheologii.* Vol. 1. Tomsk, Russia: N.p.

Friedrich, J. 1966. *Geschichte der Schrift.* Heidelberg, Germany: Carl Winter.

Gamkrelidze, T. V., and V. V. Ivanov. 1984. *Indoyevropeiskii yazyk i indoyevropeitsy.* Vols. 1–2. Tbilisi, Georgia: Izdatel'stvo Tbilisskogo Universiteta.

Gimbutas, M. 1977. The first wave of Euroasian steppe pastoralists into Copper Age Europe. *Journal of Indo-European Studies* 5 (4): 277–338.

Gimbutas, M. 1985. Primary and secondary homeland of the Indo-Europeans. *Journal of Indo-European Studies* 13 (1–2): 185–202.

Giperboreiskaia vera rusov. 1999. Moscow: FAIR-Press.

Globa, P. P. 1999. Vozrozhdenie Giperborei. *Prezident. Parlament. Pravitel'stvo (politiko-pravovoi zhurnal)* 5:60–64; 6:62–64.

Godwin, J. 1993. *Arktos: The Polar Myth in Scientific Symbolism, and Nazi Survival.* London: Thames and Hudson.

Gornung, B. V. 1964. *K voprosu ob obrazovanii indoyevropeiskoi yazykovoi obshchnosti (Protoindoyevropeiskie ili inoyazychnye substraty?).* Moscow: Nauka.

Griffiths, F. 1991. The Arctic in the Russian identity. In *The Soviet Maritime Arctic*, ed. L. W. Brigham, 83–107. London: Belhaven Press.

Grinevich, G. S. 1991. Skol'ko tysiacheletii slavianskoi pis'mennosti? *Russkaia mysl'* 1:3–28.

Grinevich, G. S. 1993. *Praslavianskaia pis'mennost': Rezul'taty deshifrovki.* Vol. 1. Moscow: Obshchestvennaia Pol'za.

Grinevich, G. S. 1994. Praslaviane v Etrurii. *Moskovsky Zhurnal* 10:53–56.

Grishchenko, N., and Y. Kolontaevskaia. 2002. Ariitsev ishchut vozle El'brusa. *Stavropol'skaia Pravda*, June 26.

Gromov, V. 1996. "Vavilon" otkryt na Severe. *Rossiiskaia gazeta*, Oct. 18, p. 27.

Gudz', A. V. 1995. Indoyevropeiskaia istoriia Yevrasii: Proiskhozhdenie slavianskogo mira (Predislovie k monografii). *Russkaia mysl'* 1–6:32–36.

Gudz'-Markov, A. V. 1995. *Indoyevropeiskaia istoriia Yevrasii: Proiskhozhdenie slavianskogo mira*. Moscow: Rikel, Radio i sviaz'.

Gudz'-Markov, A. V. 1997. *Istoriia slavian*. Moscow: N.p.

Guk, Y. P. 2000. Rasovye korni slavian. In *Rasovyi smysl russkoi idei*, ed. V. B. Avdeev, 1:140–152. Moscow: Belye al'vy.

Gusev, O. M. 1994. Pomory, ainy i . . . Lev Tolstoi. *Za russkoe delo* 1:2–3.

Gusev, O. M. 1996. Vozvrashchenie boga. *Za russkoe delo* 4:3–6.

Guseva, N. R. 1977. *Induism*. Moscow: Nauka.

Guseva, N. R. 1991a. Glubokie korni. In *Dorogami tysiacheletii*, ed. V. P. Yankov, 4:3–27. Moscow: Molodaia Gvardiia.

Guseva, N. R. 1991b. Prarodina yazyka. *Slovo* 1:25–29.

Guseva, N. R. 1992. Gde iskat' sledy. *Slovo* 10:10–13.

Guseva, N. R. 1994a. Arkticheskaia rodina v Vedakh. In Guseva 1994c, 1:6–20.

Guseva, N. R. 1994b. Aryi, slaviane: Sosedstvo ili rodstvo? In Guseva 1994c, 1:26–40.

Guseva, N. R., ed. 1994c. *Drevnost': Aryi, slaviane*. Vols. 1–2. Moscow: Vitiaz'.

Guseva, N. R. 1994d. *Indiia v zerkale vekov: Religiia, byt, kul'tura*. Moscow: Institute of Ethnology and Anthropology.

Guseva, N. R. 1995. *Induism: Aryi, Slaviane*. Moscow: Institute of Ethnology and Anthropology.

Guseva, N. R. 1997a. Arkticheskaia kolybel'? *Rodina* 8:81–83.

Guseva, N. R. 1997b. Drevnee drevnosti. *Chudesa i prikliucheniia* 6:54–56.

Guseva, N. R. 1997c. Ob ariistve mnimom i real'nom. *Nasledie predkov* 4:29–34.

Guseva, N. R. 1997d. Ob aryiakh, Vedakh i natsionalizme. *Ekonomicheskaia gazeta* 9–13.

Guseva, N. R. 1997e. O vitkakh spirali. *Ekonomicheskaia gazeta* 20:8.

Guseva, N. R., ed. 1998a. *Kto oni i otkuda? Drevneishye sviazi slavian i aryev*. Moscow: Institute of Ethnology and Anthropology.

Guseva, N. R. 1998b. *Russkie skvoz' tysiacheletiia: Arkticheskaia teoriia*. Moscow: Belye al'vy.

Guseva, N. R. 2002. *Slaviane i arii: Put' bogov i slov*. Moscow: Grand, Fair-Press.

Guseva, N. R. 2003. *Russkii Sever—prarodina indo-slavov*. Moscow: Veche.

Hitler, A. 1971. *Mein Kampf*. Boston: Houghton Mifflin.

Hobsbawm, E. 1992. Ethnicity and nationalism in Europe. *Anthropology Today* 8 (1): 3–13.

Informatsionnyi paket 2002. Informatsionnyi paket ekspeditsii "Kavkazskii Arkaim—2002." www.clubato.ru/club/kiyar/press2.html (accessed fall 2004).

Ivanchenko, R. P. 1996. *Istoriia bez mifiv: Besidi z istorii ukrains'koi derzhavnisti*. Kyiv: Ukrains'kyi pis'mennik.

Kaganskaya, M. 1986. The Book of Vlas: The saga of forgery. *Jews and Jewish Topics in Soviet and East European Publications* 4:3–27.

Kalashnikov, V. L. 2000. *Slavianskaia tsivilizatsiia.* Moscow: N.p.

Kandyba, V. M. 1997. *Istoriia russkoi imperii.* St. Petersburg: Efko.

Khaburgaev, G. A. 1994. *Pervye stoletiia slavianskoi pis'mennoi kul'tury: Istoki drevnerusskoi knizhnosti.* Moscow: Moscow State University Press.

Kifishin, A. G. 1977. Vetvi odnogo dereva. In *Tainy vekov,* ed. V. Sukhanov, 1:179–182. Moscow: Molodaia Gvardiia.

Kifishin, A. G. 1996. Zhretsi z Chatal-Guiuka na Kam'yanii Mogyli 6200 r. do n. e. *Ukrains'kyi svit* 4–6:6–7.

Kirillin, S. 2000. Rasovaia istoriia i "ukrainskii vopros." In *Rasovyi smysl russkoi idei,* ed. V. B. Avdeev, 86–105. Moscow: Belye al'vy.

Kobzev, I. 1971. *Vitiazi.* Moscow: Sovietskaia Rossiia.

Kochemasov, G. 1998. V serdtse Luiavrurta. *Nauka i religiia* 1:34–36.

Konstantinovsky, A. 1994. Zlatye kryliia prarodiny. *Nauka i religiia* 9:29.

Koreniako, V. A., and S. V. Kuz'minykh. 2007. O professional'noi etike v sovremennoi otechestvennoi arkheologii. *Rossiiskaia arkheologiia* 2.

Korey, W. 1995. *Russian Antisemitism, Pamyat, and the Demonology of Zionism.* Chur, Switzerland: Harwood Academic Publishers.

Kritov, A. 1995. Drevneishaia istoriia i mifologiia indoyevropeitsev v svete teosofskogo ezotericheskogo ucheniia. In *Mify i magiia indoyevropeitsev,* ed. A. Platov, 212–228. Moscow: Menedzher.

Krylov, Y. 1993. Troianskoe nasledstvo. *Rossiianin* 4: 2, 8.

Kuklina, I. V. 1985. *Etnogeografiia Skifii po antichnym istochnikam.* Leningrad: Nauka.

Kuz'mina, Y. Y. 1994. *Otkuda prishli indoarii?* Moscow: MGP "Kalina."

Laitin, D. D. 1998. *Identity in Formation: The Russian-Speaking Populations in the Near Abroad.* Ithaca, NY: Cornell University Press.

Larionov, V. Y. 2000. Rasovye i geneticheskie aspekty etnicheskoi istorii russkogo naroda. In *Rasovyi smysl russkoi idei,* ed. V. B. Avdeev, 16–42. Moscow: Belye al'vy.

Larionov, V. Y., and A. V. Semenov. 2001. Kto my, yesli ne ariitsy? *NG—religii,* June 14, p. 6.

Lazarev, Y. S. 1997. Sviatynia zapoliarnykh gor. *Nauka i religiia* 12:44–45.

Lazarev, Y. S. 1998a. Molitva Giperboreev. *Nauka i religiia* 9:34–35.

Lazarev, Y. S. 1998b. Runy Graalia nad Belym morem. *Nauka i religiia* 10:44–45.

Lazarev, Y. S. 1998c. Sviatynia Lovozerskikh gor. *Zhivaia Arktika* 3 (12): 4–7.

Lazarev, Y. S. 1999a. El'fiiskaia tverdynia na Russkom Severe. *Nauka i religiia* 8: 31, 35.

Lazarev, Y. S. 1999b. Zdes' molilis' bogine Zari i bessmertiia. *Nauka i religiia* 2:17, 64.

Lazarev, Y. S. 2000. Voistinu yest' . . . *Nauka i religiia* 2:21–22.

Lesnoi, S. 1966. *"Vlesova kniga"—yazycheskaia letopis' doolegovskoi Rusi.* Winnipeg: Trident Press.

Luchin, A. A. 1997. Slaviane i istoriia. *Molodaia Gvardiia* 9:261–351.

Malik, Y. 2004. Drevnee gosudarstvo Ruskolan' nakhodilos' na El'bruse. *Komsomol'skaia Pravda*, July 20.

Mallory, J. P. 1989. *In Search of the Indo-Europeans: Language, Archaeology, and Myth*. London: Thames and Hudson.

Mallory, J. P. 1997. The homelands of the Indo-Europeans. In *Archaeology and Language*, vol. 1, *Theoretical and Methodological Orientations*, ed. R. Blench and M. Spriggs, 93–121. London: Routledge.

Malygina, I. V. 1995. Natsional'noe samosoznanie rossiiskoi provintsii. In *Sotsiologiia molodezhnoi kul'tury: Dukhovnost' provintsii*, 3rd ed., ed. O. V. Romakh, 38–46. Tambov, Russia: Izdatel'stvo MINTs.

Matveev, A. V. 1998. *Pervye andronovtsy v lesakh Zauralia*. Novosibirsk, Russia: Nauka.

Medvedev, Y. 1983. Chasha terpeniia. In *Kolesnitsa vremeni*, by Y. Medvedev, 7–165. Moscow: Molodaia Gvardiia.

Medyntseva, A. A. 1998. Nadpisi na amfornoi keramike X—nachala XI v. i problema proiskhozhdeniia drevnerusskoi pis'mennosti. In *Kul'tura slavian i Rus'*, ed. Y. S. Kukushkin, 176–195. Moscow: Nauka.

Melikova, N. 2005. "Prosvetlenie dlia istinnogo ariitsa." *Nezavisimaia gazeta*, May 17, pp. 1–2.

Milov, V. A. 1993. Kazhdyi iz nas v otvete za svoiu istoriiu. *Stranitsy Rossiiskoi Istorii* 1:1–2; 2:2–3.

Miroliubov, Y. P. 1981. *Rig-Veda i yazychestvo*. Munich: O. Sagner.

Miroliubov, Y. P. 1983. *Materialy k preistorii rusov*. Munich: O. Sagner.

Mochalova, I. V. 1996. *Vedicheskie znaniia na perekrestke geopolitiki: Osnovy antimaterial'noi metodologii (Vozvrashchenie Kryshenia)*. Moscow: Volia Rossii.

Moiseev, L. 1995. Svoboda, a ne demokratiia. *Ataka* 72:18–21.

Moleva, S. V. 1996. "Slovo ob Aryakh": Pamiatnik russkoi pis'mennosti X–IX vv. do R.Kh. In *Rech*, ed. S. V. Moleva and M. Y. Ustinov, 5–36. Pskov, Russia: Otchina.

Moleva, S. V. 2000. *Yedinorodnoe slovo*. Pskov, Russia: N.p.

Morozov, Y. F. 2000. Bunt neprikasaemykh. In *Rasovyi smysl russkoi idei*, ed. V. B. Avdeev, 153–162. Moscow: Belye al'vy.

Nechiporenko, Y. 1996. Samyi drevnii text na zemle. *Nezavisimaia gazeta*, May 14.

Nikitin, Y. A. 1985. Akhill. In *Dalekii svetlyi terem*, by Y. A. Nikitin, 95–113. Moscow: Molodaia Gvardiia.

Nikitin, Y. A. 1995. *Giperborei*. Moscow: Ravlik.

Nikulina, M. 2000. Pro starinnoe zhutie i pro tainuiu silu. *Ural* 6:165–179.

Novgorodov, N. 2000. Tretia Rus'—Tomskoe Lukomorie—Taimyr—Giperboreia. In Demin 2000b, 480–534.

Nud'ga, G. 1979. Promin' u taemnytsiu. *Zhovten'* 10:124–135.

Perlov, B. 1977. Zhivye slova Terterii. In *Tainy vekov*, ed. V. Sukhanov, .1:171–179. Moscow: Molodaia Gvardiia.

Platov, A. V. 1995. *Runicheskaia magiia*. Moscow: Menedzher.
Ponomariov, A. 1994. *Ukrains'ka etnografiia: Kurs lektsii*. Kyiv: Lybid'.
Ponomariov, V. 1995. Slavlennia Agni. *Geneza* 1 (3): 182.
Prarodina i mify drevnikh ariev. 1995. Interview P. V. Tulaeva s Yu. A. Shilovym po sluchaiu prezentatsii yego knigi "Prarodina ariev." *Nasledie predkov* 1:11–15.
Quinn, M. 1994. *The Swastika: Constructing the Symbol*. London: Routledge.
Rechkin, M. 1998. Sibirskii Kitezh-grad. *Nauka i religiia* 10:12–15.
Renatus, Q. F. 1922. Svastika. *Narodni Politika* 40:337.
Rosenthal, B. G., ed. 1997. *The Occult in Russian and Soviet Culture*. Ithaca, NY: Cornell University Press.
Rybakov, B. A. 1961. Istoricheskii vzgliad na russkie byliny. *Istoriia SSSR* 5:141–166; 6:80–96.
Rybakov, B. A. 1981. *Yazychestvo drevnikh slavian*. Moscow: Nauka.
Rybakov, B. A. 1985. Russkii epos i istoricheskii nigilizm. *Russkaia literatura* 1:155–160.
Rybakov, B. A. 1987. *Yazychestvo drevnei Rusi*. Moscow: Nauka.
Rybakov, B. A. 1994. Glubokie korni—moguchaia krona. *Rossiiskaia provintsiia* 2:14–18.
Rybakov, B. A. 1997a. Drevnie slaviane i antichnyi mir. *Derzhava* 1 (8): 19–25.
Rybakov, B. A. 1997b. Ya pisal o tom, chto mne interesno. *Ves'ma vazhnoe litso* 32–33:25–27.
Rybakov, B. A. 1998. Predislovie. In *Vozzvanie k slavianam*, by N. I. Kekishev, 3–4. Moscow: Mezhdunarodnaia assotsiatsiia pisatelei batalistov i marinistov.
Saratov, I. Y. 1988. Stroki kamennoi letopisi. *Pamiatniki otechestva* 1:63–75.
Serkov, D., and A. Alekseev. 2003. Po sledu solntsa. *Itogi* no. 20, May 20.
Serov, A. 1992. Tysiacha let na . . . razmyshleniia. *Za Rus'* 3:4.
Shambarov, V. Y. 1999. *Rus': Doroga iz glubin tysiacheletii*. Moscow: Aleteia.
Shcherbakov, V. I. 1987. Tropoi Troianovoi. In *Dorogami tysiacheletii*, ed. A. Smirnov, 1:161–202. Moscow: Molodaia Gvardiia.
Shcherbakov, V. I. 1988. Veka Troianovy. In *Dorogami tysiacheletii*, ed. M. Kovalev, 2:60–116. Moscow: Molodaia Gvardiia.
Shcherbakov, V. I. 1991. *Asgard—gorod bogov*. Moscow: Molodaia Gvardiia.
Shcherbakov, V. I. 1995. Tainy etruskov rasseivaiutsia. *Chudesa i prikliucheniia* 8:10–14.
Shilov, Y. A. 1992. Doskyts'ki tsyvilizatsii Podniprovia. In *Kosmos drevn'oi Ukrainy*, ed. V. Dovgych, 109–124. Kyiv: Indo-Evropa.
Shilov, Y. A. 1993. Shliakhami Dyva, Appolona, Odyna. . . . *Ukrains'kyi Svit* 1–2:30–35.
Shilov, Y. A. 1994a. Aktual'neishye zadachi istorii i rodstvennykh nauk. *Russkaia mysl'* 1–6:3–15.
Shilov, Y. A. 1994b. Aratta—derzhava trypil'tsev. *Rus' Kyivs'ka* 1 (1): 13.
Shilov, Y. A. 1994c. Indoyevropeisko-semits'ko-kartvel'ski zviazky Naddnyprianshchyny. *Ukrains'kyi Svit* 3–4:14–17.

Shilov, Y. A. 1995. *Prarodina ariev.* Kiev: CINTO.
Shilov, Y. A. 1996a. Oriis'ka viis'kova doktryna. *Ukrains'kyi Svit* 1–3:8–14.
Shilov, Y. A. 1996b. Skhid i Zakhid Ukrainy i Indo-Evropy. *Ukrains'kyi Svit* 4–6:8–10.
Shilov, Y. A. 1997a. Aratta. *Nasledie predkov* 3:6–8.
Shilov, Y. A. 1997b. Troia-Illion i etnogenez slavian. *Nasledie predkov* 4:16–18.
Shilov, Y. A. 2000a. *Istyna "Velesovoi" knyhi.* Kyiv: N.p.
Shilov, Y. A. 2000b. *Pobeda.* Kiev: N.p.
Shnirelman, V. A. 1995. Alternative prehistory. *Journal of European Archaeology* 3 (2):.
Shnirelman, V. A. 1996a. The faces of nationalist archaeology in Russia. In *Nationalism and Archaeology in Europe,* ed. M. Diaz-Andreu and T. C. Champion, 218–242. London: UCL Press.
Shnirelman, V. A. 1996b. *Who Gets the Past? Competition for Ancestors among Non-Russian Intellectuals in Russia.* Washington, DC: Woodrow Wilson Center Press; Baltimore: Johns Hopkins University Press.
Shnirelman, V. A. 1998a. *Neoyazychestvo i natsionalizm: Vostochnoyevropeiskii areal.* No. 114 in the series Issledovaniia po prikladnoi i neotlozhnoi etnologii. Moscow: Institute of Ethnology and Anthropology.
Shnirelman, V. A. 1998b. *Russian Neo-Pagan Myths and Antisemitism.* Jerusalem: Hebrew University.
Shnirelman, V. A. 1999a. Archaeology of north Eurasian hunters and gatherers. In *The Cambridge Encyclopedia of Hunters and Gatherers,* ed. R. B. Lee and R. H. Daly, 127–131. Cambridge: Cambridge University Press.
Shnirelman, V. A. 1999b. Mify diaspory. *Diaspory* 2–3:6–33.
Shnirelman, V. A. 1999c. Passions about Arkaim: Russian nationalism, the Aryans, and the politics of archaeology. *Inner Asia* 1 (2): 267–282.
Shnirelman, V. A. 2001a. The "Aryans" and the "Khazars": Some peculiarities of anti-Semitic propaganda in contemporary Russia. In *Remembering for the Future: The Holocaust in an Age of Genocide,* ed. M. Levy, 1:884–896. London: Palgrave.
Shnirelman, V. A. 2001b. Nazad k yazychestvu? Triumfal'noe shestvie neoyazychestva po prostoram Yevrazii. In *Neoyazychestvo na prostorakh Yevrazii,* ed. V. A. Shnirelman, 130–169. Moscow: Bibleisko-Bogoslovskii Institut.
Shnirelman, V. A. 2001c. Strasti po Arkaimu: Ariiskaia ideia i natsionalism. In *Yazyk i etnicheskii konflikt,* ed. M. B. Olcott and I. Semenov, 58–85. Moscow: Carnegie Foundation.
Shnirelman, V. A. 2001d. *The Value of the Past: Myths, Identity, and Politics in Transcaucasia.* Senri Ethnological Studies, 57. Osaka: National Museum of Ethnology.
Shnirelman, V. A. 2002. *The Myth of the Khazars and Intellectual Antisemitism in Russia, 1970s–1990s.* Jerusalem: Vidal Sassoon International Center for the Study of Antisemitism, Hebrew University of Jerusalem.

Shnirelman, V. A. 2006. *Byt' alanami: Intellektualy i politika na Severnom Kavkaze v XX veke*. Moscow: NLO.

Shnirelman, V. A., and G. A. Komarova. 1997. Majority as a minority: The Russian ethno-nationalism and its ideology in the 1970–1990s. In *Rethinking Nationalism and Ethnicity: The Struggle for Meaning and Order in Europe*, ed. H. R. Wicker, 211–224. Oxford: Berg.

Skurlatov, V. I. 1977a. Sled svetonosnykh. In *Tainy vekov*, ed. V. Sukhanov, 1:327–332. Moscow: Molodaia Gvardiia.

Skurlatov, V. I. 1977b. Uvidevshie vse do kraia mira. . . . In *Tainy vekov*, ed. V. Sukhanov, 1:188–194. Moscow: Molodaia Gvardiia.

Skurlatov, V. I. 1987. Etnicheskii vulkan. In *Dorogami tysiacheletii*, ed. A. Smirnov, 1:203–224. Moscow: Molodaia Gvardiia.

Skurlatova, O. 1979. Zagadki "Vlesovoi knigi." *Tekhnika-Molodezhi* 12:55–59.

Slezkine, Y. 1994. *Arctic Mirrors: Russia and the Small Peoples of the North*. Ithaca, NY: Cornell University Press.

Smith, A. D. 1984. National identity and myths of ethnic descent. *Research in Social Movements, Conflict, and Change* 7:95–130.

Smolin, M. B. 1999. Imperskoe myshlenie i imperskii natsionalizm M. O. Men'shikova. In *Pis'ma k russkoi natsii*, ed. M. O. Men'shikov, 5–26. Moscow: Moskva.

Stefanov, Y. 1995. Velikaia triada Fabra d'Olive. *Volshebnaia gora* 3:177–184.

Sternhell, Z. 1976. Fascist ideology. In *Fascism: A Reader's Guide*, ed. W. Laqueur, 315–376. Cambridge: Cambridge University Press.

Susloparov, M. 1996–1997. Trypil'tsi i my. In *Onuky Dazhbozhi: Pokhodzhennia ukrains'kogo narodu*, ed. V. Dovgych, vols. 1–2: 50, 53. Kyiv: Indo-Evropa, Taki spravy.

Sviatopolk-Chetvertynskii, I. 1998. " . . . U kogo razum v izobilii imeetsia." *Rodina* 4:28–31.

Sylenko, L. 1979. *Maha vira*. Spring Glen, NY: Society of the Ukrainian Native Faith.

Telegin, D. 1996–1997. Khto zhe nashy prapredky? In *Onuky Dazhbozhi: Pokhodzhennia ukrains'kogo narodu*, ed. V. Dovgych, 1–2:54–58. Kyiv: Indo-Evropa, Taki spravy.

Terebikhin, N. M. 1993. *Sakral'naia geografiia Russkogo Severa: Religiozno-mifologicheskoe prostranstvo severnorusskoi kul'tury*. Arkhangel'sk, Russia: Pomorskii Mezhdunarodnyi Pedagogicheskii Institut.

Tilak, B. G. 2002. *Arkticheskaia rodina v Vedakh*. Moscow: Grand.

Torop, V. 1995. Russkie pis'mena, otkuda oni? *Chudesa i prikliucheniia* 3:40–43.

Torop, V. 1996. Dykhanie Boreia. *Chudesa i prikliucheniia* 11:36–39.

Trekhlebov, A. V. 1998. *Taina praslavianskoi tsivilizatsii: Arkheologicheskie i pis'mennye pamiatniki Drevnei Rusi i rezul'taty ikh deshifrovki*. Moscow: Vekhi istorii.

Troshin, Y. 1997. Magiia drevnikh run. *Rodina* 12:24–26.

Trubachev, O. N. 1976. O sindakh i ikh yazyke. *Voprosy yazykoznaniia* 4:39–63.

Trubachev, O. N. 1977. Linguisticheskaia periferiia drevneishego slavianstva: Indo-ariitsy v Severnom Prichernomorie. *Voprosy yazykoznaniia* 6: 13–29.

Trubachev, O. N. 1979. "Staraia Skifiia" Gerodota i slaviane: Linguisticheskii aspekt. *Voprosy yazykoznaniia* 4:29–45.

Trubachev, O. N. 1984a. Indoarica v Skifii i Dakii. In *Etnogenez narodov Balkan i Severnogo Prichernomoriia*, ed. L. A. Gindin, 148–152. Moscow: Nauka.

Trubachev, O. N. 1984b. Svidetel'stvuet linguistika. *Pravda*, Dec. 13, p. 6.

Trubachev, O. N. 1991. *Etnogenez i kul'tura drevneishikh slavian*. Moscow: Nauka.

Trubachev, O. N. 1992. *V poiskakh yedinstva*. Moscow: Nauka.

Trubachev, O. N. 1997. Vzgliad na problemu prarodiny slavian. *Derzhava* 1 (8): 26–31.

Tvorogov, O. V. 1990. "Vlesova kniga." In *Trudy Otdela Drevnerusskoi Literatury*, 43:170–254. Leningrad: Nauka.

Tvorogov, O. V. 1996. Drevnerusskaia literature. In *Ocherki istorii kul'tury slavian*, ed. V. K. Volkov, 363–377. Moscow: Indrik.

Valentinov, A. 1998. Kogda my umeli letat'. *Rossiiskaia gazeta*, Feb. 20.

Vaganov, A. 2000. Drevneishaia kniga slavianskoi tsivilizatsii. *Nezavisimaia gazeta*, Dec. 20, p. 9.

Vasilenko, G. 1988. Taemnyche tysiacholittia. *Kyiv* 4:161–165.

Weissmann, K. 1991. *Schwarze Fahnen, Runenzeichen: Die Entwicklung der politischen Symbolik der deutschen Rechten zwischen 1890 und 1945*. Dusseldorf, Germany: Droste.

Williams, S. 1991. *Fantastic Archaeology: The Wild Side of North American Prehistory*. Philadelphia: University of Pennsylvania Press.

Wistrich, R. S. 1991. *Antisemitism: The Longest Hatred*. London: Themes Methuen.

Yanin, V. L. 2001. Drevneishaia slavianskaia kniga. *Nauka i zhizn'* 2:7–9.

Yanov, A. 1987. *The Russian Challenge and the Year 2000*. Oxford: Basil Blackwell.

Yeliseev, A. 1994. Bestsennoe nasledstvo rasy. *Za russkoe delo* 7:3.

Yerofeeva, V. 2005. Arkaim. *Zavtra* 33 (August): 8.

Zalizniak, A. A., and V. L. Yanin. 2001. Novgorodskaia psaltyr' nachala XI v.—drevneishaia kniga Rusi (Novgorod, 2000 g.). *Vestnik RGNF* 1:153–164.

Zdanovich, G. 1989. Za dve tysiachi let do Troi. *Vokrug sveta* 3:36–41.

Zharnikova, S. V. 1985. Arkhaicheskie motivy severorusskoi narodnoi vyshivki i ikh paralleli v drevnikh ornamentakh naseleniia Yevroaziiskikh stepei. *Informatsionnyi bulleten' Mezhdunarodnoi assotsiatsii po izucheniiu kul'tur Tsentral'noi Azii* 8:13–31.

Zharnikova, S. V. 1986. K voprosu o vozmozhnoi lokalizatsii sviashchennykh gor Meru i Khary indoiranskoi (ariiskoi) mifologii. *Informatsionnyi bulleten' Mezhdunarodnoi assotsiatsii po izucheniiu kul'tur Tsentral'noi Azii* 11:31–44.

Zharnikova, S. V. 1988. Arkhaicheskie motivy severorusskoi ornamentiki (k voprosu o vozmozhnykh praslaviansko-indoiranskikh paralleliah). PhD diss., Institute of Ethnography, Moscow.

Zharnikova, S. V. 1989. Gde zhe vy, gory Meru. *Vokrug sveta* 3:38–41.

Zharnikova, S. V. 1994. Drevnie tainy russkogo Severa. In Guseva 1994c, 2:59–73.

Zharnikova, S. V. 2000. Dorogami mifov (A. S. Pushkin i russkaia narodnaia skazka. *Etnograficheskoe obozrenie* 2:128–139.

Zhukov, D. 1977. Tysiacheletie russkoi kul'tury. *Ogonek* 3:29.

Zhukov, D. 1979. Iz glubin tysiacheletii. *Novyi mir* 4:278–281.

Zhukova, L. 1981. "O svezhii dukh berezy!" In *Fantastika-80*, ed. A. Kuznetsov and V. Shkiriatov, 288–293. Moscow: Molodaia Gvardiia.

Zhukova, L. 1982. Proshu tebia, pripomni. . . . In *Fantastika-82*, ed. I. Chernykh, 226–239. Moscow: Molodaia Gvardiia.

Zhukova, L. 1989. Pisali "chertami i rezami" In *Dorogami tysiacheletii*, ed. A. F. Smirnov, 3:159–166. Moscow: Molodaia Gvardiia.

Zhuravskii, V. 1988. Azbuka neolita. In *Tainy vekov*, ed. V. Sukhanov, 1:54–59. Moscow: Molodaia Gvardiia.

Znoiko, A. P. 1984. Rus' i etruski. In *Ostrov purpurnoi yashcheritsy*, ed. S. Plekhanov, 267–301. Moscow: Molodaia Gvardiia.

Znoiko, A. P. 1989. *Mify Kyivs'koi zemli ta podii starodavni*. Kyiv: Molod'.

TWO

The Challenges of Church Archaeology in Post-Soviet Crimea

MARA KOZELSKY

Crimea, the large peninsula that juts out into the Black Sea, is known variously as the site of the Yalta agreement and the Russian Riviera; it has also been called "the Slavic Pompeii," a toponym that represents its well-preserved array of ruins. Typically the term refers to the Grecian ruins that are so visible in the ancient city of Chersonesos (fig. 2.1); however, these compose only a small portion of Crimea's rich material evidence of the past.

Located on the Black Sea, a body of water that has separated the world's great empires for millennia, Crimea has contained over the years one of the most diverse populations in Europe. Archaeological remnants of many different cultural groups abound. Christian markers, old manuscripts, icons, frescoes, and churches that date from the early Byzantine period through the fifteenth century overwhelm the peninsula and spread from one corner to the other. Crumbling mosques and minarets built by Crimean khans stretch throughout the peninsula. The city of Bakhchisaray, which was the capital of Crimea's Muslim population, contained the old khan's palace and ruins of Zincirli Medrese, the oldest Islamic educational institution in Europe. Cave cities hint at memories of long-forgotten settlers, while burial mounds give evidence of the Scythian past. In several places

Figure 2.1. "Slavic Pompeii": Chersonesos with a view of the Black Sea. Photograph by M. Kozelsky.

in Crimea, layers of these ruins are found, with centuries of religious and cultural groups mixed into one another.

Because of the number of ruins and the variety of confessional groups that claim them, Crimea offers a unique opportunity to examine the relationship between religious nationalism and archaeology. As Phil Kohl and others have argued, ruins and their study sit at the forefront of identity discourse.[1] In Crimea, this identity discourse is particularly complicated, because the Russian Orthodox Church initiated archaeological research and restoration. The active involvement of the Church in archaeological study reflects the prerogatives of a long-standing discipline in Russia, called church archaeology (*tserkovnaia arkheologia*), that studies Christian ruins as relics of the Church. In Crimea the discourse of identity is permeated by a discourse of faith, and the field of archaeology is caught in the middle.[2]

Given the active role of the Church in excavation and renovation of ruins in Crimea, broader theoretical issues surrounding the muddled intersection between faith and science, as well as the connection between nationalism and archaeology, underlie my approach. As I intend to demonstrate, for the Russian Orthodox Church, ruins constitute sacred objects requiring special study and veneration. The Church quite literally views ruins as *sviatyni,* or "holy items," comparable to relics and icons in their ability to reveal God. The role of archaeologists, according to the Church, is to study and preserve ruins, enabling them to become present-day objects of veneration. Christian ruins from the Roman and Byzantine eras denote a holy history by virtue of centuries of Orthodox tradition. The Church views Crimea and its Christian ruins, therefore, not only as the birthplace of Russian and Ukrainian Christianity, but as a holy place on a par with Jerusalem or Mount Athos in Greece. This religious approach to archaeology began in the early to middle nineteenth century, when priests and prelates worked alongside professional archaeologists. In Russia priests and prelates published mainstream histories, guided excavations, and opened museums. By the 1870s and 1880s, the Church's involvement became institutionalized in the subfield of church archaeology, defined, as one scholar put it, by the confluence of theology and history. With the use of ruins as evidence, Christian scholars depicted Crimea as the cradle of Russian Christianity.

Inevitably, this faith-based approach to archaeology produced a nearly impenetrable discourse of Christianity, which has significant and perhaps unintended repercussions for Crimea's other inhabitants, especially Muslims. Although Crimea's Christian presence dates to the early Byzantine era, the peninsula was Islamized in the fifteenth and sixteenth centuries. The Islamization of Crimea's inhabitants, who were a mixture of European settlers and shamanistic Turkic nomads, formed a new *ethnos* called Crimean Tatars.[3] Crimean Tatars are considered the indigenous population in this multiethnic, multiconfessional peninsula and are one of the more unusual populations of Europe. After a couple hundred years of semi-independent association with the Ottoman Empire, the Tatars were colonized by Russia in the late eighteenth century and have fought an often losing battle to preserve their lives and heritage ever since. Most dramatically, after World War II, approximately two hundred thousand Crimean Tatars were forcibly removed from their homes and scattered throughout the Ural Mountains and Uzbekistan after Joseph Stalin accused them of collaborating with German occupiers. Almost half of all deportees died as a result of the deportation, prompting survivors to designate the catastrophic event as genocide. After decades of decimation and exile, they are returning to Crimea and reclaiming their heritage and their homes.[4] Once the dominant group on the peninsula, now they constitute only 13 percent of Crimea's total population. As they assert their ancestral rights, the Tatars have a special stake in religious landmarks and constructions of Crimea's past.[5] Given the return of the Tatars, the religious nature of archaeological research has potentially dangerous consequences.

The restoration of Christian ruins also intersects with the larger identity conflict between Ukrainians and Russians. Khrushchev officially attached Crimea to Ukraine in 1954. After the dissolution of the Soviet Union, Crimea has remained attached to Ukraine following a short-lived bid for independence. However, the majority of its population is Russian-speaking. Crimea is the symbolic southern capital of Russia and is the home of the famed Black Sea naval fleet. Given the strong Russian-leaning population, Crimea's relationship with Ukraine is at best tenuous. Therefore, it is significant that the Russian Orthodox Church, rather than the various splinter branches of the Ukrainian Orthodox Churches, leads restoration.

In this chapter I trace the development of the unique discipline of church archaeology and its influence over Crimea's identity. In order to explore the complex interplay between faith, science, and identity that remains evident in Crimea today, I describe the Christian legends of Crimea and the early association with archaeology. Next, I show how one archbishop, Innokentii Borisov, used archaeology to support a program of Christian renewal. This later developed into the distinct disciplinary field of church archaeology. And finally, I discuss the reemergence of church archaeology in the post-Soviet era today. Whether as a province of the Russian empire or as an autonomous republic attached to Ukraine, Crimea presents no clear-cut case of nationalism and archaeology. Rather, there are competing versions of national identity to which Orthodox Christianity contributes one powerful strain. In this case, the Church treats archaeology as a means to attract Christians, to discover more about God, and to respect holy histories. Yet the association of ruins with Christian legends may generate a harmful discourse of religious nationalism in an era in which Crimea's identity and political future are still uncertain.

The Archaeology of Christian Legends

Before Russia annexed the peninsula in 1783, Crimea was a semi-independent Tatar khanate attached to the Ottoman Empire. Tatars were the majority population and Islam was the official religion. At the time of annexation, Crimea also had a Christian minority, whose roots, according to some theories, dated to the first century CE. This population dwindled to nearly nothing during the Russo-Turkish Wars, but it had been replenished by the mid-nineteenth century by consistent waves of Orthodox refugees fleeing the Ottoman Empire. As Russian imperial rule strengthened in this corner of the world, so did the role of archaeology; historical legitimacy gave the state a reason for being there.

Because its rich array of ruins attracted scholars from across the Russian Empire, Crimea is often considered the birthplace of Russian and Ukrainian archaeological traditions. In 1811 one of Russia's first provincial museums opened in Feodosia, and fifteen years later another opened in Kerch.[6] Most of the empire's archaeologists received their training in Crimea, because the region contained such a rich array of ruins. A. S. Uvarov, the man who defined the Russian archaeological tradition for a half century, produced his first major work on lands in and around Crimea. The relationship between Church, archaeology, and nation is illustrated by the fact that A. S. Uvarov was the son of none other than S. S. Uvarov, the master architect of Russia's 1833 nationality platform, "Orthodoxy, Autocracy, and Nationality."[7]

The earliest archaeological research in Crimea revolved around classical antiquity, a development that was much in line with the rise of philhellenism that Suzanne Marchand notes in Germany in the eighteenth and nineteenth centuries.[8] More to the point, perhaps, archaeological research in Crimea, which was colonized by Greeks in the fifth century BCE, provided Catherine II with evidence to support a Western pedigree for Russia. It also helped buttress her own Greek Project, in which she envisioned Russia as the heir of the Byzantine Empire and aspired to place her grandson, Constantine, on the throne of Constantinople.[9] With the Greek War of Independence, however, the philhellenic movement in Russia transformed into a phil-*Orthodox* movement, and the study of Christian ruins took a higher priority.[10] In 1827 the Black Sea Naval Fleet even sponsored a dig to uncover Christian artifacts in Chersonesos. This dig and later attempts to excavate Crimean Christianity reflected a shift in Russian imperial policy regarding the Tatars. Initially, the state followed a laissez-faire approach to Crimea's Muslim population and resisted any movement of Christianity in the region for fear of inciting an uprising among the Tatars. As tensions with the Ottoman Empire mounted, however, nationalists inside and outside of state structures began to look at Crimea as crucial terrain contested between Christians and Muslims, as well as the center of Russia's Black Sea aspirations. Church scholars played a leading role in bringing Crimea's past to the fore of Russian national consciousness.

Christian scholars revived several legends to give Crimea a holy pedigree. One of the most important was a debate about whether or not Scythia, then considered the proto-Slavic nation, was the apostle Saint Andrew's mission field.[11] After closely comparing legends with texts from the Middle Ages, however, one famous Church historian concluded that Saint Andrew not only visited the southern shores of the Crimean peninsula but also penetrated deeply into the northern Black Sea littoral and other areas of the Russian empire in a mission to the Scythians in 63 CE.[12] They further believed that several early, first-century Christian communities formed, including a population of more than two thousand near Chersonesos.[13] Work of Church scholars legitimated the myth of Saint Andrew by offering a "scientific analysis" based on exegesis of medieval chronicles. This line of interpretation became one of the cornerstones of Crimea's holy pedigree—conversion by a first-century apostle—and one of the main myths that archaeologists tried to substantiate.

Other legends include the life of Saint Clement, the first-century pope exiled to Crimea by the Roman emperor Trajan. Many believe that Saint Clement found Christian communities inspired by Saint Andrew and converted more Christians himself. Subsequently, according to many estimates, Crimea had more than seventy-five churches in the first century CE, a number drawn from the life of Saint Clement but also reflected in archaeological surveys of the "cave cities."[14] Other highlights of Crimea's Christian history included the seven martyrs of Chersonesos, who were first dispatched to Crimea in 310, when Jerusalem's patriarch sent a mission to Tauride.[15] Scholars also celebrated the life of Saint Martin, who was incarcerated in Chersonesos in the mid-seventh century, and Cyril and Methodius, the famous apostles to the Slavs believed to have studied Khazar and Jewish languages in the Crimean city.[16] Following the 1827 dig and the explosion of Christian scholarship, archaeologists spent the next several decades exploring sites of these early Christians; most associated the cliff churches at Inkerman with the first-century apostles and the sainted popes.

While first-century roots may have created a holy pedigree for Crimea, the legend of Saint Vladimir became the center of Russian Orthodox identity in the Black Sea region. According to *The Chronicle of Nestor*, Prince Vladimir accepted baptism in Chersonesos after conquering the city in 988.[17] Many scholars believed that Prince Vladimir's conversion defined Russia. It gave the people a Christian identity, drew them together as a nation, and created a state.[18] Thus, the legend of Saint Vladimir provided the most significant link between Crimean and Russian Christianity and became a fundamental rationalization for the Church's expansion in

Crimea. It also enabled Russian nationalists to argue that Orthodoxy was present before Islam and, subsequently, that Russia was the rightful heir to the region. For the Church, however, the baptism of Saint Vladimir was not merely a rationale for expansion but the moment of its inception in all of Slavdom. The Church believed it had a responsibility to uncover ruins associated with Prince Vladimir and to raise them for veneration.

Archbishop Innokentii and the Birth of Church Archaeology

The real impetus for Church archaeology in Crimea came during the mid-nineteenth century, when the Church attempted to consolidate its position there. It did so through the person of one of its most famous Orthodox prelates, Archbishop Innokentii Borisov, a typical nineteenth-century intellectual who dabbled in many areas of research.[19] By the time of his appointment to the Kherson-Tauride diocese, Innokentii Borisov had become famous inside and outside the Church. His supporters widely considered him to be Russia's first "modern" theologian and most prolific preacher; his collected sermons, catechisms, and acathists (Orthodox hymns), as well as political and philosophical treatises, fill eleven volumes.[20] His accomplishments, moreover, attracted attention within secular Russian educated circles and were frequently reviewed in nonreligious journals.[21] Like many other prelates of his time, he had contacts throughout various fields of research and held memberships in multiple academic societies. Many intellectuals outside the church recognized him as a legitimate social scientist.[22]

When Innokentii moved to his post in Kherson-Tauride, he took an active role in the predominant scholarly society of the region, the Odessa Society of History and Antiquity, founded in 1839. As soon as he arrived in Odessa, he continued his predecessors' projects and immediately advocated further study of Crimea's Christian past. However, he took archaeological and historical research much further in a campaign designed to recognize Crimea as a special holy place of the Russian Empire, based largely upon the peninsula's spectacular Byzantine ruins.[23] Innokentii's approach to archaeology served as the basis for religious science in Crimea for seventy-five years and is evident in Church archaeology today. Principally, Innokentii characterized his work as a "distinct field of archaeology," a "holy archaeology," depicted by "cognitive study of good and evil" and analysis of the "first traces of God among humanity."[24] Thus, whereas other scholars might have pursued archaeology for the sake of abstract knowledge or the explicit service of the state, Innokentii pursued another, more sacred agenda. He was interested in archaeology's ability to reveal God and believed that ruins should be incorporated into religious rituals or, in the case of ancient churches that were relatively intact, be renovated to hold Orthodox services.

Throughout his post as the archbishop of Kherson and Tauride, Innokentii supported and publicized the society's research on Crimean Christianity in area newspapers such as the *Odessa Herald* and through correspondence with bureaucrats, prelates, and nationalists scattered widely across Russia.[25] He also patronized the society scholars' work and maintained an active correspondence with other local researchers.[26] And although Innokentii produced no formal scientific studies, he incorporated his findings into all other areas of his activity, including sermons. He did publish several articles for a popular readership in *Odessa Herald,* the local newspaper. Most importantly for this discussion, Innokentii was responsible for bringing several of Crimea's archaeological sites into the orbit and control of the Russian Orthodox Church. It was he who formulated the plan to cast Crimea as a holy place of the Russian Empire based on the peninsula's fantastic array of ruins.

In a seminal document titled "Notes on the Renewal of Ancient Holy Places in the Crimean Mountains," he proposed building a network of several monasteries on sites deemed most holy.[27] Innokentii provided a brief narrative about each site, explaining legends or miracles that contributed to their special holiness. Some sites, such as the springs of Cosmas and Damian, constituted natural phenomena considered sacred by local populations. The other sites were to be built on ruins that had been studied by historians and archaeologists. The most significant sites of archaeological interest were the Dormition Monastery, the ruins of Chersonesos, and the cliff churches in Inkerman.[28] He proposed that the renewed monasteries be called "Russian Athos" after one of the most famous holy places in the Eastern Orthodox world, Mount Athos in Greece.

For Innokentii, the continuity between past and present was fundamental. Throughout his proposal and his writings elsewhere, he argued that Christians had a holy duty to uncover, study, and restore Crimea's ancient churches. Nowhere was this connection between ruins and restoration more apparent than in Chersonesos.[29] These ruins, he argued, were among the most holy in all of Russia, yet they had been completely ignored. In one of his sermons, he expressed shock over their condition: "The church that according to all probability was the place that St. Vladimir was baptized, and from which began the enlightenment of the faith for all of Russia . . . was left to the trampling of animals, who destroyed the remaining grasses that covered our cradle of Orthodoxy."[30] Literally, the ruins of Chersonesos, which bore witness to Saint Vladimir's baptism, had become pastureland for farmers' herds, and according to the archbishop, the local Orthodox believers had betrayed their duty to protect them. Later, during the Crimean War, Innokentii's passion for restoring the old monasteries rose to a much higher level, when wartime sermons drew parallels between Russia's losses and the neglect of antiquity in Crimea. "Maybe," he told his congregants, "this fiery battle has risen as a response to our former coldness to our holy history."[31]

Abandonment of the ruins to the ravages of time was tantamount to sacrilege, for as Innokentii drilled into his parishioners before, during, and after the war, the ruins themselves were holy. Russian pilgrims and travelers in the Sevastopol area were deeply disappointed not to see a monument to Saint Vladimir, who had turned Russians away from "idolatry and into the saving light of the Gospel." Thus, Innokentii concluded, it was important "for all of Russia . . . to build a church in memory of the Christianizing of St. Vladimir."[32] Church-building and restoration in Crimea was not a matter of historic preservation, or even of national representation, but of honoring and perpetuating the faith. Because the archbishop perceived the ruins as having a holy past, Christians had an obligation to rescue them from oblivion.

Innokentii asserted that recent archaeological studies and travel narratives, especially those by scholars noted for their work in Crimea, P. I. Keppen and S. N. Montadon, rescued "Crimea's holy memories from oblivion" and proved that it had a long history of early ascetic monasticism.[33] Not only did the ruins contain evidence of a glorious Christian past and visitation of saints; they continued to attract respect and admiration from local inhabitants. Even the Tatars themselves, who were at one time Christian, "express their memory of their former beliefs in their occasional pilgrimages to places sanctified by Christianity."[34]

A short yet revealing petition from Orthodox believers in Crimea accompanied his proposal to the synod. Signed "Residents of the cities of Simferopol, Bakhchisaray, the village of Alushta, and other neighboring cities and villages," this petition reiterated many of the points made in the proposal. The petition reveals some popular support for the Church's appropriation of the ruins.[35] Like Innokentii's proposal, this petition called upon legitimating discourses of history and archaeology to advocate restoration: "History clearly shows that the Crimean peninsula from the first centuries of Christianity was familiar with the Gospel of Christ and had abundant Christians, and martyrs for Christ. Many Christian monuments, particularly the remains of the churches in the Crimean mountains and cliffs, provide evidence of how many Christians were here."[36] The petition reveals two fundamental impulses. First, Crimean ruins held a special Christian significance for many believers. Second, they should be restored for active use of the faith. Emblematic of Christianizing discourses, the petition emphasized Crimea's sacred Christian history, which dated to the first century, and stated that the ruins, especially the cave churches, constituted evidence of Crimea's holiness. Thus, instead of advocating further study and research into Crimean Christian ruins, the petition encouraged restoration and active use.[37] With the selection of sites for restoration, the proposal and the petition inscribed Russian Orthodox authority over sacred landscapes and laid claim to noted landmarks. Therefore, this Christian science also produced a nationalist discourse of rule. Resurrection of Christian history legitimated Russian expansion into a Muslim territory. The new communities also relied heavily upon a carefully reconstructed past and the manipulation of ruins.

By the end of Innokentii's administration, the Church and archaeologists had worked together to project plans for restoration of several communities. The most impressive was the monastery dedicated to Saint Vladimir in the ruins of Chersonesos.[38] This monastery literally incorporated ruins of an older church into its foundation. Scholars worked closely with priests to restore the ruins of the church to represent the exact style of the Byzantine church in which the prince would have been baptized (fig. 2.2). The Church even established at the monastery an archaeological museum staffed by priests.

The monastery in the Inkerman cliffs represented another impressive joint effort between archaeologists and clergy. Inkerman is one of the most curious places in Crimea, and one of the most picturesque. It is an ancient city, which in the past was inhabited by successive waves of settlers and their conquerors; its origin is contested and unknown. Only seven kilometers from Sevastopol, ruins of the ancient city spread along the mouth of the Black River through the seaside cave city of Calamita, where remnants of a fortress and its encircling wall overlook the sea. Here, the Church renewed the ruins of an ancient church that some scholars dated to the Middle Ages and other more optimistic Christian archaeologists liked to date to the first century (fig. 2.3).[39] It is located in a cave-city complex, with remnants of more than two hundred structures built into the cliffs, eighty of which archaeologists determined were churches.[40]

Inkerman was a hot-spot of archaeological and scholarly research, generating far-reaching controversy among the era's most prolific academic writers.[41] The Calamita fortress and its caves, according to most scholars,

Figure 2.2. St. Vladimir Church under renovation in the ruins of Chersonesos. Photograph by M. Kozelsky.

Figure 2.3. The Inkerman Monastery. Photograph by M. Kozelsky.

Figure 2.4. The Dormition Monastery. Photograph by M. Kozelsky.

dated to the eighth century, when Byzantine icon-worshippers fled to Crimea during the empire's iconoclastic period.[42] However, archaeological findings produced a diverse, often contrasting body of scholarship. An article in *New Russian Calendar* (1855) sorted through some of the controversies, especially the debate over whether the Scythians or the Byzantines founded the Inkerman fortress.[43] Coincident with the controversy over the monastery's founding, scholars also debated the origin of Christianity there, for like many other monasteries in Russian Athos, Inkerman also has a sacred history, or legends of saints, martyrs, and miracles. In fact, many Christian scholars hypothesized that this was the site of the seventy-five cave churches inspired by the proselytizing of Saint Andrew and Saint Clement.

The Dormition Monastery, which is situated between the Karaite ruins in Chufut Kale and the remnants of the khan's palace in Bakhchisaray, was renewed also. Like the Inkerman Monastery, it is built into the cliffs (fig. 2.4). The earliest surviving records of its history date to 1625, but Russians believed that the monastery had been in operation centuries before. Once the center of Orthodoxy in Crimea, the monastery was rumored to be especially holy; every year on its holy day, August 15, pilgrims from all around streamed into Bakhchisaray for the annual journey to the cave church,[44] while travelers, antiquarians, and archaeologists visited the monastery to study its cave architecture. Before the Greeks left

Crimea in the eighteenth century, the Dormition Monastery operated as the diocesan seat and became a meeting place for Crimea's multinational Orthodox population. Because the monastery was centrally located in the khan's capital, however, its role was far more ambiguous than Innokentii's sacred history revealed, for it often constituted a contentious contact zone between Tatar and Orthodox populations. It is precisely due to its real historical role and contentious presence that the Dormition Monastery became the most logical site to begin the process of Church expansion. Opening a Christian monument in a city celebrated for its Islamic heritage marked an assertive step forward in the competition between confessional landscapes.

Innokentii's active scholarship and fund-raising used archaeology to legitimate Church expansion and building in a predominantly Muslim area. Ruins themselves were resurrected and transformed into objects of faith. The monastery at Chersonesos was considered particularly holy because it contained traces of the original structure in which Saint Vladimir was presumed to have been baptized, while the cave churches of Inkerman were to be equally revered for their remnants of devout eremitic Christians who were believed to have lived there from the first century. In Crimea, archaeology played a crucial role in mediating believers' relationship with God and nation. Although Innokentii is considered one of the founding fathers of Crimea's church archaeology, he himself did not use that term. The focus on Christian archaeology acquired a unique rubric at the end of the century, after the field of archaeology began to specialize.

Church Archaeology in Crimea

Given the importance of archaeology in Crimea and the high visibility of the Church in excavation there, it is no great surprise that a foundational attempt to define the field of church archaeology came from the region. Initially, religion blended indistinguishably with the developing field of archaeology. Early on the study of archaeology was combined with history in imperial societies such as the Imperial Society of History and Antiquity (1804) and, later, the Odessa Society for History and Antiquity. By the mid-nineteenth century, however, the first imperial society exclusively devoted to archaeology had formed, and by 1869 the very first national archaeological conference met in Moscow. For decades, the center of archaeological study closest to Crimea in the nineteenth century was the New Russia University, located in Odessa.

In the 1880s, the scholar N. F. Krasnosel'tsev, a professor at the New Russia University, was prompted by the increasing specialization within archaeology to define church archaeology as a subfield. Church archaeology, according to Krasnosel'tsev, was any form of archaeological excavation that focused on religious and specifically Christian artifacts. It included the study of ruins of churches, utensils, icons, frescoes, and even cults. Because such exploration illuminated the history of the Russian Orthodox Church, he argued that church archaeology had an ambiguous position. It was a historical science. But because the subject was Christianity, church archaeology was also a subject of theology. Therefore, church archaeology, like the history of the Church, provided believers with evidence to support their faith. In essence, because it straddled history and theology, church archaeology was an "interdisciplinary" science, although Krasnosel'tsev did not use that term.[45]

Krasnosel'tsev did not distinguish between researchers who studied religious artifacts from a viewpoint of faith and those whose viewpoint was science. For Krasnosel'tsev and all others who followed in his footsteps, the only determinant of "church archaeology" was that it studied something related to the Church. In other words, he identified researchers as "church archaeologists" whether or not the authors placed themselves in that category. Thus, for example, the majority of the seven national archaeology meetings held by the time he wrote the article had distinct rubrics for church archaeology in their programs.[46] In the 1884 meeting, held in Odessa, however, there was no distinct category made for church archaeology.[47] Krasnosel'tsev nevertheless concluded that the field was woven throughout the program, "reflected in general archaeology," arguing that "church archaeology" was too organically related to Russian archaeology for program organizers to make an exception. This connection was most prevalent, he pointed out, in the study of the Middle Ages, when religion permeated politics, culture, and everyday life.[48] Thus, he implied, all archaeological excavation associated with the Byzantine era was church archaeology. As an interesting reflection of his point, archaeologists who attended the national convention of archaeologists in Odessa took a steamboat to Crimea at its conclusion to view the Byzantine-era ruins, many of which by then had been transformed by Archbishop Innokentii's Russian Athos program into live monasteries.[49]

Krasnosel'tsev's article captures an important, recurring theme: Orthodoxy permeated archaeology in Crimea as much as and as indissolubly as nationalism permeated archaeology elsewhere.[50] In nineteenth-century Crimea, archaeology was perceived as having an important religious function and a crucial role in supporting faith. The consequence of this line of thought was that the Church exercised control over those sites believed to be of Christian value. It enjoyed ownership privileges over the sites and could decide who dug there and for what purposes.

The role of the Church in archaeology was reflected further in the development of scholarly societies in Crimea itself. In the late 1880s, Crimea's first major independent scholarly society formed, the Tauride Archival Commission, which later became the Tauride Society for History, Archaeology, and Ethnography. Previously, most local scholarship had been conducted through the Odessa Society. Following the precedent set by Archbishop Innokentii in the Odessa Society, clergy composed a significant number of the Tauride Archival Commission's three-hundred-strong membership. Among them were Iriniarkh, bishop of Berezovsk; Dmitrii, archbishop of Tauride and Simferopol; Feofan, bishop of Poltava; and many local priests. Church archaeology remained a chief focus in both organizations, evident in the agendas of their meetings and in their publications, which produced only about 40 percent of the meeting proceedings. One of the earliest journal issues of the Tauride Archival Commission (vol. 5, 1888) was dedicated entirely to the matter of church archaeology and published a series of primary documents related to the excavations and building of the Saint Vladimir Church in Chersonesos. Alexander Kristianovich, one of the founding members of the commission, in fact advocated producing this 1888 volume in honor of the anniversary of Prince Vladimir's Christianization of Rus.[51]

The professionalization of archaeology in the nineteenth century was accompanied by a popular acceptance that ruins had religious meaning. One of the most widely read travel guides for Crimea, which was written by F. V. Livanov and published in Moscow in 1875, takes this connection for granted and illustrates the degree to which archaeology, religion, and nationalism developed into a seamless line of discourse. This lengthy narrative, composed of more than fifty chapters, which were often reprinted as separate pamphlets, describes the history and contemporary status of Crimean ruins, monasteries, and holy sites in great detail. Livanov's depiction of Chersonesos reflects the degree to which the trope of holiness lasted through the prerevolutionary period: "What fortune for Russia, that she possesses the first baptistery of its Christianity, there on the same corner of earth where Vladimir converted from paganism to Christianity, and where receiving higher inspiration, burning with zealotry, enlightened all of pagan Russia with Christianity . . . ! This place, like Palestine and Jerusalem, is truly holy for Russian Christians."[52] This pamphlet, needless to say, encouraged tourists to visit the ruins out of their religious devotion. In nineteenth-century Crimea, we see a strong connection between faith, ruins, identity, and tourism, which has reappeared today.

By 1917 many of Crimea's most celebrated Christian ruins that were actively researched by archaeologists had been transformed into real, working monasteries, most evidently in Chersonesos, Inkerman, and Bakhchisaray. The Church erected a monastery serving fifty brothers in Chersonesos on top of ruins that dated to the fifth century BCE and founded a museum for the storage of religious artifacts. Dormition Monastery, sandwiched between Chufut Kale on one side and the khan's palace on the other, had five small churches, numerous brothers, and was still growing. Inkerman Monastery had fifty brothers.[53] Based on a complicated Christian history and an extensive array of ruins that testified to its Christian past, Crimea acquired the reputation of being a special holy place in the Russian Empire, and these ruins and monasteries attracted pilgrims from all over the Slavic world.[54] In just a few decades, priests, prelates, and archaeologists had imbued a predominantly Muslim region with a Christian identity, and with the example of its ruins, Crimea became especially holy.

Church Archaeology Today

As one may expect, the field of church archaeology in Crimea all but disappeared in the decades of Soviet rule. Elsewhere scholars have well documented the Soviets' disdain for regional studies and even greater distaste for religion. Thus, not only did the study of religious ruins in Crimea decline, but the Tauride Archival Society was disbanded as well. Archbishop Innokentii's renovated churches and monasteries became storage facilities for nuclear weapons and other such things, while Crimea's regional history was simply ignored, unless a narrative of workers' consciousness could be culled out from the evidence.[55] However, the climate of glasnost under Gorbachev and Ukraine's declaration of independence in 1991 led to a rapid reconception of historical and archaeological fields. In Crimea the Church surfaced to fill the void left by the absence of traditional Soviet-style scholarship. Now Orthodoxy in Crimea seeks to reclaim its prerevolutionary status, influence, and land. Thus, one of the interesting conundrums facing archaeologists and the Church today, fifteen years after the collapse of Soviet rule in Crimea and the creation of the Autonomous Republic of Crimea in Ukraine, is who has authority over ruins that are considered to be holy. Authority over the ruins is

further complicated by the diversity of faith and cultural groups seeking to justify status by using the past. The Orthodox Church itself has splintered into several branches, each aspiring to represent the Orthodox believers of Ukraine, while Crimean Tatars are returning to their homeland, seeking to reestablish themselves after decades of exile. Each of these groups, and others, has a stake in regulating Crimea's historical landscape.

Before moving on to discuss the problems facing church archaeology today, however, it is important to note that the Church's perspective on the role of archaeology has not changed substantially. In a preface to a recently published collection of articles about church archaeology in Crimea, *Orthodox Antiquities of Tauride* (*Pravoslavnye drevnosti Tavriki: Sbornik materialov po tserkovnoi arkheologii*) Metropolitan Lazar of Simferopol and Crimea discussed the importance of the field for faith and science, as well as the essential connection of Christianity in Crimea.[56] Lazar paralleled the ruins to other holy objects like icons, writing that "Material evidence" of the past reveals "Orthodox truths" and draws observers closer to God. For reasons of faith, Orthodox followers should "preserve valuable material relics of past epochs: ancient churches and their ruins, holy places, reminders of Holy Traditions, Byzantine frescoes and icon paintings."[57] The editors of the collection, themselves archaeologists, concur with Lazar, arguing that a knowledge of religious history is essential. "For the church-going person," they write, "studying and learning historical truth is not a leisurely past-time, but a spiritual obligation and necessity." However, they take this a step further, to warn against dereliction of religious duty: "Without knowledge of the sources of our spiritual traditions, we risk a cataclysmic breach with God, trading Holy Truth for deceitful superstition, the threshold of emptiness."[58] The study and preservation of ruins is paramount, for it is conducted not merely for understanding the past, but to come into a closer relationship with God.

Like their predecessors, the contributors to this collection argue that there is something unique about Crimea's Christian past. In what appears to be an echo of nineteenth-century philosophies, Metropolitan Lazar wrote: "Material in this collection convincingly shows the truth, that Tauride earth from ancient times has a direct relationship to the history of the Eternal Church. It convinces us that the Cradle of Orthodoxy appears in Crimean lands. . . . Present here is the unique sensation of ancient Christian history of Crimean lands, amazing with the abundance of religious treasures, material incarnation, which reveals the richness of

Church archaeology."[59] Just as decades before the Soviet Union existed, the Church again views Crimea as the cradle of Christianity, a holy place of unique importance.

It should be emphasized that the Church continues to see archaeology as having the ability to make a critical contribution to faith. In fact, after decades of repression under the Soviet Union, much of the population that would traditionally be Orthodox—the Russians and the Ukrainians—are now atheists. Thus, the authors argue that studying Christian antiquities can provide a doorway to faith. "For many people," they write, "still not accepted into the Christian Church, but trying to love antiquity, knowledge of Orthodox antiquities might be their first step on the path to Christ." In other words, church archaeology and the preservation of religious monuments have the power to convert or facilitate entry into the Church. Church archaeology, according to the editors, can also counter the proliferation of sects, foreign missionaries, and pagan cults in the post-Soviet era. Knowledge of the Orthodox past, from this perspective, serves to combat the "newly appearing sects and dishonest scholars" that make claims of being closest to original Christianity.[60]

Despite its primary goal of protecting and preserving holy artifacts, church archaeology has the potential to generate controversy and to seriously influence Crimean identity politics. Because the Church still considers ruins tantamount to other holy items like icons, it desires jurisdiction over them as in the past. The Church views the sites of Inkerman, Dormition Monastery, and Chersonesos as holy and arranges pilgrimages there for Orthodox believers. Just as they did more than a century ago in Tsarist Russia, churches and their ruins constitute a main attraction for Crimea tourists.[61] However, this sanctification of historical monuments encounters obstacles in present-day Crimea, including conflict between the Church and archaeologists.

One of the more controversial moves of the Church has been its involvement in Chersonesos. The site at Chersonesos is one of the central stages of the post-Soviet Orthodox revival, for it is believed to contain the baptismal font of Saint Vladimir, the "converter of all of Russia."[62] In 1997, against the express wishes of Ukraine's Ministry of Culture and the museum directors of the National Preserve of Tauric Chersonesos, the Orthodox Church hired a helicopter to install a gazebo over what is believed to have been the font in which Prince Vladimir, the tenth-century saint credited with converting Kyivan Rus, was baptized.[63] The gazebo is placed directly in the middle of an impressive array of ruins that date back to the fifth century BCE and include remnants of Hellenic, Roman, and Byzantine cultures (fig. 2.5).

Figure 2.5. The baptistery in honor of St. Vladimir (installed in the ruins in 1997). Photograph by M. Kozelsky.

On the outskirts of the ruins, but still very much in the center of the archaeological preserve, the Church has renewed the cathedral in honor of Saint Vladimir that was initially built in the middle of the nineteenth century. The visual contrast between a newly renovated model of a Byzantine cathedral and the Greek ruins for which Chersonesos is primarily known is striking (fig. 2.2). Yet this sight of the imposing church on the ruins in Chersonesos is only one example of many. The Church and the archaeologists will have to negotiate for the future of ruins deemed to be holy. And although museum directors have not turned over the old monastery buildings, which now house the museum and its offices, it does cooperate with the large church on the ruins. The Saint Vladimir church has an indefinite lease on the square in which it sits, and pilgrims are allowed to visit it without purchasing tickets to the museum complex.[64] This compromise stands as a testimony to the unusual relationship between religion and archaeology in Crimea.

Apart from rethinking its relationship with archaeologists, the Church must also negotiate with other religious groups that lay claim to Crimean landmarks. In Crimea, where Ukrainians, Russians, and Crimean Tatars are competing for control over the past, the challenges for the role of archaeology in identity formation are perhaps particularly pronounced. One of the central issues involves the struggles between the mainly Russian and Ukrainian residents who lived in Crimea during the Soviet regime and the Crimean Tatars who are now returning to their homeland after decades of exile. A well-publicized conflict between Tatars and Christians over moderating the past has occurred at Dormition Monastery. Situated between Chufut Kale and Bakhchisaray, the monastery, it seems, shares a much-contested space with Zincirli Medrese, the oldest Muslim educational institution in Europe. Like the khan's palace in Bakhchisaray, it is treasured as one of the most important historical monuments of Crimean Tatar culture.[65] Each of these institutions has its own set of scholars who seek to establish legitimacy based on the past, and the square of the monastery has been the site of more than one protest.

Finally, something might be said about the splintering of the Orthodox Church and control over the ruins. After the Soviet Union dissolved and power devolved to Ukraine, the Russian Orthodox Church, which was the official Orthodox Church of the Soviet Union, followed suit and began to splinter along national lines. Several new Orthodox Churches were created, each vying to represent the new nation of Ukraine: the Ukrainian Orthodox Church Moscow Patriarchate (UOC-MP), the Ukrainian Orthodox Church of the Kyiv Patriarchate (UOC-KP), and the Ukrainian Autocephalous Orthodox Church (UAOC). These branches are locked in dispute over who should represent the new Ukraine; issues range from whether the churches should follow the patriarch in Moscow or the one in Kyiv, whether liturgies should be conducted in Russian or in Ukrainian, and who inherits property that belonged to the Russian Orthodox Church before 1917. In Crimea, the UOC-MP is the dominant church, reflecting the fact that there is a very large population of Russians there who consider themselves loyal to the patriarch of Moscow and not the patriarch of Kyiv. The restoration of religious ruins in Crimea has thus far been primarily led by the UOC-MP, which in turn lays claim to the monuments. In their preface to the collection of articles about Crimea's church archaeology, the editors make this explicit: "Russian Orthodoxy is beyond time and borders—it is a unique phenomenon in the history of the world, the source of which is located in Crimea. In this appear the mystical ties united through Chersonesos's Christening of Vladimir of Kyiv, 'Second Rome' in Constantinople, and Third Rome in Moscow." The excerpt above demonstrates the challenges of church archaeology. It is a scientific discipline based in faith, yet plagued by competing discourses of nationalism. The editors associate Chersonesos, its ruins, and the legend of Saint Vladimir not merely with Orthodoxy, but with *Russian* Orthodoxy. The editors note, for example, that "Russian Orthodoxy is beyond time and borders."[66] Such a comment implies that although Crimea is technically attached to Ukraine, it is still Russian. This line of reasoning draws a spiritual continuum between Chersonesos and

Moscow and is highly reminiscent of nineteenth-century religious-nationalist platforms that attempted to link Russia to Crimea through the baptism of Vladimir, an argument that the other Ukrainian national churches are likely to find unappealing.

In Crimea, and in Russian archaeology as a whole, faith has constructed scientific knowledge in crucial ways, while ruins themselves have become integrated into religious practices.[67] One of the most remarkable outcomes of this "religious science," has been the transformation of ruins into relics. From the early to middle years of the nineteenth century, Christian scholars argued that Crimea was the cradle of Russian Christianity, drawing upon legends of Crimea's choir of saints. Even today, the Church continues to view archaeology as having a critical contribution to make to faith. This nexus between faith, archaeology, and identity is much more pronounced for Orthodox than for other Christians, or perhaps those of other faiths as well. This is because Orthodoxy privileges material expressions of faith, such as relics, icons, and ruins, as conduits to God. Thus, whereas Catholics and Protestants might visit ruins in Jerusalem to learn more about the life of Jesus, pilgrims visit ruins in Crimea to transcend their worldly experience and interface with God.[68]

This spiritual conception of ruins is even more complicated by nationalism. Ruins in Crimea are perceived as having not only a special Orthodox significance, but a special *Russian* significance as well. Archaeology in this case, and undoubtedly elsewhere in the Orthodox world, has become an instrument of faith and a link between Church and state. And ironically, the state in question is not Ukrainian, but Russian. In the nineteenth century, Tatars and Jews found their landscapes reinscribed in a sacred Russian Orthodox geography supported by science. Today, archaeology appears to be reprising its prerevolutionary role.

Notes

1. See, for example, Philip L. Kohl, "Nationalism and Archaeology: On the Constructions of Nations and the Reconstructions of the Remote Past," *Annual Review of Anthropology* 27 (1998): 223–246; Philip L. Kohl and Clare Fawcett, *Nationalism, Politics, and the Practice of Archaeology* (Cambridge, U.K., 1995).
2. According to archaeologists excavating in Chersonesos at the time of publication, the influence of the Church over archaeology has receded in recent years. While this may be the case in Chersonesos, it is not necessarily so for other parts of Crimea. In the small village of Golubinka, for example, the Church has been at odds with local Muslim groups over the restoration of a holy site. Archaeologists have been called in to consult on the affair, and

the Church plans to build a structure with glass floors so that ruins are visible below the surface. For the starkest expression of controversy in the affair, see Natalia Kiseleva, "Slabost' vlasti i bezzakonie porozhdaiut tatarskii terrorizm," *Vremia Krymskoe,* June 22, 2006, 4; and for the Tatar perspective, Ibraim Abdullaev, "Torg s istoriei ne umesten!" *Golos Kryma,* no. 28, July 7, 2006.

3. My understanding of Crimean Tatar ethnogenesis is derived almost entirely from Brian Glyn Williams, *The Crimean Tatars: The Diaspora Experience and the Forging of a Nation* (Boston, 2001), 7–38. See also Brian Glyn Williams, "The Ethnogenesis of the Crimean Tatars: An Historical Reinterpretation," *Journal of the Royal Asiatic Society* 11 (2001): 3.
4. Many of these issues received international attention when the Tatars commemorated the sixtieth anniversary of their exile. See the statement issued by the Mejlis: "The Statement of the Participants of the All Crimean Mourning meeting, Dedicated to the Memory of the Victims of the Deportation of the Crimean Tatar People," www.qurultay.org/eng/ayrinti.asp?HaberNo=2004051803 (accessed May 25, 2004). For English-language sources devoted to the study of Crimean Tatars as well as this terrible episode of Crimean history, see Williams, *Crimean Tatars;* Alan Fisher, *Between Russians, Ottomans, and Turks: Crimea and Crimean Tatars* (Istanbul, 1998); Alan Fisher, *Crimean Tatars* (Stanford, CA, 1986); E. Allworth, ed., *Tatars of the Crimea: Their Struggle for Survival* (Durham, NC, 1988); Greta Lynn Uehling's excellent and compassionate analysis of Crimean Tatar memory, *Beyond Memory: The Crimean Tatars' Deportation and Return* (New York, 2004). For Crimean Tatars as a case of ethnic cleansing in larger works, see Svetlana Alieva, ed., *Tak eto bylo: Natsional'nye repressii v SSSR, 1919–1952 gody* (Moscow, 1993); N. F. Bugai, "K voprosu o deportatsii narodov SSSR v 30–40kh godakh," *Istoriia SSSR* 6 (1989); Aleksandr M. Nekrich, *The Punished Peoples: The Deportation and Fate of Soviet Minorities at the End of the Second World War,* trans. George Saunders (New York, 1978); J. Otto Pohl, *Ethnic Cleansing in the USSR* (Westport, CT, 1999).
5. For more information on Crimean Tatars and their political representation, see Natalya Belitser, "'Indigenous Status' for the Crimean Tatars in Ukraine: A History of a Political Debate," www.iccrimea.org/scholarly/elections2002.html (accessed May 26, 2004). The most up-to-date English-language information on the present conflict surrounding the Crimean Tatars' return can be found in the work of Idil Izmirili. See, for example, "Regionalism and the Crimean Tatar Political Factor in the 2004 Ukrainian Presidential Election," *Journal of Central Asia and the Caucasus* 1 (1) (Apr. 2006): 138–152; and "Return to the Golden Cradle: An Overview of Post-Return Dynamics and Resettlement Angst of Crimean Tatars in Crimea," in *Finding Home: Population Movements in Eurasia,* ed. Cynthia Buckley and Blair Ruble (Washington, DC, forthcoming). See also Gul'nara Bekirov, *Krym i krymskie tatary, XIX–XX veka* (Moscow, 2005); and *Krymskotatarskaia problema v SSSR (1944–1991)* (Moscow, 2004).

6. For more on early museums in southern Ukraine, see A. A. Nepomniashchii, *Razvitie istoricheskogo kraevedeniia v Krymu XIX–nachale XX veka* (Simferopol, Ukraine, 1995), 47; and G. C. Lebedev, *Istoriia otechestvennoi arkheologii, 1700–1971* (St. Petersburg, 1992).
7. For more on the nationality platform, see Nicholas V. Riasanovsky, Nicholas I and Official Nationality in Russia, 1825–1855 (Berkeley, CA, 1967); and Cynthia Whittaker, The Origins of Modern Russian Education: An Intellectual Biography of Count Sergei Uvarov, 1786–1855 (DeKalb, IL, 1984).
8. See Suzanne L. Marchand, *Down from Olympus: Archaeology and Philhellenism in Germany, 1750–1970* (Princeton, NJ, 1996).
9. For more on the Greek-Russian connection during Catherine's reign, as well the importance of Christian monuments in the Crimean landscape, see Gregory L. Bruess, *Religion, Identity, and Empire: A Greek Archbishop in the Russia of Catherine the Great* (New York, 1997).
10. See Theophilus Prousis, *Russian Society and the Greek Revolution* (Dekalb, IL, 1994); and Mara Kozelsky, "Ruins into Relics: The Monument to St. Vladimir on the Excavations of Chersonesos, 1827–1857," *Russian Review* 63 (4) (Oct. 2004): 655–672.
11. S. A. Beliaev, "Istoriia khristianstva na Rusi do ravnoapostol'nogo kniazia Vladimira i sovremennaia istoricheskaia nauka," in *Istoriia russkoi tserkvi: Kniga pervaia, istoriia khristianstva v rossii do ravnoapostol'nogo kniazia Vladimira kak vvedenie v istoriiu russkoi tserkvi* (Moscow, 1994), 37. The German historian A. L. Schlozer had successfully dismissed this claim at the end of the eighteenth century, but Russians reopened the question in the nineteenth century.
12. Metropolitan Makarii (Bulgakov), *Istoriia russkoi tserkvi*, 105–106.
13. Ibid., 91–100.
14. Ibid., 110.
15. These saints are known as the Holy Priest-Martyrs Basil, Ephrem, Eugene, Elpidias, Agathodoros, Etherias, and Kapiton and are celebrated on March 7/March 20. For a comprehensive list of Crimean saints, see "Kratkii Krymskii Paterik," in *Pravoslavnye drevnosti Tavriki: Sbornik materialov po tserkovnoi arkheologii*, ed. V. Iu. Iurochkin (Kyiv: Stilos, 2002), 175–178.
16. Makarii, *Istoriia Russkoi Tserkvi*, 114.
17. *Povest vremennykh let* (The Hague, 1969); *The Russian Primary Chronicle, Laurentian Text*, ed. and trans. S. H. Cross and O. P. Sherbovitz-Wetzor (Cambridge, MA, 1953), 96–116. For a discussion of the various versions and editions of the *Chronicle*, see 3–6.
18. Albeit with greater qualification and fewer Christian sentiments, most historians would agree that Prince Vladimir's conversion to Christianity forever changed the course of Russian history. Yet, historians do not come to any consensus over the date and location of this event, largely because the earliest accounts provide conflicting details. In the *Life of St. Vladimir* recorded by James the Monk, Vladimir accepted baptism in Kyiv, before

proceeding to Chersonesos. Although this question seems relatively minor, its resolution has enormous repercussions for theories of the Byzantine state, as well as respective local identity issues. For a brief review of the interpretations, see Dimitri Obolensky, "Cherson and the Conversion of Rus': An Anti-Revisionist View," *Byzantine and Modern Greek Studies* 13 (1989): 244–256; Inok Iakov, "Pamiat' i pokhvala kniaziu russkomu Vladimiru," *Khristianskoe chtenie* 2 (1849), 317–329; E. Golubinsky, ed., *Istoriia russkoi tserkvi*, (Moscow, 1901), 1:238–245; and Andrzei Poppe, "The Political Background to the Baptism of Rus': Byzantine-Russia Relations between 986–989," *Dumbarton Oaks Papers* 30 (1976): 195–244.

19. A. Dobroklonskii, *Rukovodstvo po istorii russkoi tserkvi: Sinodal'nyi period, 1700–1890* (Moscow, 1893), 268–271.
20. There are two different collections of Innokentii's works: *Sochineniia Innokentiia arkhiepiskopa khersonskago i tavricheskago,* 11 vols. (St. Petersburg, 1908–1911); and *Sochineniia Innokentiia arkhiepiskopa khersonskago i tavricheskago,* 10 vols. (Moscow, 1872–1877; reprint, 1901, with 12 vols.).
21. Lev Matseevich, *Vysokopreosviashchennyi Innokentii Borisov, arkhiepiskop khersonskii i tavricheskii: Materialy i zametki* (Minneapolis, 1983), E.
22. Gosudarstvennyi Arkhiv Odesskogo Oblast' (GAOO), Odessa: f. 167, op. 1, d. 3, 1.2; l. 14–34; Rossiiskii Natsional'naia Biblioteka (RNL), St. Petersburg: f. 313, d. 42; l. 228.
23. See Archbishop Innokentii, "Nasazhdenie i uspekhi khristianstva v drevnem Khersone," in *Sochineniia* (1877), 11:383–386.
24. GAOO, f. 167, op. 1, d. 3, l. 34.
25. Innokentii's contributions to *Odesskii vestnik* are far too many to recount here. See Matseevich (cited above, note 21) for a detailed biography.
26. Anton Ashik to Archbishop Innokentii, Oct. 20, 1848, and June 24, 1850, in "Materialy dlia russkoi istorii pervoi poloviny XIX sloletiia: Pis'ma raznykh lits arkhiepiskopu Innokentiu Borisovu," *Chteniia v imperatorskom obshchestve istorii i drevnostei rossiiskikh* 4 (Oct.–Dec. 1884): 41–42; see Anton Ashik, *Vosporskoe tsarstvo s ego paleograficheskimi i nadgrobnymi pamiatnikami, rospisnymi vazami, planami, kartami i vidami* (Odessa, 1848), part 3. See, for example, I. G. Mikhnevich to Archbishop Innokentii, Dec. 23, 1849, RNL, f. 313, d. 42, l. 294. This correspondence has been published in a series of letters from Mikhnevich to Innokentii in "Materialy dlia russkoi istorii pervoi poloviny XIX sloletiia: Pis'ma raznykh lits Arkhiepiskopu Innokentiu Borisovu," *Chteniia v imperatorskom obshchestve istorii i drevnostei rossiiskikh* 4 (Oct.–Dec. 1884): 62–67.
27. Archbishop Innokentii, "Zapiski o vostanovlenii drevnikh sviatykh mest' po goram krymskim," part 3, an addition to *Khersonskie eparkhal'nye vedomosti* 1861; reprinted in "Arkhivnye dokumenty, otnosiashchiesia k istoriiu khersonesskago monasteryia," *Izvestiia Tavricheskoi uchenoi arkhivnoi kommissii* 5 (1888): 81–105.

28. Ibid.
29. Ibid., 89.
30. Innokentii, "Slovo v den' pamiati sv. Bezsrebrennikov Kozmy i Damiana," in *Sochineniia* (St. Petersburg, 1901), 5:309–310.
31. "From a sermon at Simferopol St. Alexander Nevsky Cathedral, July 1, 1855, ibid., 5:309.
32. Innokentii, "Zapiski o vostanovlenii drevnikh sviatykh mest' po goram krymskim," 181.
33. Ibid., 95; P. I. Keppen was one of the more prolific writers on Crimean antiquity; he published several archaeological studies and travelogues during the 1820s and 1830s on the cave cities. See P. I. Keppen, "Opisanie tuakskoi peshchery v Krymu," *Trudy vysochaishe utverzhdennogo Vol'nogo obshchestva liubetlei rossiiskoi slovesnosti* 14 (1821): 220–249; P. I. Keppen, "O krymskikh peshcherakh," *Russkii zritel'* 5–6 (1828): 132–136.
34. Innokentii, "Zapiski o vostanovlenii drevnikh sviatykh mest' po goram krymskim," 88.
35. Ibid., 81–83.
36. Ibid., 81.
37. Y. M. Mogarichev, *Peshchernye tserkvi Tavriki* (Simferopol, 1997), 97.
38. There have been few lengthy studies devoted to the monastery at Chersonesos. One notable exception, a master's thesis, has investigated the controversies around its restoration through 1917 and beyond. See Kelly O'Neill, "Rebuilding from the Ruins: A Study of Architecture and Ideology of Vladimir Cathedral, Khersones" (Harvard University, 2000).
39. Rossiiskii Gosudarstvennyi Istoricheskii Arkhiv (RGIA), f. 797, op. 20, d. 44614, l. 10.
40. M. Obolenskii, "Skazanie sviashchennika Iakova," *Z.O.O.I.D.* 2 (1850): 687–692. The first description of Inkerman, as this article reveals, appeared in the writings of Priest Iakov; See also V. F. Filippenko, "K istorii inkermanskogo peshchernogo monastyria (pervyi etap sushchestvovaniia)," in *Istoriia i arkheologiia Iugo-Zapadnogo Kryma* (Simferopol, 1993).
41. See chapter 3 of my dissertation, "Christianizing Crimea: Church Scholarship, "Russian Athos," and Religious Patriotism of the Crimean War" (PhD diss., University of Rochester, 2004), 111–118.
42. A. G. Gertsen and O. A. Makhneva, *Peshchernyie goroda Kryma* (Simferopol, 1989); T. Y. Iashaeva, *Peshchernyi kompleks v okruge Khersona: Problemyi istorii i arkheologii Kryma* (Simferopol, 1994), 93–94.
43. I. Danevskii, "Ocherk istorii Inkermana," in *Novorossiiskii kalendar na 1855* (Odessa, 1855), 398–413.
44. Ibid.
45. N. F. Krasnosel'tsev, "O znachenii arkheologicksikh otkrytii dlia obrabotki drevnei tserkovnoi istorii," in *O znachenii arkheologicksikh otkrytii dlia obrabotki drevnei tserkovnoi istorii* (Odessa, 1889), 2–3.

46. The archaeological meetings were held in 1869 (Moscow), 1871 (St. Petersburg), 1874 (Kyiv), 1877 (Kazan), 1881 (Tiflis), 1884 (Odessa), and 1887 (Iaroslavl).
47. N. F. Krasnosel'tsev, "Tserkovnaia Arkheologiia na Russkikh Arkheologicheskikh s"ezdakh, po povodu VII arkheologicheskago s"ezda v Iaroslavl," in *O znachenii arkheologicksikh otkrytii*, 1–28.
48. Ibid., 7–9.
49. "Zapiska ob ekskursii, sostoiavsheisia posle zakrytia VI Arkheologicheskago s"ezda v Krym," in *Trudy VI Arkheologicheskago s"ezda v Odesse* (Odessa, 1889),78–80.
50. Phil Kohl, "Archaeology and Nationalism," in *Encyclopedia of Nationalism*, ed. Alexander Motyl (San Diego, 2001), 2:29.
51. S. B. Filimonov, "Voprosy istorii khristianstva v dokladakh krymskikh kraevedov kontsa XIX-pervoi tretii XXvv," in *Pravoslavnye drevnosti Tavrike*, 15–16.
52. F. V. Livanov, "Khersonesos," in *Putevoditel' po Krymu s istoricheskim opisaniem dostoprimechatel'nostei Kryma* (Moscow, 1875), 1. Each chapter is paginated separately.
53. A. A. Pavlovskii, *Vseobshchii illiustrirovanyi putevoditel' po monastyriam i sviatyim mestam rossiiskoi imperii i afonu* (Nizhni Novgorod, 1907; reprint, New York, 1988), 645–650 (page references are to 1988 ed.).
54. V. G. Tur, *Krymskie pravoslavnye monastyri XIX–nachala XX veka: Istoriia: Pravovoe polozhenie* (Simferopol, 1998), 56–108.
55. Filiminov, "Voprosy istorii khristianstva," 16–17.
56. *Pravoslavnye drevnosti Tavrike.*
57. Metropolitan Lazar, "Slovo vysokopreosviashchenneishego Lazaria, mitropolita simferopol'skogo i krymskogo," in *Pravoslavnye drevnosti Tavriki*, 3–4.
58. I. Iurochkin et al., "K chitateliami sbornika," in *Pravoslavnye drevnosti Tavriki*, 7.
59. Lazar, "Slovo vysokopreosviashchenneishego Lazaria," 4.
60. Iurochkin et al., "K chitateliami sbornika," 7.
61. Palomnicheskie marshruty, "Krym pravoslavnyi," http://orthodox.sf.ukrtel.net/palomnik/index.htm (accessed Aug. 5, 2004).
62. For more on this controversy, see Kristin M. Romey, "Legacies of a Slavic Pompeii," *Archaeology*, Nov.–Dec. 2002, 18–25. For other issues, see also Leonid Marchenko, "Preserving the Global Cultural Heritage in Post Cold War Ukraine," speech delivered at Rutgers University, Oct. 31, 1998, www.utexas.edu/research/ica/pubs/leonid/ (site discontinued; accessed Nov. 18, 2002).
63. For more on Chersonesos and the problems of archaeological preservation, see the Institute of Classical Archaeology and the National Preserve of Tauric Chersonesos, *Crimean Chersonesos: City, Chora, Museum, and Environs* (Austin, TX, 2003).

64. I wish to express gratitude to Larisa Serikova, the vice director of excavations in Chersonesos, as well as to Adam Rabinowitz, the field codirector of the excavation in Chersonesos sponsored by University of Texas—Austin, for sharing their experience and insights. Of course, this chapter reflects my own conclusions, and any failings are my own.
65. I owe special thanks to Inci Bowman of the Crimea-L list-serve for pointing out this controversy. The buildings and land under dispute are located in the Marya-Dere valley in the outskirts of Bakhchisaray and were most recently inhabited by a "psycho-neurological" institution. Orthodox and Muslim groups have been contesting ownership of the territory since 1993. On July 25, 2001, Crimean Tatars led a demonstration against an illegal transfer of deed to the monastery, and a year later on July 10, 2002, the *mejlis* (governing council of the Tatars) appealed it. The monastery's possession of land is also contested by government offices, including the Ukrainian Ministry of Culture, the republic's Committee for the Preservation of Historical Heritage, and the Governing Board of Architecture. For more on this controversy, see "Conflict around Dormition Monastery Continues," Religious Information Service of Ukraine, Nov. 7, 2002, www.risu.org.ua/eng/news/article;1784/; "Monastery and Madrassah Dispute in Bakhchysarai," Sept. 13, 2006, www.risu.org.ua/eng/news/article;11892/ (accessed Sept. 25, 2006). Anna Vassilyeva, "Ukraine: Muslims Protest against 'Secret' Property Decision," Keston News Service, July 19, 2001. For a more recent article that reflects the emotional nature of the conflict, see Oleg Markelov, "Do Afona rukoi podat'," *Krymskoe vremia,* no. 47, Apr. 28, 2005, 19.
66. Iurochkin et al., "K chitateliami sbornika," 7.
67. The influence of faith over science has been little studied. An exception is the recent work of Loren Graham, who has made a pioneering contribution to understanding the penetration of Orthodoxy into Russian scientific thought. He concluded that an epistemological basis in mystical Orthodoxy enabled Russians to make advances in set theory that French Cartesianists could not. While Graham's study by no means offers a direct correlate to archaeology, it does suggest that the particularities of faith can inform scientific traditions. For more, see Loren Graham and Jean-Michael Kantor, "Russian Religious Mystics and French Rationalists: Mathematics, 1900–1930," *Bulletin of the American Academy* (2005), www.amacad.org/publications/bulletin/spring2005/graham.pdf (accessed May 15, 2006); and similarly, Loren Graham and Jean-Michel Kantor, "A Comparison of Two Cultural Approaches to Mathematics: France and Russia, 1890–1930," *Isis* 97 (1) (Mar. 2006): 56–74.
68. Jill Dubisch explains why scholars have had a tendency to overlook Orthodoxy: *In a Different Place: Pilgrimage, Gender, and Politics at a Greek Island Shrine* (Princeton, NJ, 1995), 48. Although to my knowledge no one has posed questions about how particular religious traditions inform

archaeological research, one anthropologist has undertaken the complicated different Christian approaches to holy places. See, for example, Glenn Bowman, "Christian Ideology and the Image of a Holy Land: The Place of Christian Pilgrimage in the Various Christianities," in *Contesting the Sacred: The Anthropology of Pilgrimage,* ed. John Eade and Michael J. Sallnow (Chicago, 2000; originally published in 1991), 104–106.

THREE

The Writing of Caucasian Albania

Facts and Falsifications

MURTAZALI S. GADJIEV

In the early to middle 1990s, a sensation swept newspapers, journals, and magazines in Daghestan when a handful of amateur scholars discovered the so-called *Albanian Book*, an eighth-century manuscript that recorded the long-obscured early history of a patchwork of ethnic groups in the Caucasian mountains. In this small corner of the world, the eponym *Albania* bears no relation to the modern nation-state located on the Balkan Peninsula. The reference is to Caucasian Albania instead, an ancient multiethnic state that was located in a smallish territory stretching over the current border between southern Daghestan and northern Azerbaijan. Caucasian Albania existed from the end of the first millennium BC until the beginning of the seventh century AD (fig. 3.1). Today, those ethnic groups who can establish a backward lineage to the ancient Albanians can claim to be native and therefore the rightful heirs to this coveted mountain region. When the *Albanian Book* appeared, it gave Daghestan's many ethnic groups a rare and precious opportunity to claim the distant past. After much analysis, scholars ascertained that the ancient language reflected in the *Albanian Book* most closely resembled that of the Lezgis, a relatively populous group that inhabits both southern Daghestan and

Figure 3.1. A map of the Caucasus (London, 1729) showing the ancient states of Colchis, Iberia, and Albania based on the data of Claudius Ptolemy's geography

northeastern Azerbaijan. Suspiciously, however, it was Lezgi scholars who discovered this text and constructed the interpretation.

A coterie of scholars concocted a new body of literature around this *Albanian Book* to create a glory-filled past for the Lezgis, complete with rich cultural legacies, impressive heroes, and triumphs over invading Roman armies. Careful analysis of the *Albanian Book* text, however, shows it to be a forgery, a fake, a product of the perestroika period and of the post-Soviet time when numerous national (often nationalist) movements arose. Shortly after scholars proved that the *Albanian Book* was a forgery, however, another researcher discovered new clues into the Albanian past: an ancient Georgian text that, when wiped away, exposed an authentic original masterpiece composed in the ancient Albanian language. Now scholars believe that ancient Albanian is closest to present-day Udi, a language spoken by an ethnic group called Udins. While most experts agree that this particular palimpsest is indeed authentic, Lezgi nationalists continue to "find" new texts to support their claims. In the Caucasus, research into murky historical details of the elusive Albanian past has perhaps greater propensity for danger and deceit than for enlightenment.

Even legitimate historical discoveries, such as the palimpsest described above, can become fuel for nationalist fires.

The contest over history is particularly heated in the post-Soviet space. After the Soviet Union collapsed, numerous national movements arose demanding self-determination and the creation of separate sovereign states. The small Caucasian Autonomous Republic of Daghestan in southern Russia, where more than thirty recognized nationalities reside, acutely reflects the problem of national conflict. Here, roughly ten mononational political movements emerged during the 1990s. One of these was the Lezgian National Movement, or "Sadval" (Unity) party, that was formed in July 1990 and officially registered in May 1992. The main tasks for "Sadval" were first to reunite the Lezgis, a people recently divided between the sovereign states of Russia and Azerbaijan, and then to form the independent state of Lezgistan. Another equally persuasive nationalist strategy involved manipulation of the historical record. It is here that that the discovery of the *Albanian Book* fits in.

An item listed in the official Lezgis' Nationalist Program specified: "The History of the Lezgis requires objective research and interpretation without ideological and nationalistic violence." Subsequently, two large nationalistic and mythologized books appeared that were written by the leader of the movement, professor of physics and mathematics G. A. Abduragimov: *Caucasian Albania—Lezgistan: History and Modernity* (St. Petersburg, 1995, 607 pages) and *Lezgis and the Ancient Civilizations of the Near East: History, Myths, and Stories* (Moscow, 1998, 479 pages). In them the author "proves" "the direct genetic connection" between the modern Lezgis and famous ancient peoples—the Sumerians, the Hurrians, the Urartians, and the Albanians. Such a historical connection with famous ancestors and great ancient civilizations helps legitimate the contemporary political aspirations of the Lezgis by demonstrating that they have an ancient written culture and a tradition of independent statehood (cf. Shnirelman 2000: 22–23). Moreover, the author's connections with an official university lent an air of authenticity to the nationalist claims. His work paved the way for the appearance of the fake *Albanian Book* discussed in this chapter (fig. 3.2).

In this chapter I closely analyze the *Albanian Book* as a cautious tale of the manipulation of archaeological and historical data in an age when national identities and self-governance are uncertain, yet bound to reconstructed pasts. Because it was my research that exposed the *Albanian Book* as a fake, a significant portion of the chapter dwells upon the evidence I assembled to discredit it. In particular, I demonstrate that the revelation of the text was dubious at best and that its chief supporter, Y. A.

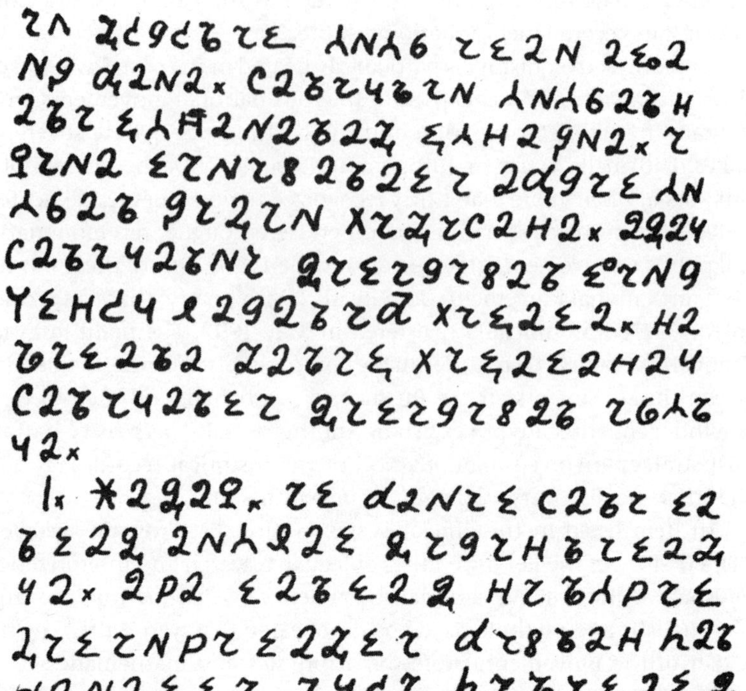

Figure 3.2. A page of the forged *Albanian Book*

Yaraliev, was himself an active Lezgi nationalist. I also analyze the inconsistencies in the language and content that reveal the *Albanian Book* as a forgery, and a poorly constructed one at that.

Writing is one of the most important indicators of the development of society and is tied closely to the histories and cultures of people. Ancient manuscripts preserve memories of ethnic groups, peoples, and civilizations that would otherwise have disappeared from view altogether. Linguists, historians, and archaeologists all are attracted to ancient writing and generate hot and lively debates over indecipherable texts from past centuries and millennia. Among the most mysterious of literary cultures of ancient times remains the writing of Caucasian Albania, the first mention of which appears in the first century BC.

The Testimonies of Written Sources

At the beginning of 65 BC, in the Alazani Valley in the southern foothills of the Caucasus Mountains, the Roman general Gnaeus Pompeius Magnus and his legionnaires defeated the troops of Orod (Horod, Orois, Orhoz), king of Albania. In his defeat, King Orod was forced to send costly tribute to this "favorite of Fortune," with a letter requesting a "restoration of peace." Pompeius "gladly accepted" the letter (Plut. *Pomp.* 45; Oros. 6.4, 8) and "granted peace to the Albanians" (Dio Cass. *Roman History* 36.51; see also App. *Mith.* 103; Eutr. 6.14; Flor. 1.40, 28). A few hundred years later, in AD 260 in a battle close to Edessa (modern Urfa in Turkey), the army of the Sasanian "Kings of Kings" Shapur routed the larger Roman army, capturing Emperor Valerian himself, along with many of his soldiers and legionnaires. King Shapur recorded a lengthy account of his victory and sent it to the kings of Armenia, Albania, and Iberia. The Armenian king advised Shapur to free Valerian, saying that otherwise, "you will not only lose the victory, but will be visited by another war" (Julius Capitolinus *Val. Duo* 6; see also Tebellius Pollionis *Val. Duo* 3.1). Julius Capitolinus informs us that the kings of Albania and Iberia also "did not accept the letters of Shapur but sent an epistle to the Roman leaders, promising to help free Valerian from the captors" (Julius Capitolinus *Val. Duo* 7; see also Tebellius Pollionis *Val. Duo* 4.1). Later, at the beginning of the fourth century, according to Agathangelos (fifth century), the Armenian king Trdat (Tiridat) sent a letter inviting various Caucasian nobles, including the Albanian emperor, to his court on the occasion of a Christian celebration (Agafangel 1909: 114; see also Lafontaine 1973).

This evidence from various ancient authors allows us to conclude that there was a literary culture among highly ranked administrators in Caucasian Albania. More evidence comes from Koryun, who wrote about the fifth-century Armenian monk Mesrop Mashtots, the man who "renewed the alphabet" of Albania and taught the "new alphabet" (Langlois 1869: 10, 12). The phrases "renewed the alphabet" and "new alphabet" used by Koryun, the biographer of Mashtots, indicate that an older version of the Albanian alphabet and writing existed previously. Unfortunately, there are no surviving examples of ancient Albanian writing, not even the international diplomatic correspondence described by ancient authors above.[1] It might be reasonably and carefully suggested, however, that Albania used the Aramaic script and language that functioned as the lingua franca of the Middle East, including Armenia and Iberia. It is possible, therefore, with the establishment in Albania of the Arsacid Parthian Dynasty, which ruled Iran from the late third century BC through the early third century AD, that the language and literature for the administration and the record-keeping of the imperial chancellery for external affairs naturally became Parthian and that that system in turn was based on the Aramaic script.

The first independent or original Caucasian Albanian script dated from the beginning of the fifth century AD, when Mashtots, in conjunction with the priest and translator Albanian Benjamin, worked with the consent of the higher secular and religious authorities of the country, King Ahswahen and Bishop Jeremy, to create the original Albanian alphabet. Thus a new page was opened in the history of Caucasian Albanian writing (Trever 1959: 306–314; Mamedov 1993: 100–114). Information about this important event in the history and culture of Albania was recorded in the fifth century (Koryun 1962: 15; Khorenaci 1978: 3.55), as well as by the seventh-century Kalankatuaci-Dasxuranci (Dasxuranci 1961: 2.3). According to these sources, a school existed for the study of the new Albanian language. Initially created for the study of religious literature, Albanian became the language of official correspondence.

In addition, by the middle of the fourth century, the Sasanids, an Iranian dynasty that ruled from the early third century AD until its defeat by the Arabs at Qadasiya in AD 637, entered Albanian territory. Iranian administrators and servants, as well as Zoroastrianism, spread the Middle Persian language and literature throughout the Albanian higher elite and administration. This process was a consequence of strong dynastic ties between the Arsacids of Albania and the Sasanids. Thus, King Urnayr (fourth century) married the sister of Shapur II (309–379). King Ahswahen (fifth century) married the daughter of Yazdigird II (439–457), and

King Vache II (mid-fifth century) was a nephew of Shah Hormizd III (457–459) and Peroz (459–484) and also married their niece. Finally, a zealous adherent of Christianity and disseminator of Albanian script and literacy, King Vachaghan III the Good-Honourable (ca. 485–510) was associated with the "Royal family of Persia"; Mihran, Duke of Ghardman, who founded a new dynasty of Albanian administrators, also came from the Sasanids.

The relationship between Iran and Albania is further demonstrated in archaeological artifacts. For example, the Christian gem-seal of the fifth and sixth centuries AD, which is stored in the collection of the National Library in Paris, has a Middle Persian cursive inscription, "Great Catholicos of Albania and Balāsagan" (Göbl 1973: pl. 33, 102a; Lerner 1977: 31, pl. 1, fig. 13; Gignoux 1978: 64, no. 7.5, pl. 23; 1980, pl. 1, fig. 1; Kolesnikov 1989: 249–250; Kasumova 1991: 23–24; Gyselen 1993: 155, no. 60.13, pl. 42, no. 60.13). It is worth emphasizing that the official seal of the chief Christian church of Albania was inscribed with Middle Persian writing, for it clearly demonstrates the large cultural and political influence of Iran and shows that the Middle Persian language and writing permeated not only the Albanian elite but also the ecclesiastical elite. Moreover, the central image of a Christian symbol, a cross, is coupled with the Zoroastrian symbols, a half moon and a six-ray star.

Another example involves an Albanian king's gem-seal, which is located in M. A. Pirousan's collection of Sasanian intaglios (Gignoux 1975: 17, pl. 1, fig. 2.2) and which I recently read and identified (Gadjiev 2003: 102–119). In the circle of this gem is the Middle Persian inscription "Ahswahen, King (*Shah*) of Albania," but in the center of its image is the Zoroastrian symbol (*neshan*) representing the so-called Moon-Wagon. This symbol is presented as the emblem of Ahswahen, but it could also be the emblem of the entire Arsacid dynasty of Albanian kings. It is significant that we are speaking of a king's seal created in an epoch in which Christianity consolidated its position in Albania, a development that in turn facilitated the origin of Albanian literature.

To summarize the argument briefly, it is evident that the Middle Persian language and writing had official status in early medieval Albania. Probably the Middle Persian inscriptions of Derbent, both informal and official, which were made on behalf of Darius, a high official, or *amargar*, of the region *shahr Adurbadagan,* refer to an area that included Albania (and all the Caucasian provinces of Sasanian Iran) in the sixth century.[2]

Researchers did not doubt the existence of an original system of Albanian writing, but they had long considered it irretrievably lost. In 1937 Professor Ilya Abuladze discovered the Albanian alphabet contained in an Armenian manuscript from the fifteenth century AD (preserved as no. 7117 in the Matenadaran—the Institute of Ancient Manuscripts, Armenia). This Albanian alphabet was depicted in a series with other alphabets, including Arabic, Greek, Syrian, Latin, Georgian, and Coptic.

The Facts of Archaeology

Ten years later, in 1947, archaeological excavations in Mingechaur (Azerbaijan) under the guidance of S. Kaziev found the first remains of Albanian writing—a stone altar post with an inscription around its border that consisted of seventy letters. Subsequently, the excavations at Mingechaur from 1948 to 1952 recovered six Albanian epigraphic artifacts with brief texts (containing from five to fifty letters), including candlesticks, a tile fragment, and a vessel fragment.[3]

Unfortunately, as scholars have repeatedly observed, the decipherment of these examples of original Albanian writing was complicated by a number of objective factors, including their limited lengths, the insufficient number of inscriptions, the essential differences in the external shapes of the letters of the Albanian alphabet of the manuscripts from the fifth and sixth centuries compared with the letters of inscriptions from the sixth to eighth centuries, the lack of established forms and phonetic meanings for a large series of the letters, and so forth. Further success in the study and decipherment of the Albanian script required subsequent research and augmentation of this limited corpus of Albanian inscriptions.

Modern Forgery

This brings us to the beginning of 1991, when the journal *Lezgistan* published a mysteriously produced copy of a handwritten page of a manuscript with simple marks (fig. 3.2), accompanied by an explanatory note informing the reader that before us was "a page of an unknown *Albanian Book*" and "a text-book written with Albanian letters that have not yet been read" ("Stranitsa iz neizvestnoy" 1991: 29, 63). The anonymous note mentioned that the owners of the manuscript had presented a copy to the journal for the benefit of its readers. Strangely, however, the editor of the journal did not disclose how the "pages of the old book" fell to her or how she was informed about the owner of the book. Nor does any further information about these people appear in print.

Two years later, after it appeared that this exciting excerpt was all but forgotten, a scholar announced that he had unlocked the mysteries of the text. Professor of chemistry Y. A. Yaraliev successfully deciphered the text of this page, using the contemporary (modern) Lezgi language. He published his conclusions widely in the spring and summer of 1993 in the newspapers *Alpan, Samur, Sadval, Lezgistandin Habarar, Lezgi Gazet,* and *Daghestanskaya Pravda.* Shortly thereafter, a forty-nine-page manuscript, which received the name *Albanian Book,* was discovered. Yaraliev first translated and published it in the papers *Rikin Gaf* (1995, no. 1) and *Lezgi Gazet* (April 14, 1995) and then produced a separate book. The book included a facsimile copy of the manuscript and a translation from Albanian and pseudo-Albanian epigraphs, together with commentaries on the translations of the epigraphs and the manuscript and an essay about Caucasian Albania and the genetic roots of the Lezgi language (Yaraliev 1995).

The relatively large book consisted of four independent chapters. The first chapter is devoted to the history of Caucasian Albania from biblical times (starting with Adam) to the Arabian conquest and accounts for more than half of the book (28 pages). The second is a short fragment (2 pages) from a "Book about the Stars" written by a certain ancient scientist, Shanatil. It tells about the stars and constellations known to the Albanians and about the Albanian calendar. The next chapter (4 pages) presents information about past Albanian writers, architects, scientists, generals, and musicians. The fourth chapter (16 pages) is devoted to religious commandments and essential injunctions.

The "discovery" of the *Albanian Book* was highly celebrated in the local press and was compared to the discovery of Troy. Its authenticity was not questioned. In an interview in the paper *Lezginskiy Vestnik* (1995, no. 3), the rector of the YUZHDAG (Southern Daghestan) Institute, Nariman O. Osmanov, proclaimed that "Prof. Ya. A. Yaraliev solved the secret of ancient Albanian writing." Osmanov went so far as to claim that Yaraliev "will be nominated by his Institute as a candidate for the Nobel Prize." Obviously, however, only associates of the Nobel Committee have the ability to recommend candidates for the prize. Outlandish statements such as these characterize the "scholarship" surrounding the *Albanian Book.* It becomes almost ludicrous to note the level of political and territorial ambitions disguised as historical and cultural discovery. Needless to say, Y. A. Yaraliev himself is a Lezgi, and the chief supporters of this hoax were Lezgis. At the initial "discovery" of the *Albanian Book,* no one appeared skeptical despite the dubious circumstances surrounding its finding and despite the obvious political overtones. Those who later questioned its authenticity were branded as antipatriotic. Consequently, the majority of challenges to the text later came from non-Lezgis, such as myself. The research into the *Albanian Book* quickly became not an academic inquiry but a heated nationalist battle.

In his foreword, Yaraliev reported that a photocopy of the manuscript was preserved in the archive of the deceased Lezgi poet Z. Rizvanov and had been transferred by his son. He continued that the manuscript itself, consisting of "a volume of fifty separate sheets of dense yellow-faded paper with bluish fringe," was located in the poet's papers. Subsequently, however, all traces of the original manuscript disappeared (Yaraliev 1995: 119). In the first place, it is strange that the manuscript was "in a volume of fifty distinct sheets." Obviously the "copyist," in a departure from medieval norms, used only one side of the paper for writing, an odd practice for a time when the economic value of paper required using both sides of the sheet. In the second place, in an article in *Daghestanskaya Pravda* about the "discovery" of the *Albanian Book,* the poet's son, R. Rizvanov, says nothing about the origin of the manuscript and its copies, noting only that it is a "miracle" that the Albanian texts had been "preserved" (Rizvanov 1993a, 1993b).

It is immediately evident that neither the decipherers nor the journalists writing about the "discovery of the ancient Albanian manuscript" had seen it. One's suspicions are raised about the absence of the original itself. Allegedly someone owned it, but somehow it strangely "disappeared." Nevertheless, copies "leaked out." And it is perhaps more surprising that a text said to have been written ten centuries ago should contain "clear Lezgi text, understandable as if it were written yesterday" (Negidhul 1993: 1). This claim raises a series of questions that relate to the secrecy around the discovery and the production of the text and its copy. Because the original was never produced, we must ask whether the manuscript was a "fake foundling" written yesterday. Apart from the circumstances of the text's "discovery," there are several other indications that call its authenticity into question.

First, the character of the handwriting more closely resembles contemporary writing than medieval Caucasian cursive (Armenian and Georgian). It is logical to expect Albanian writing to share parallels with both Georgian and Armenian scripts, since neither existed in isolation from the other. Punctuation provides another clue. Visible are not only indentations, but also daggers (used as reference marks or to indicate a death date), each separate from the other. Yet one expects the colons and *troetochie* (three vertical points) used in native Armenian and Georgian systems of writing during the Middle Ages. Colons were a customary form of punctuation, for example, in an Avaro-Georgian inscription from Khunzakh, Oroda. I should note that Yaraliev interprets this last inscription (from Oroda) as Albanian and undertakes an unsuccessful attempt at reading it on the basis of the Lezgi language (Yaraliev 1995: 113, 114, 116), although doing so requires far-reaching assumptions and conclusions. Next, the use of signs in the manuscript signifying numbers contradicts the norms of Caucasian writings. A. G. Shanidze was the first to argue that in Albanian writing, as in Armenian and in Georgian, the characters also had figural/numeric designations (Shanidze 1957: 34). Later marshalling a series of arguments, A. G. Abramyan (1964: 34) and G. A. Klimov (1990: 495–496) supported this view.

An analysis of the *Albanian Book* shows that it used thirty-seven symbols in the text, but the Albanian alphabet contains fifty-two letters and two ligatures. To compensate for the contradiction, the author of the manuscript asserted that "Saint Misrup [i.e., Mesrop Mashtots] created a good alphabet, composed of thirty-seven letters" (Yaraliev 1995: 131). This compilation of signs is more or less comparable with the known phonetic meanings and quantity of signs in the epigraphs from Mingechaur. The author of the manuscript has basically used the real letters of the Albanian alphabet with their sounds established by experts but has changed the form of a series of letters, giving them, as well as the entire alphabet, a more accomplished or more modern appearance.

Even if we assume that this book is truly an original Albanian manuscript created in the middle of the eighth century AD and repeatedly copied, as the decipherer claims to believe owing to the presence of numerous borrowings from the Arabic and Turkish languages (Yaraliev 1995: 151), there remains an insuperable contradiction: the essential difference between the number of letters in the manuscript (37) and used, ostensibly, in the eighth century and in the following centuries (the period when the manuscript was supposedly copied), and the number of characters in the Albanian alphabet contained in the Armenian manuscript (52). Moreover, the presence of Arabic and Turkish words in the pages of the manuscript suggests a later date for the last copy of the manuscript, no earlier than the tenth to eleventh century, when Arabic and Turkish diffused throughout the eastern Caucasus, implying that at this later time the Albanian alphabet still contained 37 characters. However, the political, social, and cultural realities of Azerbaijan and southern Daghestan at that time argue against this conclusion. Rather, it is likely that by the tenth to eleventh centuries the Albanian alphabet and writing had already undergone significant, cardinal changes and that the alphabet had expanded by 15 characters, reaching the total of 52 that are recorded in an Armenian manuscript of the first half of the fifteenth century titled "Albanian Written Marks." It is unlikely that the Albanian alphabet changed after the tenth century, or the time of the "triumph" in the eastern Caucasus for the Arabic and Persian scripts and languages, in which the representatives of the peoples of Azerbaijan and Daghestan (e.g., Nizami Ganjevi, Abu Bakr Muhammad al-Darbandi, Abd ar-Rashid al-Bakuvi, Mammus al-Lakzi, Yusuf al-Lakzi, and Masud ibn Namdar) wrote their works.

To be sure, the *Albanian Book* itself accounts for this discrepancy. On page 28, the manuscript suggests that "from this time [namely, the second half of the seventh century], Udins, Tsakhurs, Kitashes, and Kurks composed a new alphabet for themselves based on the letters created earlier by the outstanding genius Misrup" (Yaraliev 1995: 136). But if this were true, then the later author of the Armenian grammar of the fifteenth century must have made a mistake, for that text included not the Mesropian alphabet of thirty-seven letters, but the fifty-two-letter alphabet, and it was called "Albanian." However, we have no reason to doubt that the medieval Armenian philologist produced another alternative alphabet, differing essentially from that of the Mesropian Albanian alphabet in the number of its characters.

I have mentioned the large number of loan words from Arabic appearing in the *Albanian Book*. It is not possible to analyze them in detail here, but I can address a few of the more frequently recurring examples: *kele* 'citadel, fortress' (Arabic *kala*), *imir* 'governor, sovereign' (Arabic *amir*), *hebil* 'tribe' (Arabic *qabila*), *makil* 'province, district, principality' (obviously an artificial word created by the author of the manuscript from the Arabic *mahalla*), *kisan* 'good, better' (Arabic *hasan*), and *dene* 'world, earth' (evidently from Arabic *dunya*). The presence of such words in the manuscript reveals the forged character of the *Albanian Book*. Given the temporally restricted period of influence of Arabic on Albanian, it is impossible for such words to have entered the working lexicon of the Albanian language and to have replaced their native equivalents.

Particularly revealing is the interdependence of the word *kilis* 'church' and the names of the weekdays in the section of the manuscript called "Book about the Stars." The word *kilis* in the manuscript is not designated as 'Sunday' (Lezgian *h'yad*; compare Avarian *hatan k'o* 'church day'), as one might expect, but as 'Thursday'. 'Sunday' carries the name *kerki*, a clear parallel to Udinian *kerkets* 'church' (a term borrowed from Armenian). But in the manuscript the term used for 'church' is *kilis*, not a word rooted in *kerki, kerkets*. This is particularly surprising because the original author and the copyists of the manuscript present themselves as zealous adherents of Christianity. Apparently these Christians quickly forgot the word for church in their native language and used it only to signify a day of the week—Sunday—even though the text was allegedly written when the Albanian Church was still strong, during the eighth to tenth centuries. Anticipating a bit, it should be noted that 'church' is designated by the term *eklesia,* of Greek origin (Alexidze 2002: 25), in the recently discovered original Albanian manuscripts (see below, "The Modern Genuine Discovery").

Other evident borrowings include the Armenian ethnonyms *Utik/Udik* used in the text of the manuscript alongside the ethnonym *Udi.* The use of such an Armenianism (the *-k* ending of the suffix) to signify one of the leading Albanian tribes is not only surprising but also unpardonable for an "ancient" author, shedding light on the origin of the manuscript. Evidently, the creator of the *Albanian Book* was suggesting that *Udi* and *Utik/Udik* are two parallel Albanian forms of the ethnic term.

Concerning ethnonyms, which are richly represented in the manuscript, we meet both familiar and unfamiliar names of tribes. Among more than thirty listed ethnonyms, we encounter such recognized tribal names as *Leg, Lek, Lezg, Sul, Chur,* and *Chul.* However, they appear as independent terms, although it is known that many of these ethnonyms (e.g., *Leg, Lek, Lezg*) simply represent language variants for the same ethnic group. The same applies to the ethnonyms *Sul, Chur/Chul,* which also were used by the ancient authors to designate not an Albanian tribe, but a Turkic tribe that lived along the eastern bank of the Caspian Sea during the fifth–sixth centuries and was led by a Chol-khagan.

According to the manuscript, "Suls and Chuls settled on the slope of the mountain Jilga [Mount Jalgan near Derbent] and built a large fortress with two gates. This fortress was called Kvevar ["two gates" from the Lezgian, i.e., citadel of Derbent]" (Yaraliev 1995: 121). The text thus placed these "Albanian" tribes in the Derbent region, which was known in the early Middle Ages in Armenian and Georgian as *Čor/Čol,* in Greek as Τζοῦρ (Procop. *Goth.* 4.3), in Syrian as *Tūrāyē* (Michael Syrus *Chronikon* [d. 1199]) (see Altheim and Stiehl 1959: 110), and in Arabic as *Sul.* But the author of this manuscript made a huge error not only in labeling as Albanians these tribes of Turkish origin that appeared only in the fifth century in Central Asia, not in the Caucasus, but also in associating the Turkic ethnonym *Chur/Chul, Sul* with the similar-sounding toponym signifying ancient Derbent. The ancient designation of Derbent and the Derbent pass—*Čor/Čol* > Τζοῦρ, *Tūrāyē, Sul*—has, as is well known, a reliable

Iranian etymology (compare Yaghnobian *čor* 'narrow place, narrow pass' [see Khromov 1966: 134]). This blunder, for an Albanian author of the eighth century, is not insignificant.

One more example is the use of Albanian to describe the tribe called *Mushks*, "which settled at the mouth of the Kulan-vats [i.e., the Samur River on today's border between Daghestan and Azerbaijan]" (Yaraliev 1995: 121). Obviously, the Mushks are to be identified with the ethnonyms and ethnotoponyms *Maskut, Maskat/Mashgata/Mashtaga, Mushkyur*. But the Maskuts are an Iranian tribe, first settling on the littoral plain of southern Daghestan and northeastern Azerbaijan not in the biblical epoch but in the first centuries after Christ. As shown by archaeological data, they preserved their ethnic characteristics, and their kingdom existed, according to ninth- and tenth-century Arabian authors, until the beginning of the eighth century, or close to the presumed time of the *Albanian Book*. An eighth-century author who was excellently informed about the politics and ethnic history of Albania and bordering nations (as the text seems to indicate this author was), must have known about the Iranian origin of the *Maskuts* (*"Mushks"*). After all, the author knew dozens of names of various governors of Albania and its principalities (naturally, the majority of these names are not in line with written sources and so appear to have been a product of the author's imagination). Excluding the names of a series of Albanian kings, dependent on Kalankatuaci-Daskhuranci, the fabricated names include seventeen princes of Mushkyur (among these, Sanas, Selasen, and Sanasal are kings' names produced from the historically certified name of the Maskut King Sanesan and have an Iranian etymology).

The author did, however, know about real historical events that were significantly more removed in space and time. For example, he described "the collapse of the state of the Persian King Daria in the battles with the Greek Philip Iskander (Alexander)" (Yaraliev 1995: 122). I will not dwell on the pages related to the names but note only that the author probably was familiar with the work of the historians of Alexander and maybe with the *Romance of Alexander*, which circulated widely in the East; or with the Persian writer Aphraat's essays, composed in Syrian at the beginning of the fourth century; or with the Syrian chronicler of the city Karka de bet Seloh, who described Alexander's victory over Darayavuš (Middle Persian Dariuš, Dārāy).

Those are only a few of the ancient writers known to the *Albanian Book*'s author. The book includes many other descriptions of historical events occurring in the first century BC. One episode recounts the battle of the Albanian military with the Roman general Gnaeus Pompeius and his legionnaires at the beginning of 65 BC. This part of the text has many parallels with ancient sources. In the ancient sources, the Albanian king is called *Orois* (Horod, Orod), but in the Albanian manuscript, *Aran*; Plutarch gives the name of the king's brother as *Kosis*, but in the manuscript he is *Kasik*. According to Plutarch, Kosis "rushed on Pompeius and stuck a spear in his coat of mail, but Pompeius won by piercing him with his own hand [or by personally stabbing him]" (Plut. *Pomp.* 35); in the *Albanian Book*, the author advises that "Kasik stuck a heavy sword in the chest of the general Pumpi. A poisoned arrow shot by Pumpi pierced the throat of Kasik. After this the battle stopped" (Yaraliev 1995: 123). (It should be noted that Roman generals did not use bows and arrows.) Another interesting parallel relates to what the Romans, according to Appianus and Plutarch, called "Amazons" among the dead and captured Albanians. These accounts are corroborated by the *Albanian Book*, which describes the participation of "Albanian girls and brides" in the battle.

Despite several similarities in the account of the Albanian battle, the *Albanian Book* and the ancient authors ended the battle differently. According to the evidence of the ancient authors, the Romans won the battle, but according to the patriotic attitudes of the authors of the manuscript, after "a victory in the seven day battle, the Roman army turned back" (*Yaraliev* 1995: 123). Who should be believed? The ancient authors who described the Caucasian campaign of Pompeius created their narrative of events from eyewitness-participants' accounts. How, one should ask, did the author of the *Albanian Book* arrive at his version? Certainly, he could not have recorded this history from national memory, which after the passage of eight centuries could not be expected to preserve such nuances, in such striking concordance with ancient authors. More likely, the author was familiar with the works of Plutarch and Dio Cassius and others, probably in Russian translation.

There is still one more observation to make about this particular passage. According to the manuscript, the dead in this battle of Albania were buried in collective graves and *kurgans* (or barrows/tumuli; "*kuntar*" in Lezgian). But here the author shows his ignorance of the burial customs and rites of Caucasian Albania. According to archaeological data, the Caucasian Albanians utilized diverse burial customs and structures, but they did not bury their dead in *kurgans* or raised barrows; this practice has not been documented archaeologically and is absolutely not characteristic for Albanian tribes.

Elsewhere in the text, we encounter similar misrepresentations of the historical record. For example, the author asserts that the princes of Mushkur, Lezgi, Pakul, Shakan, Tsakhan, Mukan, and Kyura, headed by a certain Ashtik, king of Alupan (i.e., Albania), gathered in the "Great Alupanian residence" "in the big town of Chur," as a "Consultative Council" convened in response to an incursion from the north of a nomadic tribe of Cimerics (i.e., Cimmerians). But at what date does the manuscript allege this incursion to have happened? According to this particular passage, the "Consultative Council" decided to request aid from the Iranian king Sasan (Yaraliev 1995: 124); that is, the speech concerns an event purported to have taken place about the end of the second century AD.[4]

This account, like the rest of the *Albanian Book*, contains tremendous and, for the professional historian, stupefying myths and inaccuracies. First, the author's mention of the Cimmerians, who lived in the early Iron Age (ninth–seventh centuries BC), not in the first centuries AD, is surprising. Moreover, the "Alupian residence," that is, the capital of Albania, was not the city Chur (or, more exactly, Chor), but Cabala, and from the second half of the fifth century it was Partav. The Iranian king Sasan never existed; where the name Sasan is mentioned (at the end of the second and the beginning of the third century) as the founder of the Sasanid Dynasty, and in official Sasanian texts (for example, Shapur's Inscription on Ka'aba-i Zardušt, Karnamag-i Ardašīr), he has the title *hwataw*, the title given to sovereigns of small local principalities, not the title of king or shah.

Furthermore, many of the names of the Sasanian kings (*shahanshahs*) that are mentioned in the *Albanian Book* are given in the New Persian form or something closely resembling it: Gurmuz, Gubad, Bahram, Feruz. (Apparently the Middle Persian names were changed to New Persian names during this period [i.e., during the time the manuscript was purportedly written and transcribed]). It was imprudent for the author of the manuscript to include the inaudible spirant *f* in the many words and names of persons included in the text. All linguists who have studied ancient Albanian writing know that this spirant is not found in the Albanian alphabet. It appears later only in the contemporary languages of the Lezgi group of languages. The author of the *Albanian Book* introduced it. Its form corresponds to the forty-ninth letter of the Albanian alphabet, which is called *c'ayn* in the Armenian transcription and whose name, apparently, reflects its phonetic significance.

I will touch on one more passage from the historical part of the manuscript. The *Albanian Book* describes

> the Iranian King Shabur [judging by the text, Shahpur III, who ruled in AD 383–388] who placed his brother-in-law Basla [absent from the written sources] on the throne

of Alupia. He also built a long wall in the foothills of the river Ghil that stretched from the mountain to the sea. This same year, the Emperor Basla died. His son Farim [also not mentioned in the written sources] ascended the throne. Within a year, the weak youth died. Sanas, Duke of Mushkur [Sanesan, King of Maskuts, who ruled in the 330s] took his place. At this time the Iranian Emperor was Yazdagir [i.e., Yazdigird I, 399–420]." (Yaraliev 1995: 126)

This small excerpt contains notable chronological discrepancies, as well as other errors. For example, the long wall the *Albanian Book* describes clearly refers to the fifty-kilometer-long Ghilghilchay defensive wall, which, according to archaeological and narrative sources, was constructed at the beginning of the sixth century during the rule of Shahanshah Kavad (488–531), certainly not as early the fourth century. If the author of the *Albanian Book* had lived and written in the eighth century, he would have known about this, because the wall was known at this time by the Middle Persian name *Apzut Kavat* 'Kavat is exalted' (Corène 1881: 27; *Ananias of Shirak* 1992: 2:12–13). And the idea that Sanas, prince of Mushur [i.e., Sanesan, king of Maskuts], was the king of Albania undoubtedly "wandered" into the pages of the manuscript from the pages of contemporary literature, where this has become a myth.

Space does not permit dwelling on all the absurdities, contradictions, and inventions about the history, ethnonyms, geography, calendars, and cultures of Caucasian Albania that fill the pages of the *Albanian Book*. Such a long list would include a brilliant assemblage of about forty otherwise unknown names of Albanian writers, poets, architects, generals, and other persons active in science and culture. The author even discovered a "writer of genius" named Jamag, who wrote "a large book about the love of Khosrow and Shirin" and who is presented as the predecessor (and possibly the inspirer) of Nizami Ganjevi, the great Azerbaijani poet of the eleventh century.[5] Some leaders of the Albanian Church, not mentioned in the known lists of Albanian patriarchs, are also listed in this roster.

Comparison of the *Albanian Book* with credible historical data sufficiently illustrates that here before us is not an ancient Albanian manuscript, but a forgery created during our day that rudely falsifies history. The goal of the forged manuscript is to depict a specific people as exceptional and superior and to establish the antiquity of that group's civilization, political system, and high culture—in order to legitimate the political aspirations of the Lezgis during the social and economic crises, the processes of separation, and the aggravated ethno-political problems that occurred during the immediate post-Soviet period. A close analysis of the text reveals that its creator was a person who was familiar with the history and culture of Caucasian Albania and who possessed a creative and fanciful imagination. In fact, there are close parallels between the historical narratives in the *Albanian Book* and a series of works by Z. and R. Rizvanov, especially the *History of the Lezgins*, which were published before the discovery and decipherment of this "ancient manuscript."

It is worth quickly describing, therefore, some of the most revealing parallels. In the first place, the toponym Kvevar ('two gates', from the Lezgian) repeatedly appears in the *Albanian Book* and more than once in *History of the Lezgins* as the Albanian name of Derbent (Rizvanov and Rizvanov 1990: 7, 8, 53). Because such a toponym has never been recorded among a diverse body of specialists, linguists, historians, ethnographers, archaeologists, and geographers, it appears to have been invented by the Rizvanovs. Second, the toponym Kvepele ('two hills', from the Lezgian) is mentioned both in the *Albanian Book* and in the *History of the Lezgins* as the Albano-Lezgian name of Cabala, the capital of Albania (Rizvanov and Rizvanov 1990: 6–7); this toponym has never been recorded anywhere else, so it appears similarly artificial. Third, according to the *Albanian Book* and the *History of the Lezgins*, the Filan principality is depicted as an Albano-Lezgian political formation situated in southern Daghestan. Here, the author reflects the dated opinion shared by Professor V. F. Minorskii (Minorsky 1963: 137–138). However, the late professor A. R. Shikhsaidov clearly substantiated the location of Filan in central Daghestan, in the territory of the Akusha-Dargo (Shikhsaidov 1976). Fourth, the tribes *Kas, Kyur/Kur, Bil/Fil, Shar/Sharv*, which do not appear in any other sources, are named among the Albanian tribes in both the *Albanian Book* and the *History of the Lezgins* (Rizvanov and Rizvanov 1990: 5; Rizvanov 1991: 10).

Fifth, according to the *Albanian Book,* "Mikran [i.e., the founder of the new Albanian dynasty of Mihranides] emigrated to Alupan together with 200,000 men from Kurdish tribes" (Yaraliev 1995: 133). And in Z. Rizvanov's article with the revealing title "Two Fragments of Scientific Falsifications," published four years before the decipherment of the *Albanian Book* in the same issue of the *Lezgistan* magazine that "discovered the page of an unknown *Albanian Book,*" we read that a "small Kurdian principality not far from Ganja was created for the first time by the Kurdian Mihran. Offspring of this Kurdian family of Mihranides included the famous general Jawanshir" (Rizvanov 1991: 8). Not one written source, however, mentions the Kurdian descendant of Mihran or Mihranides or the family's ties with the Kurds. Contradicting both the *Albanian Book* and Z. Rizvanov is Kalankatuatsi-Daskhurantsi (Dasxuranci 1961: 2:17), who pointed out that the Persian descendants of Mihran appeared in the family of Khosrow II of Parviz. Persians and Kurds were and are different peoples, and ancient and medieval authors clearly distinguished them.

Sixth, in contradistinction to the record put forward by the classic authors, the patriotic authors of the *History of the Lezgins* believe that the "united resistance of the local tribes" forced Pompeius to leave Albania (Rizvanov and Rizvanov 1990: 6). This interpretation of events is very consonant with the passage from the *Albanian Book* analyzed above.

Seventh, according to the *Albanian Book*, Shirin, Shahanshah Khosrow's wife, was Udian (i.e., Albanian) (Yaraliev 1995: 133). This assertion parallels the opinion of R. Rizvanov, who called her the Albanian queen (R. Rizvanov 1993). But according to more traditional chroniclers, including contemporaries of Khosrow and Shirin (in Theophylactus Simocatta's *History*, Evagrius Scholasticus's *Ecclesiastical History*, Sebeos's *History*, and Syrian Anonym's *Chronicle*), Shirin was Aramaean, a native of Khuzistan and a countrywoman of Gregory of Firat (or the Euphrates).

Finally, in the twelve-part division of the "Lezgian-Albanian" calendar given in the Rizvanovs' work and in the *Albanian Book*, the names of six months correspond with each other: Ibne and Ibne, Nava and [Nava]-sardum, Tul and Tulen, Baskum and Baskum, Funduk and Funduk, and Ekhen and Eknakh (*Rizvanov and Rizvanov* 1990: 36; *Yaraliev* 1995: 137). The names refer to the names of the months of the real twelve-part Albanian calendar—Khaba (Khibna), Navasardon, Tulini (Tulen), Bochkon, Bontoke, and Ekhnay (Ekhna)—that were fixed by medieval Armenian authors and that were the subject of research by the linguists E. Agayan, A. Shanidze, A. Abramyan, and V. Gukasyan (some of the names of months have Udian etymologies). However, the professional ethnologists who studied the Lezgian national calendar (A. Trofimova, S. Agashirinova, and G. Gadjiev) discovered a twenty-four-part division, and the names of these periods of the year do not correlate with the names of the months of the Albanian calendar.

For all these reasons and others, the authenticity of the so-called *Albanian Book* is suspect, and questions arise about the motives behind its falsification. The calendar system in particular suggests the aim of "joining the Ancient Albanians with the Lezgis, who are their direct descendants" (Rizvanov and Rizvanov 1990: 5). Thus, it appears that the author or authors of the *Albanian Book* endeavored to create a written manuscript linking the Albanian alphabet with the contemporary Lezgi language (diluted with two hundred created words that purportedly occupied the intersection of the two languages) and subsequently feigned joy over "discovering" their own decipherment.

The "discovery" and decipherment of the *Albanian Book* enabled some amateur scholars or dilettantes to assert that "the Lezgian language forms the basis of Albanian writing and was the State language" (Mirzebegov 1995: 1) and that the Albanian language "is preserved essentially in the modern Lezgian language" (Yaraliev 1995: 188). Referencing the *Albanian Book*, "Alup [according to the manuscript, the younger son of Targum, ethnarch and eponym of the Albanians] occupied lands from the Lower Sea [the Mediterranean, according to the decipherer] to the Upper Sea [the Caspian] and from the lower mountains to the peaks" (Yaraliev 1995: 120). They wrote that "the peoples spoke in proto-Lezgian or close to their own language, lived in the southern Balkan peninsula, occupied the Near East and Asia Minor, and spread over a large part of the Caucasus" (Mirzebegov 1995: 1).) Their amateur efforts demonstrated the genealogical connection between the contemporary Lezgian language and Hatti (proto-Hittite), Minoans (Mycenaeans), Pelasgians, Sumerians, and so on (Yaraliev 1995: 167–181; Abduragimov and Abduragimova 1998: 5–98). Thus, for example, these researchers assert that the "Sumerians have a straight genetic connection with the Lezgis" and that "the culture of the Akkadians, Babylonians and Assyrians on the whole was the culture of Lezgian peoples—Sumerians and Hurrians."

In Yaraliev's opinion, the "decipherment of the Albanian manuscript enables us to confirm I. M. D'iakonoff's conclusions about the commonalities of the Hurro-Urarto-Albano-Lezgian languages" (1995: 174). However, neither I. M. D'iakonoff nor S. A. Starostin argued for such a commonality; they wrote more circumspectly about the common origin of the Hurro-Urartian and eastern Caucasian languages (Diakonoff and Starostin 1976). In addition to the Lezgian language itself and Lezgian-related language groups, there are significant other languages spoken within the family of eastern Caucasian languages, for example, Lakian and the Avaro-Ando-Didoian, Darginian, and Nakhian languages. Similarly overemphasizing a single language, this ethnic formulation is unfaithful to the presentation of the glottochronology of the Daghestano-Nakh languages and the ethnogenesis, history, and culture of its carriers. In sum, it vulgarizes and corrupts a complicated picture of historical reality.

Unfortunately, Y. A. Yaraliev, who deciphered the *Albanian Book*, deciphered the original Albanian and the pseudo-Albanian epigraphic texts using a false key—the alphabet of the *Albanian Book* (in which, it is true, the phonetic meaning of nearly thirty of thirty-seven letters had long been established by specialists). This fact illustrates the incorrectness of his translations (Yaraliev 1995: 96–118). As shown above, in addition several letters in a series of inscriptions were corrupted. As a consequence of these mistaken assumptions, the author incorrectly interpreted the most extensive Albanian inscription at Mingechaur on a pedestal as the epigraph for the tombstone of a certain Miyakhtsa (Yaraliev 1995: 108–109). But the form of the pedestal and the context of its discovery during the excavations (in the center of the altar section of the second Mingechaur church of the sixth–eighth centuries) demonstrate that it was not a tombstone, but the base for an altar cross. A pedestal with similar measurements, form, and construction, together with fragments of a massive stone cross, was found in situ during excavation of the altar of Church no. 2 of the seventh–eighth centuries in Verkhniy Chiryurt, Daghestan (Magomedov 1983: 162, fig. 65). Finally, it is important to note that Yaraliev ambitiously hurried to establish "his priority for revealing the mystery of the decipherment of the well-known and recognized monuments of Caucasian-Albanian writing" (1995: 5). And it was on April 14, 1993, which was not the date of a scientific conference but of a meeting of the Lezgian Democratic party of Azerbaijan, that he first announced the results of his decipherment (113).

In conclusion, the fact that until recently all discoveries of Albanian inscriptions were rather brief, limited, and unsatisfactory has invited creative readings and links to different languages, whether Daghestani, other Caucasian, or unrelated languages. The extremely limited nature of the originally available Albanian epigraphic remains was such that it was possible also, for example, to decipher and read the Mingechaur inscription on the pedestal as Azerbaijanian (i.e., Turkic) (Mustafaev 1990: 23–25), an unsuccessful attempt, like numerous others, to demonstrate a long-standing Turkic ethnic and linguistic affiliation with such eastern Caucasian tribes as the Albanians, the Gargars, and the Udins (see Gadjiev 1997: 25–27). Such falsifications, pseudoscientific discoveries, and conclusions are not only formidably shortsighted but also rather dangerous, especially for the development of interethnic and international relations in multiethnic Daghestan and the Caucasus. The task of scientists is not to ignore but to oppose and to expose the "sensations" feeding the roots of nationalism.

The Modern Genuine Discovery

The International Scientific Conference "Ethnic and Cultural Heritage of Caucasian Albania" took place in Baku, Azerbaijan, at the end of May 2001. At this conference the director of the K. Kekelidze Institute of

Manuscripts of the Georgian Academy of Sciences, Zaza Alexidze, reported a sensational discovery that he made while working in the ancient Christian Monastery of St. Catherine on Mount Sinai, which houses a rich collection of manuscripts and icons. There Alexidze found two ancient Georgian manuscripts (N/Sin-13 and N/Sin-50) layered over Albanian texts (Alexidze 2001: 37–38). These are called palimpsests—manuscripts written over preexisting texts that had been scrubbed away. Alexidze established that the manuscripts were completely covered with the earlier Albanian texts, nearly two hundred of three hundred pages that yielded a reliable reading.

As Alexidze notes, "the Albanian text represents a Lectionary that is a basic part of the Holy liturgy. Lectionaries are collections of the Liturgical Lessons read throughout the year and consist of readings from the Old and New Testaments. The existing Albanian palimpsests represent Lessons from the Gospels (chapters from Mathew, Luke and John), Catholic Epistles of the Holy Apostles (Peter's, Jacob's and John's Epistles), Epistles of the Holy Apostle Paul (I and II Corinthians, Ephesians, I and II Thessalonians, I and II Timothy, Titus and Hebrews)." Alexidze especially emphasized that "the discovery of a complete Lectionary in the Albanian language and script directly indicates the existence of the highly developed Christian Ecclesiastic Writing in Caucasian Albania. The discovery of the Albanian Lectionary at the same time proves the information given in some sources concerning Albanian translations of the Books of the Prophets, Gospels, Acts of the Apostles and Epistles of the Apostles" (Alexidze 2001: 37–38).

He argued, "The language of the Albanian texts is undoubtedly closer to [the] Udian language in its lexis, phonetics and in grammar forms, though still different. . . . Nevertheless, the rebuilding of [the] ancient Albanian language is quite real by means of the comparative study of the ancient Albanian text with the modern Udian and in general with the southern Daghestanian group of languages" (Alexidze 2001: 38).[6] Earlier famous linguists had pointed out the closeness of contemporary Udin and the ancient Albanian languages, but now, thanks to Alexidze's discovery, this hypothesis has been irrefutably confirmed. Scholars at the time of this report showed snapshots of the pages of the Albanian manuscript and read a few excerpts in the presence of Udins who were at the conference. The sound of living Albanian speech was heard for the first time in centuries!

The further study of the manuscripts has allowed Alexidze to reach a number of major conclusions and postulate certain assumptions (Alexidze 2002: 15–20). Among them are these:

At the time of the creation of the Albanian lectionary, Albanian writing already had reached a high level of development.

Soon after the Albanians accepted Christianity, a complete Albanian translation of the Bible was available.

The Albanian lectionary probably represents the earliest stage of the development of such lectionaries and is dated to the second half of the fourth century; the translation of the books of the Bible preceded its composition.

The Albanian language is a near ancestor of the Udinian (not of the Lezgian) language from the points of view of both its lexicon and its morphology.

The Albanian literary language was completely generated during the creation of the lectionary and existed for a long period after that.

The Albanian lectionary is not a translation from Georgian, Armenian, or Syrian, but its source is apparently a Greek lectionary that has not come down to us.

Meanwhile Other "Discoveries" Continue to Appear

Despite the consequences of Alexidze's discovery, there appeared a new attempt to "reinvent the bicycle" and to receive "universal recognition." Thus, in September 2001 an amateur scholar, A. Umarov, published an article entitled "Solution of the Alphabet of the Caucasian Albanians" (Umarov 2001). Remarkably, this article notes that the discovery of Alexidze "might be considered premature." In 2002 a new article by the same author was published in which he deciphers the ancient Albanian epigraphic texts on the basis of the Avarian, Chamalalian, Tsakhurian, Dargian, and other Daghestanian languages (Umarov 2002). A year later, in 2003, he issued a brochure in which he concluded: "The Avarian and the languages of the Andian group closely resemble the ancient Albanian language" (Umarov 2003). A. Umarov must have been inspired by the unsubstantiated and dated (beginning of the twentieth century) views of the famous linguist N. Y. Marr. As is well-known, Marr asserted not only that the Avars were descendants of the Albanians, but that the "Avars are Albanians . . . [a] principle . . . [demonstrated by] not only one linguistic way" (Marr 1917: 307–338; see also Marr 1933: 70–71; 1947: 7–14). Marr never established or substantiated this opinion, and neither his "Japhetic theory" nor his "New Doctrine about Language" has stood the test of time. Rather, both have been seriously criticized. Nevertheless, A. Umarov now plans "to publish the data on the names of the peoples of Caucasian Albania, its cities, regions and rivers. Thus we shall reach the most ancient civilizations on earth. The Caucasus has great importance in the history of the peoples of the planet; the Caucasus became the

Мировая сенсация!

Впервые разгадана тайна «Фестского диска» - в Дагестане, в институте «ЮЖДАГ»

В 1908 г. во время раскопок дворца в древнем городе Фесте, на острове Крит (Эгейское море), итальянский археолог Л.Пернье случайно обнаружил небольшой глиняный диск, на котором имеется штампованная надпись. Установлено, что этот, так называемый "Фестский диск" изготовлен примерно к 1700 г. до н.э. и относится к догреческой крито-микенской культуре.

Копия одной стороны "Фестского диска" приведена на рисунке. Попытки большого числа специалистов и дилетантов дешифровать надпись на диске не увенчались успехом: надпись до сих пор не только не дешифрована, но и не определены ни направление чтения, ни начало и конец письма, ни обозначения знаков, ни происхождение письма.

И вот, наконец, тайна "Фестского диска" разгадана: надпись полностью расшифрована профессором института "ЮЖДАГ" (г.Дербент, Республика Дагестан, Россия) Я.А.Яралиевым. Язык надписи, предполагаемый минойским, оказался близким к одному из кавказских языков.

Figure 3.3. "A World Sensation! For the first time, the Secret of the Phaestos Disc is solved—in Daghestan at the YUZHDAG Institute." *Daghestanskaya Pravda*, May 17, 2000.

center of life after the World Flood, and they settled worldwide from here" (Umarov 2002). We "impatiently" await these publications.

And in another update, the decipherer of the forged *Albanian Book* is again "conquering new peaks" and creating a "world sensation." This accomplishment is none other than the decipherment of the enigmatic Phaestos Disc from Crete (the famous six-inch clay disk with spirally located marks on both sides that was found by Italian archaeologists in

1908 during the excavations of a palace complex [dated to the twentieth–eighteenth centuries BC] of the Crete/Minoan-Mycenaean culture). A May 2000 announcement published in *Daghestanskaya Pravda* (fig. 3.3) informs us that "the language of the inscription, which had been previously presumed to be Minoan, really turned out to be close to one of the Caucasian languages." Shortly thereafter, Y. A. Yaraliev published a monograph about the decipherment of the disk, in which, as expected, he demonstrated the Lezgian affiliation of the famous Phaestos Disc (Yaraliev 2001). Unfortunately, Yaraliev and other aspiring decipherers cannot understand that the brevity of the inscription, its pictographic character, and the uniqueness of its text allow it to be read, according to one's desire, in any language of the world. Meanwhile, scholars and experts remain skeptical of any claimed decipherment of this object.

The appearance of a series of pseudoscientific researches and discoveries began with *perestroika,* with the growth of national consciousness under the flags of national identity. As Mikhail Gorbachev then liked to say: "process *poshel*" (the process is under way). And processes of nationalist reclamation colored archaeological and historical discoveries, producing artificial sensations and falsifications. Unfortunately, these processes will continue for a long time to come.

Notes

This chapter was translated and annotated by Mara Kozelsky.

1. There are two known inscriptions—one in Greek, the other in Latin—from the first and second centuries AD that have been found within the territory of Caucasian Albania. They were composed, respectively, by the Greek Ailios Iason (the epitaph from Beyuk-degne) and by L. Julius Maximus, centurion of the Twelfth Fulminata legion (the inscription in Beyuk-dash). See Trever 1959: 339–345.
2. About the newly discovered Middle Persian inscriptions of Derbent (nos. 26–31), see Gadjiev 2000: 116–129.
3. On the discovery and later study of the Albanian alphabet and epigraphic monuments, see Trever 1959: 306–312, 336–339; Abramyan 1964; Muravyev 1981; Klimov 1990: 494–503.
4. Philip L. Kohl points out that this was roughly a millennium after the Cimmerians initially invaded the Near East.
5. Y. A. Yaraliev (1995: 151) relies on the *Albanian Book,* which mentions Jamag, the author of the book about Khosrow and Shirin, and which does not

mention Firdousi and Nizami Ganjevi. As a result he dates the *Albanian Book* no later than the tenth to eleventh centuries AD.

6. The Udins are a small ethnic group of Daghestan origin living today in three villages in the territories of Azerbaijan and Georgia. The language of the Udins is related to the Lezgian subgroup of the Daghestano-Nakh group of languages. One part of the Udins are Grigorian Christians, another Orthodox, and the third Muslim.

References

Abduragimov, G. A. 1995. *Kavkazskaya Albania—Lezgistan: Istoriya i sovremennost'.* St. Petersburg.

Abduragimov, G. A., and D. G. Abduragimova. 1998. *Lezgi i drevneyshie civilizacii Peredney Azii: Istoria, bili, mifi, skazania.* Moscow.

Abramyan, A. G. 1964. *Deshifrovka nadpisey kavkazskih agvan.* Yerevan, Armenia.

Agafangel. 1909. *History of Armenia.* Tbilisi, Georgia.

Alexidze, Z. 2001. Preliminary account on the identification and deciphering of the Caucasian Albanian text discovered on the Mount Sinai. In *History of the Caucasus,* vol. 1 of *The Scientific-Public Almanac.* Baku, Azerbaijan.

Alexidze, Z. 2002. What a Georgian-Albanian palimpsests, discovered in St. Catherine Monastery of Mt. Sinai, can tell us about the history of the Caucasian Albanian Church. In *History of the Caucasus,* vol. 2 of *The Scientific-Public Almanac.* Baku, Azerbaijan.

Altheim, F., and R. Stiehl. 1959. Michael der Syrer über das erste Auftreten der Bulgaren und Chazaren. *Byzantion* 28 (1959): 105–118.

Ananias of Shirak. 1992. *The Geography of Ananias of Shirak (Ašxaracoiz): The Long and the Short Versions.* Trans. R. H. Hewsen. Wiesbaden.

Corène, M. 1881. *Géographie de Moïse Corène d'après Ptolémée.* Trans. P. A. Soukry. Venice.

Dasxuranci, M. 1961. *The History of the Caucasian Albanians by Movses Dasxuranci.* Trans. C. J. F. Dowsett. London.

Diakonoff, I. M., and S. A. Starostin. 1976. *Hurro-Urartian as an Eastern Caucasian Language.* Munich.

Gadjiev, M. S. 1997. Sovremennie tendencii v izuchenii problemi etnicheskoy definicii plemen Kavkazskoy Albanii. *Tezisi dokladov nauchnoy konferencii: Sovremennoe sostoyanie i perspektivi razvitiya istoricheskoy nauki Dagestna i Severnogo Kavkaza.* Makhachkala, Daghestan, Russia.

Gadjiev, M. S. 2000. Novie nahodki i topografiya srednepersidskih nadpisey Derbenta. *Vestnik drevney istorii* 2.

Gadjiev, M. S. 2003. Gemma-pechat' tsarya Albanii Asvagena. *Vestnik drevney istorii* 1.

Gignoux, P. 1975. Intailles sasanides de la collection Pirousan. In *Monumentum H.S. Nyberg. Acta Iranica* 6. 2nd ser.

Gignoux, P. 1978. *Catalogue des sceaux, camées et bulles sasanides de la Bibliothèque Nationale et du Musée du Louvre.* Vol. 2 of *Les sceaux et bulles inscrits.* Paris.

Gignoux, P. 1980. Sceaux chrétiens d'époque sasanide. *Iranica Antiqua* 25.

Göbl, R. 1973. *Der sāsānidische Siegelkanon.* Brunswick, Germany.

Gyselen, R. 1993. *Catalogue des sceaux, camées et bulles sasanides de la Bibliothèque Nationale et du Musée du Louvre.* Paris.

Kasumova, S. Y. 1991. Le sceau du catholicos d'Albanie et du Balasagan. *Studia Iranica* 20. Facsimile.

Khorenaci, M. 1978. *History of Armenia.* Trans. Robert W. Thomson. London.

Khromov, A. 1966. Novie materiali po leksike yazika yagnobtsev. *Acta Orientalia* 30.

Klimov, G. A. 1990. O sostave agvanskogo (kavkazsko-albanskogo) alfavita. *Izvestiya AN SSSR. Seriya Literaturi i Yazika* 49 (6).

Kolesnikov, A. I. 1989. Problemi atribucii administrativnoy toponimii na oficial'nih sasanidskih pechatyah. *Vostochnoe istoricheskoe istochnikovedenie i special'nie istoricheckie disciplini* 1. Moscow.

Koryun. 1962. *Zhitie Mashtotsa.* Trans. S.V. Smbatian and K. A. Melik-Ogandjanian. Yerevan, Armenia.

Lafontaine, G. 1973. La version grecque ancienne du livre arménien d'Agathange. *Publications de l'Institut Orientaliste de Louvain* 7.

Langlois, V. 1869. *Collection des historiens anciens et modernes de l'Armenie,* vol. 2. Paris.

Lerner, J. A. 1977. *Christian Seals of the Sasanian period.* Leiden.

Magomedov, M. G. 1983. *Obrazovanie Khazarskogo kaganata.* Moscow.

Mamedov, T. M. 1993. *Kavkazskaya Albania v IV–VII vv.* Baku, Azerbaijan.

Marr, N. Y. 1917. Nepochatiy istochnik istorii kavkazskogo mira. *Izvestiyz Akademii Nauk* 6 (5). St. Petersburg.

Marr, N. Y. 1933. *Izbrannie trudi.* Vol. 1. Leningrad.

Marr, N. Y. 1947. Albanskaya nadpis'. *Kratkie soobscheniya Instituta istorii material'noy kul'turi* 15. Moscow.

Minorsky, V. F. 1963. *Istoriya Shirvana i Derbenda* X–XI vekov. Moscow.

Mirzebegov, A. A. 1995. Ot redaktora. *Rikin Gaf* 1.

Muravyev, S. N. 1981. Tri etyuda o kavkazsko-albanskoy pis'mennosti. *Annual of Ibero-Caucasian Lingvistics* 8. Tbilisi, Georgia.

Mustafaev, K. 1990. Epigraphic monuments of Azerbaijan. *Science and Life* 11–12. Baku, Azerbaijan.

Negidhul, F. 1993. Sensaciya v mirovoy albanistike. *Sadval* 6 (29).

Rizvanov, R. 1993a. Raskrita tayna drevnih pis'men. *Daghestanskaya Pravda,* May 13.

Rizvanov, R. 1993b. Zagovorili drevnealbanskie rukopisi. *Daghestanskaya Pravda,* July 31.

Rizvanov, Z. 1991. Dva fragmenta o nauchnih fal'sifikaciyah. *Lezginstan* 0.

Rizvanov, Z., and R. Rizvanov. 1990. *Istoriya lezgin.* Makhachkala, Daghestan, Russia.

Shanidze, A. G. 1957. Poryadok bukv gruzinskogo, armyanskogo i albanskogo alfavitov. *Materiali po istorii Azerbaijana* 2. Baku, Azerbaijan.

Shikhsaidov, A. R. 1976. O lokalizacii Filana. *Onomastika Kavkaza*. Makhachkala, Daghestan, Russia.

Shnirelman, V. A. 2000. Tsennost' proshlogo: Etnotsentristskie istoricheskie mifi, identichnost' I etnopolitika. *Real'nost' etnicheskih mifov*. Moscow.

Stranitsa iz neizvestnoy albanskoy knigi. 1991. *Lezginstan* 0.

Trever, K. V. 1959. *Ocherki po istorii i kul'ture Kavkazskoy Albanii*. Moscow.

Umarov, A. 2001. Razgadka alfavita kavkazskih alban. *Daghestanskaya Pravda*, September 5.

Umarov, A. 2002. Albanskie nadpisi i alfavit. *Dagestanskaya Panorama*, nos. 19, 20, May 16 and 23.

Umarov, A. 2003. *Alfavit i nadpisi kavkazskih alban*. Makhachkala, Daghestan, Russia.

Yaraliev, Y. A. 1995. *Alupanskaya (Kavkazsko-Albanskaya) pis'mennost' i lezginskiy yazik*. Makhachkala, Daghestan, Russia.

Yaraliev, Y. A. 2001. *Deshifrovka "Festskogo diska."* Derbent, Daghestan, Russia.

FOUR

Archaeology and Nationalism in *The History of the Romanians*

GHEORGHE ALEXANDRU NICULESCU

The publication of *The History of the Romanians* (*Istoria Românilor*), which starts with the Paleolithic period, provides an interesting opportunity to examine how archaeological data and interpretations are used in a narrative about the origins of a nation under changing political and ideological circumstances.

Besides identifying the archaeological contribution to the building of the main points of the extended narrative of *The History of the Romanians*, I attempt to show in this chapter to what extent the archaeological knowledge present in this work, which is meant to be authoritative, is normal knowledge produced within the limits of the paradigm of cultural history that supports a nationalist representation of society. This perspective has been maintained even when archaeologists have tried to avoid what appeared to them as nationalism. I also call attention to the interpretive devices—many of them incompatible with any kind of scientific reasoning—that were employed by some of the authors in order to provide "scientific" backing for a particular version of the national genealogy of the Romanians.

The History of the Romanians presents itself as the apex of Romanian historical and archaeological research in a long tradition of national histories that started before the birth of the Romanian national state and continued with the works of Alexandru D. Xenopol, Nicolae Iorga, and Constantin C. Giurescu. This tradition continued after World War II with the work published in 1960–1964 as the official history of Romania under the aegis of a Romanian Academy "reformed" by the Communist leadership of the country. That work, titled *History of Romania*, ended with volume 4, principally because of rapidly changing views on Romania's recent past. A new version was planned in the second half of the 1970s, but the preparations ceased in 1980 (Babeş 2002: 9; Iliescu 2002: 7) when the authors of the first volume refused to comply with the view of the national past favored by an influential part of the Communist leadership. After 1989 the Romanian Academy, reinforced by the return of more than fifty research institutes under its authority, including those of history and archaeology, tried to reassert its position as the leading scientific institution of the country. It decided that the interrupted work on the new version should be resumed, but it did not seriously consider a change of perspective. One of the editors of the third volume sees the resulting 2001 work, *The History of the Romanians*, as "the editing of a continuously renewed old project" (*IR3*, Theodorescu: x),[1] words in which, following Zygmunt Bauman's thoughts (1992: 685–686), an imperative of nationalism can be recognized: the outcome of research on the origins of the nation has to consist of what was already known.

If we compare the first three volumes of *The History of the Romanians* with the relevant literature from the 1980s, the continuity is unmistakable. There is almost no change in the depiction of the origins of the nation, and this shows "the absence of a long-term regeneration effort, of debates and recuperation projects, of a systematic effort to detect and mend the lacunae of Romanian historiography" (Papacostea 2002). Many of the texts intended for the project aborted in 1980 were recycled for *The History of the Romanians*. At a meeting in 1994 to set up the editorial boards for the volumes, Ştefan Pascu declared that the third volume was "already written" (Alexandrescu 2002), and in 1995 Răzvan Theodorescu summoned the authors of the same volume and established as a principle that the old texts should be revised by the authors and eventually "actualized" (Iliescu 2002: 6).

The continuing importance of national history is linked with what happened in Romania after the end in 1989 of Ceauşescu's dictatorship, a regime particularly interested in legitimating itself by the use of the national past, a regime that mobilized for that purpose the whole range of ideological and academic teaching and research institutions of the state. The "transition period," marked by the building of democratic institutions and of a market economy, started as an apparently "clean break" with the Communist past, in which, nevertheless, as in other countries of the region, the former *nomenklatura*, lower-level party officials, secret police, and personnel attached to the administration of party assets, as well as managers of the socialist economy and entrepreneurs of the informal one, occupied the leading positions. In these circumstances the nationalist ideology proved to be most appropriate for facilitating the transformation of the old politically and economically dominant groups into the new ones. It had the peculiar property of being both a sign of continuity with the last two decades of the Communist regime and a sign of renewal, of bringing to life an idealized pre–Word War II Romania and consequently appealing to the revived "historical parties."[2] The nationalist ideology has allowed those who have made careers of "defending national interests" to justify the positions held during the Communist dictatorship and to keep them after 1989 by promoting the fiction of the incompatibility between communism and nationalism.

After lingering a few years in an atmosphere of relative indifference and skepticism about the purpose of a new grand work on national history, the project suddenly became a priority in 1999 when the institutes were pressured to produce the necessary texts, the Academy going so far as to make their delivery a condition of long-overdue salary raises. This change of pace might have been related to the introduction in the same year of alternative high school history textbooks by the Democratic Convention government, a coalition of promarket and pro-European parties that won in the 1996 elections and then lost in the 2000 elections. The opposition, especially the nationalist Greater Romania Party, but also the winner of the 2000 elections, the Social Democratic Party, both linked with the former Communist elite, reacted unfavorably and sometimes angrily.[3] Blaming politicians and historians for their irresponsibility toward our nation, some public figures, many of whom were connected with the opposition, demanded from the Romanian Academy "the highest forum of science and culture," a comprehensive and "true" synthesis of national history. The Romanian Academy accepted the legitimacy of alternative textbooks but repeatedly criticized one of them and the curriculum because, instead of starting from "the necessities of *national education*, they mechanically implemented external models" (Berindei 1999: 1, original emphasis). One introductory text in *The History of the Romanians* mentions "the denigration of historical personalities" in the alternative textbooks, thus evaluating the official *IR* as a work of sober patriotism while criticizing "the exaggerations of the 'demythologization'"

(*IR1,* Berindei: xix), an allusion to the works of Lucian Boia, a professor in the History Department of Bucharest University, who, in several books (esp. 1997), has successfully attempted to prove the mythical nature of much of what is known about the Romanian past, especially about the origins of the nation.

The authors of *The History of the Romanians* define their position also against the version of the purely Dacian origins of the Romanian nation, a theory that was particularly influential in the 1980s, when it was supported by some Communist Party leaders and promoted by some people in the party's Institute of History. "Thracomania," as it is usually called in the Romanian academic environment, traces the origins of the Romanian nation, and eventually of all European civilization, to the Dacians and presents the Romans as conquerors and foreigners. This theory has a long history, starting in the nineteenth century (Verdery 1991: 36–40; Boia 1997: 101–107), and in recent years has been noisily advocated by an organization, the *Dacia Revival International Society,* led by the U.S.-based physician Napoleon Săvescu, who claims that the Dacians form the matrix of all European peoples. Săvescu uses, among other arguments, misinterpretations of ancient DNA evidence.[4] In the few attempts after 1989 to discuss nationalism in Romanian archaeology, such "excesses," which were seen as among the worst consequences of the party's control over historical and archaeological research during the 1980s, were the main, if not the only target (Mihăilescu-Bârliba 1997), reinforcing a widespread distinction between "good" and "bad" nationalism. *The History of Romanians* rejects Thracomania, and the historians who have resisted criticizing the Romans are praised for their patriotism (*IR1,* Berindei: xix).

The History of the Romanians is justified on the bases of its importance for the nation, its proportions, and its quality. In his introduction, the president of the Romanian Academy exhibits an irritated defensiveness: "Why . . . a ten volume Handbook about a history with already too many myths and too many statues, and far too many heroes which prevent us from our entering Europe!? . . . The Romanians deserve an integral history, neither mythologized, nor minimized; written, as Braudel demanded, with *exigent passion*" (*IR1,* Simion: xiii–xiv).

Along similar lines, the head of the Historical Sciences and Archaeology Section of the Romanian Academy, Dan Berindei, argues that in the contemporary process of reducing the distances between the peoples, we have to "preserve our distinguishing traits . . . in order to enter the big round dance of the European nations . . . with our spiritual dowry." The Romanians need their national history: without it, they would be "gravely affected by the complicated and complex processes facing them" (*IR1*: xvii). The work binds the Romanian citizens together, fulfilling "a necessity of our society," and it is "beneficial . . . for the complex process of transition we are living, for the normalization and stability we hope to see established" (xix).

The History of the Romanians is presented as an "ample synthesis, . . . the result of the information from the sources and of the works of interpretation offered by our modern and contemporary historiography after an evolution of 200 years," written by the "best specialists" (*IR1*, Berindei: xviii), and as a fruit of recently gained freedom, which makes possible this "synthesis of the achievements of national historiography, . . . without any political conditioning, . . . in the spirit of historical truth" (xix). The emphasis on "specialists" can be understood not only as a reaction against Thracomania, which has been promoted mostly by amateurs, with little or no education in ancient history and archaeology, but also as an assertion of the authority of those authorized by the state to write about the origins of the nation. The "specialists" in Romanian archaeology deserve a closer look. Employed by the state in appropriate positions, they are empowered to speak about their field; but in the absence of an institutionalized qualitative evaluation of their work, their level of professionalism is almost entirely dependent on personal initiative and dedication and is variably related to social recognition. This situation explains the differences in quality between the volumes and the chapters of *The History of the Romanians*.

The responsibility of coordinating tens of historians and archaeologists was assumed for each volume by two coordinators and an editorial secretary. Together with the editors of the whole series, they have attempted "to solve difficult situations . . . in order to ensure a unitary, relatively similar and organized character to the volumes" (*IR1*, Berindei: xviii). Dan Berindei finds that the main impediments *The History of the Romanians* had to overcome included insufficient funding and "the weakening of the links between the Academy and the research institutes, chapter authors being recruited only of their free will" (xix).

To accommodate differences of opinion, the coordinators of the first volume found the following solution: "The different interpretations" are introduced with expressions such as "the author of these lines believes" (*IR1*, Petrescu-Dîmboviţa and Vulpe: xxii). While this policy might represent progress compared with the authoritative writing (disguised as collective authorship) of the 1980s, it would unfortunately lead us to believe that whenever such an explanatory introduction is missing, we are reading not an interpretation but "historical truth."

In the published reactions to *The History of the Romanians* (e.g., Papacostea 2002; Iliescu 2002; Alexandrescu 2002), the most discussed problem has to do with the use made in volumes 3 and 4 of the texts prepared for the version aborted in 1980 and of previously published literature. An official answer of the Romanian Academy to the accusations of Şerban Papacostea describes how volume 4 was produced: the editors used parts of the chapters written for the version abandoned in 1980 and articles written by their authors afterward "without being able to specify the paternity of each fragment." The authors' names were merely mentioned in the foreword to the volume and listed in the bibliographies of the chapters. This blatant infringement on authorship rights appears to these editors as somewhat natural, and the use of the name of another author for a text written by Şerban Papacostea, who refused to take part in *The History of the Romanians* project, is regarded only as a "regrettable negligence" (Biroul de presă 2002).

Several authors of chapters in the second and the third volumes have discovered in their texts changes of which they did not approve; at times, they did not even recognize the text published under their name as theirs. Especially in the third volume, there are chapters attributed to several authors that appear to the reader as having been written only by Ştefan Olteanu. A shocking decision was to name Radu Popa, who died in 1993, as coauthor with Ştefan Pascu and Olteanu even though, in one of the few direct attacks against the local ideological tradition of writing history, Popa had chosen Pascu's and Olteanu's works as targets (1991). Therefore, we cannot always be sure that the texts in *The History of the Romanians* were indeed written by the named authors. Nevertheless, I will cite the authors as published, even when I strongly suspect they have not written the chapter.

The choice of *The History of the Romanians* as a title, which was not particularly popular among the archaeologists from my institute, was justified in one of the introductory texts by the fact that before World War II similar works had this title, allowing the historians to take into account "the history of the entire nation, both within the state and outside the borders" (*IR1*, Berindei: xviii). Since the authors do not mention the Romanians until toward the end of the second volume, what justifies the use of the title *The History of the Romanians* for the first volume? What can a history of the Romanian national territory before the Romanians mean?[5] The million years covered by the first part of the first volume are thought to be of paramount importance for Romania's subsequent history; they are seen as "the foundation of the whole building of the subsequent evolution," as "the inheritance of the past, without which the subsequent evolution of the history of the Romanian people, from the Middle Ages to the present, would not be understood" (*IR1,* Petrescu-Dîmboviţa and Vulpe: xxi). There is no elaboration on what was inherited and on how this has shaped the Romanian nation, but the construction and the content of the first volumes of *The History of the Romanians* show that indeed the nation was born before its birth.

Archaeology

In *The History of the Romanians,* archaeology is defined as "a discipline with its own methods, which . . . has the task of complementing the data from the written sources, and, when these are missing, is the only source of information about extinct prehistoric populations" (*IR1,* Petrescu-Dîmboviţa: 43). The dominant attitude about how different kinds of sources should be used by the historian or the archaeologist stems from the idea that the "[written] sources interweave . . . harmoniously with the archaeological ones, thus contributing to a better approach to the historical phenomenon." Therefore, mixed argumentation, the use of knowledge produced in various disciplines, represented as "historical evidence" without a proper consideration of its paradigmatic context,[6] appears as an imperative: "the confrontation of [the written sources] with other source categories, whenever this is possible, is somewhat mandatory in the determination as correctly as possible of the facts" (*IR2,* Protase: 5). A few of the *History of the Romanians* authors, it should be noted, are aware of the dangers of this approach. Alexandru Vulpe warns about mixing the methods of archaeology and history, because they have different "probability coefficients" and because "there is nothing to justify the interpretation of the historical data as a premise for ordering the archaeological material" (*IR1,* Vulpe: 399). Mircea Babeş (*IR1*: 525) has a similar opinion: when writing about the identification of the Bastarnae with the Poieneşti-Lukashevka culture, he mentions the independent analyses of the written sources and of the archaeological record leading to this interpretation. Archaeology as a provider of historical information when better sources are missing is an outcome of a long local tradition: in Romania all the archaeological teaching at university level is done in history departments. Archaeology is not taught as an autonomous discipline. Even though after 1989 the number of archaeology courses has increased in many old and new Romanian universities, this increase has brought no visible change in the status of the discipline: archaeology is an auxiliary discipline to history. With a historian's goals, the archaeologist is supposed to combine digging and analytical techniques with "historical thinking" in writings where the specificity of the approach is limited to description, typology, and chronology, any interest in social realities being usually limited to the detection of ancient identities that are thought to explain everything else of importance.

Whereas in other paradigms and traditions of archaeological research, archaeological knowledge about society is built on theories linking material culture with social realities, the paradigm at work in Romania expects archaeologists to use the ancient authors to understand the ancient societies, whenever this is possible. The social sciences are usually ignored, a few remnants of the kind of Marxism imposed in Romania by the Soviet occupation being of little consequence. The role of the social sciences is played by the common knowledge about society, structured by nationalist representations.

The importance of archaeology for the reconstruction of the past varies, sometimes even in texts by the same author. It is particularly important for the crucial period after the abandonment of the Roman province of Dacia in AD 271 because it produces "direct evidence" (*IR2,* Protase: 259) and offers "sure documents" of the continuity of the "Daco-Romans" (555), whereas the written sources stubbornly mention only "migratory peoples" on the future national territory. We learn from the same author, however, that the historian encounters great difficulties in reconstructing the ways of life and the social-economic structures of the indigenous population after the withdrawal of the Romans because he has "to rely on data, frequently vague and incomplete, which archaeology and numismatics can offer" (581). Nevertheless, when they are badly needed, archaeological data can be more reliable than written sources. For instance, we are told that the written sources on the fifth to seventh centuries contain "errors"—by which confusions between our ancestors and the "migratory peoples" are meant—that archaeological research is supposed to be able to "correct" (e.g., *IR2,* Teodor: 641, 725, 729–730). The archaeological sources, as "direct sources," by "their materiality" (*IR2,* Protase: 605), do not deceive as the written sources do. Ştefan Pascu even states that the information offered by archaeological excavations has the value of a main historical source, because most of the written sources about the seventh to fourteenth centuries do not come from the Romanian environment, which diminishes their credibility, especially when they contain "faulty or tendentious interpretations." The archaeological sources in many cases complement the written information, "verifying and correcting it" (*IR3*: 3). They are most relevant because of their authenticity (*IR3,* Zaharia, Teodor, and Theodorescu:

288) and because they offer "a credible, concrete image of the material and spiritual culture values . . . of these territories" (*IR3,* Rusu, Olteanu, Popa, and Székely: 44).

The main task of archaeological research appears to be the separation of "our ancestors" from other peoples, usually following the assumption, embedded in the use of the "archaeological culture" concept, that we are able to recognize them in the archaeological record because peoples "have" distinctive cultures. Attempts to define the concept of the "archaeological culture" are to be found only in the first volume, and most of them, if not all, belong to Alexandru Vulpe:

> The concept of the *archaeological culture* is understood, in the traditional sense, as representing merely a combination of characteristic traits from the material obtained in archaeological excavations, which constitutes itself in a *rule,* delimited in space and time from other similarly made combinations. The *rule* must include more (as many as possible) categories of finds—not just one. Thus conceived, the culture is an image of the organization of the archaeological material, behind which real situations, historical, social or of other natures must not necessarily hide. . . . the majority of the [Bronze and Iron Age] "cultures" are made of groups of pottery shapes and decoration, the style of the latter being the defining element. It is evident, therefore, that such groupings of the archaeological information do not necessarily imply ethnic groups; a grouping of pottery forms with a certain decoration might indicate a group of related tribes, as well as ethnically different populations. (*IR1*: 211–212, original emphasis)

This position, a radical one in the Romanian context, does not significantly modify the account of national origins: Vulpe describes the Iron Age Basarabi culture as "a complex synthesis of material culture which *certainly* also mirrors cultural-historical processes" (*IR1,* Vulpe: 327, my emphasis). He is not questioning culture history as a useful paradigm for archaeologists—this paradigm at work in Romania has no name, because it is archaeology *tout court*—as the remark about a conception being "unsatisfactory from a culture-historical point of view" shows (215). His repeated warnings against the ethnicization of archaeological cultures do not lead to a decisive reformulation of Romania's ethnic past. The nature of ethnic phenomena is not questioned; it is only what archaeologists, with their limited means, can do to recognize them in the archaeological record that is problematic. Central to their representation is still the belief that people speaking the same language are an ethnic group, an assumption essential for the construction of the national past,[7] for the ethnogenesis of the Romanians that is treated in *The History of the Romanians* as similar and intimately related to the formation of the Romanian language (*IR2,* Protase: 167; see also *IR3,* Pascu and Theodorescu: 24), despite the linguists' opinion that the formation process of the Romance languages "should not be confused with the formation process of the Romanic *peoples*, which is one of an ethnic nature" (*IR3,* Sala and Mihăilă: 111, original emphasis).

In most of his warnings, Vulpe allows the interpretation of archaeological cultures to indicate ancient peoples but does not offer any hint regarding how such an interpretation might be validated. Following the traditional understanding of an archaeological culture, he tries to give the concept more consistency by adding to pottery styles metallurgy, funerary customs, and other cultural traits. Most importantly, he assumes the existence of human groups—difficult to imagine as something other than ethnic groups—associated with the archaeological cultures. These are made of the "bearers" of archaeological cultures to whom behaviors are assigned: for example, "the economy of bearers of the Coţofeni culture" (*IR1,* Vulpe: 231) or "the metallurgical activity of the bearers of the Tei culture" (269). Despite Vulpe's concerns about the interpretation of archaeological cultures, most contributors to *The History of the Romanians* understand them as "cultural-historical phenomena" (e.g., *IR1,* László: 297), and almost everywhere in the three volumes there is little doubt about their ethnic significance. Starting with the Neolithic, the archaeologists make the archaeological cultures the main actors in the historical narrative. Thus "the Starčevo-Criş communities" are enclosed with shallow ditches, "maybe to defend themselves against the first Vinčan tribes"; "[t]he departure point of the Dudeşti communities lies in northwest Anatolia" (*IR1,* Ursulescu: 143); cultural groups can have an "organic, continuous evolution" (*IR1,* László: 313), and their "bearers" occupy territories (320–321).

The ethnic meaning of the traditional concept is present in a sequence of cultures understood as stages in the evolution of the autochthonous population into Romanians: the Daco-Roman stage (the Bratei-Ipoteşti-Costişa culture, fourth to sixth centuries AD), the Romanic stage (the Ipoteşti-Cândeşti-Botoşana-Hansca-Filiaş culture, sixth to seventh centuries AD), and the ancient Romanian stage (the Dridu culture, eighth to eleventh centuries AD) (*IR3,* Zaharia, Teodor, and Theodorescu: 288). One of the alleged authors of this scheme presents a different view when he is named as the only author: archaeological cultures (Costişa-Botoşana-Hansca, Ipoteşti-Cândeşti-Ciurel, Bratei-Ţaga-Biharea) appear as "regional aspects" of the "autochthonous civilization" of the fifth to seventh centuries. He argues that they are "identical in origin and evolution" and cover the whole territory once inhabited by the Geto-Dacians" (*IR2,* Teodor: 652, 654). Such cultural distinctions can be ignored altogether: in the third volume the archaeological finds of the seventh to fourteenth centuries are presented as "the material culture of the population identified . . . on the whole territory of ancient Dacia." Everything demonstrates "its Romanic character, its Latin origin," including agricultural implements and household annexes (*IR3,* Rusu, Olteanu, Popa, and Székely: 45).

We, the "Autochthons"

The main plot of the first volume is the compact inhabitation of the national territory, since the beginnings of the Neolithic, by an uninterrupted genealogy of archaeological cultures. Such inhabitation suggests or is interpreted as a succession of inheritances from one culture to another that continues until an unspecified ethnic content, after traveling through the ages, reaches and determines the Romanian nation. Just one example illustrates how an element of this genealogy is built: "For the origin of the Verbicioara culture a contribution of the groups with striated pottery of Gornea-Orleşti type is assumed, defined exclusively on criteria of typological selection of the pottery, groups which should have also contributed to the genesis of the cultural aspect Corneşti-Crvenka from the Banat and Serbia—all with roots in the Early Bronze Age" (*IR1,* Vulpe: 267). The cultural unity of the future national territory emerges with the Iron Age Basarabi culture, "a stage in the natural evolution of the local Hallstatt" (327), showing analogies in pottery decoration with long-disappeared Bronze Age cultures, a situation explained by the survival of "a patrimony of [decorative] motives . . . preserved on perishable materials." In contrast to the Bronze Age cultures, which were well individualized on restricted territories, the Basarabi culture has a large area; it is "a syncretic and unitary image" that mirrors "to a great extent" a cultural unity of the communities from the respective area, explained "very probably" as a religious one, not necessarily linked to a certain ethnic identity (327–329). Then the author mentions as a hypothesis his interpretation from 1979 that defined the "content of the Basarabi culture" as belonging to a community of tribes of different origins (Illyrians, Pannonians, Thracians, and maybe unknown others) among which "it is plausible to distinguish the Northern Thracian communities—named by convention Geto-Dacian—as a dominant element. Only thus can be justified the later contribution of the Basarabi culture to the genesis of the Geto-Dacian civilization. The fact that the area of the Basarabi culture coincides to a great extent with that of the five centuries later 'classical' Geto-Dacian civilization makes plausible the hypothesis that sees in this cultural community a manifestation of a unity of [religious] belief, characteristic especially for the Northern Thracian tribes" (331). This "spiritual unification" is imagined as an "accelerated diffusion" from one community to another, a consequence of ever more sustained contacts among their members, of a much more intense circulation in the entire Carpatho-Danubian area, a phenomenon supposed to explain, in great part, the cultural syncretism and one that could favor the emergence of a single language for the mutual understanding of all these communities. This process should have begun much earlier—at the end of the Bronze Age. While the Basarabi culture is allowed, however cautiously, to take on an ethnic content, this does not happen with the Scythian culture; such a hypothesis is not even suggested: "By 'Scythian' culture we mean a conventional term, which generically designates all the cultural-archaeological manifestations from the Northern Pontic area of the Late Hallstatt (7th–4th centuries BC). In no circumstance should any ethnic character be assigned to this concept" (410).

The same happens with another "intrusion" into the "Geto-Dacian" area, the "Illyrian cultural area," which is declared a convention not to "be confused with the aerial spread of the populations speaking proper Illyrian" (*IR1,* Vulpe: 414).

Once the presence of cultural uniformity on the future national territory of Romania is established with the Basarabi culture, a strong and pervasive dichotomy is instated between the local population, continuously evolving to become Romanian, and the foreign peoples.[8] The purpose of all these endeavors from now on will be to reconstruct "the thread of the history of the autochthonous population" (*IR1,* Vulpe: 463), which will continue uninterrupted up to 1918, when all the territories inhabited by Romanians were united in a single state.

The "autochthonous" population is frequently presented as civilized, unlike its barbarian neighbors. In this perspective, the Dacian kingdom from the first century AD, viewed as "a strong client kingdom," was "a trusted ally of Rome against the continuous threats from the Germanic and Sarmatian tribes, who were always looking for loot and strife" (*IR1,* Petolescu: 675). The high level of civilization enables the local population to act as a cultural mediator, especially between the Roman Empire and the barbarians, one of the frequent hypostases of peripheral claims to civilization in eastern Europe and central Europe.

Who Were the "Geto-Dacians"?

After the Basarabi "cultural unity," one can speak about a single "autochthonous society" with a "traditional culture" (*IR1,* Vulpe: 468). Professor Vulpe is one of the few Romanian archaeologists to make a clear distinction between the Getae and the Daci and to argue against the long tradition of considering them one and the same, expressed in the concept of "Geto-Dacians" (417–418), which creates the fiction of a uniform population inhabiting the Romanian national territory. Nevertheless, he needs, for unspecified reasons, "a generic term to designate all the Carpatho-Danubian peoples" and writes about the difficulties of finding one, recognizing that "the names of the *Getae,* of the *Daci,* and of all other peoples had their own history and certainly their own significance that has evolved in the course of time" (417).

Although the first mention of the Getae is from the fifth century BC and the first one about the Daci from the first century BC, and although Strabo (7.3.13) describes them as two peoples inhabiting different territories, Alexandru Vulpe supports the use of "Geto-Dacians," understood as a modern and conventional concept, "designating all the Northern Thracian tribes which have inhabited the Carpatho-Danubian space." It is a concept that does not imply "an absolute ethnic, linguistic or historical unity" (*IR1,* Vulpe: 418–419). Another convention with a similar function is to name Dacia the territory inhabited by the "Geto-Dacians." Vulpe carefully points out that "nothing allows us to understand a more ancient use of this term for the whole area inhabited by the *Getae* and the Dacians," although he thinks this "is plausible for the time of Burebista" (first century BC) (421). However, he believes that "the Romanian historiographical tradition" entitles us to use Dacia as an alternative name for the Carpatho-Danubian space, "in order to designate all the territories inhabited by the *Getae,* the Dacians, and other North Thracian peoples" (423). The diversity suggested by the tribal names known to the ancient authors is downplayed in these "other" peoples, and when Vulpe refers to other ethnonyms than the Getae or the Dacians, which are mentioned by ancient sources on the territory of present-day Romania, he supposes that they were "related" to the Getae, if not Getic tribes (424). Alexandru Suceveanu gives the same treatment to such names (*IR2*: 307–309).

Vulpe seems to believe there is more to the "Geto-Dacians" than mere convention; he sees the Getae and the Dacians related in a way typical of modern thinking, not of antiquity, and his further arguments tend to establish this concept as an accurate description of an ancient reality. He claims that "the ancient sources are unanimous in asserting that the

Getae and the *Daci* were the same people, the differences being regional," but quotes only Strabo (7.3.13) for the assertion that the Getae and the Daci spoke the same language. Here the representation of ancient peoples as nations leads Vulpe to understand that Strabo considered the two to be one people because they were speaking the same language, although the ancient geographer clearly states that they were two distinct peoples.

Thus the "Geto-Dacians," adequately characterized by Karl Strobel as a sui generis social form (1998: 75), end up being recognized as a people (*neam* in Romanian) permanently inhabiting the Carpatho-Danubian territory, something confirmed "to a great extent" by archaeological research. They are often contrasted to the "foreign populations" who settled in Dacia, imagined as "temporarily constituting enclaves that were in the end absorbed" (*IR1,* Vulpe: 421). The "Geto-Dacians" have a "civilization" (429) and a "religion" (439, 444), and they are singled out by a remarkable uniformity, which still allows even an autochthonous ethnic diversity (648). During the first century BC and the first century AD, the Getae and the Dacians made a "veritable ethno-cultural unity" (*IR1,* Babeş: 301). Mircea Babeş distinguishes for the second century BC to the first century AD a central area, in which the main components have local antecedents, and a peripheral one. This central area "must be defined" as "the permanent living hearth of the Getic and Dacian tribes"; in addition, "significantly," "this territory coincides to a great extent with the formation area of the Romanian people. This ascertained fact is of paramount importance, suggesting the role of biological, cultural and ethnic substratum which the Geto-Dacian element has played in the formation of the Romanian people" (760). Once the equivalence of the Getae with the Dacians and the link with the Carpatho-Danubian territory are firmly established, anything that happens on this territory happens to the indigenous population. For example, the finding of Greek coins from Istros on the "indigenous territory" indicates that the Getae have entered into "closer commercial relations with the Greek world" (*IR1*, Vulpe: 645). This inaugurates an interpretative device of great further use: in every action, every inhabitant of the future national territory of Romania represents his people (no women are mentioned in the *History of the Romanians* volumes reviewed here).

The reign of Burebista (ca. 80–44 BC), the first important "Geto-Dacian" ruler (Strabo's clear statement [7.3.11] that he was *aner Getes* receives no attention) to extend his domination over a vast territory, assumed to be that of present-day Romania or even greater, is interpreted as a period of political unification of an already culturally homogeneous population. His actions are seen as the consequence of high political aspirations. He did not destroy the fortifications of his rivals because they were "vital for Dacia" (*IR1,* Glodariu: 640). He attacked the Greek colonies not with vulgar hopes of gaining wealth, like previous local dynasts; beyond "financial necessities" he acted for a superior good, that of Dacia (649); and he had a "superior political plan," that of "strengthening the eastern flank of his recent political construction" (646). Finally, the Greek colonies were not simply plundered; they were "integrated in his kingdom" (647).

The interpretation of the archaeological data that make up the "Geto-Dacian" culture leads to a conclusion "of deep historical significance": the culture is "unitary" throughout its entire area, and the unity is "most pregnantly" illustrated by the uniform aspect of hand- and wheel-made pottery (*IR1,* Babeş: 759). This unity is ascribed to "a defining structure," which was not affected by "particularities" issued from contact with other populations (*IR1,* Glodariu: 762).

Economic activities on the future national territory are described as the economic life of Dacia (in terms reminiscent of propaganda during Ceauşescu's time): "The rapid increase of all the branches of the economy . . . , the continuous intensification of the commercial relations with the Hellenistic countries, then especially with the Roman world." This development is traced to the progress of iron metallurgy, which sustained and "favored the evolution of the agriculture and of the other crafts" (*IR1,* Glodariu: 762) and the intensification of internal commercial exchanges (774). We find a similar description for the end of the first millennium AD: the economy of the "Carpatho-Danubian society" has mutually conditioning economic branches, defining "the structures of human communities" and "exports" (*IR3,* Rusu, Olteanu, Popa, and Székely: 50, 54).

According to this narrative, the "Geto-Dacians" lived in village communities (*IR1,* Glodariu: 777), where land was common property. At the same time primary elements and small replicas of a nationlike entity and spaces of ethnic uniformity and social equilibrium, they are imagined as perennial and basic forms of organization of the local population. Yet, there is no convincing archaeological argumentation supporting their existence; they are inferred from social realities studied in some parts of Romania at the beginning of the twentieth century, as well as from late medieval documents (Stahl 1969). The village communities barely survived during the time of the Roman province (*IR2,* Protase: 171), but after the end of Roman rule they became again ubiquitous (581).

The Survival and Romanization of the "Geto-Dacians"

The survival of the "Geto-Dacians" after the final defeat of king Decebalus (AD 106) and the organization of the Roman province of Dacia are key elements in the narrative of Romanian national origins. They extend the Romanians back into prehistory, and as such they must be well defended against opponents who argue that the "autochthonous" population was exterminated by the Romans. *The History of the Romanians* argues that this is an "aberrant thesis" put forward "for chauvinistic political reasons" by foreign historians and rejected by "the entire Romanian historiography and by a series of foreign scholars, eminent experts in the history of the Roman Empire" (*IR2,* Protase: 137). Of course, Dumitru Protase does not deny that Romanian historians from Transylvania had the same opinion at the end of the eighteenth century and in the first half of the nineteenth, but he thinks that unlike those foreign historians, they were supporting the extermination of the Dacians "in good faith, although naively . . . in order to demonstrate the pure Roman origin of the Romanian people" (138). This survival is supported by "archaeological culture" reasoning: "The Geto-Dacian culture from the province of Dacia has close relationships, evidently of a genetic nature, with that of the second Iron Age from the same area, from which it derives" (*IR1,* Babeş: 798). The interpretation of this survival allows for two contradictory processes: (1) the maintaining of collective identity by living in isolation—in settlements clearly differentiated from those of the Roman colonists, settlements characteristic of all Free Dacians (*IR1,* Babeş: 799)—and (2) Romanization. The solution is peculiar: these two opposed processes are presented as noncontradictory; and the outcome, the "Daco-Romans," are as autochthonous as the "Geto-Dacians."

Romanization is described as a "linguistic and ethnic mutation, of spiritual *habitus,* of ways of thinking and of living" (*IR2,* Protase: 165). It is a "beneficial synthesis, the basis of the evolution towards Romanianness" (168). The social aspect of the process is generally played down, and even when the phenomenon is examined in a chapter about social structure, it is considered "decidedly determined by the cultural factor" (*IR2,* Suceveanu: 350–351). Romanization is presented as a civilizational upgrade of a particularly homogeneous and receptive, that is, an already highly advanced, population (*IR2,* Protase: 160). The "power and prestige of Rome" are "efficient psychological factors in the assimilation of the autochthons to [*sic*] Romanization" (166). *The History of the Romanians* also hosts a different opinion: the local population was not at all prepared for the new values—for example, writing was scarcely used until the conquest—and Romanization was a "spiritual" shock to the Dacians, "because nothing specific to the autochthons (e.g. the Zalmoxian religion or the sacred architecture) survives" (*IR2,* Bărbulescu: 225; see also 249–251).

A distinction between culture and ethnicity is noticeable in the presentations of the Romanization process: Romanitas appears to be mostly cultural, whereas ethnicity is Dacian, as "Daco-Roman" seems to indicate. Ethnicity is understood as a demographic and biological objective reality, the economic basis of the province (*IR2,* Protase: 163–164). No arguments support this economic role, which would be more conducive to ethnic dichotomization than to Romanization.

The progress of the Romanization process is not described, archaeologically or otherwise. It is simply asserted that "in the 3rd century the ethnic differences between the newcomers and the autochthons, the old adversity between the Dacians and the new masters, disappeared, being replaced by general cooperation," but this is not its end—as one might expect—because Romanization "did not stop on the territory of the former province after the withdrawal of the army and of the administration . . . under the reign of emperor Aurelian, but continued and accomplished itself as a natural process within the Daco-Roman population until the 5th century. . . . the Romanized elements from the cities . . . continued to bring [to the rural areas] higher forms of civilization: Latin, the Roman way of living, Christian belief."

One of the most difficult parts of the construction of the national past is the Romanization of the Free Dacians, a process that was supposed to end just in time for the Slavs to find on the future national territory of Romania "a compact mass of Romanic population, Latin-speaking, and Christian" (*IR2,* Protase: 167).

The "Free Dacians"—the shift from "Geto-Dacians" to "Dacians" suggests an increasing ethnic uniformity—are the Dacians who inhabited territories outside the Roman province. The concept, another "convention," recognized as a modern historiographical creation (*IR2,* Ioniţă: 401), helps establish the idea that "Dacia," as the future Romanian national territory, continued to be inhabited by a homogeneous population. To that effect, the persistence of "traditional relations" between the Dacians from the province and the Free Dacians is emphasized and explained by family ties and commercial exchanges with Roman products (404).

For the Free Dacians of Muntenia, the process of Romanization is described as "authentic" and as developing "intensely and alertly" after the

Daco-Roman wars. While the Romans acted by their "nominal domination," with an occasional presence of persons for production activities, commerce, and the "collection and acquisition of the products necessary for the military units on the *limes*," the Dacians "were attracted by the force of the Roman civilization to which they remained faithful to the end" (*IR2,* Ioniţă: 421–422). Romanization appears here less as a social process to be explained than as a destiny to be fulfilled. Later the same author takes a more rational approach: the Free Dacians from Muntenia "were compelled to come closer to the Roman civilization and to assimilate it to a greater extent, which also meant the gradual renunciation of many specific Dacian elements" (430). The Romanization of the Free Dacians is usually extended beyond the end of the third century, and its agents are the nearness of the Empire and the Christianization process (*IR2,* Teodor: 652).

The Foreign Peoples

While the autochthonous population is presented as compactly inhabiting the future national territory, the foreigners are almost always presented as intruders, as "infiltrating themselves," usually by taking advantage of the incapacity of the local population, for example of "the weakening of the power of the Geto-Dacians [after the fall of Burebista]" (*IR1,* Petolescu: 671). The slow, surreptitious movements of small groups of people on the national territory, which is already packed with the "autochthonous" population, might be conceived as the inverse of *Landnahme,* a central concept for the origin-myths of other nations, which makes not the local population, imagined as shapeless and retarded, but the people on the move the true heroes of civilization.[9]

The presence of foreign peoples on the national territory, which is always viewed as a historical accident, sometimes violent, always short-lived, and opposed to the principles of historical evolution embodied in our ancestors, has only one significance: they slowed, or even, for a short time, stopped the evolution of the "autochthonous society." Conversely, in the absence of the "migratory peoples," the local communities enjoyed a steady progress. Thus toward the end of the first millennium, Romanian society, "freed . . . from the specter of destructions by the nomads, steps on the path towards a sensible progress" (*IR3,* Pascu, Olteanu, Teodor, and Iliescu: 183). More specifically, the foreign peoples hamper the natural evolution of the local society toward state formation; for example, the "Celtic military and political domination in central and western Dacia has certainly prevented an earlier unification of the *Getae* and the Dacians" (*IR1,* Babeş: 503).

The foreign peoples do not typically mix with the local population on the Romanian national territory. When this happens, in Crişana for instance, the foreigners are so few that they can exert no durable influence (*IR2,* Ioniţă: 405). This is especially true when the foreigners are imagined as "migrators," or peoples always on the move, unable to create anything durable, lacking the healthy cohesion of the "autochthonous population," and therefore short-lived; they "have always been dominant ethnic enclaves . . . who lived mostly on what the autochthonous village community of farmers, herdsmen, and craftsmen with old traditions peacefully produced and realized" (*IR2,* Protase: 603). The foreigners are rarely imagined as the common people; rather, "we" were the common people. The idea that they must have lived in "enclaves" is stronger than what the archaeological evidence suggests: even when the archaeological finds assigned to the local population are thought inseparable from those of other populations, as happens with those from the second half of the fifth and the sixth century in Transylvania, when "the living together of the migrating people with the local population determined unitary aspects of the material culture," the Gepids are still imagined as "ethnic enclaves" (*IR2,* Bârzu: 716–717).[10]

One of the maps (*IR2,* Protase: 37, fig. 1), representing finds of the first to third centuries AD, offers support to this kind of reasoning: it presents a Roman center of Romania, with a homogeneous Free Dacian periphery from which diversity—such as the differences between Militari-Chilia from Muntenia and the Carpian culture of Moldavia—is eliminated. Most intriguingly, only two Sarmatian find spots are shown—Stejaru and Viespeşti—out of the seventy-nine known in Muntenia (Niculescu 2003: 200–203); they are completely absent from the eastern part of the Walachian Plain, where nothing other than Sarmatian burials dating from the second and first half of the third century AD has been found. Sarmatian finds like those from Ulmeni and Lişcoteanca are presented as Dacian. Another map, illustrating the finds from the fourth to sixth centuries, uses a similar procedure (*IR2,* Protase: 557, fig. 70): the presence of the "migrators" is minimized simply by eliminating sites or assigning them to the "autochthons." For instance, the Goths have no settlements and only 10 cemeteries (4 in Transylvania, 5 in Muntenia, and only 1 in Moldavia). There is no indication why these mostly Cernjakhov culture cemeteries were selected as Gothic; anyway most Cernjakhov find spots (1,915, among which are 158 settlements and 206 cemeteries, burial groups, and isolated burials)[11] are ignored on this map.

The relations between the Dacians and other barbarian peoples are not always presented as the consequences of natural enmity. Sever Dumitraşcu interprets the Zemplin cemetery (Slovakia, first century BC to second century AD) as an illustration of the cohabitation of the Dacians and the Vandals "in conditions of freedom . . . that is without dominating each other" (*IR2:* 445). The interpretation changes when the presence of a Germanic population on the future Romanian national territory (in Crişana) is discussed: "these enclaved Germans will not change the local ethnic structure" (447). Similarly, after struggling to demonstrate the lack of Sarmatian influence over the Dacians in Moldavia, Ion Ioniţă accepts the cohabitation of the Sarmatians and the Dacians in the same settlements outside the Romanian national territory, in Hungary (*IR2:* 454). However, there are authors in *The History of the Romanians* who admit cohabitation on the national territory (*IR3:* Barnea and Diaconu: 393).[12]

The relations with the foreign peoples usually consist of unbalanced mutual influences. For example, the "Daco-Romans" took from the Goths pottery with burnished decoration, certain combs, and some brooches (i.e., what archaeologists use as ethnic indicators), thus making the Goths invisible,[13] while the Goths took from the "Daco-Romans" some pottery forms, brooches, the use of bricks for graves, and the "occasional" use of coins (*IR2,* Protase: 601–602); that is, cultural traits that spread as a consequence of the Roman influence throughout many territories of the Barbaricum at that time. The "migrators" either lost their "ethnocultural identity," having been assimilated because of their demographic and cultural inferiority,[14] or they left. One of the more elaborate illustrations of this conception is the following:

> The vastly superior number of the Romanics in all the regions east and south of the Carpathians, the solid internal structure of the village communities, the higher social and economic development stage, as well as the superiority of the autochthonous material and spiritual culture compared to that of the various migrators, to which was added the direct or indirect support of the Empire, offered through multiple and permanent economic, cultural and spiritual links, and the sustained military activity against the foreigners . . ., were some of the principal causes which laid the ground and then oriented the direction in which, starting with the 7th century, the process of assimilating the newcomers into the mass of the autochthonous population took place gradually, everywhere north of the Lower Danube. (*IR2,* Teodor: 662)

The Local Population after the Withdrawal of the Romans from Dacia

One other delicate moment for the national narrative is that of the end of the Roman province in AD 271. The withdrawal of the Romans from the province is conceived in such a way that the poor, that is, "the autochthons," the majority, the "demographic and economic basis," do not leave; the only ones to emigrate are those who once came to Dacia, "the city-dwellers, great landowners of the Roman provincial past" (*IR2,* Protase: 561). The poor wanted to "be masters again of lands they once owned and to fully benefit from material goods, of which they had been previously frustrated to a great extent." This interpretation produces an uninterrupted autochthony by connecting the survival of the "Geto-Dacians" with the continuity of the "Daco-Romans." The local population, "the ethnic basis of the historical processes," appears to be the same as the one before the conquest, only even more civilized than before. In other words, the historical role of the Romans was to quickly civilize the local population and then to withdraw: "The Roman graft on the Dacian stock proved resistant and viable" (267).

One way to emphasize the Dacianness of the "Daco-Roman" population is the interpretation of the presence in the former Roman province of groups of Carpi and "other Free Dacians" as "strengthening the Dacian component of the Romanized population" (*IR2,* Ioniţă: 453); their presence was supposed to partially compensate for the demographic losses following the withdrawal of the Romans (*IR2,* Protase: 578). The arrival of the Free Dacians was peaceful (571), unlike that of the "migrators," and, most importantly, it happened after the abandonment of the province. Dumitru Protase deplores that in "the last decades some authors have claimed— . . . even tendentiously, with evident Roeslerian substratum— that the Free Dacians-*Carpi* from Moldavia were colonized by the Romans and that they founded settlements of their own in the province since the reigns of Marcus Aurelius or Commodus or towards the middle of the 3rd century." He argues that through this idea about the early colonization of Free Dacians in the Roman province, "*nolens volens* the documentary fund about the massive existence of the Dacians in Roman Dacia was reduced and they were robbed of a great part of their cultural dowry" (572). Without using the chronological arguments one might expect here, the author emphasizes the damage that is being done to the national interests by the interpretation he is resisting.

However, a problem persists for Protase: did the "Daco-*Carpi,*" who had immigrated into the province, settle exclusively in new places, or did they also settle by "*joining* the existing Daco-Roman communities"? (*IR2,* Protase: 573, original emphasis). This is to him a legitimate question because the Carpi are not "migrators" who live in ethnic enclaves: these are ethnic brothers, and here the peculiarity of the Romanization concept employed is again at work. The Romanized Dacians, that is, the "Daco-Romans," are still Dacians, and even if the Free Dacians had attacked the province for loot, as Ion Ioniţă admits (*IR2*: 451), all autochthons are related in the great autochthonous society, no matter how Romanized they are.

The entire archaeological construction of the continuity of the local population is based on attributing everything belonging to the Roman tradition—artifacts, coins, Christianity, and so forth—to the "Daco-Romans" (e.g., *IR2,* Protase: 555–556). The former Roman cities belong exclusively to them, while the "migrators" settled "in open spaces, adequate to their tribal life" (556). Two Gepidic burials found in a former Roman camp, strikingly foreign to the local tradition, are declared to be of "no major ethno-cultural significance for the general situation in Potaissa" (558). This reasoning allows the archaeologists to assign all the finds in the former cities of the province to the "Daco-Romans" and to imagine their life as completely separated from the "migrators," not "significantly influenced" by the civilization of the Goths and the Gepids (560).

After the Romans abandoned the province, its population is supposed to have preserved Roman traditions and permanent links with the Roman-Byzantine world that are assumed to exert a considerable influence over culture and religion, over the economy and the techniques of the "Daco-Romans," an influence "which created, in some respects, a certain superiority towards the foreign elements and towards the neighboring populations who had not lived in the Roman Empire" (*IR2,* Protase: 584).

Up to the end of the sixth century, important traits of civilization are extended from territories still part of the Empire (Scythia Minor [Dobrogea] and several cities on the northern bank of the Danube), where they were indeed present, to the whole Romanian territory. For example, the problem of writing during the fourth to eleventh centuries is presented in such a way that one is led to believe that "some" of the Romanians and their immediate ancestors used writing continuously; the argumentation mingles data from the Late Roman and Byzantine cities with data from the Early Middle Ages (*IR3,* Olteanu, Rusu, and Popa: 79–81). The same procedure is applied to the ecclesiastical organization: by mentioning some real bishoprics in Dobrogea and some highly dubious ones in

Muntenia, *The History of the Romanians* extends ecclesiastical organization to the "rest of the country" without any shred of evidence (92–93). The links with the Empire after the withdrawal of the Romans from Dacia are considered essential for the survival of the Romanitas north of the Danube (*IR2,* Protase: 604–605; Popilian: 607). They were economic and political, "ethno-cultural" and linguistic (*IR2,* Popilian: 614).

Surprisingly, the presence of the Late Roman and then Byzantine fortifications is as beneficial to the Romanitas north of the Danube as their absence: one author believes that after the Danubian *limes* was destroyed by the Slavs and the Avars toward the end of the sixth century, "thus cutting the links between the Byzantine world and the autochthonous population north of the Danube," "the demise of the Romano-Byzantine border . . . created new facilities for the economic and ethno-cultural relations between the *Romanitas* south of the Danube and that from old Dacia." The links with the Empire are believed to be so intense that the whole territory north of the Danube might be considered "a Roman-Byzantine cultural province" (*IR2,* Popilian: 616).

The economic preeminence of the local population is extended outside the province, and so, for Ion Ioniţă, the quality of the manufactured items in the Cernjakhov culture settlements, the great number of the workshops, and the fact that their population practiced mainly agriculture justify its presence in a chapter dedicated to the local population (*IR2,* Ioniţă: 619–620), although he is also one of the few authors of the *IR* to recognize that the Goths ("migrators") had the capacity to practice agriculture (689).

Metallurgy continues to be considered an exclusively "autochthonous" occupation, explained by the "perpetuation in the same ethnic community of the appropriate technical knowledge" (*IR2,* Pascu, Olteanu, Teodor, and Iliescu: 179–180). During the sixth to seventh centuries, the "autochthons" were the main producers of food, implements, and weapons for the "newcomers" (*IR2,* Teodor: 559, 562), and agriculture during the fourth to seventh centuries is ascribed exclusively to "the autochthonous population," because it was incompatible with the nomadic character of the "barbarians" (*IR3,* Olteanu and Rusu: 102–103). Such views are not shared by all the authors of *The History of the Romanians*: some recognize that the Bulgarians and the Alans, perhaps even the Magyars, practiced agriculture (*IR3,* Spinei, Diaconu, and Ferenczi: 251). Accordingly, one of them rejects the idea that the foreign peoples relied exclusively on the production of the local population (*IR3,* Spinei: 269).

In addition to their economic role, the social organization of the "Daco-Romans" is an expression of their identity and of their superiority.

According to "archaeological results" (i.e., "the distribution of family plots, that of the houses, that of the deceased in the cemeteries"), they were organized in nuclear families, while the "migrators" were organized in "large patriarchal families," corresponding to the "gentile community" (*IR3,* Olteanu, Zaharia, and Popa: 64–65; see also Teodor: 641–642). The method to arrive at such conclusions seems to be a crude form of pattern recognition. For example, in the first settlement from Davideni, out of 8 dwellings, 4 make a "nest" (i.e., they are grouped), while the rest are isolated; in the second settlement, out of the 15 dwellings, 3 make a "nest," the rest being dispersed and "lonely." The "nests" are interpreted as the house of the "nuclear family and those of the children," while the isolated houses belong to the foreigners accepted by the village community (*IR3,* Olteanu, Zaharia, and Popa: 65–66).

These village communities are supposed to form groups, "confederations" for common defense and economic interests, based on "ethnolinguistic community and similar stage of socio-economic development, culture, and [Christian] spiritual life." Dan G. Teodor, after Nicolae Iorga ([1924] 1984), calls the communities "popular *Romaniae*"; that is, they are "strong, stable demographic and linguistic cores of Romanic culture" (*IR2*: 642). A gradually increasing social differentiation is accepted, with a clear preference for feudal lords raised from the village communities, to whom the obligations of the peasants were more of "a familial character... under the control of the collectivity and constantly limited by the power of the traditions" (*IR3,* Pascu, Olteanu, Rusu, Matei, Popa, and Iliescu: 349). To these considerate local lords the foreign merchants are contrasted; the latter constituted "a negative aspect" because they "disadvantaged Romanian society by making great profits" (*IR3,* Olteanu and Iliescu: 543).

"[A]lthough sufficient and explicit documents are not available"—there is no interpretation of the archaeological material to that effect—"in principle and analogically" we are told that we have to admit that the local village communities, producing the majority of the material goods necessary to everyday life, were "collectively subjected" to the new masters (Goths, Huns, Gepids), not individually or by families (*IR2,* Protase: 603). This subjection was possible only because the Romanic population, "in its evolution towards Romanianness, was not able to rise to superior forms of socio-political organization" (*IR2,* Protase: 603).

The political organization is considered "of paramount importance in the history of the Romanian people, associating itself, through its probative capacities, to the fundamental problem of our historical permanence." Again positions contrary to "ours" are deplored—in this case those that place the beginnings of the political organization of the Romanians in the fourteenth century—and assigned to "foreign historians, adversaries, for political reasons, to the affirmation of our historical continuity." These people are supposed to ignore "the capacity and the continuous effort of political organization [of the "autochthonous society"], starting from inferior forms, like those represented by the territorial rural community, to the mature ones, embodied by the state" (*IR3,* Olteanu, Rusu, and Popa: 93–94).

The method of identifying political organization and its complexity in the fourth to ninth centuries is the same as that described above: "groupings" of "urban settlements [*sic*]" are detected; for example, for the third to fifth centuries, twenty-five such groupings were found on the territory of ancient Dacia. Over time their number decreased as the number of settlements included increased (*IR3,* Olteanu, Rusu, and Popa: 94–95). The whole process is imagined as a continuous evolution toward state formation, a capacity inherent in the local population. It is viewed as a political maturation (*IR3,* Constantinescu, Olteanu, Matei, and Ştefănescu: 563), a result of the union of "pre-state formations" (*IR3,* Ştefănescu: 589).

Similarly, Christianity is described as a cultural-historical phenomenon of universal importance and, "not less important, a solid testimony of the massive continuity of the Latin-speaking indigenous population in post-Roman Dacia" (*IR2,* Protase: 587). For most of the authors of *The History of the Romanians,* this cultural phenomenon seems interesting mainly for its utility as an ethnic marker. Its beginnings are so important for the origins of the nation that during the last two decades of the Communist regime, the research—mostly the continuous discovery of new evidence, even if sometimes highly questionable—was constantly encouraged. After 1989 the Christianization of the ancestors of the Romanians by the apostle Andrew became a dogma for the Orthodox Church, and some historians and archaeologists have accepted it (for an opposing perspective, see *IR2,* Bărbulescu: 257). The recent emphasis on early Christianization, beginning in the second half of the first century AD, is echoed in a chapter about Dobrogea, where, following "Church traditions," against "the reservations of some researchers," it is suggested that Andrew had founded the bishopric of Tomis, an idea apparently supported by the assertion that the local population of Dobrogea was "in a superior evolutionary stage" (*IR2,* Rădulescu: 370–371, 530, 532).

From there, *The History of the Romanians* suggests that Christianity spread throughout the future national territory by the end of the fifth century (*IR2,* Protase: 596). Dumitru Protase thinks "we are logically and necessarily" to suppose the existence of cult buildings on the "whole Daco-Roman territory," from the withdrawal of Aurelian to the end of the sixth century, although he admits that the only ones we know about are the one from Sucidava, a Roman city on the northern bank of the Danube, at that time a part of the Byzantine Empire, and two other (highly) questionable constructions in Porolissum and Slăveni. The more than one hundred paleo-Christian objects, worship places, and cult buildings, "even though they have an unequal scientific weight and their Christian significance remains uncertain, indicate the high number of those who embraced the new creed" and "decidedly argue for the widespread existence of cult buildings, even though they have not been detected . . . by the archaeological excavations." We are warned that many were wooden constructions and therefore, Protase believes, archaeologically undetectable (591–592).

The exclusive access to Christianity of the "autochthons" is explained by the fact that Christianity could not spread spontaneously in the "tribal world, incapable of massively receiving the new religion. . . . Among the 'barbarian' peoples . . . organized in tribes and with their ancestral beliefs, Christianity could not establish itself."[15] Protase plays the archaeological evidence against the evidence of the translation of the Bible by Ulfilas and that of the Gothic martyrs, to claim that the Goths from the territories north of the Danube were not Christians (*IR2,* Protase: 594–595),[16] and he declares that any paleo-Christian find of the fourth and fifth centuries was exclusively that of the "autochthonous population" (595–596).[17]

Ethnogenesis

The process of ethnogenesis, or the emergence of the Romanians after the withdrawal of the Romans, is described as a gradual qualitative change of the local population. It became more uniform in all its cultural manifestations, more Romanized, and more Christian. Significantly, the concept most frequently used to designate the sameness of all the "autochthons" is not the descriptive *uniformity,* but *unity.* Although unity allows some cultural diversity (if it turns into complementarity), its main function is to convey the social and political solidarity to be expected from the members of a nationlike entity. Thus settlements and dwellings, the burial rite and rituals, the specific artifacts, the same weight of the Christian elements and of the artifacts imported from the Empire—all are taken as indisputable evidence of the "*unity* of material culture and spiritual life," a consequence of "the same socio-economic development," of the existence of "the same ethno-linguistic elements" (*IR2,* Teodor: 654, original emphasis).

The emergence of the Romanians is placed in the seventh century without any kind of argumentation. In the second volume of *The History of the Romanians,* the local population after the abandonment of the Roman province of Dacia is named "Daco-Romans" or, less frequently, Romanics. The third volume, which begins with the seventh century, designates the local population exclusively as "Romanians." At the end of their ethnogenesis, the Romanians are the only population of Romanic origin in eastern Europe, with ancient social and economic regulations and with Christian mental structures preserved from the Roman and Roman-Byzantine times (*IR3,* Pascu and Theodorescu: 110).

With one exception (namely, Alexandru Vulpe when writing about the origins of the Thracians [*IR1*: 286]), ethnogenesis—"one of the key problems of the history of each people" (*IR3,* Ferenczi and Nägler: 412)—is a concept used only for the Romanians, although one could legitimately inquire about a Getic ethnogenesis, a Dacian one, a "Geto-Dacian" one, or a "Daco-Roman" one. Ethnogenesis is conceived as a synthesis of (carefully identified) demographic and cultural components, a process of natural evolution (*IR2,* Protase: 604). As such it does not differ from the birth of an archaeological culture or, for example, that of the "Daco-Romans," which is defined as "a symbiosis and later an ethnic and cultural synthesis between the winners and the vanquished" (*IR2,* Protase: 143). How ethnogenesis is different from these other "syntheses" remains unexplained, but the importance of ethnogenesis appears with clarity. All that we know about events prior to it constitutes its "premises," and everything that follows is its consequences.[18] As usual in nationalist ideologies, the origins explain the present,[19] and the profound structural changes that make Romanians much more similar to the Hungarians or the Bulgarians than to the Dacians or the Romans, in the entity whose continuity is assumed, the ethnomorphoses (Kohl 1998: 232), are ignored or downplayed to predictable, "normal" evolution.

Conclusions

The authors of the first three volumes of *The History of the Romanians* have various attitudes toward its main narrative, the ethnogenesis of the Romanians and its "premises." Some ignore the narrative altogether, and this is possible especially when writing about matters peripheral to it or by making the narrative peripheral[20] (therefore their names are seldom mentioned here). A few (e.g., Alexandru Vulpe when discussing the "archaeological culture" concept and Mircea Babeş when discussing the elements of Dacian discontinuity in the Roman province [*IR1:* 800–802]) confront from scientific positions some of its key issues, without questioning the core of the construction, while others support it following an ideological tradition. This welcome variety of attitudes does not affect the construction of an ancient past for the Romanians in *The History of the Romanians*. Its structure and main elements are the same as before 1989.

It is not my purpose to assess the overall quality of the work or the merits of each author. There are very important qualitative and editorial differences between the chapters and the volumes of *The History of the Romanians*. However, most of the archaeology used in it for the building of the national narrative is simply bad archaeology. There is no need to compare it with other paradigms and other conceptions of society in order to pass such a judgment. It is enough to examine it against the criteria of traditional culture historical archaeology, the dominant paradigm in Romania. With the remarkable exception of the efforts made by Vulpe to "clean" the archaeological culture concept of its ethnic and therefore political implications, the archaeological interpretations made with the purpose of reconstructing the national ancestry follow Gustaf Kossinna's concepts of culture, archaeology, and ethnicity but are used with less rigor. The poor understanding of the archaeological record, its sloppy documentation, the frequent contradictions, the double standards employed for the ancestors of the Romanians and the foreign peoples, and the reduction of the past to "premises" of the present and of archaeology to the role of providing "concrete evidence" for already existing representations of the national past are all likely to make any archaeologist unhappy.

The low quality of the interpretation stems mostly from the subordination of archaeological knowledge to political goals: many interpretations are not meant to lead to a better understanding of the past, nor are they made for colleagues to read and critique. Rather, they are expected to be appreciated and rewarded by politicians, based on their interests and their common knowledge. Such constructions are not evaluated against archaeological criteria of validation; instead, they are matched to the perceived imperatives of the political present, to "the national interest" to which normative, ritualized discourses about the nation, disguised in knowledge about the past, are offered.

If what matters is conformity to the political present, not the quality of the interpretation, the limited autonomy of archaeology in Romania and its auxiliary status become easier to explain. When the outcome of the research is validated from the outside, no wonder that lack of confidence and purpose sets in: "Restricted to the information offered by archaeology, even when correlated with ethnographic models, the researchers have to remain in the world of hypotheses, without any chance of verification, with the risk of projecting modern models and obsessions" (*IR1,* Monah: 173).

I suggest that this condition is not inherent to archaeology but represents a local state of despondency to which the intervention of political priorities has contributed by discouraging the formation of professional criteria of validation and procedures. The professional criteria have a dynamic of their own, developing in a framework that is not that of the national state and is capable of resisting the imperatives of local political situations. An independent and professional milieu would also limit the readiness of archaeologists to accommodate contradictory evidence (Kohl 1998: 239) and enable them to trust their fragile scholarship more than the sacred truths of the national ideology.

Notes

A version of this paper was presented as a lecture at the Institute of Archaeology "Vasile Pârvan" in May 2003. I am grateful to my colleagues for their comments and support for this line of inquiry.

Translations from non-English works are my own.

1. *The History of the Romanians* (*Istoria Românilor*) is cited throughout in this manner: *IR1*, *IR2*, or *IR3*, indicating one of the three volumes, often along with the names of one or more contributing authors within the volume. See the list of references for further information.
2. On nationalism in Romania immediately after 1989, see Verdery 1993.
3. For a chronological presentation of the alternative-textbook debate, see Pecican 2002.
4. Statements and papers presented at the "International Congresses of Dacology" are available at www.dacia.org.
5. See, e.g., the title used by Jean Guilaine (1980) or the subtitle of Wolfram 1987.
6. For a discussion of this subject, see Wenskus 1979.
7. See, e.g., *IR3*, R. Theodorescu: x on the value of including in the Romanian national history all the people speaking the same language.
8. A remarkable exception: for A. Suceveanu (*IR2*: 307–309), in Dobrogea not only the Getae were autochthonous, but also the Scythae, the Bastarnae, and the Sarmatians.

9. See the studies published in Müller-Wille and Schneider 1993.
10. A different view deserves to be mentioned: V. Spinei admits that Turkic nomads became sedentary on the future national territory and that there was a symbiosis with the local population (*IR3*: 266).
11. Petrescu 2002: 19 (based only on literature, without a new determination of the finds). For more (ernjakhov finds than on the map of D. Protase, see *IR2,* I. Ioniţă: 618, fig. 89 (in a chapter on the local population), where the finds are nonetheless still grossly underrepresented.
12. These authors allow for the cohabitation of the local population with "barbarians" at Dinogetia-Garvăn in the second half of the twelfth century AD and at the beginning of the thirteenth.
13. See Harhoiu 2003: 138 on the capacity to absorb cultural indicators, assigned by many Romanian archaeologists to the autochthons.
14. See *IR2,* D. Protase: 602–603 about the Gepids.
15. The absence of any evidence about the organization of the church on the future Romanian national territory outside the Empire and the pressure of the nationalist representation of society lead D. Protase and many others to defend the thesis of a "popular" Christianity, with no hierarchy (*IR2,* D. Protase: 599–600), echoing the "popular" basis of the Romanian ethnogenesis.
16. A different opinion is expressed by Ion Ioniţă, who believes that the Christianization of the Goths is visible for the archaeologist (*IR2*: 691).
17. The exclusive use of the Christian objects by the "autochthons" is supposed to last only until the end of the fifth century, when the first Christian objects belonging to a Germanic population are dated (*IR2,* D. Protase: 596).
18. In guidelines to teachers and textbook authors for the twelfth grade, backed by the authority of the Ministry of National Education, this is all one finds out about ethnogenesis: "the premises and consequences of the synthesis" (Cerkez et al. 1999: 32). There is nothing more to indicate the nature of the process. How far back in time the "premises" can go is apparent in one textbook (Dumitrescu et al. 1999: 6), where, in a lesson dedicated to those premises, the chronology begins with the orogeny of the Carpathians, "ca. 65,000,000 years BC."
19. How important the origins continued to be after 1989 in Romania is shown by the length of Romanian politicians' discussions of the history of the nation during the debates on a new constitution in 1990–1991 (Preda 2001).
20. For instance, by writing *ad narrandum* (Suceveanu 1999), as some of the authors of the second volume of *The History of the Romanians* have done. I am grateful to the author for allowing me to use this text, an afterword to the second volume. Suceveanu's manuscript was rejected by D. Protase for reasons that might have to do with some unorthodox ideas presented in it, such as the possibility that the national territory was inhabited at times by an ethnic mosaic and the rejection of a global characterization of the "migrators."

References

Alexandrescu, Petre. 2002. "Volumul III din Istoria Românilor: O istorie în trei acte şi un deznodămînt." *22* 13, no. 18 (634): 12.

Babeş, Mircea. 2002. "Archäologie und Gesellschaft am Anfang des 21. Jahrhunderts." *Mitteilungen des Humboldt-Clubs Rumänien* 6:7–12.

Bauman, Zygmunt. 1992. "Soil, blood, and identity." *Sociological Review* 40 (4): 675–701.

Berindei, Dan. 1999. "Uitarea trecutului ameninţă viitorul oricărei naţii!" *Academica* 9, no. 12 (108): 1, 14.

Biroul de presă al Academiei Române: Comitetul de redacţie al volumului IV la Tratatului de Istoria Românilor. 2002. "Comunicat." *22* 13, no. 14 (630): 10.

Boia, Lucian. 1997. *Istorie şi mit în conştiinţa românească*. Bucharest: Humanitas; 2nd ed., Bucharest: Humanitas, 2000. Published in English as *History and Myth in Romanian Consciousness* (Budapest: Central European University Press, 2001).

Cerkez, Matei, Mihaela Singer, Laura Capiţă, Lucian Ciolan, Dan Crocnan, Daniel Oghină, Ligia Sarivan, and Firuţa Tacea. 1999. *Curriculum naţional: Programe şcolare pentru clasa a IX-a. Volumul al III-lea*. Bucharest: Editura Cicero. In spite of the subtitle, this publication includes the curriculum for the twelfth grade.

Dumitrescu, Nicoleta, Mihai Manea, Cristian Niţă, Adrian Pascu, and Mădălina Trandafir. 1999. *Istoria Românilor: Manual pentru clasa a XII-a*. Bucharest: Humanitas Educaţional.

Guilaine, Jean. 1980. *La France d'avant la France: Du néolithique à l'âge du fer*. Paris: Hachette.

Harhoiu, Radu. 2003. "Quellenlage und Forschungsstand der Frühgeschichte Siebenbürgens im 6.–7. Jahrhundert." *Dacia*, n.s., 43–44 (1999–2000) [2003]: 97–158.

Iliescu, Octavian. 2002. "Erata la 'Istoria românilor.'" *22* 13, no. 39 (676): 6–7.

Iorga, Nicolae. [1924] 1984. "'Romania' dunăreană şi barbarii în secolul al VI-lea." In *Studii asupra evului mediu românesc*, by Nicolae Iorga, 29–38. Bucharest: Editura Ştiinţifică şi Enciclopedică. First published in French in *Revue belge de philologie et d'histoire* 3 (1) (1924): 35–50.

IR1. See Petrescu-Dîmboviţa and Vulpe 2001.

IR2. See Protase and Suceveanu 2001.

IR3. See Pascu and Theodorescu 2001.

Kohl, Philip L. 1998. "Nationalism and Archaeology: On the Construction of Nations and the Reconstructions of the Remote Past." *Annual Review of Anthropology* 27:223–246.

Mihăilescu-Bârliba, Lucreţiu. 1997. "Nationalism in Romanian Archaeology up to 1989." *Studia Antiqua et Archaeologica* 3–4:161–164.

Müller-Wille, Michael, and Reinhard Schneider, eds. 1993. *Ausgewählte Probleme europäischer Landnahmen des Früh- und Hochmittelalters: Methodische Grundlagediskussion im Grenzbereich zwischen Archäologie und Geschichte* I. Sigmaringen: Jan Thorbecke Verlag.

Niculescu, Gheorghe Alexandru. 2003. "Die sarmatische Kultur im Zusammenhang der kaiserzeitlichen archäologischen Funde aus Muntenien—unter besonderer Berücksichtigung der Funde von Tîrgşor," with a contribution by Nicolae Miriţoiu: "Sarmatische Gräber mit künstlich deformierten Schädeln in Muntenien." In *Kontakt—Kooperation—Konflikt: Germanen und Sarmaten zwischen dem 1. und dem 4. Jahrhundert nach Christus*, ed. Claus von Carnap-Bornheim, 177–205. Neumünster: Wachholtz Verlag.

Papacostea, Şerban. 2002. "O nouă sinteză de istorie românească: metodă şi probitate." *22* 14 (676): 7.

Pascu, Ştefan, and Răzvan Theodorescu, eds. 2001. *Istoria Românilor.* Vol. 3, *Genezele româneşti* (*IR3*). Bucharest: Editura Enciclopedică.

Pecican, Ovidiu. 2002. "Cronica unei conflagraţii anunţate: Fragmente dintr—un documentar." *Observator cultural* 99 (January 15–21): 7–12.

Petrescu, Florin. 2002. *Repertoriul monumentelor de tip Cerneahov-Sântana de Mureş de pe teritoriul României.* Bucharest: Ars Docendi.

Petrescu-Dîmboviţa, Mircea, and Alexandru Vulpe, eds. 2001. *Istoria Românilor.* Vol. 1, *Moştenirea timpurilor îndepărtate* (*IR1*). Bucharest: Editura Enciclopedică.

Popa, Radu. 1991. "Observaţii şi îndreptări la istoria României din jurul anului *O Mie*." *Studii şi cercetări de istorie veche şi arheologie* 42 (3–4): 153–188.

Preda, Cristian. 2001. "La nation dans la constitution." *Romanian Political Science Review* 1 (3): 733–762.

Protase, Dumitru, and Alexandru Suceveanu, eds. 2001. *Istoria Românilor.* Vol. 2, *Daco-romani, romanici, alogeni* (*IR2*). Bucharest: Editura Enciclopedică.

Stahl, Henri H. 1969. *Les anciennes communautés villageoises roumaines: Asservissement et pénétration capitaliste.* Bucharest: Editura Academiei; Paris: Éditions du CNRS.

Strobel, Karl. 1998. "Dacii: Despre complexitatea mărimilor etnice, politice şi culturale ale istoriei spaţiului Dunarii de Jos I." *Studii şi cercetări de istorie veche şi arheologie* 49 (1): 61–95.

Suceveanu, Alexandru. 1999. "Încheiere." (Afterword prepared for the second volume of *The History of the Romanians*, not published.)

Verdery, Katherine. 1991. *National Ideology under Socialism: Identity and Cultural Politics in Ceauşescu's Romania.* Berkeley: University of California Press.

Verdery, Katherine. 1993. "Nationalism and National Sentiment in Post-Socialist Romania." *Slavic Review* 52 (2): 179–204. Reprinted in *What Was Socialism and What Comes Next*, by Katherine Verdery, 83–103 (Princeton, NJ: Princeton University Press, 1996).

Wenskus, Reinhard. 1979. "Randbemerkungen zum Verhältnis von Historie und Archäologie, insbesondere mittelalterliche Geschichte und Mittealterarchäologie." In *Geschichtswissenschaft und Archäologie*, ed. H. Jankuhn and R. Wenskus, 637–657. Sigmaringen, Germany: Jan Thorbecke Verlag.

Wolfram, Herwig. 1987. *Die Geburt Mitteleuropas: Geschichte Österreichs vor seiner Entstehung: 378–907*. Vienna: Sielder Verlag.

2

The Near East

FIVE

The Rise of the Hittite Sun

A Deconstruction of Western Civilization from the Margin

WENDY SHAW

Near the end of Orhan Pamuk's 1995 novel *The Black Book*, the protagonist Galip comes across a photograph of his missing wife, Rüya. He understands that the photograph is recent because she is wearing a necklace that he gave her for her last birthday, shortly before her disappearance. It is a pendant representing the Hittite sun.

This necklace could not be more typical, and that, no doubt, is why Pamuk chose it. Yet its power of identification contains ambiguity. What does it mean to wear as a symbol a miniature reproduction of an artifact whose original meaning had been lost for four thousand years when the object was unearthed and which can never fully be deciphered? When people wear a symbol, they declare something about their identity. Jewelry often represents something far more valuable than the material of the object to its wearer: religion, in the form of a cross, a Qur'anic verse, or a star of David; or good luck in the form of a simple and personal charm. What does it mean, then, to wear the Hittite sun? If this is indeed a symbol, then what does it signify, and how is its meaning produced?

Approximately four millennia ago, the bronze sculpture that today sits on a red velvet throne in the Museum of Anatolian Civilizations must have had a purpose, either physical

Figure 5.1. One of several Hittite Suns or bronze symbolic standards on display at the Museum of Anatolian Civilizations in Ankara

or representational, or perhaps both, for why else would such a carefully crafted object have been produced (fig. 5.1)? However, that purpose or meaning had long since been lost by the time the sculpture was found during 1935 Turkish excavations, led by Remzi Oguz Arik, at a site known as Alacahöyük, to the northeast of Ankara. Further archaeological and textual work in Hittitology has suggested that the object once functioned as the finial of a ceremonial staff and probably represented the world and the stars. But in 1935, in the absence of such textual guidance, it bore no clear meaning. Thus, with its rebirth into the modern age, the object became a signifier without a signified; it was available as a blank sign, a tessera. The object, and symbolic images of it, acquired a name—the Hittite sun—and thereby began to signify with significations that proliferated over the course of the twentieth century, establishing its own discourse of Turkish identity within that of nationhood and independent of changing archaeological discourses. Although I bear in mind the contemporary archaeological and linguistic discourses pertinent to the Hittite sun, my primary concern in this study is with the livelihood of a sign that has created a world of meaning independent of the scientific discourse that might otherwise frame comprehension of it.

Today when we look at the Hittite sun, in its many reproduced manifestations and variations based on the original group of artifacts, it represents not simply the value assigned to it in 1935, but the changing values that it has lost and acquired since then. It has at times symbolized such vastly different concepts as an essentialist Turkish identity, a pagan culture, and the enlightened, secular state developed under Atatürk.[1] As these changing values become more recent, they become increasingly familiar. The meanings of the sign have been imbricated in the layered moments of contestation when it has emerged, been suppressed, and reemerged since its discovery. Although the excavation of this object occurred in 1935, the excavation of its meanings begins now, at the moment when it continues to mean.

In March 2003, after a long series of court cases, the Hittite sun was restored to Ankara as the emblem of the city. It had been replaced in 1995 by the government of the Islamist Welfare Party (Refah Partisi), which suggested that a symbol extending to Turkey's pre-Islamic past was an inappropriate representation for a country that is today 99 percent Muslim. This action was contested in court soon after the government changed to a centrist coalition (under the strong influence of the secularist army, in what has often been labeled a "silent coup") in 1997. The matter was only recently resolved, notably under the new, more centrist Islamist leadership of the Justice and Development Party (Adalet ve Kalkinma Partisi).

Opponents to the changing of the emblem in 1995 felt that the new government had no right to replace the sign that had represented the city for so long. They saw it as a symbol not of paganism but of the existing order within the Turkish state, which is not, of course, pagan, or even atheist, but secularist—a difference that secularists emphatically insist upon. The primary debate concerning secularism and Islam revolves around this very tension: while secularism is based on personalizing religion, Islamists see religion as a mode of life that necessarily includes the public sphere. Even in the face of the laical policy that has been the cornerstone of the republic since 1923, this conflict clearly emerged in the emblem the Islamists used for the city for eight years, between 1995 and 2003. This emblem superimposed the silhouette of the massive Ottoman-style Kocatepe Mosque (complete with extensive underground parking garages and a shopping center) built in Ankara in 1987 with the new Atakule tower built in the 1980s with a revolving restaurant that provides a panoramic view of the city, cradled in a crescent moon, the symbol of Islam.

The new Islamic symbol represented the modernity of the state as part and parcel of its religion, as opposed to the preceding sign, which had identified the modern state with a primeval link to Turkish prehistory. Yet this use had not been continual since the 1930s. The Hittite sun was first used symbolically on several commercial goods, including those of the Eti biscuit company (founded in 1961) and Maltepe Cigarettes. It became the symbol of the Ministry of Tourism at the time of its foundation in 1973. In 1977 the planned erection by the Anatolia Insurance Company of another, this time greatly enlarged, model of one of the bronze sculptures found at Alacahöyük was heavily criticized as a pagan monument. While not identical in form to the Hittite sun used for the Second Congress of the Turkish Historical Association, the original statuette on which this sculpture is based was part of the same excavation and attributed with the same meanings as the more abstract Hittite sun used most frequently as an emblem, and thus it belongs to the same class of Hittite sun figures. In response to its planned erection, for eight months the minister of the interior refused to approve anything coming from the Ankara municipality. Labeling the approach of the ministry as "horrifyingly ludicrous," Republican People's Party mayor Vedat Dalokay summarized the situation by inviting the minister of the interior to explain his point of view about the "symbol of the Ministry of Tourism, the symbol on the packet of Maltepe Cigarettes in his pocket, and the symbol on the ashtrays in parliament" before objecting to the monument. "If he can't," the mayor asserted, "let us make it clear: within two months the Minister of the Interior will pass in front of that monument every day and thereby learn to respect the civilization which it signifies." Why, one might ask, would one want a contemporary minister to respect a prehistoric civilization? Alternatively, why might the notion of such respect be so offensive that a minister would cut off all communications with a municipality? Clearly, what was at stake here is less a discussion of history than of historical value. How can a monument to a prehistoric civilization come to represent respect to a modern one? Indeed, the question Dalokay raises is, Precisely whose civilization is the monument understood to represent?

Today, this monument of the Hittite sun in Sihhiye Square marks a central point between the poles of activity that take place within the capital. Its site is the intersection of three major urban arteries leading directly to the Kocatepe Mosque (on Midhatpasa Caddesi), to the ministries and military headquarters (on Necatibey Caddesi), to the presidential residence, Çankaya (on Atatürk Boulevard), and to Ulus, the early center of the city with the original parliament (the other way on Atatürk Boulevard) (fig. 5.2). The visibility of both the Kocatepe Mosque and the Hittite emblem from Atatürk Boulevard serves as a permanent marker of

Figure 5.2. The monument to the Hittite Sun with the Kocatepe Mosque in the background

the covalent tension between these symbolic identities. Whichever city symbol is currently in use, the monuments provide a constant reminder of the ideological spectrum of the nation at an intersection along which people in government, as well as those using the mosque and its underground shopping facilities, frequently pass, much as Dalokay predicted.

The symbolism of a modern and mammoth mosque intended as both a religious and a commercial hub of the capital clearly refers to the political aims of populism and capitalism of the Motherland Party that sponsored it during the 1980s, but that of the Hittite sun is far less clear. How has an artifact whose original significance has been erased over the illegibility of time come to signify enlightenment and secularism? If one considers the Hittite sun as a sign that ties the modern nation-state of Turkey to a prehistory whose focal point was Anatolia, this idea says more about the modern state's use of history to construct and justify its effectively natural borders than about secularism as such. Indeed, while various groups in Turkey have expressed a desire for close links with other countries, both Islamic and Turkic, considered to be within the Turkish purview and sometimes within the memory of Ottoman suzerainty, few would openly argue for a direct modification of these borders. As such, the Hittite sun could be a noncontroversial symbol of them. Yet it is not.

One explanation for the seeming conflict between these two meanings emerges from the symbolic value of the sun itself. For the Hittite sun rose to prominence once in 1935, but then it was scarcely used at all from the end of World War II through the government of the Democratic Party during the 1950s. Its modern symbolic life emerged in 1961, when the postcoup government assigned it as the emblem of Ankara for the first time. This moment gave it its current meaning as a reaffirmation of Turkey's faith in Atatürk's leadership and ideals. If one of the ideological reasons for the 1950 change in political power had been a movement away from the secularism and statism of Atatürk's Turkey, this new sign came to symbolize a new era of reaffirmation of the Atatürk ideology as a whole.

But what had connected the Hittite sun with Atatürkism in the first place? Why did an archaeological artifact—and why did *this* archaeological artifact—become a metonymic device evoking an entire national ideology? To answer this question, one must consider both the circumstances of the Hittite sun's emergence into the modern world and the context of that world. Turkey was a very new nation-state in which all adults remembered the fear and grave risk of colonialism that they had faced at the end of World War I and the great hardships that they had suffered in order to become one of the few non-European nations never under colonial suzerainty. The resistance to colonialism, as much as the emerging nationalist ideology, which facilitated the construction of the new state, remained a driving force in the construction of a collective Turkish identity. That identity was already forming in various institutions, in part through the concerted efforts of the Turkish Historical Society, instituted in 1932, and the Turkish Linguistic Society, instituted in 1933.

Turkey built its modern identity within a context of resistance to European incursion, both in terms of its near colonization immediately after World War I and in terms of impending invasion during World War II. It also built this identity within the context of the pervasive ideologies of the 1920s and 1930s, next door to a Europe in the grip of not only various forms of fascism but also racialist ideologies. Modernism was based on Enlightenment ideals of the progressive development of humanity that naturalized the superiority of European civilization. Both the writing of the history of peoples, in the march of civilization westward, and the writing of the history of languages—with its philological emphasis on Indo-Europeanism—were, and remain, the primary understanding of the ordering of history and peoples, not only in postfascist Europe but in much of the rest of the world as well, where a European writing of history as a positive discursive field has taken hold. It was in this context, the clash of European scientific ideologies with rising Turkish nationalism, that the Hittite sun was produced. A brief review of these ideological crosscurrents will assist in understanding how Turkish archaeologists came to interpret their find in 1935 as the Hittite sun.

Archaeology, like linguistics, grew into a science alongside the concurrent revolution of evolutionary biology and during an era when the myth of nationalism required both long-standing national entities, such as England and France, and more nascent ones, like Italy and Germany, to reinforce their national territorial affiliations through increasingly mythologizing their autochthonous ancestral pasts. Yet these disciplines also participated in the broader production of a pan-European identity, familiar under the rubric of Western civilization, which was based not on the indigenous character of modern nations but on a set of coterminous, often collinear, almost always westward, asynchronous migrations of people and diffusions of "culture." The mutual acceptance of such coterminous origin myths suggests the boundaries that define a culture, in this case the Western one that they forged.

The narrative production of the migratory histories of modern Europe can be read as a process of the decreasing hegemony of the church and thence the core narratives of the Bible on the minds of European intellectuals. The migratory narratives that have framed western Europe present a striking similarity to their religious forebears: like the fall from the Garden of Eden and the myth of the Tower of Babel, both recounted in Genesis, Western origin myths rely on a pure source of unity from which dissolution has led to the fragmentation of races, languages, and cultures. Whether or not such a model bears historical truth is less relevant here than the persistent search for that source. The search itself suggests that the modern world perceives itself in a permanent state of inadequacy because of its imaginary perception of a complete and perfect self in a historical mirror.

In much European scholarship, the narrative of Indo-European origins on the linguistic front, racial origins on the physical anthropological front, and archaeological origins on the historical front came to supplant the Genesis account. Nevertheless, the notion of a single ideal source continued to provide an impetus for teleological narratives that produced Europe as the subject of historical identity, and produced it from an ideal root source akin to the Garden of Eden in that this source held the seeds of the perfection of the Western civilization that was to come. The composite of these overlaid tales of migration produced a border along a predominantly Christian narrative of the West made secular by the persistent reproduction of the East as its developmental stage.

Led by both ideological and political exigencies to speak against this border, the young Turkish Republic not only adopted the predominant mode of discourse producing Western civilization—developmental narratives of migration from a unitary origin in the East—but also rearranged the methods and components of such narratives into a story producing an Other destination, a Turkish destination, as the unitary subject of world history. The result, which emerged and reached its apogee during the 1930s, was the Turkish Historical Thesis. Long critiqued and ridiculed for its questionable methodology and even more questionable conclusions,[2] drawn through its adaptation of information exclusively from contemporary Euro-American sources, the theory nonetheless acts with deconstructive agency as a historiographic moment derived from the same practices of teleological narcissistic historiography as those used to create a history of Western civilization as a unitary subject in its own right. The Turkish text functions as a bricolage of disassembled European texts, thus mimicking a European form through the utilization of footnotes to guarantee legitimacy.

The Turkish Historical Commission (Türk Tarihi Heyeti) was established as an extension of the Turkish Hearth organization during its sixth congress on April 23, 1930. The first product of the commission's work, *A General Outline of Turkish History (Türk Tarihinin Ana Hatları)*,[3] directed under the auspices of Atatürk himself, emerged in the form of a single-volume, limited edition of one hundred copies distributed to a select few in 1930. By the following year, a four-volume set of history books following this general outline had been distributed for high school use. The outline was intended as a guide for sixty-six follow-up projects, many of which were published in 1933 and 1936. Thus, the first phase of the production of Turkish history that emerges from these studies has a public outlook and was designed to present a worldview appropriate for the indoctrination of the citizens of a new nation.

The four-part purpose of the educational histories produced after 1930 was (1) to secularize not only Turkish history but also the historical worldview through scientific understandings of the universe and the world; (2) to eliminate the Eurocentric focus of world historiography as produced in European texts by focusing historiography eastward rather than westward; (3) in doing so, to produce the Turks as the linking phase between eras and cultures of the East, thus giving world history a pan-Turkic flavor; and (4) to "expose" the archaism of the Ottoman system as a feudal society that used religious ideology to maintain itself. The history was structurally anticolonial and antireligious, then, as much as its content was ethnonationalist and statist. It was not a purely nationalist history, in the sense that a nationalist history focuses solely on the historical justification of national integrity. Rather, it was intended also as a history of resistance to an existing world order that had been produced through the nineteenth-century colonization of the world by Europe and that had occurred in concert with the European writing of the world's history as its own.

Rather than attempting to write an original, source-based history for the young nation, the authors of the new Turkish history hoped to use already established "facts" to trace a narrative that had been elided by the European practitioners of the historical sciences. This was not simply laziness; it was a politically charged narrative method in which a repetition of the European voice at once promised servile imitation and produced the last laugh of mastery. With a strong faith in positivism, the authors contended that facts, as established by sciences such as geology, archaeology, and linguistics, were neutral, but that European practitioners had long avoided reading them so that the latent primacy of the Turks would be evident. They accepted European primacy as expressed in its constituting texts in order to undermine it, at least within Turkey.

The attempt was a complex enterprise indeed, incorporating myriad texts culled from all over the European corpus of history, linguistics, anthropology, biology, and geography. It granted equal value to old and new texts, depending on which facts suited the needs of a particular writer. Thus it conceived of the European corpus as a discourse in the Foucauldian sense—a self-referential set of texts set within particular epistemic principles of truth. It brought together many writers, both Turkish and foreign, in the attempt to construct a new master text.

After all, the new narrative argued, even the bare minimum of facts showed the antecedence of Eastern history: it was well known that human origins could be traced to Asia, where the New Stone Age began in 12,000 BC, five thousand years before it reached Europe; by that time Asia was experiencing the Bronze Age with the beginnings of Sumerian civilization (*Türk Tarihinin Ana Hatları*, 40). Such general oversights were supposed to be widespread and provided the impetus for the development of the new historical thesis. Reşit Galip summarized the confusion concerning human origins in contemporary European discourse by pointing out that

> more than the spirit of science, a movement born of emotional and political thoughts [in the mid-nineteenth century], a sort of European nationalism or European pride, found it more appropriate to look for the roots of humanity and civilization in Europe than in Africa and Asia. . . . unable to find a cradle for the perfect human type which they called, periodically, Aryan, Homo-European, Homo-Nordicus, Indo-Aryan, and Indo-European, they moved him from the West and Eastern slopes of the Pamir mountains to the Oxus river valley, from there to European Russia . . . [and even] to the skirts of the Taunus mountain in Germany.[4]

He interpreted these apparent indications of what we might now call Eurocentrism as signs of an active avoidance of the centrality of Turkish and Islamic history in that of mankind. "What might have given birth to this mentality," Reşit Galip asks, "which we could liken to wounding thorns that stubbornly become ever sharper as they are hoed into a field with poor and limey soil? We will find two sources: One is that Turkish migrations left Europeans in fear until as recently as three centuries ago; the other is the blood feuds between Christianity and Islam."[5]

The new history would serve as a corrective by "opening the road leading to the creative abilities of our nation, exposing the secret genius and character of Turks, showing Turks their own specialties and strength, and showing that our national development is tied to deep racial roots."[6] Yet the notion of race was even more fluid here than that used in Europe; it was more a nationally imposed category of demarcation between Turks and others than a suggestion of biological unity.

As race became central to the production of modern European identity, the originary locus of the Indo-Europeans gained importance as the homeland of the Aryans, which brought linguistic categorization to the fore as evidence for racial migrations. Each author seemed to put forward a new proposition for the homeland of the Aryans; included were Central Asia, Southeast Asia, and Mesopotamia. Reşit Galip found the confusion over Indo-European origins to be clear evidence of politically motivated obfuscation, but Gordon Childe, in his 1926 work *The Aryans*, could interpret this diversity of interpretation as a healthy debate in a community of scientists working toward the solution of a common set of problems. As he explained, scholars were utilizing the deductive process of "Linguistic Paleontology" to determine the characteristics of early Aryan civilization: they had domesticated animals, raised grain and wool, spun and wove, used wheeled vehicles, had a patriarchal family structure, distinguished between a mortal body and a soul, and worshipped gods. They used horses, probably of the type found in the plateaus of Central Asia. The climate of the cradle was cold and snowy in winter, hot in summer. "Such a climate," Childe points out, "reigns almost anywhere in the Eurasiatic continent north of the mountain axis and east of the Alps." Another distinguishing feature was that there had been some form of early contact between the Finns and the Aryans; in fact, some philologists suggested that the Indo-European and Ugro-Finnic linguistic families might have emerged from a common agglutinating stock. Childe lists Central Asia, Bactria, Armenia, Anatolia, South Russia, the Danube Valley, Lithuania, Germany, and Scandinavia as regions that could have served as a cradle for the Aryans. "Yet," he points out, "all are open to certain more or less grave objections."[7] Whereas in *The Aryans* Childe favored an original site in the plains of southern Russia, in his later work *Prehistoric Migrations in Europe,* published in 1950, he favored an Anatolian origin for the Indo-Europeans on the basis of increased information from Hittitology.

Much as Childe could argue that the spread of the Indo-European language across a wide range of cultures indicated its functional and aesthetic superiority, which reflected the mental and physical superiority of its creators, Turks could argue that the same qualities reflected the superiority of the Turkish race without any concern for the ensuing conflation of race and language that they had so carefully guarded against. Thus their reading of the very racial, linguistic, and cultural discourses that had constructed Indo-European migration, Aryanism, and Western civilization constructed a homogenization of races within Turkey.

As opposed to the trend in Western scholarship, the Turkish narrative said the people of the Indo-European and Turkish narratives were the same. Turks had begun to migrate from Central Asia nine thousand years ago and had continued to do so until seven hundred years ago. Lest such migrations be associated with primitive nomadism, it was pointed out that the Turks of Central Asia were endowed with all the signs of civilization as defined by European historians: they had, already in Central Asia, practiced agriculture and animal husbandry, developed weaving and metallurgy, and even constructed early architectural forms such as menhirs and tumuli. The very characteristics that identified Indo-Europeans as Central Asian for Childe were indeed remarkably similar to the characteristics of nomadic Turkic tribes who still live in the region and travel within Turkey (designated as *Yörük*)—not surprising since communities acquire such characteristics through intercourse with their environment. These were less the traits of Indo-Europeans than of herders and nomads, tied not to a language or a culture but to a mode of survival that might be labeled a civilization, if one were to consider a civilization as a discourse in which various cultures coexist under a shared umbrella of lived reality that they might recognize as truth.

The Turkish Historical Thesis used the historically verified nomadism of Turkic tribes as evidence for the Turkic identity of prehistoric migrations. According to the thesis, the Turks migrated from their Central Asian homeland first to nearby China and soon after to India, where they established the civilizations of Mohenjo-daro and Harappa. In both locations, the "true natives had no civilization."[8] Thereafter, Turkish migrations were always moving westward, along a northern route from between the Ural Mountains and the Caspian Sea along the north coast of the Black Sea to the Danube River valley and Thrace, and along a southern route that was more convenient after the glaciers had retreated and left swamps in their wake. The southern route took Turkish tribes to Mesopotamia and Anatolia. From there some members of the tribes moved on to the Italian Peninsula (as the Etruscans), to the Aegean islands (particularly Crete), and eventually to mainland Greece; others traveled across Syria, Palestine, and Mesopotamia (as the Sumerians and the Elamites) to Egypt (as the conquerors from the north). Of these civilizations, the Turkish Historical Thesis laid particular claim to those whose languages had not yet been categorized—Sumerian and Etruscan, which are still unclassified, and Hittite, which was at the time under investigation as a potential proto-Indo-European tongue. Categorically, all of these languages were subsumed under the designation "Turkish." The linguistic category "Turkish"—like the racial category—thus can be described more clearly as what it was not (Indo-European) than as what it was: the odd array of languages to which it laid claim. Such associations affiliated Turks with the very foundations of Western civilization—Sumer and Egypt no less than Greece and Rome.

On the one hand, the range of these migrations appears comically narcissistic. On the other, they not only overlap with the later historical migrations of Turkic tribes from Central Asia recorded after the eighth century, but they also invert the migratory paths established by Eurocentric origin myths. Rather than imagining an ideal form of the world in the Garden of Eden, European scholars transferred the desire for an original state of perfection—before the fragmentation of humanity into nations—onto archaeological and linguistic sources. Through the narratives of migration and of adaptive evolutionary radiation, civilizations flung far and wide around the world could be read as teleologically leading to the superior civilization of Europe, and thus they could be disassociated from their more recent histories.

In addition to responding to European scientific discourses on Aryanism, the Turkish Historical Thesis and the subsequent creation or signification of the Hittite sun also drew on European excavations in Mesopotamia that were highly invested in finding the physical traces of biblical times. In the 1840s, Austin Henry Layard conducted some of the earliest excavations in Mesopotamia when he went to Mosul in order to uncover what was believed to be the ruins of the biblical city of Nineveh. Interest in Mesopotamian archaeology soared in the 1870s after George Smith published a clay tablet from Nineveh containing a Babylonian account of the deluge. Similarly, the early work of the Palestine Exploration Fund and the Egypt Exploration Society focused on portions of the Nile Delta associated with biblical accounts. Even in 1929, Leonard Woolley interpreted archaeological evidence of a flood plain in Mesopotamia as a sign of the biblical deluge. With a selection of ancient cultures discovered on lands already biblically associated with the West, the acceptance of a line of civilizational descent from the Near East simply amounted to transferring the narrative. Much as Christians of the Middle Ages had read the events of the Old Testament as foreshadowing the New Testament, the grand civilizational narrative of the West in the post-Christian secular era built a narrative that began in Mesopotamia (Palestine), passed through Egypt (with the Israelites), and then came to be disseminated via ancient Greece (where the apostles later effected the first conversions to Christianity). In *Narrow Pass, Black Mountain,* a narrative of the discovery of Hittite civilization in Anatolia, C. W. Ceram made this parallel explicit: "This land, which is now Turkey, has from the beginning been a highway for armies, a battleground, and a melting pot of nations. Here history played itself out in its full savagery, and the stakes were death or survival—as they always have been down to our own day whenever East and West have collided. That is why for us of the twentieth century *after* the birth of Christ there is a strange contemporaneity about what took place in this arena twenty centuries *before* Christ."[9] Rather than allowing the ancient world to be read as a network of civilizations that bore their own patterns of expansion and contact, the interests that chose the sites of archaeological excavation at the end of the nineteenth century and into the early twentieth forced the ancient world to become read as a transcription of the grand narratives built into the Christian traditions of Europe.

It is in this light that we can reread the migratory narratives that carry the Aryans from their "source" and that also carry civilization westward from ancient Sumer. Many scholars produced similar narratives drawing upon different evidence. L. A. Waddell, for example, asserted in 1929 that Cappadocia was the cradle of Aryan civilization, basing his claim on the relatively recent identification of Hittite and proto-Hittite sites in Anatolia and their entry into the search for the proto-Indo-European language.[10] In 1834, while looking for the ancient city of Tavium, where invading Celts had settled during Roman times, Charles Texier happened upon the ruins of a massive sphinx gateway near the village of Bogazköy in central Turkey. The following year, William Hamilton—familiar with the pilfering of antiquities from his experience beside Lord Elgin during his youth—also visited the gateway, and he found the ruins of Alacahöyük nearby. In 1879 the biblical scholar Archibald Henry Sayce's *The Hittites in Asia Minor* identified the ruins with the civilization formerly known only by a passing reference in the Bible. By 1882 the archaeologist Karl Humann had drawn a map of the ruins, and by 1884 William Wright's *Empire of the Hittites* had compiled all the knowledge to date. While extensive written records in cuneiform on clay tablets found at excavation sites both at Bogazköy and at Zincirli indicated that the civilization had spread across Anatolia, it was not until 1917 that the Czech scholar Bedrich Hrozny deciphered the Hittite language. During the 1920s and 1930s, scholars were still trying to determine whether it was an Indo-European language and, if so, whether it was the *Ursprache* of the family that had been sought for so long. However, from a Turkish point of view, the identification of Anatolia as the homeland of the Indo-Europeans, which this identification made possible, relied on the linguistic exclusion of the Turks, a thesis that was unacceptable from a nationalist perspective.

The role of Anatolia as the crossing point of so many theories of Indo-European origins helped frame the Turkish Historical Thesis. While the European origin myths are coterminous—all civilization beginning elsewhere culminates in Europe—the Turkish myths are concentric, insisting in reply that those migrations share the same loci, a Turkish one doubly inscribed on Central Asia and on Anatolia. The Turkish narrative of prehistoric migrations thus insinuated itself into the premise of Western civilization, into its very origins, by adopting the narrative framework of archaeologically and linguistically—scientifically—provable migrations. Much as the histories of Mesopotamia, Egypt, India, and Greece could become at least as much European as local through the migratory matrix, these same histories could become Turkish through a palimpsest-like overlay of Turkish migration. "It can be said that these authors rightfully looked at the matter [of Turkish race] from its lining, and when this lining is turned inside out [and the truth is shown], it can be said not that Turks were Europeanized, but that they performed a daunting task when, through their constant migrations and close interactions, they Turkified the originally Protonegroid and Protoaustraloid Europeans."[11]

It was in this clash between European and Turkish claims over the origins of civilization that the object later identified as the Hittite sun was excavated in 1935. This round disc, which carried few or no clues to its meaning, was attributed a signification based not on evidence but on archaeological theories heavily influenced by highly politicized colonial discourses. When Remzi Oguz Arik's team excavated a series of small objects with no apparent use that varied between abstract forms and representations of deer, both the Turkish Historical Thesis and the Sun-Language theory (described below) were still quite new. Arik interpreted the finds in this context. In his 1937 monograph about the excavations, he explains that "having arrived at a depth of 6.20–6.25 meters, we found works in bronze, iron, and even silver which we called 'solar disks.'" But why, and why did this initial attribution become conclusive? Arik does not say. Nonetheless, by the end of the book, the name had stuck:

> Among the votive monuments of the three tombs, the different "solar disks" remain the most truly unique documents. In all these "solar disks" the horn of the ox, the stag, the idea of the sun remain in common and dominate. The images of the stag, so obstinately repeated on each occasion, either separately or such that they furnish the principle theme on these ex-voto take us above all to Central and Northern Asia. Does not the "swastika" symbolize the sun and heavenly continuation? In all the cases, one encounters the same constitutive elements of the discs in the monuments of Mesopotamia.[12]

Why conclude that this object represented the sun?

Arik was no doubt influenced by the Sun-Language theory, which had emerged in late 1934 as an alternative to Western schemata for the origin and categorization of languages and thereby cultures. The Sun-Language theory posited that language first appeared as people pointed toward the sun and said, "Ah!" in amazement. In order to understand why the disks were interpreted as sun disks, one must not only understand how this theory made the sun into the object of primordial pointing; one must also consider the sun as it was understood within a broader context of Indo-European and Aryan identity.

The nineteenth-century popularizer of philology Max Müller, in his *Essay on Comparative Mythology* of 1869, explained the primacy of the sun

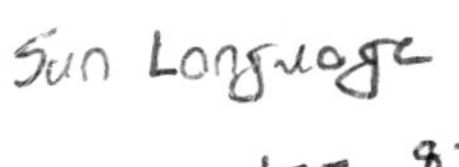

for primitive man. He considered the sun as the key element linking Aryan mythologies. Moreover, with an inconsistent flourish connecting all languages with the Indo-European languages, Müller declared, "Never in the history of man has there been a new language. What does this mean? Neither more nor less than that in speaking as we do, we are using the same materials, however broken-up, crushed, and put together anew, which were handled by the first speaker, i.e. the first real ancestor of our race."[13] Thus the sun already had an identity within Aryanism nearly as strong as its identity in Central Asia. The interpretation of the artifact discovered in 1935 at Alacahöyük can be understood only in terms of the linguistic and archaeological associations built within the frame of this palimpsest of layered migrations between Central Asia and Anatolia.

Arik's interpretation of the findings was well in line with that of the first Turkish Historical Thesis, which drew heavily from the work of Raphael Pumpelly in an attempt to link the Sumerians with Anatolia. Although Pumpelly had excavated at Anau, a site in modern Turkmenistan, between 1903 and 1908, in the search for the homeland of the Aryans, he had found his work too inconclusive to publish.[14] The authors of the Turkish Historical Thesis seized on this ambiguity and conflated the contemporary and prehistoric inhabitants of the site, constructing a continuous narrative of Turkic habitation in Central Asia that served as the root of Turkic migrations to Anatolia. For the Turks, the primary importance of the links between Anau and southward migrations was that they provided a narrative that allowed the Hittites of Anatolia both to be the initial inhabitants of Anatolia and to be Turkish, thus making Turks autochthonous to Anatolia and also equivalent in level of development to their cousins the Sumerians, already widely credited as the source for Western civilization. And yet there was more. For the first time, local archaeological finds utilized images like the swastika, although it was not the first time that somebody had used archaeological finds to suggest that the swastika had actually been a Turkish icon.

While the discovery of an object decorated with a swastika design brought this claim home to Anatolia, the one decorated with swastikas was not chosen as the new Turkish icon. The new objects fit with Aryan symbolism, but they were also used to subtly distinguish between Turkish race theories related to Aryanism and the use of the swastika by the Nazis. The Hittite sun was specifically not a swastika; it was chosen to replace the swastika, both with an autochthonous Anatolian symbol and with the theories of Turkish migration from Central Asia supporting the notion that the Hittites were actually Turks and represented the first wave of Turkish migration to Anatolia, centuries before any modern people.

Figure 5.3. Afet Inan at the Second Turkish Historical Congress in 1937 beneath an enlarged image of the sun disk

By the time of the Third Linguistic Congress in 1937, it had all come together. With an enlarged image of the sun disk behind the podium, Afet Inan (fig. 5.3) explained the role of the sun as she introduced the congress:

> The Turkish revolution, which has squeezed the work of centuries into years, has discovered its own *mihrab*, that of the sun. In the voyage of history, it is we the Turks who most frequently encounter the traces of the sun's inspiration. The Turkish race discovered its culture in such a place that there the sun was the most productive. The Turks who had to leave their first home chose their primary routes of migration by following the guidance of the sun. . . . They spread to the East and to the West; in those wide countries, they left the documents of their exalted existence. And our ancestors the Hittites, the first to establish the culture of our own home Anatolia, made a symbol of the sun. They made it the subject of the intricacy of their arts. Several sun disks found during the Turkish Historical Foundation's excavations at Alacahöyük provide incontestable proof of this. . . . These sun disks, decorated with various geometrical designs, will take an important position in our history as the symbol of Turkish thought and art.[15]

Thus a chronologically prehistoric artifact became defined as the symbol for a thought and an art yet to be defined, a symbol that would designate a race and, through it, a nation, by way of linguistics. "It is not," Afet Inan explained, "that in the world of knowledge there are no scientists who do not consider language essential to race. This [the idea that language is not essential to race] might be true for some societies. But never for Turks."[16] Childe had conceived of language as the trace of the superior mind that had developed it, but he had made allowance for diffusionist rather than migrationist explanations for its spread. In contrast, the Turkish language theory, dubbed the Sun-Language theory, postulated that the root language had been spread through the migration of the Central Asian Turks who had invented it and that the languages of "East Asia, America, India, the Iranian plains, the Mesopotamian valleys, near Asia, Phoenicia, Egypt, North Africa, from the Ural Mountains and the shores of the Volga River to the Danube, Vistüla, and Rhine rivers, and the Atlas Ocean" had emerged from it.[17] As the general secretary Saffet Arıkan explained:

> Once we learned that hundreds of words in the Mayan language of Mexico, in the south of the American continent, are Turkish, and keeping in mind the Maya mountain to the west of Gevgili in Macedonia, we read in European histories that in the era that America first encountered European invasion the inhabitants of Peru worshiped "Günesh" [the Turkish word for sun] and that the native leader, who gave his life in fighting against the Europeans, was named "Atahualpa", that is "Ata Alp" [*Ata* means "patriarch" or "elder" or "forebear"]. From European geography and history experts we also learned that, in contrast to the assertion that the continent was named after Amerigo Vespuchi, Nicaraguan natives already used the name "America." Then in Yakut dictionaries we found that the word "Emerik" is still in use. After seeing all these traces of the spread of Turkishness, Turkish culture, and the Turkish language around the entire world, is it possible not to realize that the sun of truth has risen?[18]

Clearly, the subtext here is not merely linguistic, but one that aims to reclaim knowledge, using the voice of the European expert as an anticolonial weapon, indeed denying the reality of European colonialism and suzerainty on a global level. By undercutting the power of Europeans to name, Turkey may not have removed the physical reality of imperial history and the threat that had until recently been so palpable (and could once again threaten in the form of the Third Reich), but Turkey had requisitioned the symbolic power of naming ironically to a simultaneously native and Turkish agency.

The immediate assumption of the artifact as a symbol becomes clear through its use both as a backdrop at the second historical congress and as a line drawing on the first issue of the Historical Society's publication,

Belleten. Far from innocent, the sun was clearly also a sign of racial, and thereby political, affiliation. As indicated by Hamid Zübeyir Koşay's discussion of Alacahöyük at the Historical Congress the following year, the primary Hittite site to be excavated solely by Turks to date during the republican era, archaeology was not simply a nationalist activity in its marking of territoriality; it produced an inherent link between the antiquity thus unearthed and the modern age.[19] Eugene Pittard's presentation supported this new view of Turkish nationalism: not only were Turks from Central Asia, a migratory people identified with the Indo-European migrations, but they were also the living relatives of the Hittites, and thus autochthonous. He wrote:

> Who could imagine that a name change in any state could change the physical composition of its people? . . . In the canton of Vale in Switzerland, four languages were spoken over the course of four successive eras: first they were Celts; after the Roman invasion they spoke Latin; later they were Germanized; and finally they re-Latinized as many came to speak French. Over the course of these centuries, the only thing to change was the language spoken by these people. This people physically stayed the same. . . . With regards to the invasions undergone in Anatolia, it is clear that the people who produced and administered these invasions were mostly of the same race, and were people of the same components. Let me repeat: it is not possible for it to be otherwise. A look at the racial map around Anatolia confirms this. Today the people known as Kurdish, Armenian, and Laz, who are to a large extent brachyocephalic, came to existence out of these primitive groups. As for the invasions known as Semitic, these were performed by people of another race, since Arabs come out of the dolicocephalic race, which is primitive, and some Jews and Syrians also emerged from this race.[20]

By this point, one of the primary aims of the Sun-Language theory had clearly moved beyond its original interest of affiliating Turks with Europeans to a much more specific interest in producing them as Aryans, or, more to the point, of revealing the Aryans as Turks. For the first time, Abraham Necmi Dilmen's introduction of the theory to the conference utilized a derivation of the word *Ari*, or *Aryan*, as the primary explanation of the theory. Thus, he explained, the Aryans are actually Turks. Along similar lines, the Celts could be shown to be related to the "Seltçuks," and Ankara could be proven to be the name of a river in Central Asia. So a modern city was named, as it were, by the ancient Hittites.[21] Such an assertion may not be as misguided as the evidence used at the time would suggest: recent excavations suggest evidence of Celtic habitation in central Turkey.

With an unprecedented emphasis on physical anthropology, including craniometric studies and analyses of comparative blood groups and fingerprints, the second historical congress generally eschewed any more than a passing glance at historical-era presentations and focused instead on reinforcing Turkey's prehistoric identity with regard to race, language, and ethnic unity and universality. This emphasis must be conceived in the contemporary intellectual and political milieu, which was responding to the increasing fragmentation of Europe and to the high tide of anti-Semitic racism in Germany.

The Sun-Language theory and the sun disk did not, of course, remain cloistered in scholarly conferences. Explanations of the theory in the newspaper *Cumhuriyet* used diagrams comparing the role of language to the solar system. The solar disk became the symbol of the state-controlled Eti (Hittite) Bank, founded in 1935 to finance mining. In the meantime, articles in the main daily newspaper, *Cumhuriyet,* explained that the Hittites had brought metallurgy and mining to the world.[22] It became the symbol of the nation's first biscuit company and the symbol on its most popular brand of cigarettes.

The political urgency of the Sun-Language theory and the Turkish Historical Thesis is perhaps best indicated by the quick demise of their high ideological rhetoric by the end of World War II. Having served its central ideological purpose in resisting the Aryanism that threatened to drag Turkey into the war and that rejected Turks as inferior, this symbol became transformed. By the time the third historical congress convened in 1943, the Turkish Historical Thesis and the Sun-Language theory had entered the realm of historical truths of the nation, still "the light of truth erasing error," but no longer in need of elaborate racial elaboration and support from the four corners of the earth. Despite residual mention of nation, race, and language, interest in national identity overrode the production of a transcendent universal theory; the evidence of physical anthropology was relegated to the end of the conference. Presenting the six-year report on archaeological excavations, the secretary of the Turkish Historical Society, Muzaffer Göker, explained that, in contrast to earlier universalist renditions of Turkish identity, "there are few nations which have come into contact with as many nations as the Turks. Thus it is natural for us to consider not only written sources in our own language, but in those of the Eastern and Western nations (China, India, Iran, Arabia, Byzantine, Armenian, Assyrian, and others) with which we have been in contact." Along similar lines, he suggested comparatively modest objectives for archaeological projects: "(1) to bring the Paleolithic period of Anatolia to light; (2) to expose documents that settle the issues of the movement and settlement patterns of ancient cultures; (3) to ascertain the spread and points of passing of the Hittites, who established a large state in Anatolia; (4) to investigate the links between the oldest Anatolian culture and the cultures of Central Asia, Mesopotamia, the Aegean basin, Southern Russia, and Eastern Europe; (5) and, in the end, to bring to light documents concerning the more recent history of Anatolia, which has been the place of settlement for many important civilizations."[23]

Rather than grounding comparative investigations in linguistic and historical theory, he proposed to maintain close contact with excavators in diverse regions, but he did so without any mention of the racial connections that had constituted the core of the discourse at the previous congress. Moreover, while the congress was still concerned with prehistoric archaeology, work on the historical eras of Anatolia began to regain center stage. Similarly, although Ahmet Cevat Emre, one of the authors of the Sun-Language theory, still supported the notion of a protolanguage emerging in Central Asia, he makes no mention of the mechanics of the Sun-Language theory and instead favors morphemic comparisons between languages that make fewer racial assertions.[24]

When the Hittite sun became the symbol of Ankara in 1961, it was no longer the antiswastika but rather the symbol of the possibility of a purely Turkish ideology and identity that had been possible in Turkey's formative years and under the auspices of Atatürk. Since only parts of this ideology survived, and many other parts became transformed and diluted, the Hittite sun became a sign flexible enough to symbolize new interpretations of and emphases on various aspects of Atatürkist thought as needed for the changing contemporary world. Rather than symbolizing Atatürk's power within the language reform per se, it became a much broader sign for adherence to his reforms as a whole, the most penetrating of which was secularism.

Thus during the 1960s revival of the discourse of Hittite ancestry, Arın Ergin could repeat the general cultural and racial arguments put forward in the first version of the Turkish Historical Thesis thirty years earlier, but he restricted linguistic analysis to word comparisons and made no mention of Aryanism.[25]

What remained most palpably from the historical and linguistic theories was the historical periodization that still constitutes the framework for the official national narrative of the Turkish past: prehistoric eras (the Paleolithic, Mesolithic, and Chalcolithic eras and the Bronze Age), the Hittite era; the Phrygian era; the Hellenistic and Roman periods; the Byzantine Empire; the Seljuk and Beylik periods; the Ottoman Empire. Like all periodizations, such a taxonomy of time represents a diagrammatic view of groups that apparently followed one from another and apparently covered the same territory with similar degrees of autonomy and comprehensive cultural unity. Reduced to a popular reading of history through mass education, such periodization produces an impression that the Hittite empire may have had a single administrative structure akin to that of the Byzantine; that during the Phrygian era, the Phrygians covered the same territory that the Seljuks inhabited later; that the Byzantine and Seljuk eras were temporally exclusive; and that one era flowed neatly into the next without ruptures such as the massive shifts of populations and centuries of discord that often make up more comprehensively detailed historical reality. Indeed, this was the *explicit* function of history suggested by the president of the organization, Professor Semseddin Günaltay, who explains, "History is not just a signboard of fate. It is the never ending source of the energy and excitement which a nation needs in its struggle to maintain its existence, support its progress, and secure its development."[26]

As Afet Inan had predicted soon after its discovery, the Hittite sun became a sign of Turkish thought, representative less of an ancient civilization per se than of the geography and the ideology that it was made to evoke. In the 1930s, the Hittite sun for a brief historical moment provided a metaphoric condensation of an entire historico-linguistic thesis designed to produce an internally unitary race and an externally indomitable nation based on the mythic universality of that race. But what precisely does it represent today? If the Hittite sun simply symbolized Turkey's geographic relationship to the Hittites as the inheritor of Anatolia, few would probably argue with its symbolism. But the production of a competing sign in the 1990s of a mosque and a tower—a sign at once of Islamic and of economic globalism—reveals the emblem of the Hittite sun as less a sign of geography or history than a metonymic signal toward a national secularism always at a remove, placed in an imaginary counterpoint to the West and perhaps to the future, but rooted in the prehistoric and autochthonous Hittites.

Ironically, though initially known only from the Bible, in Turkey the Hittites became a sign of taking European origins away from biblically charged narratives of origins and repeating the secularization entailed by the post-Enlightenment racial, cultural, and linguistic theories that replaced their biblical forerunners. Likewise, the Hittite tale of origins retold existing Ottoman-Turkish origin myths, particularly that of the westward conquests of central Asian Turks, while removing them from the Islamicizing function with which those narratives had been associated. When Turks were reconceived as prehistorically pagan rather than as Muslim migrants to Anatolia, their identity as Hittites could not only reframe their origins in the modern nation; it could provide a new prehistory, which racially and even linguistically encompassed the ethnic and religious differences within the nation. It gave Turks an earlier shared identity, which could serve to mask difference both within the country and, in particular, between Turkey and Western nations.

In an era when religion was no longer overtly called on to produce the nepotistic families of mankind, theories of history and race, backed up by the absolute voice of science substituting for the absolute voice of God, insidiously stepped in to take religion's place. Thus Turkey's production of secularism was intimately bound up with the production of the Turkish race as distinct from other nations, unitary in its composition yet belonging to a broader family of nations affiliated through a common mythology. The notion that the move to secularism represented a narrative leap from the family of Muslim nations to the family of Western ones is almost a truism; less obvious is that this symbolic leap depended on racial and historical definitions at least as much as, if not more than, waning religious identifications in an era with an overt narrative (if not practice) of secular governance. Produced as common ancestors, Hittites could assure a myth of mutual relatedness, mutual recognition for "their descendants" both as ethnic groups within the nation and as national groups without. Linguistics utilized a discursive mode—that of science—designed to make the myth palatable to the modern mind. With the waning of the scientific discourses of physical anthropology and linguistic paleontology after World War II, the Hittite sun became a sign less for the thought of the early republic than for the need that had forced that thought to emerge.

The emergence of a countersign, the new emblem of Ankara, foregrounding a majority Muslim state as produced in a contemporary world, emphasizes not simply a stance against the secularist symbolism of the Hittite sun, but perhaps also a desire to recast the kinship of identity in a manner more attuned to the contemporary regionalism increasingly espoused by political units that gain their strength from pragmatic economic interests rather than from myths of cultural unity. What is the endpoint of the deconstruction of such narratives of origin? Narratives of origin developed in complicity with the categorization and hierarchical ranking of races. The theories, developed in conjunction both in logical structure and in their production of history, are complicit within each other. We cannot reproduce the historical narrative of origins without implicating the racial narratives within it. If we currently deny the reality of racial categorization, then the production of such linear historical narratives becomes hypocritical. Such a production of communal narratives then becomes, in sharp contrast to the Foucauldian model of epistemic rupture, a continual plane of narrative conjunctions and negotiations between points that emerge from their multiple conjunctions—and governments become less representing bodies than administrative units. This becomes a history ultimately of the intensely local rather than of the immensely and artificially communal, a sliding chain of synchronic and diachronic narratives that must be told within a multiplicity of dimensions, with a consciousness of necessary narrative contradictions, and with an awareness of the political agency of narrative on all sides. It is not historical "truth" that wins, since such truth is always essentially mutable. Rather, the contemporary climates force the dominance of certain spaces on the chain of narratives. Yet in the absence of race, communal historical narratives lose much of their power to separate as they bring together, and in doing so they can make way for a new era when signs can speak shortly and plainly because, rather than in spite of, their increasingly forked tongues. If shared history constitutes an alternative to racism, the increase in human mobility coupled with increased communications and the ensuing cultural mixing may construct a pooling of the very communal differences on which racial discrimination relies. What then?

Historical grand narratives, ranging from those of nation-states to those of great civilizations, are constructed for the building of a state unique from, and usually superior to, others. The greatest threat to such a narrative is not to be contested as a lie or as a fabrication—which it must be, to some extent, as competitive narratives also must be. The greatest threat is for such narratives to fail as proof of exclusivity. That such narratives can belong, equally well, to multiple owners is the threat that breaks the back of the discursive space of nationalist historiography and threatens that all borders will become just what they are: sites of transition rather than division. What must come to the fore is the archaeology of such narratives in their multiple derivations, multiple diatribes, and, most importantly, multiple possibilities. Thus may we raise the hope that "the omnipresence of human discourse will perhaps one day be embraced under the open sky of an omni-communication of its text," not through the filling of the emblem, but through the constant memory of it as a blank, as a tessera, "a coin whose obverse and reverse no longer bear any but effaced figures, and which people pass from hand to hand 'in silence,'"[27] the passive unities of historical narratives silenced by the dynamic narratives of shared imaginations and projects.

Notes

1. Mustafa Kemal (1881–1938) was the general who led the Turkish nationalist forces to victory against the waning Ottoman sultanate and against colonizing Allied forces. With the institution of the Turkish Republic in 1923, he became its first president and acquired a mythic standing as father of the country, indicated by the surname granted to him by the parliament: Atatürk, "Father of the Turks." The national cult of Atatürkism began during his lifetime and has ebbed and flowed since his death in 1938.
2. For examples of such critiques and more complete investigations into the history of the Turkish Historical Thesis, see İsmail Beşikçi, *Türk tarih tezi, güneş-dil teorisi ve Kürt sorunu* [The Turkish Historical Thesis, the Sun-Language theory, and the Kurdish problem] (Ankara: Yurt Kitap-Yayın, 1991); Behar Buşra Ersanlı, *İktidar ve Tarih: Türkiye'de "Resmi Tarih" tezinin oluşumu (1929–1937)* [Power and history: The establishment of "Official History" in Turkey] (Istanbul: Afa Yayınları, 1992); Etienne Copeaux, *Espaces et temps de la nation turque: Analyse d'une historiographie nationaliste, 1931–1993* (Paris: CNRS édition, 1997); Geoffrey Lewis, *The Turkish Language Reform: A Catastrophic Success* (Oxford: Oxford University Press, 1999).
3. *Türk Tarihinin Ana Hatları: Kemalist yönetimin resmi tarih tezi* [General outline of Turkish history] (Istanbul: Devlet Matbaası, 1930; reprint, Istanbul: Kaynak Yayınları, 1999), 25. Page references are to the reprint edition. Translations from non-English works are my own unless otherwise indicated.
4. *Türk Tarih Kongresi: Bildiriler* (Ankara: Maarif Vekaleti, 1932), 136.
5. Ibid., 151.
6. *Türk Tarihinin Ana Hatları*, 25.
7. Gordon Childe, *The Aryans: A Study of Indo-European Origins* (New York: Alfred A. Knopf, 1926), 88–90.
8. *Türk Tarihinin Ana Hatları*, 60.
9. C. W. Ceram, *Narrow Pass, Black Mountain: The Discovery of the Hittite Empire*, trans. from German by Richard and Clara Winston (London: Victor Gollancz, 1956), 3.
10. Cf. his 1929 book *The Makers of Civilization in Race and History: Showing the Rise of the Aryans or Sumerians, Their Origination and Propagation of Civilization, Their Extension of It to Egypt and Crete; Personalities and Achievements of Their Kings; Historical Originals of Mythic Gods and Heroes with Dates from the Rise of Civilization about 3380 BC Reconstructed from Babylonian, Egyptian, Hittite, Indian, and Gothic Sources* (London: Luzac, 1929).
11. *Türk Tarih Kongresi*, 158.
12. Remzi Oğuz Arık, *Les fouilles d'Alaca Höyük entreprises par la Société d'histoire turque: Rapport préliminaire sur les travaux en 1935* (Ankara, 1937), 119.
13. George William Cox, *The Mythology of the Aryan Nations* (London: Longmans, Green, 1870; reprint, Varanasi: Chowkhamba Sanskrit Series Office, 1963), 22; Müller quoted on 16.

14. Peggy Champlin, *Raphael Pumpelly: Gentleman Geologist of the Gilded Age* (Tuscaloosa: University of Alabama Press, 1994), 165.
15. Afet İnan, "Söylev" [Speech], in *Üçüncü Türk Dil Kurultayı* [Third Congress of the Turkish language] (Istanbul: Devlet Basımev, 1937), 7.
16. Ibid.
17. Safett Arıkan, "Söylev," in *Üçüncü Türk Dil Kurultayı*, 9.
18. Ibid., 11.
19. Hamid Zübeyir Koşay, "Türk Tarih Kurumu tarafindan Alacahöyükte yaptırılan hafriyatta elde edilen neticeler," in *İkinci Türk Tarih Kongresi* [Second Congress of the Turkish Historical Society] (Istanbul: Kenan Matbaasi, 1943), 31–32.
20. Eugene Pittard, "Neolitik devirde küçük Asya ile Avrupa arasında antropolojik münasebetler" [Anthropological relationships between Asia Minor and Europe during the Neolithic Period], in *Üçüncü Türk Dil Kurultayı*, 73–77.
21. İbrahim Necmi Dilmen, "Türk Tarih tezinde Güneş-Dil teorisinin yeri ve değeri" [The place and value of the Sun-Language Theory in the Turkish Historical Thesis], in *İkinci Türk Tarih Kongresi*, 89–95.
22. *Cumhuriyet*, April 5, 1937, p. 7.
23. Muzaffer Göker, "Türk Tarih Kurumu'nun altı yıllık çalışmaları" [Six years of work of the Turkish Historical Society], in *Üçüncü Türk Tarih Kongresi* [Third Congress of the Turkish Historical Society] (Ankara: Türk Tarih Kurumu Basımevi, 1948), 15–17.
24. Ahmet Cevat Emre, "Dil Davamızın Morfolojik İspatı Üzerine," in *Üçüncü Türk Tarih Kongresi*, 178–194.
25. Arın Ergin, *Atatüçülük Savaşımızda Türk Kültürü Geçmişbilimi Eti Tarihi* [Turkish culture, knowledge of the past, Hittite history in the fight for Atatürkism] (Istanbul: Atatürkkent, 1961), 42–43.
26. Şemseddin Günaltay, "Açiş Nutku" [Opening speech], in *Üçüncü Türk Tarih Kongresi*, 1–2.
27. J. Lacan, *Ecrits: A Selection* (New York: W. W. Norton, 1977), 56, 43.

SIX

The Sense of Belonging

The Politics of Archaeology in Modern Iraq

MAGNUS T. BERNHARDSSON

In Iraq there is still . . . no Iraqi people but unimaginable masses of human beings, devoid of any patriotic ideal, imbued with religious traditions and absurdities, connected by no common tie.

KING FAYSAL OF IRAQ, 1932

Antiques are the most precious relics the Iraqis possess, showing the world that our country . . . is the legitimate offspring of previous civilizations which offered a great contribution to humanity.

PRESIDENT SADDAM HUSSEIN, 1979

The main news story on April 9, 2003, in most media outlets around the world was the toppling of the statue of Saddam Hussein on the al-Fardos (Paradise) Square in Baghdad. The square is centrally located near the Palestine Hotel, where most of the foreign journalists who were covering the American invasion of Iraq were staying. In the wake of the arrival of the American army in Baghdad, a group of people had gathered by a large, Stalinesque statue of Hussein. And in front of the world's television cameras, the crowd started to throw rocks, soda cans, and other objects at the statue. They took off their shoes and used them to beat the statue. Foreign television viewers were reminded that this was a traditional way for Arabs to show disrespect. When the initial attempts seemed futile, a well-known Baghdad bodybuilder by the name of Kahdim Sharif Hussein dramatically appeared with a sledgehammer and started to beat furiously at the base of the statue, hoping that it would fall. Yet the statue of Saddam Hussein stubbornly stood firm and did not budge. The difficulties that the Iraqis had in dislodging the statue were a reflection of the fact that, after decades of attempts, they had not managed to topple the authoritarian leader themselves.

Adding to the symbolism of the moment, the American soldiers started to assist the Iraqis in their quest. Ropes and chains appeared, and they were tied to a large military vehicle. Initially an American soldier put an American flag on top of the statue, but his commanders reminded him that such a gesture sent the wrong message to the world. The Americans had come not to conquer Iraq but to liberate the Iraqi people. In its place an out-of-date Iraqi flag was draped over Hussein's head. After considerable effort and after the military equipment had pulled and pulled, the imposing statue finally fell to the ground and shattered. Because of American military intervention, the dictator had finally been overthrown. The mighty had fallen!

The commentators of the day were exuberant and hyperbolic describing this moment. The toppling of the statue was presented as a unique historic moment, perhaps similar to the fall of the Berlin Wall. The ancien régime was no longer; a new era would begin with new leaders in Iraq. The icons of the Ba'th government would no longer prevail over the cultural and political landscape. Instead, a new political dawn was on the horizon for Iraq.

But was this event the most symbolic moment of the day and indicative of what lay ahead for Iraq and its citizens? Amid the euphoria, the news broadcasts also reported widespread looting in Baghdad. Because of the breakdown of central authority, lawlessness prevailed. Instead of tyranny, there was anarchy. The society seemed to have been turned upside down. Everywhere, people of all ages were seen carrying all kinds of goods and merchandise as offices, institutes, and stores were emptied. And several days later, the world was shocked to hear about the destruction and plunder at Iraq's National Museum and other museums, cultural institutions, and libraries. A considerable portion of Iraq's artifacts and antiquities became part of the war's "collateral damage." In a matter of a few hours, Iraq's art galleries and museums suffered incredible harm. Irreparable damage was done to Iraq's archaeological heritage by anonymous perpetrators while the American military was struggling to gain control of Baghdad. The National Museum, home to priceless and unique artifacts from some of the earliest human civilizations, was basically emptied, it seemed, of anything movable and of value. Instead of being centrally located, classified, and under governmental control, Iraq's artifacts were now dispersed. Although the ruin is not nearly as serious as previously thought, this was still one of most acute cultural calamities of modern times.

The toppling of the statue of Saddam Hussein was therefore not a true symbol of what was in store for Iraq; it was not the most historic occurrence during those days in April 2003; rather, the plunder of Iraqi antiquities was what foreshadowed the Iraqi nation's future. For the last twenty years of the twentieth century, Iraq experienced an unusually turbulent and violent history. Starting with the misunderstood and forgotten Iran-Iraq War (1980–1988) and continuing right through the war that started in 2003 and the subsequent occupation, the Iraqi nation has suffered long periods of devastation, foreign invasions, and deprivation. Not only have there been human tribulations; in addition Iraq's unique archaeological artifacts and heritage have been subject to unprecedented destruction. The immense and tragic obliteration and plunder of Iraq's antiquities in April of 2003 was a stark reminder of how vulnerable the nation's archaeological objects have been throughout its history. This destruction was indicative of how closely Iraqi antiquities have been tied to the country's political history.

I argue in this chapter that Iraq's national identity has been forged to a large extent by its unique archaeological heritage. In multifaceted ways, Iraqis have sought paradigms from their history in order to define their nation. Using this cultural nationalism, or *paradigmatic nationalism*, Iraq has sought to demonstrate through archaeology how its modern and ethnically diverse population is tied to the various peoples and periods of the country's recent and distant past.[1] Archaeology also provided the props and the scientific justification for the government's legitimacy and its policies. Archaeology and ancient history thus helped foster a distinct sense of Iraqiness that has made Iraqis proud of their nation and their history.

For the modern state of Iraq, therefore, archaeology has served to unify the nation and create a sense of belonging. The obliteration of its archaeological heritage symbolizes the disparate nature of the nation today. One of the many tasks that lie ahead for the fragile Iraqi nation is to develop once again a unity. In the process, archaeological artifacts will undoubtedly again play a key role.

Iraq's National Identity

The question of national identity has been a perplexing concern for the political leaders of modern Iraq ever since its establishment in August 1921. The leaders of this new country, whose borders were decided by the Allies following World War I, were faced with the task of nation-building among a population that was diverse ethnically, religiously, and linguistically. Iraq's first ruler, King Faysal, was clearly speaking from experience when he exclaimed after eleven years of rule that there were still no "Iraqi" peoples. During the early years of the Iraqi state, therefore, "the central question of politics was not 'Who should rule?' but 'Who are we?'"[2] This latter question has continued to predominate throughout recent Iraqi political history. The answer changed from year to year as Iraqis sought different inspirations from their long and storied past.[3]

Some governments, such as those in power between 1936 and 1941 and between 1963 and 1968, emphasized archaeology and history connected to Iraq's pan-Arab, pan-Islamic ties, particularly its role as the seat of the Abbassid Caliphate in the ninth century CE. Others, especially during the reign of Abd al-Karim Qasem (1958–1961) and Saddam Hussein (1979–2003), stressed Iraq's particularism based on its unique pre-Islamic history, such as being the seat of the Babylonian, Akkadian, and Sumerian civilizations. In this way, the governments have sought different paradigms from history. The ancient empires and cultures thus became "Iraqi," and what it meant to be Iraqi was fluid and constantly changing.

In Iraq the history and practice of archaeology have gone through four stages: the international stage, from 1808 to 1921; the national or negotiated stage, 1921–1941; the independent stage, 1941–1991; and the sanctioned stage, 1991–2003. In 2003 Iraq's archaeology may have reentered the negotiated stage as Iraq has begun again to seek to reclaim its lost heritage and initiate its political and cultural reconstruction.

The International Stage: Whose Cradle of Civilization?

When the modern state of Iraq was established in 1921, neither archaeology nor Iraq's ancient history was of much concern to the Iraqi political leaders or the population at large. Before the establishment of Iraq, it was primarily Western travelers and archaeologists who showed interest in the archaeological relics of Iraq (or Mesopotamia, as it was then known).

In the eighteenth and nineteenth centuries, various travelers and archaeologists ventured into Mesopotamia to explore the land and culture, and specifically its antiquities. Enlightenment universalist apocalyptic teleology, Romantic nostalgia, and imperialist racism helped create the European fascination with the "primitive" *and* the "oriental." It was in this context that European travelers came to Mesopotamia searching for traces of ancient history.

These early explorers were products of societies still firmly entrenched in religious beliefs and influences. They were therefore, in a sense, returning to their infancy—to their "cradle"—and as they started to dig into the earth to find traces of those roots and their own ancient history, they naturally felt the need to return the artifacts they found to their current home in Europe or in the United States. Most of the sites that were excavated before World War I related to biblical history and not to Islamic history. For the Western archaeologists, biblical-era artifacts were clearly more valuable and relevant.

This search for history was conducted within the context of European imperialism and was thus invigorated by the competitive spirit of colonialism. The world, and all that was in it, was up for grabs—a view reflecting European power and progress. The scramble for colonies was also played out in the arena of Middle Eastern antiquities. The urge to discover as many magnificent antiquities as possible often resulted in crude and reckless digging in Mesopotamia, as well as rash methods in the export of the antiquities. It is clear that many sites and relics were irreparably damaged or lost in this process.

While the ruins of Mesopotamia fascinated Western travelers and archaeologists, it is difficult to gauge the attitudes of the locals toward the antiquities and toward archaeological excavations in general. Because of the paucity of surviving sources, one must rely on indirect accounts, such as those by the Western archaeologists themselves, which in this regard should be treated with skepticism. Accounts such as Austen Henry Layard's famous best-seller *Nineveh and Its Remains* were deliberately and consciously tailored to their audience back home and stressed the exotic and even, at times, almost erotic aspects of Middle Eastern culture. Therefore, as has been amply documented, travelers went to the Middle East with specific stereotypes in mind. Their own writings then typically perpetuated the stereotypes inherited from earlier accounts. Although the travelers showed considerable respect and knowledge of the area's history, the natives have a less dignified role in their narratives. The natives are most often depicted as ignorant, hotheaded zealots who had no interest in archaeological relics but were concerned if the Westerners were digging for gold and other such treasures.

Based on the lack of evidence to the contrary, one must surmise that the archaeological ruins and their study were not prominent concerns in Iraqi day-to-day life. For centuries, the ruins had been left alone, but they were not completely ignored, for certain Middle Eastern travel accounts and histories mentioned them. Most of these accounts, such as al-Qazwini's thirteenth-century narrative, comment that the locals visited ruins to carry off bricks for their houses. Before the twentieth century, then, archaeological relics were used to build houses, not a national identity. Archaeology up until World War I was therefore "international" in that it was mainly foreign institutions or organizations that conducted archaeological work in the region and expressed interest in the unearthed objects as historical and artistic artifacts. Most of the excavated artifacts did not remain in Iraq.

The National or Negotiated Stage

With the downfall of the Ottoman Empire after World War I, Britain was primarily responsible, under a mandate from the League of Nations, for establishing a comprehensive, modern infrastructure in Iraq. In order to "assist" the Iraqis to "stand alone," as the covenant of the League described the mandate relationship, British colonial officials devised a system of indirect rule in Iraq. A British official was placed in each Iraqi ministry to "advise" on and effectively approve all decisions. Although most aspects of the government involved British and Iraqi cooperation, archaeology was initially primarily a British concern.

The British had committed themselves under the mandate to serve only as "advisers" to the Iraqis, but when it came to archaeology, the British denied the Iraqis active participation. Officially they always sought Iraqi approval, but in the early years, the British made all the major decisions concerning archaeology. Archaeology became the responsibility of the British Oriental Secretary in Baghdad, Gertrude Bell. Bell, one of the most remarkable British personalities in modern Middle Eastern history, had traveled extensively in the area before the war and was familiar with the antiquities of Iraq. She had also worked with archaeologists and inspected numerous sites. As she put it, "I think I'm something of an archaeologist myself."[4]

Shortly after the establishment of Iraq, the need for archaeological preservation and control became more apparent to the British. Since several foreign expeditions had expressed interest in excavating in Iraq, Bell started to draft a new antiquities law. In July of 1922, she reported in a letter that she had received Faysal's approval "for *my* law of excavations" and that she would be appointed the director of archaeology. "I should then be able to run the whole thing in direct agreement with him." She had several meetings with the cabinet, in which she explained and defended her law. As she described it, they labored "clause by clause, for two hours," and she thought they had agreed in principle to pass it.[5]

However, the process took longer than she imagined. In September of the following year, she was still working on the bill and stated that one minister, Yasin Pasha, "had tried to rush through a law of his own while I was away."[6] Bell also encountered resistance from Sati al-Husri, the minister of education, who in the 1930s became the first Iraqi director of antiquities.

Al-Husri, an influential and leading proponent of modern pan-Arabist thought, was of Syrian origin and had played a key role in the Ottoman educational system. Through his various governmental posts, al-Husri became very influential in formulating an Arab consciousness in Iraq. Heavily influenced by the German Romantics, he believed that nations were natural divisions of the human species. He argued that the Arabs constituted a nation and ought therefore to be united into a single state. The fundamental criteria of nationhood, in his view, were a shared language and a common history. Although the Arab nations were divided into several political states, al-Husri said that because they shared the Arabic language and memories of their glorious past, the Arabs possessed all the critical ingredients for a single nationhood. Since al-Husri believed that political unification could come only as a result of a growing awareness of shared history, it is not surprising that he was interested in the archaeological legislation.

In his autobiography and in newspaper interviews in the 1930s, al-Husri describes various debates he had with Bell over the antiquities law, particularly about which ministry should be responsible for archaeological matters. Bell wanted the law to place the Department of Antiquities under the Ministry of Public Works rather than the Ministry of Education. According to al-Husri, this move was to ensure that archaeological matters could be more effectively controlled by the British, since they wielded more authority within the public works ministry.[7] Although Bell does not mention this episode in any of her surviving letters or diaries and does not say why she decided to move the department to that particular ministry, she was determined to conduct archaeological affairs in a certain manner. Therefore, her actions and her desire to have full control of archaeological matters would suggest that there is probably some truth in al-Husri's claim.

This clash between al-Husri and Bell, two very prominent and influential figures in early Iraqi political history, is indicative of the politics of archaeology of this period and was a pivotal moment in the Anglo-Iraqi struggle over the control of antiquities. The Iraqis sought a law favorable to the Iraqi state, while Bell strove to ensure that she, or the office of the Director of Antiquities, could have plenty of latitude in the execution of a law that would be lenient toward foreign excavations. It is a testament to British power and Bell's influence that despite some opposition, Bell was able to push through a law providing her with extensive powers in archaeological matters, particularly in determining the division of finds between Iraq and foreign excavators.

Bell's 1924 law provided that the excavator receive an "adequate" and "representative" share of all antiquities after the needs of the Iraqi Museum had been satisfied. This provision allowed for some discretion, since the terms *adequate* and *representative* are vague and subjective. The law stipulated that the director of antiquities would make the ultimate decision as to what constituted a "representative" share for the excavator. In the actual execution of the law, Bell went to the sites and inspected the findings to decide which objects should be kept in Iraq. As her letters reveal, she was torn in her allegiance. She had to remind herself that "in my capacity as Director of Antiquities, I am an Iraqi official and bound by the terms on which we gave the permit for excavation."[8] Although Bell was certainly committed to the Iraqi cause, she also helped foreign nationals to export large quantities of antiquities. However, at the same time, the Iraqi government was able to build up a great national collection at virtually no direct financial expenditure.

In order to house Iraq's new and growing antiquities collection, the Iraqi National Museum was established under the tutelage of Bell in 1923 and was open to the public for the first time in June 1926. At first the museum was quite small and housed relics mainly from pre-Islamic times. Al-Husri, for example, describes in his memoirs how shocked he was to find hardly any relics from Iraq's Islamic history during his first visit to the museum. A 1931 floor plan of the museum verifies this al-Husri account: only one room out of six contained objects from Iraq's Islamic period.[9]

Slowly but surely the Iraqis were beginning to become more interested in the ancient Mesopotamian history and antiquities. The British archaeologist Leonard Woolley noted and was surprised by the interest in his project shown in Baghdad. He writes, "I would like to remark specially on the interest shown by everyone in the work to be carried out by our expedition and on the practical manner in which this interest was manifested by the willingness of all to give every kind of assistance. The King was very affable and keen on the work."[10]

In the years 1921–1933, therefore, archaeology was primarily under the control of the British, who wrote the law, executed it, and held the final judiciary authority. At this stage most Iraqis were passive observers, yet some were starting to take a more active interest.

Early in 1933 Iraqi newspapers started to print stories that were critical of the state of archaeology in the country. In the paper *Sawt al-Iraq* (*Voice of Iraq*), an editorial entitled "*Our* Antiquities" (emphasis added) exemplifies this discussion. The tone of the editorial suggests that some Iraqis felt robbed of their historic treasures. It urged the government to follow more closely the division of archaeological finds: "May we throw a glance at our small museum and compare its contents with the objects unearthed in this country which have found their way into the museums which have been sending excavation missions into this country . . . and find out whether our share has been a fair one or otherwise?" The editors urged further that the government take measures to prepare Iraqis to study archaeology so that Iraq could effectively police its own antiquities.[11] Iraqi politicians also took notice and started to draft new, more restrictive antiquities legislation that would curtail the activities of foreign excavators.

Sati al-Husri was appointed director of antiquities in October 1934; he was the first Iraqi to hold that position. With al-Husri came a new orientation in the Department of Antiquities. Just as in his previous tenure in the Department of Education, al-Husri sought to make Iraqis aware of their Arab identity and its implications. For al-Husri one primary reason for the study of the nation's past was to inculcate national feeling in Arabs. With this goal in mind, he considered archaeology a political tool. During al-Husri's tenure practically all of the department's funds and energies were directed toward the restoration of Islamic monuments and the establishment of an Islamic museum. Al-Husri did not see much need for studying the ancient civilizations of Iraq that had been "buried under the sands of time for thousands of years [and] . . . to revert to those lost epochs was an attempt to revive . . . that which is dead and mummified." Ancient history seemed to him irrelevant for the present population.[12]

With al-Husri at the helm, Iraq's Department of Antiquities embarked on various projects that reflected his views of history. In February 1936 the Iraqi press reported that the Department of Antiquities planned to sponsor the first Iraqi excavation at the ruins of Wasit. The choice of Wasit marked a clear political and philosophical stance, given al-Husri's devotion to pan-Arab nationalism. Wasit was the capital of Iraq during the Ummayyad dynasty in the eighth century CE and was an important provincial city in the Abbassid period between the ninth and eleventh centuries.

His political leanings notwithstanding, al-Husri performed in 1936 his first division of artifacts with a foreign expedition. Being still under the authority of Bell's 1924 law, al-Husri pleasantly surprised the archaeologist Henri Frankfort. Frankfort wrote to the American Ambassador, "We had an excellent division . . . even of the exceptional objects we got a fair share."[13]

Despite protests from Western archaeologists and institutions, and in the face of some foreign diplomatic pressure, new antiquities legislation was brought before the Iraqi Parliament in 1936. The law contained a provision that all unique objects should be assigned to the Iraq Museum and all duplicate objects to the excavator. The spirit of this new law was similar to other such laws at the time. For example, in September 1937 the Sixth Committee of the League of Nations agreed on a resolution entitled "International Statute for Antiquities and Excavations," which emphasized that the ownership and the excavator's share should be determined by the internal legislation of the country. This resolution also declared that foreign excavators should be allowed a share of the finds, consisting of duplicates or objects that were similar to those already in possession of the home country's national museum.

Consequently, in the 1930s Iraqis came to appreciate the political potential of archaeology. Like Iraqi politics in general, the politics of archaeology was concerned with getting a bigger share, "controlling" Western activities, and proved to be very anti-Western in its stance. Although the Iraqi political leaders had little power to influence or curtail large, complex Western endeavors such as the oil industry or military affairs, archaeology was a convenient and reasonable fight for the Iraqis to pick. Hence, archaeology was deployed as a weapon in the battle against imperialism, which, during the early 1930s, was a significant issue in Iraq political thinking. The government was also able to defy Western diplomatic efforts and independently draft a new law that ensured the protection of its interests. Finally, the government started selecting which sites were to be excavated and which museums were to be built, as part of an overall political strategy. An example of how the Iraqis had become independent from the British in their archaeological affairs is that the British Foreign Office found it worthy of comment in its annual report of 1938 that new technical experts had been appointed in the Iraqi Department of Antiquities "without reference to HMG [His Majesty's Government]."[14]

The Independent and Sanctioned Stages 1941–2003

In the years 1941–2003, Iraqis experienced dizzying sequences in their governmental politics. During those years, numerous coup-d'états took place as well as several revolutions. In one of those clearings, Sati al-Husri fell out of favor and in 1941 fled the country. Shortly after World War II, Naji al-Asil became the director of antiquities and, along with two recent Iraqi graduates from foreign universities, Fuad Safar and Taha Baqir, organized the department along apolitical and scientific lines. Their first major projects were to excavate at the ruins of ancient Eridu and to initiate a major project for conservation of various important Islamic buildings.

The 1950s, an exciting period in the Iraqi art scene, were a time when the conscious development of a specific and unique Iraqi artistic vocabulary in the literary and visual arts took place—a time of fermentation and artistic vigor. During those years the work of the Baghdad Modern Art Group (Jama'et Baghdad lil Fann al-Hadith) became quite prominent and dominated the Iraqi scene, and the Institute of Fine Arts was a significant component of Iraqi intellectual life.

The Institute of Fine Arts spawned a contingent of artists of various kinds, but perhaps the most visible development was in the visual arts. During World War II, a large number of European and American Allied soldiers were based in Iraq. In the small but remarkable Polish contingency, there happened to be some acclaimed painters. Several important Iraqi painters, who later formed the influential 1950s Iraqi art group Al-Ruwad (The Pioneers), such as Faiq Hassan and Jewad Salim, sought out and studied with the Polish soldier-artists. The Poles encouraged the Iraqi artists to set aside their previously held artistic norms and instead to explore new horizons by working in an individualistic, expressionist manner.

In the years immediately after the war, the Iraqi visual arts, especially the Al-Ruwad group, really started to develop a conscious, distinct Iraqi style. The way these artists interpreted "Iraqi" was to depict nature, city, and village scenes and traditional village life. The painter and sculptor Jewad Salim, in particular, made deliberate attempts to incorporate ancient historical motifs in his art. Salim, who had studied in Paris (in

1938–1939) and Rome (in 1939–1940), often sought inspiration from the paradigms of the various periods of Iraqi history. For example, he incorporated Assyrian and Babylonian reliefs and Abbasid architectural design in his works of art. Salim had previously worked in the Department of Antiquities and was thus well aware of pre-Islamic and Islamic art forms. This synthesis and exploration is evident in his masterpiece *Nasb al-Hurriyah* (*The Monument of Freedom*), a gigantic bronze mural in downtown Baghdad. It contains twenty-five figures in which he combined Arabic characters with Sumerian and Babylonian forms clearly influenced by prevailing Western styles. It is at once universal and distinctively Iraqi.

Salim and other Iraqi artists at the time thus created cultural and nationalistic links with those earlier civilizations. They consciously and explicitly sought to "search for the features of the national personality in art" in order to connect and build upon earlier cultural phases. Ancient and medieval civilizations became "Iraqi" and highly relevant to modern citizens. Heritage or tradition was modernized, and modernity was perceived to be based on tradition.

This artistic experimentation was not confined to the visual arts. In literature, the Iraqi free-verse movement (*al-shi'r al-hurr*) started to make its appearance in the early 1950s. Poets such as Naziq al-Mala'ika, Badr Shakir al-Sayyab, and 'Abd al-Wahhab al-Bayyati "radically changed the form of Arabic poetry and constituted a direct and uncompromising challenge to the rules that had formed the traditional poetic canon."[15] This was a rejection of tradition and an indication of dissatisfaction with the old rigid, romantic practices. In many different ways, Iraqis were being inspired by multiple paradigms from the past that they utilized to define their Iraqiness.

During the 1958 revolution, the pro-British Hashemite Kingdom was overthrown, and the leader of the revolution, Brigadier Abd al-Karim Qasim, declared Iraq to be a republic. He established close ties with the Soviet Union and the rest of the Eastern Bloc and, more importantly, opposed the current pan-Arab trends advocated by Egypt's Gamal Abd al-Nasser. Qasim concentrated on building a sovereign Iraq, politically isolated from the rest of the Arab world. Iraq unveiled a new emblem and a new national flag with symbols from pre-Islamic Iraq. Large floats and displays based on ancient Mesopotamian history were featured prominently in the celebration of the first anniversary of the revolution. When Qasim was overthrown in 1963 by dissident factions within the military, led by Colonel Abd al-Salam Arif, Iraq once again entered into the pan-Arab dialogue and sought full union with Egypt.

During the presidency of Saddam Hussein, 1979–2003, an emphasis on and appreciation of Iraq's pre-Islamic history resurfaced. The full story of his fascinating, yet tragic, abuse of Iraq's ancient history remains to be written. It will be some years before we can expect a better understanding of Hussein's reign and the effects of his many abhorrent policies.

Ironically, Hussein came to power through the ruling Ba'th party, which was defined in the romantic and stirring language of its cofounder Michel Aflaq as an instrument to bring about Arab unity. A main feature in the party's platform is belief in the existence of a single Arab nation, defined by its language and the religion of Islam.

However, Hussein often looked far beyond the traditional Ba'thi historical view. Since the Iraqi Shi'is and Kurds are generally ambivalent about the Ba'thi pan-Arab doctrine, Hussein strove to find a more neutral plane on which to unite the country. The history of ancient Mesopotamia once again emerged as a useful tool, since it features civilizations, figureheads, and myths of nonsectarian appeal. The general public is not very familiar with the basic facts of that history (as compared with Islamic history), and its stories are not enmeshed in popular culture. Hence, it provided a convenient basis for the implementation of a new national identity.

Like so many features of his reign, Hussein's manipulation of archaeology was exaggerated and blatant. It is possible to argue that no government paid as much attention to archaeology as Hussein's. For him and his government, archaeology served one distinct purpose: to bolster his rule and legitimate his questionable foreign-policy actions. The Iraqi people associated archaeology and archaeological museums so much with his government's power that during times of instability and when people perceived his power to be waning, they plundered their local museums. For example, during the intifada following the Persian Gulf War in 1991 and in April 2003, when Hussein's government was clearly not in control of the streets, museums were ransacked. Although people undoubtedly had multiple motivations for these attacks, many were seeking revenge upon their government. The museums were symbols of Hussein's regime, and by attacking the museums, people were indirectly challenging the government's authority.

Hussein's government spent inordinate sums on rebuilding Iraqi archaeological sites and museums. The ostensible purpose was to preserve and maintain these historic sties and artifacts, but the real motivation seems to have been to glorify Hussein as the ultimate leader in Iraqi history.

Nowhere was this more evident than in the rebuilding of the ancient city of Babylon. Starting in 1982, Hussein and his government began to reconstruct the six-hundred-room palace of Nebuchadnezzar II. Upon the foundation that included ancient bricks with engravings praising Nebuchadnezzar, Hussein's government put about 50 million new bricks that contained inscriptions paying homage to Saddam Hussein "as the protector of Iraq" and as the one who rebuilt civilization and Babylon. Nearby, Hussein built an ostentatious new palace overlooking the site. It amounted to a claim that he and his rule were directly descendant from Nebuchadnezzar and the ancient Babylonians.

In numerous posters, murals, decorations, and paintings around the country, Hussein's image was omnipresent. In some of the depictions, he was shown alongside Nebuchadnezzar. Some had him facing Hammurabi, thus suggesting how just a ruler Hussein was. In others he was portrayed as a traditional Arab tribal leader. In the latter years of his reign, Hussein emphasized his Islamic identity. He started to build mosques and was seen more frequently praying or reciting the Qur'an.

In the Iraqi context, however, these many different depictions of Hussein were not mutually exclusive, nor was Hussein unique in utilizing many different motifs and paradigms from Iraq's history. In many ways, he was a culmination—albeit an exaggerated one—of a steady process of paradigmatic nationalism in Iraq. Iraq's national identity, so closely tied to its multifaceted ancient history and its archaeological heritage, is flexible and incorporates many different features, depending on the political circumstances.

The politics of archaeology in Iraq thus has proceeded hand in hand with the politics of nationalism, and the fate of Iraqi objects has been intrinsically tied to the political process, both international and domestic. As described above, archaeology went through several distinct stages to emerge as a component in nationalist ideology clearly identified with governmental power. After a stage of limited Iraqi interest, archaeology became a tool for anti-Westernism. It then served as a basis for a unified national identity that vacillated between pan-Arabism and Iraqi particularism. At times it has served in a "negative" stance (used to unite against something); more recently it has taken a "positive" stance (to reaffirm or redefine against Iraqis' historical selves). Ultimately, like all nationalisms, it sought some degree of unity, homogeneity, and solidarity with the very idea of the nation state.

The war that started in 2003 has, however, complicated the sense of belonging to an Iraqi national state. With large segments of the national collection now plundered, stolen, and lost, the destiny of Iraqi archaeological artifacts is unclear and complicated, just as the fortunes of the Iraqi political community are. The events of April 2003 were a reminder of how closely linked Iraq's political history is with its archaeological artifacts. The obvious connections between nationalism, politics, and archaeology in recent Iraqi history highlight how archaeology and history can and will be used and abused for political purposes, especially to promote a distinct national identity. The recent fate of Iraq's artifacts has been tragic, like that of the nation. And as the Iraqi nation seeks to rebuild itself and attain some form of political balance and stability, archaeological objects and Iraq's long and glorious history will no doubt emerge front and center in the debate over national identity.

Notes

1. Bernhardsson, *Reclaiming a Plundered Past.*
2. Makiyeh, *Republic of Fear*, 152.
3. Davis, *Memories of State.*
4. Gertrude Bell to her father, Hugh Bell, Mar. 18, 1909.
5. Gertrude Bell, letter of July 22, 1922, emphasis added.
6. Ibid., letter of Sept. 11, 1923.
7. al-Husri, *Mudhakkirati fi al-Iraq*, 2:181.
8. Gertrude Bell, letter of Mar. 6, 1925.
9. al-Husri, *Mudhakkirati fi al-Iraq*, 2:409.
10. Leonard Woolley, "Memorandum on Foreign Archaeological Expeditions in Iraq," BMCA 32/392, 1933, 44.
11. *Sawt al-Iraq* (Baghdad), May 14, 1933.
12. al-Husri, *Mudhakkirati fi al-Iraq*, 1:211–219, 2:277–280.
13. Henri Frankfort, Public Records Office, FO 371/1030/E1167, February 20, 1936.
14. "Iraq Annual Report," 1939, p. 7, FO 371/2204.
15. Deyoung, *Placing the Poet*, 192.

Bibliography

Primary Sources

British Museum Central Archives (BMCA), London
Gertrude Bell Letters, Robinson Library, University of Newcastle, U.K.
Iraq Government Gazette (Baghdad)
Public Records Office, Kew, U.K., Foreign Office (FO) 371
Sumer, Department of Antiquities, Baghdad

Secondary Accounts

al-'Azzawi, Abbas. *Ta'rikh al-'Iraq bayna al-ihtilalayn.* 8 vols. Baghdad, 1955.

al-Hasani, Abd al-Razzaq. *Ta'rikh al-wizarat al-'iraqiyyah.* 10 vols. Sidon, Lebanon, 1933–1967.

al-Husri, Sati. *Mudhakkirati fi al-Iraq* [My Memoirs in Iraq]. 2 vols. Beirut, 1967–1968.

Bahrani, Zainab. Conjuring Mesopotamia: Imaginative geography and a world past. In *Archaeology under Fire: Nationalism, Politics, and Heritage in the Eastern Mediterranean and Middle East,* ed. Lynn Meskell. London, 1998.

Baram, Amatzia. *Culture, History, and Ideology in the Formation of Ba'thist Iraq, 1968–89.* New York, 1991.

Basri, Abd al-Jabbar Daoud. *Al-Siyasah al-Thaqafiyah fi-al-Iraq* [The politics of culture in Iraq]. Baghdad, 1983.

Batatu, Hanna. *The Old Social Classes and the Revolutionary Movements of Iraq.* Princeton, NJ: 1978.

Bernhardsson, Magnus T. *Reclaiming a Plundered Past: Archaeology and Nation Building in Modern Iraq.* Austin, TX, 2005.

Dann, Uriel. *Iraq under Qassem: A Political History, 1958–1963.* New York, 1969.

Davis, Eric. *Memories of State: Politics, History, and Collective Identity in Iraq.* Berkeley, CA, 2005.

Davis, Eric. The museum and the politics of social control in modern Iraq. In *Commemorations: The Politics of National Identity,* ed. John R. Gillis. Princeton, NJ, 1994.

Deyoung, Terri. *Placing the Poet: Badr Shakir al-Sayyab and Post-Colonial Iraq.* Albany, NY, 1998.

Dodge, Toby. *Inventing Iraq: The Failure of Nation Building and a History Denied.* New York, 2003.

Fagan, Brian. *Return to Babylon.* Boston, 1979.

Fernea, Robert, and William Roger Louis, eds. *The Iraqi Revolution of 1958: The Old Social Classes Revisited.* London, 1991.

Gibson, McGuire. Cultural tragedy in Iraq: A report on the lootings of museums, archives, and sites. International Foundation for Art Research, www.ifar.org/tragedy.htm.

Hitchcock, Ann. Lessons in the fog: War and heritage preservation. *Museum News* 83 (3) (May–June 2004): 47–55.

Hudson, Kenneth. *Museums of Influence.* Cambridge, U.K., 1987.

Kabbani, Rana. *Europe's Myth of the Orient.* Bloomington, IN, 1986.

Khadduri, Majid. *Independent Iraq, 1932–1958.* London, 1960.

LaFranchi, Howard. Iraq's looted heritage makes a steady—if slow—combeback. *Christian Science Monitor,* Oct. 14, 2004.

Larsen, Mogens Trolle. *The Conquest of Assyria: Excavations in an Antique Land, 1840–1860.* London, 1996.

Lloyd, Seton. *The Interval: A Life in Near Eastern Archaeology*. Faringdon, U.K., 1986.

Longrigg, Stephen. *Iraq, 1900–1950*. Oxford, 1953.

Lowenthal, David. *The Past Is a Foreign Country*. Cambridge, U.K., 1985.

Makiyeh, Kenan. *Republic of Fear: The Inside Story of Saddam's Iraq*. New York, 1990. Originally published under the pseudonym Samir al-Khalil.

Marchand, Suzanne L. *Down from Olympus: Archaeology and Philhellenism in Germany, 1750–1970*. Princeton, NJ, 1996.

Marr, Phebe. *The Modern History of Iraq*. Boulder, CO, 1985.

Pallis, Svend Aage. *The Antiquity of Iraq: A Handbook of Assyriology*. Copenhagen, 1956.

Russell, John Malcolm. Report on the first UNESCO Cultural Heritage Mission to Baghdad, May 16–20, 2003. International Foundation for Art Research Web site, www.ifar.org/unesco.htm, originally posted July 2003.

Said, Edward. *Orientalism*. New York, 1978.

Schwab, Raymond. *The Oriental Renaissance: Europe's Rediscovery of India and the East, 1680–1880*. New York, 1984.

Sherman, Daniel, and Irit Rogoff, eds. *Museum Culture: Histories, Discourses, Spectacles*. Minneapolis, 1994.

Silverfarb, Daniel. *Britain's Informal Empire in the Middle East: A Case Study of Iraq, 1929–1941*. New York, 1986.

Simon, Reeva. The imposition of nationalism on a non-nation state: The case of Iraq during the interwar period, 1920–1941. In *Rethinking Arab Nationalism*, ed. James Jankowski and Israel Gershoni. New York, 1997.

Simon, Reeva. *Iraq between the Two World Wars: The Creation and Implementation of a Nationalist Ideology*. New York, 1986.

Sluglett, Peter. *Britain in Iraq, 1914–1932*. London, 1976.

Stocking, George W., ed. *Objects and Others: Essays on Museums and Material Culture*. Madison, WI, 1985.

Wallach, Janet. Desert Queen: The Extraordinary Life of Gertrude Bell: Adventurer, Advisor to Kings, Ally of Lawrence of Arabia. New York, 1996.

SEVEN

The Name Game

The Persian Gulf, Archaeologists, and the Politics of Arab-Iranian Relations

KAMYAR ABDI

Introduction

On November 14, 2004, the National Geographic Society (hereafter NGS) unveiled the eighth edition of its *Atlas of the World* (Lane-Miller 2004). Out of approximately seventeen thousand changes made in the eighth edition, a handful touched a sensitive nerve among Iranians around the world, reigniting a heated debate now more than a half century old. The source of the Iranian outrage was a decision by the NGS to use in its atlas the alternative secondary name Arabian Gulf, placing it in parentheses beneath the primary name Persian Gulf. Further, the atlas used the Arabic name Qeys for the Iranian island of Kish and added the Arabic name Sheykh Sho'eyb in parentheses beneath the name of the other Iranian island, Lavan. The atlas also labeled the islands of Greater and Lesser Tunb and Abu Musa "Occupied by Iran (claimed by U.A.E. [United Arab Emirates])" (fig. 7.1).

In the following weeks, a flood of e-mails protesting these changes began arriving at the NGS office in Washington, D.C., from Iran and expatriate Iranians around the world (Ala 2004). Accusations sparked over Internet forums and chat rooms, labeling the NGS "anti-Iranian," referring

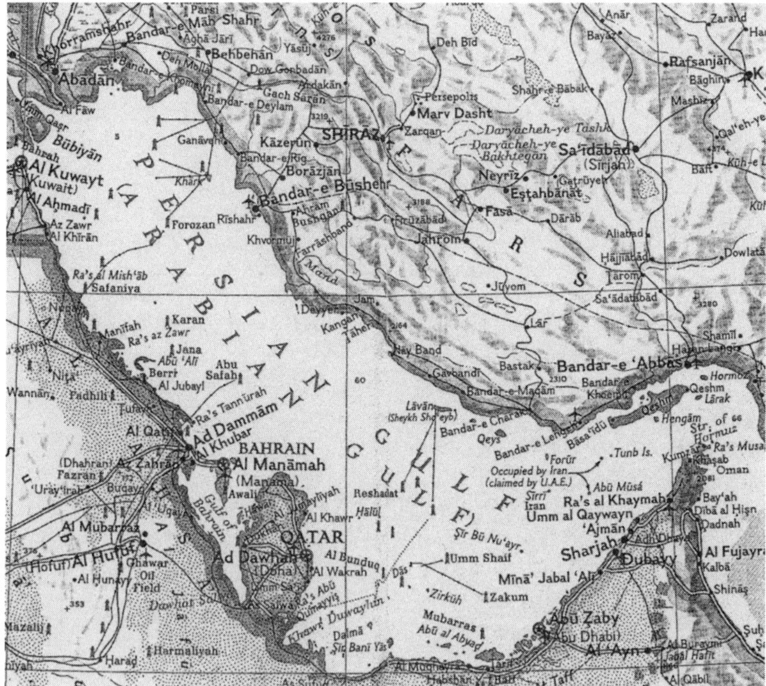

Figure 7.1. The original version of the map of the Persian Gulf region as it appeared in the eighth edition of the National Geographic Society's *Atlas of the World*

to a "sellout to Arab sheikhs' oil dollars," and even calling the NGS action "a Zionist plot to create division among Muslim nations" (Theodoulou 2004). The NGS was also accused of "selling fabricated history to Arabs" (Noor 2004). Iranians in Tehran and Los Angeles staged demonstrations to protest the changes. An online petition to reverse the changes had more than thirty thousand signatures (Anonymous 2004a). The NGS Web site was allegedly hacked, and "Arabian Gulf" was Google-bombed (Anonymous 2004b) (fig. 7.2).

After these grassroots actions, the matter gradually assumed a politically international dimension. On November 21, a week after the atlas appeared, the Iranian Ministry of Culture banned sales of the *National Geographic Magazine* in Iran and would not permit NGS reporters to enter the country (Anonymous 2004c). An invitation to a *National Geographic Magazine* editor to serve on a jury in a photo festival in Iran was withdrawn (Anonymous 2004d). In November and December, several Iranian Members of Parliament, parties, and organizations lodged official

*Other names for the Persian Gulf
Gulf of Basra

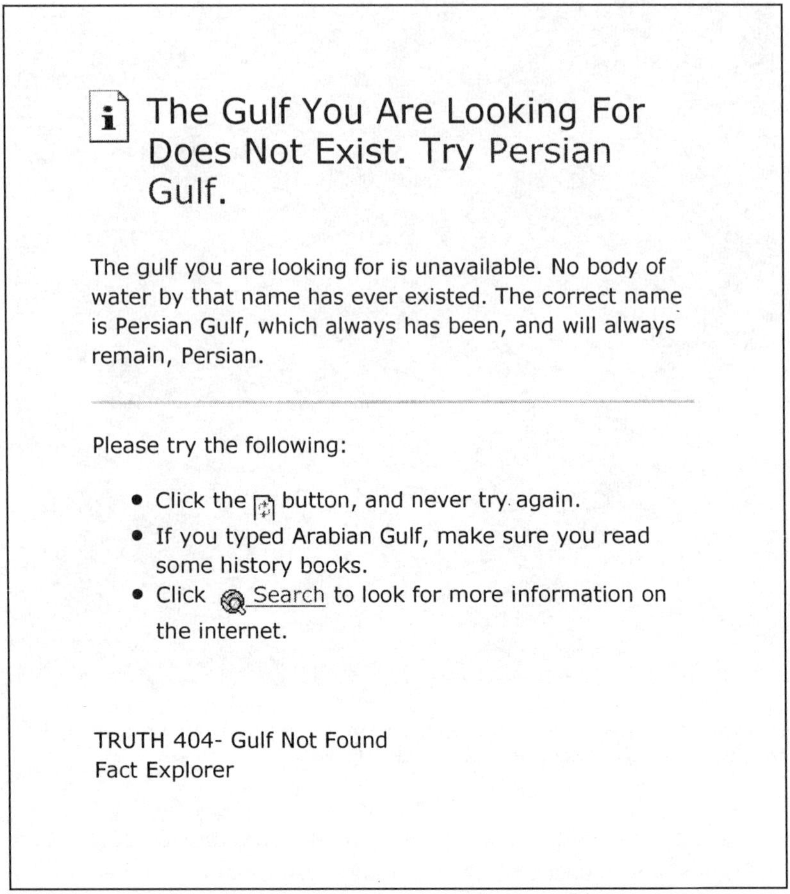

The Gulf You Are Looking For Does Not Exist. Try Persian Gulf.

The gulf you are looking for is unavailable. No body of water by that name has ever existed. The correct name is Persian Gulf, which always has been, and will always remain, Persian.

Please try the following:

- Click the button, and never try again.
- If you typed Arabian Gulf, make sure you read some history books.
- Click Search to look for more information on the internet.

TRUTH 404- Gulf Not Found
Fact Explorer

Figure 7.2. "Arabian Gulf" Google-bombed

protests against the NGS (Anonymous 2004e, 2004f); the Iranian Ministry of Foreign Affairs submitted a letter of protest to the NGS (Anonymous 2004g) and organized an exhibit of Persian Gulf historical maps (Anonymous 2004h).

On a more academic level, Iran received confirmation from UNESCO that "according to the existing documents in the UN the water way between the Arabian Peninsula and Iran is called the Persian Gulf" (Anonymous 2004i). Meanwhile, the Iranian Ministry of Culture announced plans to hold the first national Persian Gulf festival (Anonymous 2004j), and the Iranian Cultural Heritage and Tourism Organization disclosed its intention to build a chain of Persian Gulf museums along the Iranian coast (Anonymous 2004k), starting in Bushehr (Anonymous 2004l). Further, some one hundred Iranian and foreign scholars participating in the second international Iranology Conference in Tehran in December condemned the attempt to change the name of the Persian Gulf (Anonymous 2004m). At least two archaeologists, Ahmad Hasan Dani of Quaid-i-Azam University in Pakistan (Anonymous 2004n) and Ernie Haerinck of Ghent University in Belgium (Anonymous 2004o), denounced attempts to change the name of the Persian Gulf, and an ancient-history scholar, Touraj Daryaee of California State University, Fullerton, withdrew his membership from the NGS (Anonymous 2004p).

Facing mounting criticism, the NGS released a statement emphasizing that "while National Geographic considers 'Persian Gulf' to be the primary name, it has been the Society's cartographic practice to display a secondary name in parentheses when use of such a name has become commonly recognized" (Anonymous 2004q). On the question of the islands of Greater and Lesser Tunb and Abu Musa, the statement explained, "National Geographic's research determined that these islands are currently the subject of a dispute between Iran and the United Arab Emirates." The NGS statement failed to elaborate why Arabic names were used for the Iranian islands of Kish and Lavan.

Various Iranians, including representatives from the National Iranian American Council; members of the Iranian delegation to the UN; and Reza Pahlavi, son and heir of the late shah of Iran; met with NGS officials to discuss the matter. In his meeting with Reza Pahlavi, John Fahey, president and CEO of NGS, assured that "his organization was respectful and fully cognizant of the level and depth of sentiment among Iranians on the matter . . . [and that it was] in the midst of an in depth study and reflection on the merits of the use of a secondary name for the Persian Gulf" (Anonymous 2004r). In private conversations, however, the NGS officials stressed that they could not ignore the voices of millions of Arabs. In response, a sarcastic question was asked: if the NGS was so concerned with the Arab opinion, why did it not insert "Occupied Palestine" in parentheses under the name of Israel in the atlas (Hosseini 2004)?

Finally, on December 28, the NGS offered a written apology to Iran and expressed its readiness to correct the mistake (Anonymous 2004s). In a proposal to the National Iranian American Council, the NGS offered to completely delete the phrase "occupied by Iran" in reference to the islands of Greater and Lesser Tunb and Abu Musa and to use the Iranian names for the islands of Kish and Lavan. On the name of the Persian Gulf, NGS offered to use only this name on most of its maps and delete "Arabian Gulf" in parentheses, but to insert in a small font "Historically

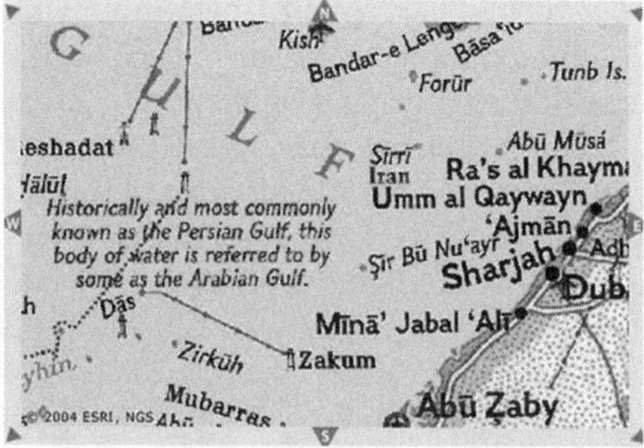

Figure 7.3. The modified version of the map of the Persian Gulf region as it appeared in the National Geographic Society Web site after Iranian objections

and most commonly known as the Persian Gulf, this body of water is referred to by some as the Arabian Gulf" and add an explanatory note on the political roots of the name Arabian Gulf (Anonymous 2004t).

These changes went into effect on December 30 (fig. 7.3) (Anonymous 2004u). Although the Iranian foreign minister called this a victory for every Iranian (Anonymous 2004v), some complained that there were still thousands of copies of the atlas in circulation with the objectionable names and phrases (Anonymous 2004w). Further, some argued that the explanatory note that NGS would be inserting in the online atlas would still give the name Arabian Gulf some sort of legitimacy (Anonymous 2004x). In the meantime, the NGS tried to downplay the political ramifications of the most recent changes under pressure from the Iranians, arguing that its maps undergo revision on a regular basis (Anonymous 2004y).

Why did such an unprecedented indignation arise on the part of Iranians, uniting a deeply divided community scattered around the world, with many religious, ethnic, political, and cultural orientations? What was so important about these NGS changes, given that names other than Persian Gulf have been around for several decades and are indicated on many other maps and atlases with international circulation?

One can think of several reasons for the Iranian outrage. First, for a long time, the NGS has been one of the very few organizations of international reputation consistently using the name Persian Gulf. The sudden change left many Iranians in a state of despair, fearing the loss of one of the last bastions of the name Persian Gulf. One should bear in mind that although the NGS is a private organization, many Iranians are under the false impression that, because of the word "National" in its title and because it is based in the United States, the NGS is affiliated with the U.S. government and therefore represents the official U.S. opinion. This concern makes sense in light of the fact that, in an ironic turn of events, the United States, despite tumultuous relations with Iran during the past quarter century, is one of a very few governments in the world formally banning the use in its official documents of any name other than Persian Gulf for the body of water in question.

More important, perhaps, is an element internal to Iranian culture. In a society so accustomed to conspiracy theories, the NGS action has all the usual suspects: Arabs, whom most Iranians hold responsible for the erosion of Iran's pre-Islamic glory and who, collectively, are believed to be the archenemy of Iranians; and the United States, which has been a thorn in Iran's side for some twenty-five years. Throw in the British, who Iranians believe are responsible, one way or another, for every problem in the Middle East, and you have all the ingredients for a perfect conspiracy theory. No wonder some of the debates on the Internet hinted at the possibility of Arab involvement in the NGS action. But even more significantly, Iranians still have open wounds from the 1980–1988 war with Iraq, a war that, in the collective consciousness of Iranians, regardless of political or social background, was imposed on Iran by an Arab state that received support and blessing from other Arab states, the United States, and the European powers (Rejaee 1997).

It is not my intention to present here the history of the name of the Persian Gulf, as that history has been documented in detail (see Wilson 1928; Eqtedari 1966; Madani 1978; Mashkour 1990) and endorsed several times. The United Nations endorsed the name twice: first by its Arab member states pursuant to the document UNAD 311/Gen on March 5, 1971, and a second time pursuant to the document UNLA 45.8.2 (C) on August 10, 1984. Further, the UN Conference on the Standardization of Geographical Names has endorsed the name Persian Gulf every five years. Moreover, a circular issued by the UN General Secretariat on August 14, 1994, contained a reminder to adhere to "the approved expression 'Persian Gulf' in all documents, correspondence and publications issued by the Secretariat" and affirmed "commitment to use [of] this expression in full, that is, Persian Gulf, and the inadequacy and incorrectness of adopting the term 'Gulf' alone, even in cases of repetition."

My purpose in this chapter is, rather, to investigate the broader nationalist and political contexts within which names other than Persian Gulf have emerged in the past fifty years and to explore the stances archaeologists working in the region have taken in response to these developments. I first examine the relations between Iran and Arabs vis-à-vis the Persian Gulf and the role of the British in shaping the geopolitical landscape of the region. Second, I look at the development of Arab nationalism in the region, along with its role in claiming the Persian Gulf as part of the Arab world. Finally, I consider the role the archaeological community, especially Western archaeologists, has assumed amid volatile Arab-Iranian relations.

Iranians, Arabs, and the British in the Persian Gulf

For more than two thousand years, ancient Mesopotamians referred to what is today known as the Persian Gulf as the Lower Sea. In the late sixth century BCE, Darius I, in his Suez inscription, referred to "the sea which goes from Persia" (Lecoq 1997: 248). While it is generally thought that this is the first reference to the body of water now called Persian Gulf identifying it as Persian, it seems that what Darius had in mind was in fact a larger geographic notion not unlike the Greek "Erythraean Sea," which included the Persian Gulf, the western Indian Ocean, and the Red Sea as one massive body of water. It was in fact Hecataeus of Miletus who coined the term *Persikos kolpos* (Persian gulf) in his *Periodos Ges* sometime around 500 BCE. This name was adopted by later geographers in various forms in different languages (e.g., Persikon Kaitas, Persicus Sinus, Al-Khalij al-Fars) and became the common name for the body of water between what is today Iran and the Arabian Peninsula.

The common use of the name Persian Gulf owes much to the fact that for most of the past twenty-five hundred years Iran (ancient Persia) has been the major regional power in the Persian Gulf littoral. From the sixteenth century, however, other powers began to arrive on the shores of the Persian Gulf. First the Ottomans came, and with them the new name of Basra Körfezi (the Gulf of Basra) for the Persian Gulf, in reference to the city of Basra, the seat of the Ottoman province of Basra. But this name appeared only in Ottoman sources and did not gain international recognition until it was revived by Arab nationalists of the 1920s and 1930s who were trying to avoid using the name Persian Gulf (see below).

Also arriving in the Persian Gulf, from the sixteenth century onward, were the colonial European powers: first the Portuguese and then the Dutch, the French, and the British; the British ultimately prevailed as the dominant colonial power in the region (Kelly 1968). Although the British adopted a predominantly diplomatic approach, punctuated with episodes of military pressure toward Iran to secure their interests in the Persian Gulf, they also tried to harness various Arab tribes and sheikhdoms on the southern shores of the Persian Gulf, and this effort proved to be a challenge. In order to protect maritime traffic to and from India, the British had to engage in negotiations with various Arab tribes, while often using military force to keep them at bay. Eventually, in 1820, the British pressed Arab tribes and sheikhdoms into a General Treaty of Peace, by which the Arabs agreed to cease plunder and piracy by sea and land (Dubuisson 1978). An Ottoman attempt to exert more influence in the Persian Gulf in the late nineteenth century (Anscombe 1997) invited more assertive British involvement that led to the signing of the Exclusive Agreement in 1892 and turned Trucial sheikhdoms (the predecessor to the United Arab Emirates) into British protectorates (Albaharna 1975: 29). The takeover of the southern parts of the Ottoman Empire after World War I paved the way for the British to create the states of Iraq and Transjordan and consolidated British control over Arab sheikhdoms. After World War I, the British continued to maintain political and military presence in the Persian Gulf region, primarily to secure immense oil resources recently discovered in the region. That discovery gradually attracted the United States also to the Persian Gulf (Palmer 1992).

The presence of the British in the Persian Gulf continued until December 1, 1971, when they terminated their treaties with Arab sheikdoms and withdrew from the Persian Gulf, allowing for the states of Bahrain, Qatar, Kuwait, and the United Arab Emirates to formally declare their independence (Balfour-Paul 1991). The British withdrawal and a perceived Soviet threat created a power vacuum in the Persian Gulf that none of the Arab states of the time were able to fill. Therefore, with implicit U.S. and British blessing, the shah of Iran, the only regional authority with the requisite military power and political weight, in spite of Arab acrimony, assumed the self-appointed position of guardian of the Persian Gulf. As part of asserting its regional authority, one day before British withdrawal, on November 30, 1971, Iran moved onto the island of Abu Musa following prior arrangements with a reluctant sheikh of Sharjah (Amin 1981: 221) and took control of the Greater and Lesser Tunb islands from Ras al-Khaimah.

Iran has had claims on the southern shores of the Persian Gulf and its islands, including Bahrain, since pre-Islamic times (Nafisi 1954; Nish'at 1965, Eqtedari 1966). In more recent history, Iran reasserted its claims in the sixteenth century when the Safavids ejected the Portuguese from the Persian Gulf with British naval support. Following the collapse of the Safavid Empire in 1722, the Arab tribes of Oman and Ras al-Khaimah took advantage of Iran's weakness and occupied many of the islands in the Persian Gulf, including the Tunbs and Abu Musa, using them as a base for piracy. Nadir Shah Afshar and Karim Khan Zand succeeded in reasserting Iran's presence in the Persian Gulf, but it fell to the British to quell the Arab piracy with a combination of military suppression and diplomatic treaties.

In 1887, in response to increased Ottoman presence in the western parts of the Persian Gulf (Anscombe 1997), the Qajars began asserting more influence in the eastern Persian Gulf. As part of their new policy in the Persian Gulf, the Qajars banished the northern branch of the Qawasim (the ruling families of Sharjah and Ras al-Khaimah) from their semiautonomous base at Bandar-i Lingah and the nearby Siri Island, the last of the strongholds they maintained, from their pirate days, on the northern shores of the Persian Gulf. In response, in 1903 the British encouraged the Qawasim to raise their flags on the islands of Greater Tunb and Abu Musa, but these were removed by the Iranian customs police. In return, the British used the threat of force against Iran to reinstate the Qawasim flag on the islands (Schofield 2001: 224). For the next few decades, Iran and Britain played a game of cat and mouse over these three islands, putting up their own flag and taking down the other's flag, ignoring each other's claims, and threatening to use force if necessary (Mojtahed-Zadeh 1994). The quarrel between Iran and Britain over the islands came to an end with the British withdrawal from the Persian Gulf in 1971. The United Arab Emirates, however, claimed sovereignty over the islands after their independence (El-Issa 1998) and, most recently, renewed their claims in 1992 following attempts by some people, including some citizens of the U.A.E., to enter Abu Musa (Schofield 1997: 150–154; Mojtahed-Zadeh 1998: 292–294).

Iran's more recent claims over Bahrain also date to the Safavid period, when Iran removed the Portuguese from this archipelago (Adamiyat 1955). Iran retained Bahrain until 1717, when it was captured by the imam of Oman, only to be recaptured by Nadir Shah and then lost again in 1783, this time to the 'Utubi Arab tribe from the mainland. Threats from Omanis and Wahhabis and rival claims by the Ottoman Empire and Iran prompted the 'Utubi sheikh of Bahrain to enter a protectorate treaty with the British in 1861, according to which, in return for British protection against external aggression, Bahrain would abstain from the prosecution of war, piracy, and slavery by sea (Aitchison 1933: 234–235). Iran, however, maintained its claim, arguing that Britain had recognized Iran's sovereignty over Bahrain once in 1822 and again in 1869 (Adamiyat 1955). Iran once again became concerned with Bahrain in 1905, when Shi'a residents of Bahrain were attacked by a mob provoked by Sunni religious leaders. The British discouraged Iran from intervention but assured protection of the Shi'ites by inducing the sheikh of Bahrain to deport some of the more fanatical Sunni leaders (Marlowe 1962: 258n6).

The quarrel between Iran and Britain over Bahrain continued throughout most of the twentieth century, and as late as the 1960s, letters bearing Bahraini stamps were treated by Iran as unstamped and returned, while passports bearing endorsements or a visa issued by British authorities for any of the sheikhdoms were not accepted in Iran (Foreign Office 1953: 20). The question of Bahrain came to a conclusion in 1970, when the shah dropped Iran's claims over Bahrain and recognized its sovereignty.

Iran's ambitions in the Persian Gulf continued throughout the 1970s, culminating in dispatching troops to help quell a rebellion by a separatist group in Dhofar, Oman. This group, initially called the Popular Front for the Liberation of the Arabian Gulf, started out as a movement aimed at ejecting the British from the Persian Gulf and spreading revolution to conservative states on the Arabian Peninsula, but when Qaboos bin-Said removed his father from the throne of Oman in 1970 in a coup assisted by the British, the movement, now called the Popular Front for the Liberation of Oman and the Arab Gulf and later the People's Front for the Liberation of Oman, increasingly shifted its belligerence toward the Omani government (Halliday 1975: 316–404). In addition to British troops, Sultan Qaboos received support from the shah, who in 1973 dispatched an Iranian army brigade, along with helicopters and artillery, to assist the Omanis in suppressing the rebellion. The rebels put up a fight against a far superior Omani-Iranian joint force for another two years before being finally subdued, with remnants fleeing to the People's Democratic Republic of Yemen (Peterson 1977).

Needless to say, Arab states viewed Iran's growing influence in the Persian Gulf region as a threat. Iraq, in particular, considering itself the stronghold of Arab nationalism in the region (see below), argued that the Arab states should preserve the Arab nature of the Persian Gulf from what was described as a systematic Iranian invasion and infiltration into the Arab lands and encouraged Arab states to repel the invader (Iran) and to preserve the Arabism of the gulf (Abdulghani 1984: 77–78). Facing the growing threat of Iranian nationalism in the Persian Gulf, Iraq described Iran's actions as "dreams of grandeur that drive them [the Iranians] to adopt policies of territorial aggrandizement in order to re-establish an empire which has been dead and buried since the time of Alexander the Great" (Abdulghani 1984: 92).

The 1979 revolution in Iran drastically changed the political configuration of the region. After the collapse of the imperial regime, the new revolutionary government disassociated Iran from military alliance with

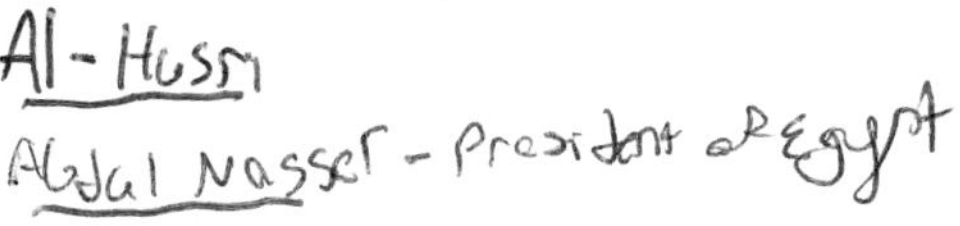

the United States, broke off relations with Israel, and withdrew its forces from Dhofar. The islands of Greater and Lesser Tunb and Abu Musa, however, remained under Iranian control. In the chaotic months after the revolution, the early revolutionary government sent mixed messages about its territorial claims in the Persian Gulf vis-à-vis Arab states. In 1979, shortly after the revolution, Sadeq Rouhani, a senior clergyman, issued threats of annexation against Bahrain, but Sadeq Khalkhali, the chief justice of the Islamic Revolutionary Courts, announced that Iran was contemplating evacuating the islands, a statement immediately denied by the Iranian Ministry of Foreign Affairs (Amin 1981: 28).

While in some quarters in the Islamic world the Iranian Revolution was hailed as ushering in a new era of pan-Islamism, it nonetheless led to apprehension among conservative Arab states, especially those on the Persian Gulf, which feared the spread of revolutionary sentiments to their countries (Menshari 1990). Partly to prevent this from happening, Iraq, now firmly under Saddam Hussein, launched a massive military campaign over its twelve-hundred-kilometer border with Iran on September 22, 1980. By the following month, Iraqi forces advanced into Khuzestan and other Iranian provinces bordering Iraq. In a letter submitted to the UN on September 25, Iraq stated that it had no expansionist ambitions in Iran, but in its communiqué to the Arab League, it declared that it was fighting in the name of Arab nations against a non-Arab state to liberate part of the Arab land occupied by Iran. This was a reference to the long-held claim by Arab nationalists that Khuzestan, the province in southwestern Iran, was an Arab land that, like Palestine, had been occupied by a foreign power (see Ramazani 1972: 41 for a brief background). Most Arab states, including those on the Persian Gulf, publicly declared their support for Iraq (Lotfian 1997).

In a series of military campaigns over 1981–1982, Iran managed to take back most of the land occupied by Iraq and even advanced into Iraqi territory, but the war dragged on until 1988, when Iran finally submitted to UN Resolution 598, calling for a cease-fire. During the eight years of the Iran-Iraq War, relations between Iran and Arab states on the Persian Gulf were tense at best, with the latter supporting Iraq both politically and financially in its war effort against Iran. In 1981 Kuwait, Saudi Arabia, Bahrain, Qatar, the U.A.E., and Oman formed the Majlis al-Ta'avon al-doval al-Khalij al-'Arabiya, commonly known in the West as the Gulf Cooperation Council (GCC) (Hollis 1993). While primarily aimed at boosting political cohesion among Arab states on the Persian Gulf, the GCC took steps to increase the military power of its members in light of a perceived Iranian threat. But, as examples such as the Tanker

War of 1984–1988 and the Persian Gulf wars of 1990–1991 and 2003 demonstrate, these states have often relied on Western, especially U.S., military support in times of crisis. The GCC thus proved to be a gateway for Western powers, especially the United States, to gain a foothold in the Persian Gulf for the first time since the British withdrawal, a development that Iran deeply resented (Ramazani 1990).

As relations between Arab states on the Persian Gulf and Iran began to improve after the Iran-Iraq War, the Arab states' relations with Iraq turned sour, culminating in Iraq's invasion of Kuwait in 1990 and the subsequent 1990–1991 Persian Gulf War. In the meantime, Iran replaced its ideologically driven attitude toward Arab states on the Persian Gulf with one more concerned about commercial and economic cooperation. Deep-rooted nationalist sentiments, however, proved difficult to overcome.

Arab Nationalism and the Persian Gulf

The pivotal role of the British in carving Arab states out of the Ottoman Empire after World War I has been subject to much study (e.g., Silverfarb 1994; Marr 2004; Simon and Tejirian 2004). Arab states in the Persian Gulf region, in particular, owed much to the British. It was British interference in the Persian Gulf that transformed Arab tribes, which were traditionally engaged in nomadic pastoralism, small-scale agriculture, maritime trade, and piracy, into sheikhdoms that ultimately formed the basis of modern Arab nation-states in the region. The British literally drew the blueprints for these states, defined their territorial boundaries (Wilkinson 1991), supported local sheikhs and later the rulers of the newly created states, and transformed their rudimentary economies with the help of massive oil revenues. Arguably, the initiative for creating a national history and identity for these countries was also undertaken by the British through conducting archaeological fieldwork and establishing archaeological services in the newly formed Arab states. This enterprise began in Iraq, where the remains of ancient Mesopotamia were coveted and unearthed.

The disintegration of the Ottoman Empire and the creation of Arab states in the Persian Gulf region coincided with rising tides of nationalism among Arab intellectuals (Dawn 1971; Khalidi et al. 1991; Jankowski and Gershoni 1997; Dawisha 2003). Having captured the southern provinces of the Ottoman Empire, the British created the state of Iraq by putting together the three Ottoman provinces of Mosul, Baghdad, and

Basra (Simon and Tejirian 2004). In the first decades of its existence, the new Iraqi state attempted to construct a national identity to serve as the basis of political hegemony (Simon 1997). The credit for formulating a doctrine of Arab nationalism in Iraq goes to a number of Arab intellectuals who emerged from the ashes of the Ottoman Empire. Two important figures in the early history of Arab nationalism in Iraq—Sati' al-Husri and Darwish al-Miqdadi—played an important role in first attempting to change the name of the Persian Gulf.

Abu-Khaldun Sati' al-Husri (1881–1968), considered one of the founders of Arab nationalism (Cleveland 1971) and described as the "intellectual prophet of Arab nationalism" (Dawisha 2003: 49), was born in Yemen to Syrian parents and studied political science and management in Istanbul during Ottoman times. Husri began his post-Ottoman political career as minister of communication after Syria gained independence. But after the French takeover of Syria, Husri moved with King Faysal to Iraq, where he served in the newly founded Iraqi government and taught at the Higher Teachers College (al-Husri 1967–1968). As the director general of education, a position to which he was appointed directly by King Faysal, Husri was instrumental in organizing Iraq's educational, intellectual, and scientific activities, thereby attaining the informal title of "Father of Iraqi public education" (al-Hadid 1932: 237). In these years, Husri was responsible for composing the curriculum, selecting textbooks, and indoctrinating the upcoming generation of Iraqi school children in Arab nationalism (Simon 1986: 75–84).

As an early ideologue of Arab nationalism, Husri stressed two interwoven principles as defining characteristics of a nation: a common language and a shared history. According to Husri, the Arabic language, originating from the Arabian Peninsula in ancient times and protected from outside influence, and the long Arab history, extending to times before the arrival of Islam, formed the essential elements of Arab national identity (Cleveland 1971: 123–126). Husri adopted the notion of *Volk* from German historiography of the 1930s that stressed an early ancestral nation that dazzled the world and disseminated the hallmarks of civilization. While German historians of the time considered early German tribes as the source of civilization, Husri argued that such a role belonged to the Semites from the ancient Near East, or what he called pre-Islamic Arabs (Simon 1997: 89).

While at the Higher Teachers College, Husri hired Darwish al-Miqdadi, a Palestinian graduate of the American University in Beirut and one of the early ideologues of Arab nationalism (Dawn 1988a, 1988b). Miqdadi was responsible for introducing the notion of a nuclear "Arab

homeland" comprising Iraq, Syria, and Arabia (al-Miqdadi 1931), based on the idea of the Fertile Crescent that was first introduced by James Henry Breasted (1916). Already a popular work among Arab nationalists with knowledge of English, Breasted's book soon appeared in an Arabic translation (Birastid 1926) and was well received in Arab lands. Miqdadi's notion of the Arab homeland received full elaboration in his *Tarikh al-Umma al-'Arabiyya* (*History of the Arab Nation*) (al-Miqdadi 1931), which soon became a standard textbook in Iraq, as well as in Syria and Palestine, and continued to influence several generations of students (Simon 1986: 42). Following Husri, Miqdadi stressed the importance of language in defining a nation, and he further argued that all the Semitic-speaking peoples of the ancient Near East, from the Akkadians, Babylonians, and Assyrians to the Hyksos, were the ancestors of the Arab people and part of a "Semito-Arab" culture.

The Semito-Arab homeland was, according to Miqdadi, occupied by Semitic-speaking people from earliest times and surrounded on both sides by hostile Aryans. From the West came a series of Aryans, starting with Alexander and the Greeks and continuing all the way to the British and the French, who held Arab lands in their control. But a greater Aryan threat to the Arabs was to their east, the Persians, who, according to Miqdadi, had a long history of aggression toward Arab lands, desiring to exert revenge on Arabs for the loss of their glory, and who had humiliated Arabs on a number of occasions and corrupted their culture (al-Miqdadi 1931; Dawn 1988b: 72). It is not surprising, then, to see that Miqdadi deliberately avoided the name Persian Gulf in his writings, using instead the defunct Ottoman name al-Khalij al-Basra (Gulf of Basra). In this, Miqdadi was perhaps inspired by Husri, who, in his extensive research and publications on the historical geography of Arab lands, also avoided using the name Persian Gulf, always referring to the "Gulf of Basra" or the "Gulf of Qatif" or simply "the Gulf" (al-Husri 1957: map 2, 196–198, 204–205).

Miqdadi's influence, transmitted to the upcoming Arab generation through his books, was immense (Ziadeh 1952; Faris 1954), laying the foundations for the Nasserism and Ba'athism of the next generation (Carré 1979) and sowing the seeds of antagonism toward westerners and Iranians among Arab nationalists (for the case of Iraq, see Bengio 1998: 127–145).

Arab nationalism received a major boost in 1952 with the rise of Gamal 'Abd al-Nasser in Egypt (Jankowski 1997) and in 1958 with the coup in Iraq; both developments expanded Arab nationalism to the eastern wing of the Arab world. The Persian Gulf was the most important

artery linking Iraq and the Arabian Peninsula to India and the Far East. Animosity toward the West, especially Britain and the United States, and Israel as a Western crony in the Arab land, was emphasized in the Arab nationalism espoused by Nasser. Iran was also branded a Western collaborator, especially after the 1953 British- and U.S.-backed coup that ousted the nationalist government of Mohammad Mossadiq and reinstalled the shah.

The 1960 de facto recognition of Israel by the shah worsened the already sour relationship between Iran and Arab states. Egypt broke off diplomatic relations with Iran and encouraged other Arab states to do the same. While few Arab states complied, the Arab League and most Arab states condemned Iran's recognition of Israel. Meanwhile, Egypt under Nasser unleashed a war of words against Iran as it was trying to expand its influence in the Persian Gulf through political and economic channels, a development that Iran observed with much suspicion (Ramazani 1972: 35–41). Egypt and Iran even engaged in a brief proxy war in 1962, when Egypt supported rebels in Yemen while Iran backed the monarchists (Schmidt 1968: 162, 280). Nasser pursued his ambitions in the Persian Gulf until 1967, when Egypt's defeat by Israel greatly diminished his prestige and curtailed his expansionist ambitions. As one observer pointed out: "The triumph of Nasserism in the Arab world, leading to effective Egyptian control of the Arab shores of the Gulf, would almost inevitably have meant an Egyptian attempt to make of the Persian Gulf an Arab lake. To Iranians this intention was forecast in Arab nationalist reference to the 'Arabian Gulf'. The failure of Abdul Nasr's wider ambitions was therefore a source of unmitigated satisfaction in Iran, where it was realized that the term 'Arabian Gulf' represents, not the shadow of an impending reality, but the ghost of a lost cause" (Marlowe 1962: 206–207).

It is commonly believed that it was Nasser who initiated the name Al-khalij al-'Arabi (Arabian Gulf). Whether this is true or not, it was thanks to him that this name gained popularity in Arab lands. In his vigorous speeches, Nasser introduced slogans such as "al-umma al-'arabiya min al-muhit al-atlasi ila al-khalij al-'arabi" (the Arab nation from the Atlantic Ocean to the Arabian Gulf) to call for Arab unity. His parlance was soon adopted by other Arab nationalists and used in spoken and written word (Dawisha 2003: 185). For example, the Iraqi propaganda machine, boosted by the 1958 coup, soon unleashed a war of words against anyone purportedly opposed to the Arabs, including Iranians, and regularly called the Persian Gulf Al-khalij al-'Arabi.

By the 1960s, all Arab states passed laws and issued decrees making the use of the name Arabian Gulf mandatory in their publications and communications with the rest of the world (Albaharna 1975: 1n1). Iran, considering the name Persian Gulf part of its national heritage, fought back by taking the matter to the UN and receiving an endorsement pursuant to the document UNAD 311/Gen on March 5, 1971, signed by all members, including the Arab states. Despite signing the UN resolution, Arab states, especially those bordering the Persian Gulf, continued to use and promote the name Arabian Gulf or a simple reference to "the Gulf." Such usage was evident in numerous Arab publications and in the 1974 establishment of the Center for Arabian Gulf Studies at Basra University, with its specialized journal *Al-Khalij al-'Arabi*; in the 1974 launching of Gulf Air, the national airline of Bahrain, Qatar, and Oman; in the 1979 founding of the Arabian Gulf University in Bahrain; in the 1978 funding of the Centre for Arab Gulf Studies at the University of Exeter (Pridham 1988), renamed the Institute of Arab and Islamic Studies in 1999, with MA and PhD programs in "Arab Gulf Studies"; and in the 1982 institution of the Gulf Cooperation Council (see above) and even the Arabian Gulf Rugby Football Union in 1974. Perhaps the most audacious move was made by the Iraqi Revolutionary Command Council in 1977 when it established the Arab Gulf Office, headed by Saddam Hussein himself, to protect the Persian Gulf from Iran's imperialism and to preserve its Arab nature (Bengio 1998: 140).

Following these developments from the 1960s to the 1980s, the archaeological literature coming out of Arab lands also underwent a process of change aimed at expunging the name Persian Gulf.

Enter the Archaeologists?

In order to understand the mechanisms through which names other than Persian Gulf have emerged in the archaeological literature in the past fifty years, it is imperative to examine in some detail the development of archaeology in Arab states in the region since World War I. Important issues include the development of archaeology in Iraq and the establishment of the Iraqi Department of Antiquities, the role of early directors of the department, the rise of indigenous Iraqi archaeology and its avoidance of using the name Persian Gulf, and the response to these developments by Western archaeologists. Finally, the rise and development of archaeology in Arab states on the Persian Gulf calls for some comment, especially the relations of these states with Western archaeologists.

Excavations in Iraq were resumed by the British after World War I even before the armistice was signed in 1918. The first postwar excavations in Iraq were carried out by Reginald Campbell Thompson, who had worked at Nineveh before the war and served during the war in Iraq as a captain in the British Intelligence Corps and also as the representative of the British Museum. Campbell Thompson launched excavations at Ur and at Eridu in 1918, using Indian troops under his command for actual digging (Lloyd 1980: 180), while H. R. Hall, who succeeded him at Ur the following year, used Turkish prisoners of war as his labor force.

The British established the Iraqi Department of Antiquities in 1922, with a British citizen as its director, first Gertrude Bell and then Sidney Smith (who later became the keeper of the Department of Egyptian and Babylonian Antiquities in the British Museum). The 1920s and early 1930s were a golden era in Mesopotamian archaeology: large-scale excavations by expeditions from different countries were carried out throughout Iraq, including efforts by the Deutsch-Orient Gesellschaft at Warka; by the Louvre at Telloh; by Oxford University and the Field Museum at Kish; by the Oriental Institute of the University of Chicago at Khorsabad and at several sites in the Diyala region, including Tell Asmar, Tell Agrab, and Khafajah; and by the British Museum and the University of Pennsylvania Museum of Archaeology and Anthropology at Ur.

On October 3, 1932, Iraq gained full independence from Britain. King Faysal died in September 1933 and was succeeded by his son King Ghazi I. With him, a group called the Iha al-Watana (National Brotherhood Party) took control of the Iraq government and embarked on a more nationalistic course. In the same year Sati' al-Husri (see above) was appointed the director of the Department of Antiquities (fig. 7.4).

Soon after assuming his position, Husri began making changes to the Antiquities Law. Meanwhile, Iraqi nationalists launched a propaganda campaign alleging that Iraq had been robbed of its national heritage by foreign archaeological expeditions operating under the liberal Antiquities Law composed by the British Gertrude Bell. The new Antiquities Law, passed in 1934, imposed severe restrictions on the rights of foreign expeditions to archaeological finds and on the export of antiquities. This led to a gradual migration of Western expeditions to Syria, which, still under French mandate, had more relaxed antiquities laws. Husri laid the foundation for an indigenous Iraqi archaeology by emphasizing national interests in archaeological research, dispatching employees of the department to gain experience by working with foreign expeditions, and

Figure 7.4. Sati' al-Husri accompanying Princess Alice of Athlone during a visit to the Iraq Museum in 1939. Seton Lloyd can be seen in the background. After Lloyd 1980: fig. 68.

sending Iraqi students abroad to receive training in archaeology and ancient languages.

Husri's support of Arab nationalists, especially during Rashid Ali al-Gaylani's government, led to his expulsion from Iraq in 1941 (Cleveland 1971). While Husri continued his research and writing on Arab nationalism, first in London and then in Cairo, the Department of Antiquities was entrusted to Naji al-Asil (1895–1963), another fervent Arab nationalist. Asil was born in Mosul and studied in Istanbul and Beirut, earning a degree in medicine. He joined the Arab nationalist movement in Hijaz and became a close friend of Sharif Husayn, representing him in London after World War I. Asil returned to Iraq in 1926, where he became a professor and later the dean of the Higher Teachers College; at that institution he made acquaintance with Husri and Miqdadi. Later he joined the Ministry of Foreign Affairs and served in Iran, where he was responsible for signing the 1937 Irano-Iraqi Boundary Treaty (Ramazani 1972: 121–124). Asil briefly served as minister of foreign affairs in 1936–1937, but he soon retired from politics, taking over the position of the director general of antiquities from Husri in 1941, a position he held until his death. Asil continued with Husri's initiatives, emphasizing indigenous archaeology. His leadership is evident in developments such as the launching of the journal *Sumer* in 1944 as the official periodical of the Iraqi Department of Antiquities.

During the Husri-Asil years, the Iraqi Department of Antiquities, having more or less cut off foreign expeditions from fieldwork in Iraq, began its own independent excavations at Samarra, Wasit, Tell 'Uqair, 'Aqar Quf, Hassuna, Tell Harmal, and Eridu. This florescence of the department owed much to two young Iraqi students returning from the University of Chicago, Taha Baqir and Fuad Safar, and their locally trained and able architectural assistant Mohammad-Ali Mostafa. The influence of Husri and Miqdadi on Safar and Baqir can be seen in their writings. For example, Safar argues that one of the objectives of his excavations at early sites in southern Mesopotamia, such as 'Uqair and Eridu, has been exploring the roots of Semito-Arab culture (Safar 1947). Baqir explored the roots of Semito-Arab culture by studying the relations between Mesopotamia, the Arabian Peninsula, and the ancient lands of Dilmun and Magan (Baqir 1948). Even at this early date we already see the Persian Gulf simply being called in their publications "al-Khalij al-Basra" or "al-Khalij" (the Gulf) (cf. Baqir 1948: 145; Baqir and Francis 1948: 175).

By the late 1950s, the name Persian Gulf had been completely expunged from the archaeological literature coming out of Iraq; it was replaced with "Arabian Gulf." This trend was gradually adopted by archaeologists from other countries working in Iraq, beginning with some of the earlier generation of Mesopotamian archaeologists such as Seton Lloyd.

In the 1930s and 1940s, the Iraqis still employed numerous foreigners at the Department of Antiquities, most importantly Seton Lloyd, who worked as a technical adviser for the department from 1939 to 1948, participating in excavations at 'Uqair, Hassuna, and Eridu. Lloyd was one of the major characters of the golden age of Near Eastern archaeology (Lloyd 1986); he had an impressive résumé that included excavations at a number of well-known sites in the Near East and some of the most widely read books on Near Eastern archaeology (cf. Lloyd 1947, 1963, 1978, 1980). The shift in Lloyd's publications from "Persian Gulf" to "Arabian Gulf" can be viewed as a model for the changing stance in the archaeological community. Throughout his earlier publications (Lloyd 1947, 1963), he consistently used the name Persian Gulf, but from the

1970s, we see him shifting to "Arabian Gulf" (see Lloyd 1978: map 1). This practice was not limited to new publications: for example, we see that the exquisite frontispiece map with the name Persian Gulf in the original edition of his classic *Foundations in the Dust* (Lloyd 1947) was replaced by two maps of inferior quality with "Arabian Gulf" in the revised edition of the same work (Lloyd 1980: maps 1–2).

Of the later generations of Western archaeologists working in Iraq, many showed no hesitation in using "Arabian Gulf" (cf. Oates and Oates 1976), but many tried to bypass the problem by using "Gulf" or "The Gulf" (cf. Postgate 1977, 1992; Reade 1978) or by simply leaving the gulf unnamed on their maps. In the meantime, archaeologists with interests in both Iran and Iraq tried to demonstrate their impartiality by using "Gulf" or "The Gulf" (cf. Wright and Johnson 1975); they would use "Persian Gulf" in publications dealing with Iran (cf. Moorey 1975) and "The Gulf" in those pertaining to Iraq (cf. Moorey 1976), or they used new names such as "Arab-Persian Gulf" (cf. Sherwin-White and Kuhrt 1993; Kuhrt 1995).

Archaeology in Arab lands on the Persian Gulf started out later than in Iraq, again with the British at the forefront (Crawford 2003). The first series of archaeological research projects on the southern shores of the Persian Gulf began with a survey of Bahrain and Qatar in 1878 by Captain E. L. Durand, a British officer attached to the British political residence in Bushehr, Iran. Durand's report on burial mounds of Bahrain piqued the interest of the British, who dispatched Colonel F. P. Prideaux, the political resident at Bushehr, to carry out a more thorough survey of the vast necropolis in Bahrain in 1908.

Sporadic work in Bahrain continued during the first half of the twentieth century by the British and the Americans, including engineers working on oil fields in the region. But the first systematic and long-term archaeological field research along the southern shores of the Persian Gulf did not begin until 1953, when the First Danish Expedition to Arabia arrived in Bahrain. Rumor has it that the Danes owed the opportunity to work in Bahrain to Sir Charles Belgrave, the British adviser to the sheikh of Bahrain (fig. 7.5). It is noteworthy that this same Sir Charles Belgrave was the first westerner to use and advocate the name Arabian Gulf, first in the journal *Soat al-Bahrain* (*Voice of Bahrain*) in 1955 (Majidzadeh 1993: 5n7) and then in his popular book *The Pirate Coast* (Belgrave 1960: 3); some twenty-five years earlier, he had published a paper on the Persian Gulf (Belgrave 1931).

Having, to his surprise, received two applications for fieldwork in Bahrain in the same week in 1953, one from the University of Aarhus in

Figure 7.5. Sir Charles Belgrave accompanying Sheikh Salman of Bahrain during a visit to London in 1953

Denmark and the other from the University of Pennsylvania, Belgrave decided to toss a coin to choose. The coin was tossed and the Danes were permitted to embark on fieldwork in Bahrain (Rice 1994: 55). I assume that the fact that Geoffrey Bibby, the liaison of the Danish expedition, was a British citizen had no impact on the decision.

Bibby was an employee of the Iraq Petroleum Company and was instrumental in putting together and launching the Danish expedition. He talked P. V. Glob, his wartime friend and later a professor of prehistory at the University of Aarhus, into dropping his fieldwork in the lush fields of Denmark and undertaking fieldwork in the sands of Arabia. After obtaining the permit for fieldwork in Bahrain, Bibby once again turned to Belgrave, who secured funding for their work through the Bahrain government (Potts 1998: 192). Interestingly enough, when the Danish expedition expanded its activities to Failaka Island, off the coast of Kuwait, in 1958, they came into contact with none other than Darwish al-Miqdadi, now the deputy director of education in Kuwait and responsible for overseeing archaeological activities (Bibby 1969: 201). In such an environment, it is fairly easy to imagine why archaeologists would quickly shift in their publications from "Persian Gulf" (cf. Glob 1960; Glob and Bibby 1960) to "Arabian Gulf" (cf. Bibby 1964, 1965, 1966).

From the 1970s onward, especially during the 1980s and 1990s, with a surge in archaeological research in Arab countries on the Persian Gulf, "Arabian Gulf" was used more frequently in the literature. For some, the change from "Persian Gulf" to "Arabian Gulf" occurred almost overnight (cf., e.g., During-Caspers 1971b ["Persian Gulf"] and 1971a ["Arabian Gulf"]), while for others it took somewhat longer to make the transition. Some started with "Persian Gulf" (Tosi 1974), went on to "The Gulf" (Tosi 1984), and finally arrived at "Arabian Gulf" (Tosi 1986). Here too, some authors tried to evade the problem by creating names such as "Persischen/Arabischen Golf" (Scholz 1990) or "Arab-Iranian Gulf" (Howard-Carter 1972) or, more commonly, simply using "Gulf" or "The Gulf" (De Cardi 1971).

The Iranian Revolution of 1979 was a turning point for archaeology in the region in general and the name of the Persian Gulf in particular. Once a bustling center for archaeological research, Iran shut its doors to foreign archaeologists and adopted a self-imposed archaeological isolation following the revolution. In despair, archaeologists who had formerly worked in Iran sought field opportunities elsewhere, and some found refuge in Arab countries. This migration brought about a change in the use of the name of Persian Gulf. Of the migrating archaeologists, some did not hold a grudge against Iran and tried to remain impartial by using "Gulf" or "The Gulf" in general (cf. several papers in Finkbeiner 1993), or "Gulf" in publications pertaining to Arab lands (cf. Haerinck 1992) and "Persian Gulf" in those pertaining to Iran (cf. Haerinck 1998). But some quickly turned to "Arabian Gulf" (cf. Potts 1978), while others delayed slightly longer taking the fateful step (cf. Tosi 1986; Whitehouse 2000), again with some making a brief stop at "The Gulf" (cf. Roaf 1990) before arriving at "Arabian Gulf" (cf. Roaf and Gabraith 1994). This trend was not restricted to Anglophone archaeologists; some Francophone archaeologists have also shifted over the years from "Golfe persique" to "Golfe" (cf. de Miroschedji 1986), "Golfe Arabo-persique" (cf. Beaucamp and Robin 1983; Salle 1987), "Golfe arabe" (Salle 1981), and "Golfe arabique" (cf. Tixier 1980; Inizan 1980). In Germany, the Tübingen Atlas von Vorderasiatische Archäologie also began its map series in mid-1977 with "Persischer Golf" but switched to "Arabische-Persicher Golf" in the late 1980s.

One can imagine that the Iranian archaeological community considers Western archaeologists' disregard for the name of the Persian Gulf and their use of other names, especially "Arabian Gulf" after shifting their fieldwork to Arab lands, to be opportunist and a betrayal of academic integrity (cf. Azarnoush 1993; Majidzadeh 1993; Alizadeh 2003). Some criticisms have been expressed in the form of reviews of books dealing with research on the Arab shores of the Persian Gulf. For example, D. T. Potts's *Arabian Gulf in Antiquity* (1990) met with much praise in Iran for gathering and synthesizing a tremendous amount of data on the southern shores of the Persian Gulf and the Gulf of Oman but was simultaneously criticized for calling the body of water "Arabian Gulf" (Abdi 1994). Of other publication using "Arabian Gulf," examples such as Harriet Crawford's *Dilmun and Its Gulf Neighbours* (1998) have been applauded for providing an accessible synthesis for the archaeology of the Arab lands on the Persian Gulf (Alizadeh 2003), whereas Michael Rice's *Archaeology of the Arabian Gulf* (1994) has been criticized for being inaccurate, anecdotal, and sometimes outright fictitious (Abdi 1995).

An alarming revelation came from Azarnoush (1993), who exposed the editors of the proceedings of a seminar on religions in pre-Islamic Central Asia—one of whom engaged in fieldwork in Arab countries (see Lombard 1981)—for deleting the adjective "Persian" from the map in Azarnoush's paper (Azarnoush 1991) without consulting him and refusing to publish his objections in this regard.

The most comprehensive rebuttal from the Iranian archaeological community was put forward by Majidzadeh (1993), who traced the archaeological connection of the attempts to change the name of the Persian Gulf and criticized Western archaeologists who switched from "Persian Gulf" to one of the other names after their fieldwork in Iran was disrupted following the 1979 revolution. Majidzadeh nonetheless argued that one way to deal with this problem was to abandon the archaeological isolation Iran had imposed on itself and to allow foreign archaeologists to resume fieldwork in Iran, a point reiterated by Abdi (1995, 1999) that may or may not have led to Iranian archaeology's rapprochement with the West in recent years (Lawler 2003).

In the past few years, as Western archaeologists are beginning to return to Iran, one can already see some changes, but not without some political implications. For example, one major advocate of the name Arabian Gulf (Potts 1990, 1992, 1993) was allowed to resume fieldwork in Iran only after a much-publicized apology to the Iranian people announced in daily newspapers and a show of redemption by using "Persian Gulf" in his recent publications (cf. Potts 1999). Others who tried to remain impartial over the years by using "Gulf" (cf. Wright 1994; Haerinck 1992; Pollock 1999) have also begun using "Persian Gulf" (cf. Wright 1998; Haerinck 1998; Pollock and Bernbeck 2005) after closer interaction with Iranian colleagues or with growing prospects of fieldwork in Iran. This development, however, has not deterred archaeologists working in Arab countries from continuing to use "Arabian Gulf" or "The Gulf," especially those who have had no prior attachments to Iranian archaeology (cf. Crawford 1998; Littleton 1998; Edens 1999; Orchard and Stanger 1999; Matthews 2000, 2003; Phillips 2001; Carter 2002; several papers in Potts et al. 2003; Beech 2004). Among the latter group, however, one can also see a gradual change from "Arabian Gulf" (cf. Magee 1999) to "The Gulf" (cf. Magee 2004; Weeks 2003), and finally to "Persian Gulf" (Carter, 2006; Weeks n.d.) as they come into closer contact with Iranian archaeology.

Why "Arabian Gulf"?

One can obviously appreciate the attempts by Western archaeologists to be polite toward their Arab hosts by using "Arabian Gulf," but a closer inspection of the Arab attitude toward the Persian Gulf may suggest a larger design in which Western archaeologists have willingly or unwillingly become important players.

An account by a European who made the journey to Arab lands on the Persian Gulf in the mid-1950s is helpful in understanding the Arab perspective on the Persian Gulf and its name and how an outsider might react to this attitude:

> No English map shows the Arabian Gulf; a matter of some concern for those who live there. A traveler has to proceed as though bound for the Persian Gulf—will probably think that that's where he is when he reaches Kuwait or Bahrain, only to be told that that's where he isn't. Persian Gulf? The dry expanses of brown sand, those blue expanses of shallow water—and everything above and especially below—are, have been, will be, integral parts of the Arabian Gulf. This was one of the many things I did not know before going there. It was the first Arab statement of opinion I heard and it was repeated at intervals over a year of wandering until now it is an effort to think of such a place as a Persian Gulf. Since this is an account of a journey where after the initial effort I regularly took the line of least resistance, where I purposely deprived myself of purpose, willed myself to have no will and heaped the result on to the lap

of Allah, I shall refer to this burning, humid gulf of the world as "Persian" before my arrival and as "Arabian" after; for this is only polite. (Owen 1957: 13)

A courteous traveler, especially one who has chosen "the line of least resistance," can certainly use politeness as an excuse to call the Persian Gulf the Arabian Gulf so as not to offend his Arab hosts, but what about scholars who are bound by academic ethics? In order to answer this question, we need to explore the context within which archaeology operates in Arab lands, especially the Arab states on the Persian Gulf. The same traveler made the following observation about the local population of these lands: "Here were some poor people who are suddenly rich beyond their wildest dreams; and they've done nothing to deserve it, It's just chance. These undeserved riches are greater than anyone in history has amassed by hard work, merit, or even dishonesty" (14). On why westerners are eager to work in Arab lands, he adds: "Why go there? For nearly every foreigner in the Gulf there is the obvious answer: 'to earn money.' English and American companies are extracting oil. Oil royalties mean that the Arabs can buy goods and skill from the rest of the world, the Arab world, the Persian, the Indian as well as the European and American" (13). This seems to be the pattern in the recent history of Arab states on the Persian Gulf. Devoid of skills to build and maintain a country with modern amenities, but with grand ambitions and ample disposable wealth, Arabs could easily secure the best the West had to offer. Once the basics of a modern nation-state were in place by the 1950s, it was time to look into more ambitious aspirations, creating history being an important item on the agenda; and who was better qualified to do this than Western archaeologists?

A recent paper by the dean of Arabian archaeology reveals two interesting points about archaeology in Arab states on the Persian Gulf pertaining to funding and personnel. Potts's observation regarding the Arab attitude toward skilled laborers, including archaeologists, is of particular interest (Potts 1998: 193–194). He draws an analogy between the practice of slavery in Arab lands on the Persian Gulf, which continued well into the 1940s, and the skilled labor drawn to the region since the discovery of oil. In countries accustomed to slavery, cheap and disposable labor can come in many forms and colors. Once it was blacks from Africa; now it is browns from South Asia and whites from the West. Arabian archaeology functions within this system. With lavish support Arabs could easily lure Western archaeologists to carry out archaeological research in Arab countries. As for support extended to foreign archaeological expeditions, Potts points out: "In the recent past, expeditions to

Bahrain and teams in the United Arab Emirates . . . have been provided variously with accommodation, food, vehicles and workmen (some, or all, depending on the local authority) by the governments of their host countries. Air fares and other expenses . . . often come out of grants from national funding agencies as well as from local sponsors. While oil companies continue to be supportive, a wide range of other concerns such as car companies (e.g., General Motors), service companies (e.g., Dubai Duty Free), and tobacco companies (e.g., Rothmans) have given generously" (Potts 1998: 192–193). This kind of generous support would probably raise an eyebrow among archaeologists working in other parts of the world, who have to go through grilling application processes to various national or international funding agencies and scrape up whatever bits and pieces of money they can lay their hands on to carry out their fieldwork. But this also raises the question of why the Arabs are eager to support archaeological research on such a lavish scale. In other words, what do Arabs get in return for their support of archaeology? Potts believes that in return for their support of archaeology, companies earn prestige, rulers gain a reputation for being enlightened and progressive (1998: 193), and states demonstrate that they have arrived at a civilized stage by having museums and international conferences on archaeology and history. But would it be unfair to suppose that beyond these enlightened reasons to support archaeology, Arabs get much more in return? Publications by famous Western archaeologists in international journals using the name Arabian Gulf might be an example. A case in point was the comprehensive survey commissioned from 1976 onward by the Saudi Arabian Department of Antiquities, which employed, with salary, archaeologists from Britain and the United States (Potts 1998: 194) who produced literature abundantly using "Arabian Gulf" (Adams et al. 1977; Potts et al. 1978; Zarins et al. 1979, 1980, 1981, 1982).

The question remains, however: why are Arabs trying so hard to change the name of the Persian Gulf? Renaming a place is a common practice in many cultures. It is a sign of taking possession or signals the ascendancy of a new regime. Well-known examples of this practice include Constantinople being renamed Istanbul after the Ottoman conquest in 1452, or St. Petersburg being renamed Leningrad in 1924 following the consolidation of the Bolshevik regime. Arabs are no exception to this practice. Yathrib was renamed Medinat al-Nabi (the city of the prophet) after the Prophet Mohammad and his followers migrated from Mecca and settled there in 622 CE, and the Pillars of Hercules was renamed Jabal al-Tariq (Gibraltar) after Tariq ibn Ziyad, the Muslim commander who crossed the pass and marched into Spain in 711 CE (Amin 1981: 32).

It seems that the renaming of the Persian Gulf by Arabs is an attempt in the same vein. By calling this body of water Arabian Gulf, Arabs seem to be trying to signal the end of Iran's regional supremacy and to emphasize their own rising star. But we see that Arab attempts to change the name of the Persian Gulf did not reach an international level until the 1970s, when westerners—including archaeologists—began calling it the Arabian Gulf. In other words, what Arabs failed to do on their own, westerners, including Western archaeologists, managed to do for them.

Going back to the question of academic integrity among archaeologists, one may ask whether using "Arabian Gulf" is a precondition for working in Arab lands. Not necessarily; Arabs may try to influence Western archaeologists to use "Arabian Gulf" by promises of financial support, or Arabs may try to intimidate archaeologists by rejecting their work permits, but Arabs have no legal leverage to enforce use of the name Arabian Gulf, at least no international leverage. To establish this point, we see that many archaeologists still use the name Persian Gulf despite having to shift their research from Iran after the 1979 Revolution to Iraq (cf. Carter 1990) or other Arab countries (cf. Wenke 1999). There are also those who have worked in Arab lands for years but still use the name Persian Gulf (cf. Nissen 1988; Vita-Finzi 1998). In this group one can also include scholars whose research is primarily concerned with ancient Mesopotamia but who do not allow current politics to cloud their judgment (cf. Bottéro 1992, 2001; von Soden 1994; Snell 1997; Van De Mieroop 2004). Arabs may explicitly or implicitly push archaeologists to use the name Arabian Gulf, but ultimately it is up to individual archaeologists to implement the change.

Conclusion

Despite signing two UN documents (UNAD 311/Gen on March 5, 1971 and UNLA 45.8.2 (C) on August 10, 1984) endorsing the name Persian Gulf, Arab states continue to use and promote the name Arabian Gulf in various forms. For example, a recent study (Atrissi 1998) shows that despite different perspectives on Iranians (past and present) in textbooks across the Arab world, ranging from indifference (e.g., in Morocco) to a mild courteousness (e.g., in Syria) to deep resentment (in Iraq), they are unanimous in using "Arabian Gulf" to refer to this body of water. In fact, statements such as the following suggest that the Arabs are enjoying this name game: "There is a big Gulf, but the biggest gulf that separates us from the Iranians is that they insist and will remain calling it Persian, and that it is our victory that the seven Arab Gulf states and the other fourteen Arab states call it Arab" (commentary in *al-Watan,* Dec. 24, 1994, quoted in Marschall 2003: 4). Whether or not this disregard of UN documents is a violation of international laws is up to political bodies to determine, but, depending on their disposition, Iranians find it either amusing or disconcerting. The former president of Iran expressed this view: "It is not at all wise for a group of countries to . . . decide on their own to change the name of what has been historically known as the Persian Gulf to 'Arabian Gulf.' What purpose does it serve, when your honorable neighbor is offended or a sense of insecurity is created in the region?" (Hashemi-Rafsanjani 1990: 465). On the international level, it is up to the Iranian government to apply direct and sustained pressure on Arab states to drop the name Arabian Gulf; but that is an undertaking that it is unwilling to enforce, fearing undesirable consequences for Iran's improving but fragile economic and commercial ties with Arab states. Incidents like that arising from the latest edition of the NGS atlas will continue until Iranians and Arabs reach an understanding regarding their proper place vis-à-vis the Persian Gulf.

Acknowledgments

I would like to thank Dale Eickelman, Dan Potts, and Henry Wright for reading and commenting on earlier drafts of this paper. Needless to say, they disagreed with me on some interpretive points, for which I assume sole responsibility.

References

Abdi, Kamyar. 1994. Review of Potts 1990 [in Persian]. *Iranian Journal of Archaeology and History* 13–14:126–129.

Abdi, Kamyar. 1995. Review of Rice 1994 [in Persian]. *Nashr-e Danish* 15:51–55.

Abdi, Kamyar. 1999. Iranian Archaeology and Lessons from the Practice of Archaeology in Other Countries [in Persian]. *Nemaye Pajouhesh: The Journal of the Deputy for Research, Iranian Ministry of Culture* 9–10:56–67.

Abdulghani, J. M. 1984. *Iraq & Iran: The Years of Crisis.* Baltimore: Johns Hopkins University Press.

Adamiyat, Fereydoun. 1955. *Bahrain Islands: A Legal and Diplomatic Study of the British-Iranian Controversy.* New York: Praeger.

Adams, Robert M., P. Carr, M. Ibrahim, and A. al-Mughannum. 1977. Saudi Arabian Archaeological Reconnaissance. *Atlal* 1:21–40.

Aitchison, C. U. 1933. *A Collection of Treaties, Engagements, and Sanads Relating to India and Neighbouring Countries*. Delhi: Manager of Publications.

Ala, Mohammad. 2004. Morale Issue Confronts Iranians in Renaming of Persian Gulf. www.payvand.com/news/04/dec/1014.html.

Albaharna, Husain M. 1975. *The Arabian Gulf States: Their Legal and Political Status and Their International Problems*. 2nd ed. Beirut: Librairie du Liban.

Alizadeh, Abbas. 2003. Review of Crawford 1998. *International Journal of Ancient Iranian Studies* 3 (1): 95–97.

Amin, S. H. 1981. *International and Legal Problems of the Gulf*. London: Middle East and North African Studies Press.

Anonymous. 2004a. Persian Gulf Will Remain Persian. www.petitiononline.com/persian/petition.html.

Anonymous. 2004b. We "Google-Bombed" Arabian Gulf. iraniandiaries.blogpost.com/2004/11/we-google-bombed-arabian-gulf.html.

Anonymous. 2004c. Iran Warns "Gulf" Is Persian. www.middle-east-online.com/english/?id=11953=11953&format=0.

Anonymous. 2004d. National Geographer Staffer Excluded from Festival Jury. *Iran Daily*, Dec. 2, p. 12.

Anonymous. 2004e. Outcry against Distortion of Persian Gulf Continues. www.payvand.com/news/04/dec/1030.html.

Anonymous. 2004f. Iranian Reformist MPs to Take a Stance on Fictitious Name for Persian Gulf. www.payvand.com/news/04/dec/1225.html.

Anonymous. 2004g. Iran Follows Up Issue of Distortion of PG Name. http://iranmania.com/News/ArticleView/Default.asp?NewsCode=28212&NewsKind=Current%20Affairs.

Anonymous. 2004h. Exhibition of Persian Gulf Historical Maps Opens. www.payvand.com/news/04/dec/1144.html.

Anonymous. 2004i. UNESCO Confirms Persian Gulf. www.iranian.com/iran_news/publish/printer_5161.shtml.

Anonymous 2004j. Iranian Culture Ministry to Hold First National Persian Gulf Festival. www.payvand.com/news/04/dec/1229.html.

Anonymous 2004k. Persian Gulf Museum Will Be Built in Iran. www.chn.ir/english/enewsprint.asp?id=4541.

Anonymous 2004l. International Competition for the Persian Gulf Museum. www.payvand.com/news/04/dec/1257.html.

Anonymous 2004m. Iranologists Condemn Deliberate Distortion of Persian Gulf's Name. www.payvand.com/news/04/dec/1206.html.

Anonymous 2004n. Persian Gulf Included Oman Sea in Olden Times. http://iranmania.com/News/ArticleView/Default.asp?NewsCode=27928&NewsKind=Current%20Affairs.

Anonymous 2004o. World-Famous Belgian Expert on Iran Criticizes Attempts to Change the Name of Persian Gulf. www.payvand.com/news/04/dec/1160.html.

Anonymous 2004p. Iranian Cancels Membership at NGS. http://daneshjoo.org/generalnews/article/publish/printer_9852.shtml.

Anonymous 2004q. National Geographic's Statement on Persian Gulf. www.payvand.com/news/04/nov/1224.html.

Anonymous 2004r. Reza Pahlavi of Iran Discusses the Persian Gulf with the National Geographic. www.payvand.com/news/04/dec/1051.html.

Anonymous 2004s. National Geographic Issues Written Apology to Iran. www.en.rian.ru/rian/index.cfm?prd_id=160&msg-id==5265273&startrow=1&date=2004-12-29&do_alert=0.

Anonymous 2004t. Proposal on National Geographic Maps Considered by NIAC Membership. www.niacouncil.org/pressrelease/press232.asp.

Anonymous 2004u. National Geographic Updates Map in the Wake of Iranian Protests. www.payvand.com/news/05/jan/1010.html.

Anonymous 2004v. National Geographic Retreat Victory for Every Iranian: FM. www.payvand.com/news/05/jan/1018.html.

Anonymous 2004w. National Geographic Society Retreats. www.rozanehmagazine.com/JanFeb2005/amarzporgohar.html.

Anonymous 2004x. National Geographic Falls Short on Changes Proposed to the Iranian-American Community. www.niacouncil.org/pressrelease/press233.asp.

Anonymous 2004y. www.niacouncil.org/pressrelease/press233.asp.

Anscombe, Fredrick F. 1997. *The Ottoman Gulf: The Creation of Kuwait, Saudi Arabia, and Qatar.* New York: Columbia University Press.

Atrissi, Talal. 1998. The Image of Iranians in Arab Schoolbooks. In *Arab-Iranian Relations,* ed. Khair el-Din Haseeb, 152–198. Beirut: Center for Arab Unity.

Azarnoush, Massoud. 1991. The Manor House of Hâjîâbâd and the Chronology of the Sasanian Governors of Kûsânshr. In *Histoire et cultes de l'Asie centrale préislamique: Sources écrites et documents archéologiques: Actes du Colloque international du CNRS (Paris, 22–28 novembre 1988),* ed. Paul Bernard and Frantz Grenet, 79–83. Paris: Editions du CNRS.

Azarnoush, Massoud. 1993. The Persian Gulf, the Orphan Gulf [in Persian]. *Negah-e Nou* 15:205–209.

Balfour-Paul, Glen. 1991. *The End of the Empire in the Middle East: Britain's Relinquishment of Power in Her Last Three Arab Dependencies.* Cambridge: Cambridge University Press.

Baqir, Taha. 1948. Relations between Mesopotamia and the Arabian Peninsula [in Arabic]. *Sumer* 5:123–158.

Baqir, Taha, and Francis Bashir. 1948. The Babylonian Story of Creation [in Arabic]. *Sumer* 5:175–214.

Beaucamp, Joëlle, and C. Robin. 1983. L'évêché nestorien de Mâshmâhîg dans l'archipel d'al-Bahrayn (Ve–Ixe siècle). In *Dilmun: New Studies in the Archaeology and History of Bahrain,* ed. D. T. Potts, 171–196. Berlin: Dietrich Reimer Verlag.

Beech, Mark J. 2004. *In the Land of Ichthyophagi: Modelling Fish Exploitation in the Arabian Gulf and Gulf of Oman from the 5th Millennium BC to the Late Islamic Period.* BAR International Series 1217. Oxford: Archaeopress.

Belgrave, Charles. 1931. The Overland Route to the Persian Gulf. *Journal of the Royal Central Asian Society* 18:560–563.

Belgrave, Charles. 1960. *The Pirate Coast*. Beirut: Librairie du Liban.

Bengio, Ofra. 1998. *Saddam's Word: Political Discourse in Iraq*. New York: Oxford University Press.

Bibby, Geoffrey. 1964. Arabiens arkaeologi: Dansk arkaeologisk ekspeditions 8. kampagne, 1961/62—Dansk arkaeologisk ekspeditions 9. kampagne, 1962/63; Arabian Gulf Archaeology: The Eighth and Ninth Campaigns of the Danish Archaeological Expedition. *Kuml* 1964:86–101 [in Danish], 101–111 [in English].

Bibby, Geoffrey. 1965. Arabiens arkaeologi: Dansk arkaeologisk ekspeditions 10. kampagne, 1964; Arabian Gulf Archaeology: The Tenth Campaign of the Danish Archaeological Expedition, 1964. *Kuml* 1965:133–144 [in Danish], 144–152 [in English].

Bibby, Geoffrey. 1966. Arabiens arkaeologi: Dansk arkaeologisk ekspeditions 11. kampagne, 1965; Arabian Gulf Archaeology: The Eleventh Campaign of the Danish Archaeological Expedition, 1965. *Kuml* 1966:75–90 [in Danish], 90–95 [in English].

Bibby, Geoffrey. 1969. *Looking for Dilmun*. New York: Alfred A. Knopf.

Birastid, Jayms Hanri. 1926. *'Usur al-Qadima was huwa tamhid li-dars al-tarikh al-qadim wa a'mal al-insan al-awwal*. Trans. Da'ud Qurban. Beirut: Al-Matba'a al-Amerikaniyya.

Bottéro, Jean. 1992. *Mesopotamia: Writing, Reasoning, and the Gods*. Chicago: University of Chicago Press.

Bottéro, Jean. 2001. *Everyday Life in Ancient Mesopotamia*. Edinburgh: Edinburgh University Press.

Breasted, James Henry. 1916. *Ancient Times: A History of the Early World: An Introduction to the Study of Ancient History and the Career of Early Man*. Boston: Ginn.

Carré, Olivier. 1979. *La légitimation islamique des socialismes arabes: Analyse conceptuelle combinatoire de manuels scolaires égyptiens, syriens et irakiens*. Paris: Presses de la Fondation nationale des sciences politiques.

Carter, Elizabeth. 1990. Elamite Exports. In *Contribution à l'histoire de l'Iran: Mélanges offerts à Jean Perrot*, ed. F. Vallat, 89–100. Paris: Editions Recherche sur les Civilisations.

Carter, Robert. 2002. Ubaid-Period Boat Remains from As-Sabiyah Excavated by the British Archaeological Expedition to Kuwait. *Proceedings of Society for Arabian Studies* 32:13–30.

Carter, Robert. 2006. Boat Remains and Maritime Trade in the Persian Gulf during the Sixth and Fifth Millennia BC. *Antiquity* 80:52–63.

Cleveland, William L. 1971. *The Making of an Arab Nationalist: Ottomanism and Arabism in the Life and Thought of Sat' al-Husri*. Princeton, NJ: Princeton University Press.

Crawford, Harriet. 1998. *Dilmun and Its Gulf Neighbours*. Cambridge: Cambridge University Press.

Crawford, Harriet, ed. 2003. *The Archaeology of Bahrain: The British Contribution.* BAR International Series 1189. Oxford: Archaeopress.

Dawisha, Adeed. 2003. *Arab Nationalism in the Twentieth Century: From Triumph to Despair.* Princeton, NJ: Princeton University Press.

Dawn, C. Ernest. 1971. *From Ottomanism to Arabism: Essays on the Origins of Arab Nationalism.* Urbana: University of Illinois Press.

Dawn, C. Ernest. 1988a. An Arab Nationalist View of the World Politics and History in the Interwar Period: Darwish al-Miqdadi. In *The Great Powers in the Middle East, 1919–1939,* ed. U. Dann, 355–369. New York: Holmes and Meier.

Dawn, C. Ernest. 1988b. The Formation of Pan-Arab Ideology in the Interwar Years. *International Journal of Middle East Studies* 20:67–91.

De Cardi, Beatrice. 1971. Archaeological Survey in the Northern Trucial States. *East and West* 21 (3–4): 225–289.

Dubuisson, P. R. 1978. Qasimi Piracy and the General Treaty of Peace (1820). *Arabian Studies* 4:47–57.

During-Caspers, Elisabeth C. L. 1971a. The Bull's Head from Barbar Temple II, Bahrain: A Contact with Early Dynastic Sumer. *East and West* 21 (3–4): 217–224.

During-Caspers, Elisabeth C. L. 1971b. New Archaeological Evidence for Maritime Trade in the Persian Gulf during the Late Protoliterate Period. *East and West* 21 (1–2): 21–55.

Edens, Christopher. 1999. Kor Ile-Sud, Qatar: The Archaeology of Late Bronze Age Purple-Dye Production in Arabian Gulf. *Iraq* 61:71–88.

El-Issa, Shimlan. 1998. The Dispute between the United Arab Emirates and Iran over Three Islands. In *Arab-Iranian Relations,* ed. Khair el-Din Haseeb, 237–248. Beirut: Center for Arab Unity.

Eqtedari, Ahmad. 1966. *Archaeological Remains on the Coasts and Islands of the Persian Gulf* [in Persian]. Tehran: Society for National Heritage.

Faris, Nabih Amin. 1954. The Arabs and Their History. *Middle East Journal* 8:155–162.

Finkbeiner, Uwe, ed. 1993. *Materialen zur Archäologie der Seleukiden- und Partherzeit im südlichen babylonien und im Golfgebiet.* Berlin: Deutsches Archäologisches Institut, Abteilung Baghdad.

Foreign Office. 1953. *Handbook on the Persian Gulf.* London.

Glob, P. V. 1960. Danish Archaeologists in the Persian Gulf. *Kuml* 1960:208–213.

Glob, P. V., and G. T. Bibby. 1960. A Forgotten Civilization of the Persian Gulf. *Scientific American* 203:62–71.

al-Hadid, 'Ajjan. 1932. Le dévéloppement de l'éducation nationale en Iraq. *Revue des Etudes Islamiques* 2:237–250.

Haerinck, Ernie. 1992. Excavations at ed-Dur (Umm al-Qaiwain, U.A.E.): Preliminary Report of the Fourth Belgian Season (1990). *Arabian Archaeology and Epigraphy* 3:190–208.

Haerinck, Ernie. 1998. International Contacts in the Southern Shores of the Persian Gulf in the Late 1st Century B.C.–1st Century A.D.: Numismatic

Evidence from Ed-Dur (Emirate of Umm al-Qaiwain, U.A.E.). *Iranica Antiqua* 33:273–302.

Halliday, Fred. 1975. *Arabia without Sultans*. New York: Vintage Books.

Hashemi-Rafsanjani, Ali Akbar. 1990. Address by Ali Akbar Hashemi-Rafsanjani, President of the Islamic Republic of Iran. *Middle East Journal* 44: 458–466.

Hollis, Rosemary. 1993. *Gulf Security: No Consensus*. London: Royal United Services Institute for Defence Studies.

Hosseini, Mehdi. 2004. Persian Gulf: What's Not in a Name. www.thethirdscript.org/articles/persiangulfname.html.

Howard-Carter, Theresa. 1972. The Johns Hopkins University Reconnaissance Expedition to the Arab-Iranian Gulf. *Bulletin of the American School of Oriental Research* 207:6–40.

al-Husri, Abu-Khaldun Sati'. 1957. *Arab Lands and the Ottoman State* [in Arabic]. Beirut: Dar al-'Ilm li al-Malayin.

al-Husri, Abu-Khaldun Sati'. 1967–1968. *My Memoirs in Iraq, 1921–1941* [in Arabic]. 2 vols. Beirut: Dar al-Tali'ah.

Inizan, Marie-Louise. 1980. Site à poterie "obeidienne" à Qatar. In *L'archéologie de l'Iraq du début de l'époque Néolitique à 333 avant notre ère*, ed. M. T. Barrelet, 209–221. Paris: Editions de la Centre National de la Recherche Scientifique.

Jankowski, James. 1997. Arab Nationalism in "Nasserism" and Egyptian State Policy, 1952–1958. In Jankowski and Gershoni 1997, 150–167.

Jankowski, James, and Israel Gershoni, eds. 1997. *Rethinking Nationalism in the Arab Middle East*. New York: Columbia University Press.

Kelly, J. B. 1968. *Britain and the Persian Gulf, 1795–1880*. Oxford: Clarendon Press.

Khalidi, Rashid, L. Anderson, M. Muslih, and R. S. Simin, eds. 1991. *The Origins of Arab Nationalism*. New York: Columbia University Press.

Kuhrt, Amélie. 1995. *The Ancient Near East, c. 3000–330 BC*. London: Routledge.

Lane-Miller, Chelsea. 2004. How Geographic's New Atlas Reflects a Changed World. http://news.nationalgeographic.com/news/2004/11/1119_041119_atlas.html.

Lawler, Andrew. 2003. Iran Reopens Its Past. *Science* 302:970–973.

Lecoq, Pierre. 1997. *Les inscriptions de la Perse achéménide*. Paris: Gallimard.

Littleton, Judith. 1998. *Skeletons and Social Composition: Bahrain 300 BC–AD 250*. BAR International Series 703. Oxford: Archaeopress.

Lloyd, Seton. 1947. *Foundations in the Dust: A Story of Mesopotamian Exploration*. Oxford: Oxford University Press.

Lloyd, Seton. 1963. *Mounds of the Near East*. Edinburgh: Edinburgh University Press.

Lloyd, Seton. 1978. *Archaeology of Mesopotamia*. London: Thames and Hudson.

Lloyd, Seton. 1980. *Foundations in the Dust: A Story of Mesopotamian Exploration*. Rev. and enlarged ed. London: Thames and Hudson.

Lloyd, Seton. 1986. *The Interval: A Life in Near Eastern Archaeology*. Oxford: Lloyd Collon.

Lombard, Pierre. 1981. Poignards en bronze de la Péninsule d'Oman au 1er millénaire: Un problème d'influences iraniennes de l'Age du Fer. *Iranica Antiqua* 16:87–93.

Lotfian, Saideh. 1997. Taking Sides: Regional Powers and the War. In *Iranian Perspectives on the Iran-Iraq War*, ed. F. Rejaee, 13–28. Gainesville: University Press of Florida.

Madani, S. A. 1978. *Trial of Those Who Write Persian Gulf* [in Persian]. Tehran: Tous.

Magee, Peter. 1999. Settlement Patterns, Polities, and Regional Complexity in the Southeast Arabian Iron Age. *Paléorient* 24 (2): 49–60.

Magee, Peter. 2004. *Excavations at Tepe Yahya, Iran, 1967–1975: The Iron Age Settlement.* American School of Prehistoric Research Bulletin 46. Cambridge: Peabody Museum of Archaeology and Ethnology.

Majidzadeh, Yousef. 1993. The Name of the Persian Gulf and Foreign Archaeologists [in Persian]. *Nashr-e Danish* 13 (6): 2–11.

Marlowe, John. 1962. *The Persian Gulf in the Twentieth Century*. London: Cresse.

Marr, Phebe. 2004. *The Modern History of Iraq*. Boulder: Westview Press.

Marschall, Christin. 2003. *Iran's Persian Gulf Policy from Khomeini to Khatami.* London: RoutledgeCurzaon.

Mashkour, Mohammad-Javad. 1990. The Name of the Persian Gulf [in Persian]. In *Essays on the Persian Gulf*, 11–26. Tehran: Center for Persian Gulf Research, Office of Political and International Research, Iranian Ministry of Foreign Affairs.

Matthews, Roger. 2000. *The Early Prehistory of Mesopotamia: 500,000 to 4,500 BC.* Subartu V. Turnhout, Belgium: Brepols.

Matthews, Roger. 2003. *The Archaeology of Mesopotamia: Theories and Approaches.* London: Routledge.

Menshari, David, ed. 1990. *The Iranian Revolution and the Muslim World.* Boulder, CO: Westview.

al-Miqdadi, Darwish. 1931. *Tarikh al-Umma al-'Arabiyya*. Baghdad: Matba'a al-Ma'arif.

de Mirsochedji, Pierre. 1986. La localisation du Madaktu et l'organisation politique de l'Elam a l'époque néo-élamite. In *Fragmenta Historiae Ælamica: Mélanges offerts a M.-J. Steve*, ed. L. De Meyer, H. Gasche, and F. Vallat, 209–225. Paris: Recherche sur les civilisations.

Mojtahed-Zadeh, Pirouz. 1994. Iran's Maritime Boundaries in the Persian Gulf: The Case of Abu Musa Island. In *The Boundaries of Modern Iran*, ed. Keith McLachlan, 101–127. New York: St. Martin's Press.

Mojtahed-Zadeh, Pirouz. 1998. Arab-Iranian Territorial Disputes: Cooperation in the Region, not Confrontation. In *Arab-Iranian Relations*, ed. Khair el-Din Haseeb, 287–308. Beirut: Center for Arab Unity.

Moorey, P. R. S. 1975. *Ancient Iran*. Oxford: Ashmolean Museum.

Moorey, P. R. S. 1976. *Ancient Iraq*. Oxford: Ashmolean Museum.

Nafisi, Sa'id. 1954. *Bahrain: Iran's Seventeen-Hundred-Year-Old Right* [in Persian]. Tehran: Zohori.

Nish'at, Sadiq. 1965. *Political History of the Persian Gulf* [in Persian]. Tehran.

Nissen, Hans J. 1988. *The Early History of the Ancient Near East, 9000–2000 B.C.* Chicago: University of Chicago Press.

Noor, Shahriar. 2004. National Geographic Sells "Fabricated History" to Arabs. www.iranian.ws/iran_news/publish/printer_4650.shtml.

Oates, David, and Joan Oates. 1976. *The Rise of Civilization*. Oxford: Elsevier Phaidon.

Orchard, Jocelyn, and G. Stanger. 1999. Al-Hajar Oasis Towns Again! *Iraq* 61:89–119.

Owen, Roderic. 1957. *The Golden Bubble*. London: Collins.

Palmer, Michael A. 1992. *Guardians of the Gulf: A History of America's Expanding Role in the Persian Gulf, 1833–1992*. New York: Free Press.

Peterson, J. E. 1977. Guerrilla Warfare and Ideological Confrontation in the Arabian Peninsula: The Rebellion in Dhufar. *World Affairs* 139 (4): 278–295.

Phillips, C. 2001. *Prehistoric Middens and a Cemetery from the Southern Arabian Gulf*. Arabia Antiqua 3: Protohistoric Countries of Arabia. Rome: Serie Orientale Roma.

Pollock, Susan. 1999. *Ancient Mesopotamia*. Cambridge: Cambridge University Press.

Pollock, Susan, and Reinhard Bernbeck, eds. 2005. *Archaeologies of the Middle East: Critical Perspectives*. Malden, MA: Blackwell.

Postgate, J. N. 1977. *The First Empires*. Oxford: Elsevier-Phaidon.

Postgate, J. N. 1992. *Early Mesopotamia: Society and Economy at the Dawn of History*. London: Routledge.

Potts, D. T. 1978. Towards an Integrated History of Culture Change in the Arabian Gulf Area. *Journal of Oman Studies* 4:29–51.

Potts, D. T. 1990. *The Arabian Gulf in Antiquity*. Oxford: Clarendon Press.

Potts, D. T. 1992. The Chronology of the Archaeological Assemblages from the Head of the Arabian Gulf to the Arabian Sea, 8000–1750 B.C. In *Chronologies in Old World Archaeology*, 3rd ed., ed. Robert W. Ehrich, 63–76. Chicago: University of Chicago Press.

Potts, D. T. 1993. The Late Prehistoric, Protohistoric, and Early Historic Periods in Eastern Arabia (ca. 5000–1200 B.C.). *Journal of World Prehistory* 7:163–212.

Potts, D. T. 1998. The Gulf Arab States and their Archaeology. In *Archaeology under Fire: Nationalism, Politics, and Heritage in the Eastern Mediterranean and Middle East*, ed. Lynn Meskell, 189–199. London: Routledge.

Potts, D. T. 1999. *The Archaeology of Elam: Formation and Transformation of an Ancient Iranian State*. Cambridge: Cambridge University Press.

Potts, D. T., A. S. Mughannum, J. Frye, and D. Sanders. 1978. Preliminary Report on the Second Phase of the Eastern Province Survey, 1397–1977. *Atlal* 2:7–27.

Potts, D. T., H. Al Naboodah, and P. Hellyer, eds. 2003. *Archaeology of the United Arab Emirates: Proceedings of the First International Conference on the Archaeology of the U.A.E.* London: Trident Press.

Pridham, B. R., ed. 1988. *The Arab Gulf and the Arab World.* London: Croom Helm.

Ramazani, Ruhollah K. 1972. *The Persian Gulf: Iran's Role.* Charlottesville: University Press of Virginia.

Ramazani, Ruhollah K. 1990. Iran's Resistance to the US Intervention in the Persian Gulf. In *Neither East nor West: Iran, the Soviet Union, and the United States,* ed. N. R. Keddie and M. Gasiorowski, 13–35. New Haven, CT: Yale University Press.

Reade J. E. 1978. Kassites and Assyrians in Iran. *Iran* 16:137–143.

Rejaee, Farhang, ed. 1997. *Iranian Perspectives on the Iran-Iraq War.* Gainesville: University Press of Florida.

Rice, Michael. 1994. *The Archaeology of the Arabian Gulf, c. 5000–323 BC.* London: Routledge.

Roaf, Michael. 1990. *Cultural Atlas of Mesopotamia and the Near East.* London: Facts on File.

Roaf, Michael, and J. Gabraith. 1994. Pottery and p-Value: "Seafaring Merchants of Ur" Re-examined. *Antiquity* 68:770–783.

Safar, Fuad. 1947. Excavations at Eridu [in Arabic]. *Sumer* 3:95–111.

Salle, Jean-François. 1981. Le Golfe arabe dans l'antiquité. *Annales d'Histoire de l'Université Saint-Joseph,* 1–59.

Salle, Jean-François. 1987. The Arab-Persian Gulf under the Seleucids. In *Hellenism in the East,* ed. A. Kuhrt and S. Sherwin-White, 75–109. Berkeley: University of California Press.

Schmidt, Dana A. 1968: *Yemen: The Unknown War.* London: Bodley Head.

Schofield, Richard N. 1997. Border Disputes in the Gulf: Past, Present, and Future. In *The Persian Gulf at the Millennium: Essays in Politics, Economy, Security, and Religion,* ed. G. G. Sick and L. G. Potter, 127–165. New York: St. Martin's Press.

Schofield, Richard N. 2001. Down to the Usual Suspects: Border and Territorial Disputes in the Arabian Peninsula and Persian Gulf at the Millennium. In *Iran, Iraq, and the Arab Gulf States,* ed. J. A. Kechichian, 213–236. New York: Palgrave.

Scholz, Fred. 1990. *Muscat, Sultanat Oman: Geographische Skizze einer einmaligen arabischen Stadt.* Berlin: Das Arabische Buch.

Sherwin-White, Susan, and A. Kuhrt. 1993. *From Samarkhand to Sardis: A New Approach to the Seleucid Empire.* Berkeley: University of California Press.

Silverfarb, Daniel. 1994. *The Twilight of British Ascendancy in the Middle East: A Case Study of Iraq, 1941–1950.* New York: St. Martin's Press.

Simon, Reeva Spector. 1986. *Iraq between the Two World Wars: The Creation and Implementation of a Nationalist Ideology.* New York: Columbia University Press.

Simon, Reeva Spector. 1997. The Imposition of Nationalism on a Non-Nation State: The Case of Iraq during the Interwar Period, 1921–1941. In Jankowski and Gershoni 1997, 87–104.

Simon, Reeva Spector, and E. H. Tejirian, eds. 2004. *The Creation of Iraq, 1914–1921*. New York: Columbia University Press.

Snell, Daniel C. 1997. *Life in the Ancient Near East*. New Haven, CT: Yale University Press.

Theodoulou, Michael. 2004. Ideological Gulf Inflames Iran. www.timesonline.co.uk/printfriendly/0,,1-3-1385235-3,00.html.

Tixier, Jacques, ed. 1980. *Mission archéologique française à Qatar*. Doha, Qatar: Department of Tourism and Antiquities.

Tosi, Maurizio. 1974. Some Data for the Study of Prehistoric Cultural Areas on the Persian Gulf. *Proceedings of the Seminar for Arabian Studies* 4:145–171.

Tosi, Maurizio. 1984. The Notion of Craft Specialization and Its Representation in the Archaeological Record of Early States in the Turanian Basin. In *Marxist Perspectives in Archaeology*, ed. M. Spriggs, 22–52. Cambridge: Cambridge University Press.

Tosi, Maurizio. 1986. The Emerging Picture of Prehistoric Arabia. *Annual Review of Anthropology* 15:461–490.

Van De Mieroop, Marc. 2004. *A History of the Ancient Near East, ca. 3000–323 BC*. Malden, MA: Blackwell.

Vita-Finzi, C. 1998. Ancient Shorelines of Oman and Qatar. In *Arabia and Its Neighbours: Essays on Prehistorical and Historical Developments Presented in Honour of Beatrice de Cardi*, ed. C. S. Phillips, D. T. Potts, and S. Searight, 262–272. Turnhout, Belgium: Brepols.

von Soden, Wolfram. 1994. *The Ancient Orient*. Grand Rapids, MI: William B. Eerdmans.

Weeks, Lloyd. 2003. Prehistoric Metallurgy in the U.A.E.: Bronze Age–Iron Age Transitions. In *Archaeology of the United Arab Emirates: Proceedings of the First International Conference on the Archaeology of the U.A.E.*, ed. D. T. Potts, H. Al Naboodah, and P. Hellyer, 115–121. London: Trident Press.

Weeks, Lloyd. N.d. Iran and Bronze Age Metals Trade through the Persian Gulf. In *Draya tya hacâ Pârsâ aitiy: Essays on the Archaeology and History of the Persian Gulf Littoral*, ed. Kamyar Abdi. BAR International Series. Oxford: Archaeopress.

Wenke, Robert J. 1999. *Patterns in Prehistory*. 4th ed. Oxford: Oxford University Press.

Whitehouse, David. 2000. Ancient Glass from ed-Dur (Umm al-Qaiwain, U.A.E.) 2. Glass Excavated by the Danish Expedition. *Arabian Archaeology and Epigraphy* 11:87–128.

Wilkinson, J. C. 1991. *Arabia's Frontiers: The Story of Britain's Boundary Drawing in the Desert*. London: I. B. Tauris.

Wilson, Arnold T. 1928. *The Persian Gulf: An Historical Sketch from the Earliest Times to the Beginning of the Twentieth Century*. Oxford: Clarendon Press.

Wright, Henry T. 1994. Prestate Political Formations. In *Chiefdoms and Early States in the Near East: The Organizational Dynamics of Complexity*, ed. Gil Stein and M. Rothman, 67–84. Ann Arbor, MI: Prehistory Press.

Wright, Henry T. 1998. Uruk States in Southwestern Iran. In *Archaic States*, ed. Gary M. Feinman and J. Marcus, 171–197. Santa Fe, NM: School of American Research.

Wright, Henry T., and G. A. Johnson. 1975. Population, Exchange, and Early State Formation in Southwestern Iran. *American Anthropologist* 77:267–289.

Zarins, Juris, M. Ibrahim, D. T. Potts, and C. Edens. 1979. Saudi Arabian Archaeological Reconnaissance, 1978: The Preliminary Report on the Third Phase of the Comprehensive Archaeological Survey Program: The Central Province. *Atlal* 3:9–42.

Zarins, Juris, A. Murad, and K. al-Yish. 1981. Comprehensive Archaeological Survey Program: The Second Preliminary Report on the Southwestern Province. *Atlal* 5:9–42.

Zarins, Juris, A. Rihbini, and M. Kamal. 1982. Comprehensive Survey of the Central Nejd: The Riyadh Environs. *Atlal* 6:25–38.

Zarins, Juris, N. Whalen, M. Ibrahim, A. Morad, and M. Khan. 1980. Comprehensive Archaeological Survey Program: Preliminary Report on the Central and Southwestern Provinces Survey. *Atlal* 4:9–36.

Ziadeh, Nicola A. 1952. Recent Arab Literature on Arabism. *Middle East Journal* 6:468–473.

3

Israel/Palestine

Reformers

sephus

Rabbi – Sadducees – Priests of the Temple
Levites – Moses/Aaron
Pharisees – Non Levi, non priests
Essenes – Qumran, don't like above 2
Zealots – violent revolt against Rome
Sicarii

"Sign Prophets" ~ groups reinstituting Kingdom of David

*Primary source
- miscalculations
- bias — Ancient / Contemporary
- Faulty memories
- Value difference
- Lying
- mis-translation
- Physical source itself

Problems w. Josephus:
- Possible bias
- Pro-Roman / Pro-Jewish (Pharisee)

Josephus' work corrupted by later Christian bias

Yehuda's presentation of

EIGHT

Excavating Masada

The Politics-Archaeology Connection at Work

NACHMAN BEN-YEHUDA

The topic of archaeology in the context of politics has come to academic (and nonacademic) attention in recent years. Phil Kohl and Clare Fawcett's 1995 landmark book crystallized the issue and presented works that examined the fascinating ways in which politics and archaeology had interacted in different cultures. Moreover, their book substantiated, on the conceptual and descriptive levels, the very existence of the connection between politics and archaeology. Clearly, a major goal of this connection was demonstrated to be the construction of both national and personal identities. Thus, archaeology was involved, in specific historical instances, in helping to create collective memories whose aim it was to crystallize, fabricate, and give scientific validity and credibility to specific "pasts" in a way that could be interpreted as legitimating various national claims and interpretations of the present.

One of the tasks that remain is to examine in detail how exactly this process works. For example: Archaeology is a scientific discipline. If indeed it has been interacting with politics, how has the interaction been accomplished? Have the facts themselves been altered? Have findings from excavations been falsified? Have the interpretations been biased? Based on my recent research on the Masada mythical narrative (1995) and my current research on the excavations of Masada as an illustration for the politics-archaeology

Figure 8.1. Masada, looking south. On the right side (west), we can see the natural spur on which the Roman siege ramp was built, leading to the plateau, where the remnants of the Western Palace are evident. On the left side (east), the "snake path" is easily discernible. A closer look will reveal the small cable car close to the top of the "snake path." The three levels of the Northern Palace are visible on the front of the mountain, toward the right, and on top are the remnants of the storerooms and the large bathhouse. Photograph by Albatross, Aerial Photography, Tel Aviv.

connection (2002), I provide in this chapter one culturally specific illustrative answer to this fascinating series of questions.

The Excavations of Masada

The only historical source for our knowledge about what happened in Masada is the writings of Josephus Flavius. Take Josephus away or erase him, and all we are left with is ruins in the Judean desert. Historical Masada consists of what Josephus tells us. And yet, despite this widely available historical source, the story that secular Zionism conveys—while relying on Josephus—is a very different tale. It is a fabricated mythical tale of heroism that cannot be found in Josephus.

My focus on Masada's main excavations during 1963–1965, headed by Yigael Yadin, is no coincidence. These excavations helped, in a most significant way, to provide scientific credibility and reliability to one of Israel's prime and founding heroic myths (e.g., see Ayalon 1972; Ben-Yehuda 1995; Shargel 1979; Zerubavel 1995). Moreover, not only did these excavations become world famous, but in 2001 Masada was declared a UNESCO World Heritage center because it was characterized as presenting an "outstanding universal value." Indeed, the authors of the first volume of the Masada excavations final report state that "perhaps no other archaeological endeavor in Israel has attracted such widespread attention as the excavations of Masada" (Aviram, Foerster, and Netzer 1989a: ix). To drive home the point, the authors of the volume quote Louis Feldman: "No single event in the history of the second Jewish commonwealth has occasioned more discussion in recent years than the fall of Masada, the mausoleum of martyrs, as it has been called. . . . The spectacular discoveries in the excavations of Masada by Yadin in a nation where digging is a veritable form of prayer have made Masada a shrine for the Jewish people" (Feldman 1975: 218, cited by Aviram, Foerster, and Netzer 1989a: 1). According to Silberman, "Due to [the Israelis'] efforts and their discoveries, Masada became the most famous project in the history of Israeli archaeology, and perhaps second only to the clearance of the tomb of Tutankhamen, the most publicized excavation in the twentieth century" (1989: 89).

The main archaeological excavations of Masada took place during two periods, which amounted to eleven months of excavations in all. The first was between October 1963 and April 1964, and the second between December 1964 and March 1965. The excavations constituted a major logistic effort on a difficult terrain and incorporated thousands of volunteers from Israel and other parts of the world. The Israeli army assisted this gigantic effort by contributing resources and volunteers. Participation from the Israeli army in archaeological projects is not surprising; before Yadin's academic career, he was the chief of staff of the Israeli army. All sources describing the complicated logistic efforts involved in the excavations indeed point out that these efforts were immense. It was necessary to manage transportation, communications, and provision of food, water, housing, equipment, and so forth. All this occurred in a period when only half-decent roads to Masada existed.

In terms of people who were actually involved in the excavations, Yadin had at his disposal on any given day about two hundred volunteers doing the work. However, every two weeks or so, a different set of volunteers came to the task. This rapid turnover meant that eventually thousands of Israelis and non-Israelis alike participated in the excavations and were exposed to the story of Masada in the most intimate and direct way. While it is difficult to estimate the economic cost of the excavations, it seems safe to assume that the overall cost, in May 1996 prices, was around US$2 million. The British newspaper *Observer* assumed patronage of the excavations. Much of the money needed came from outside Israel, due to Yadin's connections and the *Observer*'s support. A few families contributed funds as well, including the Sachers, the Kennedys, and the Wolfsons (see Yadin 1966a, 1966b, 1970). The direct financial support from within Israel was rather minimal, but various organizations in Israel, such as the army, contributed either manpower or equipment. All told, the excavations of Masada constituted a national and international effort. The end result was, in Yadin's words, that "we excavated ninety-seven per cent of the built-on area of Masada" (Yadin 1966a: 203). Many of the excavated structures and artifacts were reconstructed too. The architectonic findings revealed the majesty and beauty of the Herodian buildings.

There was a very significant delay in publishing the final results of the excavations. While some early reports were made available (e.g., Yadin 1965, 1966a, 1966b, 1970; see also the progress report Rabinowitz 1990), the final reports began to come out only after Yadin's untimely death and were still being processed in the early 1990s. Between 1989 and 1991 (almost twenty-six years after the excavations) three volumes were published summarizing part of the final reports.[1]

Politics and Masada

As early as 1966, Moses Finley wrote, in his review of Yadin's first book about the site, that Masada was a prime example of the politics of modern archaeology. The clear implication that archaeology can be used for political purposes received another boost in the 1980s and in the early 1990s. Moshe Dayan (1983: 21) discussed Masada in the context of Jews being massacred and claimed that killing Jews from the days of the Great Revolt was a pattern. "In one country after another," he wrote, "the Jews have met a similar fate." Narkis (1983) even draws a direct line from Masada to the Holocaust. The "Masada complex" (see Ben-Yehuda 1995, chap. 13) fits very well into this critique.

Yadin himself made some unmistakable ideological-political statements before, during, and after the excavations. For example, in an interview he gave to *Bamachane*, the official weekly of the Israeli army, published March 18, 1969, he stated:

> The public's interest in the antiquities of the land is . . . almost phenomenal. . . . This big interest does not stem from interest in archaeology as such. Everyone feels and knows that he is discovering and excavating findings and artifacts from the days of his fathers. And, every finding bears witness to the connection and covenant between the people and the land. From this aspect, archaeological research added an important national dimension. There is an element of curiosity as far as the unknown is concerned. There is the wish to decipher the past. This is a natural tendency that most certainly helped the revival of interest in archaeology. But, as far as Israel is concerned, it seems to me that the factor I mentioned—the search and building of the connection to the people and the land—must be taken into consideration. [Archaeology] in my view reinforces Hebraic consciousness, let us say, the identification and the connection with ancient Judaism and Jewish consciousness. (14–15)

The tremendous interest in archaeology in Israel that he mentions was not confined to Yadin's era as an archaeologist, nor to the time he was interviewed. Ya'acov Shavit (1986) documented that the interest in archaeology could be witnessed as early as the 1930s.

It is not too difficult to understand that secular Zionism, dealing with the difficult, unprecedented idea of a whole people returning to its homeland after almost two thousand years of living elsewhere, was only too happy to take interest in and support a scientific endeavor that could potentially validate and reinforce its moral claim to the land, especially against increasing Arab national resistance. Moreover, the possibility of discovering remnants of ancient Jews who had worked the land, who were fierce fighters, and who were willing to live and die for the land provided a rather healthy antidote for the traditional and stereotypical anti-Semitic view of Jews in Europe as parasitic, lazy, unwilling to "get their hands dirty," and unable to fight. Because the leaders of Zionism at that time came from Europe, the temptation to mold new personal and national Jewish identities by relying on archaeology must have been simply irresistible. Relying on archaeology helped in two related areas as well: it created a continuous connection to a heroic and glorious past and countered anti-Semitic images.

Furthermore, Shapira pointed out that the use of the Masada heroic mythical narrative also helped to solve a debate within the Yishuv, the Jewish community in Palestine before the state of Israel was established in 1948. That debate revolved around the question of legitimating the use of violence and force by secular Zionists. The Masada mythical narrative was most certainly utilized to give credence to the idea that using force for political and ideological purposes was indeed justifiable (1992: 45, 269, 421–433).

These ideas put some major parts of Israeli archaeology, certainly up to the 1960s, in the context of supporting the process of a new nation-building in Israel. Some like to use the term *recruited archaeology* to describe this phenomenon. Indeed, in July of 1994 a social organization called "the council for a good Eretz Israel," together with *Ma'ariv* (a Hebrew-language daily newspaper); El Al (Israeli airlines); and EMI, the association of Israeli performing artists, announced special festivities giving distinctive recognition and appreciation to Israeli archaeologists for their contribution to "expose the secrets of the land, its antiquities and heritage" (*Ma'ariv*, July 22, 1994, p. 7). By way of comparison, let me point out that no such recognition was ever offered to, say, Israeli physicists, mathematicians, biologists, economists, sociologists, or even anthropologists. In fact, I believe that only Israeli archaeologists have received this type of honor.

That Yadin had a real, personal, and national interest in Masada is obvious. That he helped give the Masada mythical narrative its scientific legitimacy and accomplished wonders in spreading the mythical narrative is obvious too (see also Silberman 1993: 270–293). Both he and Shmaria Guttman (another significant figure in developing the Masada mythical narrative before Yadin) knew, no doubt, the original historical narrative, yet they chose to tailor their version to what they felt were personal and national needs. Did that basic motivation cause Shmaria Guttman or Yadin to falsify findings of the excavations, or did their

Figure 8.2. Masada, looking from east to west. Easily seen are the following: remnants of the Roman siege ramp in the foreground, with a Roman siege camp on the lower left side of the ramp (square-shaped); the distinctive three levels of the Northern Palace (left side of the picture); and the two lines of the entries to the water cisterns, beneath the Northern Palace. The photograph is dated June 1963. Courtesy of the Israeli Government's Press Office.

view affect the physical results of their excavations? The answer must be a clear no. Yadin was so careful with the findings that the daily meetings of his staff of archaeologists were recorded. That, as Magness (1992) pointed out, was quite unusual, as well as helpful. In fact, Yadin and Guttman must have been quite disappointed that the findings did not confirm in an unequivocal way their interpretation of the historical narrative provided by Josephus Flavius. We can see here that, as in other scientific endeavors, motivation to conduct a study is separate from the actual scientific findings and that scientific findings can be separated from their interpretations. The warping of the historical narrative by Guttman and Yadin (and others) was not at the level of the excavations or the findings themselves. It was at the level of interpretation; that is, the social construction of the findings. The process of exactly how that was done certainly provides an interesting future puzzle for a separate study in the sociology of science.

The Masada Mythical Narrative

Briefly described, the Masada mythical narrative is a heroic tale. It states that in around AD 66 the proud Jews in the Provincia Judaia revolted against the oppressive Roman yoke, seeking their freedom from bondage and cruelty. The Zealots spearheaded the revolt. Unfortunately for the Jews, the Roman imperial army crushed the revolt with brute force. The fall of Jerusalem in AD 70 and the burning and destruction of the Jewish second temple signified the end of the major part of the revolt. After the destruction of Jerusalem by the Romans, the remaining Zealots escaped to Masada. The Romans laid siege to Masada. The Zealots fought valiantly and raided the Roman positions over a period of three years. However, when they realized that there was no longer any hope to win and that the choice was either death or wretched slavery, they all chose to kill themselves.

The Masada mythical narrative was invented and developed in a prolonged process. Its early elements were debated already in the 1920s in British-occupied Palestine. Mostly, a few secular Zionist moral entrepreneurs crystallized the narrative during the 1930s and 1940s. As so many point out, the fabricated crystallization of the secular Jewish Masada heroic myth in the early 1940s was necessary because the founding fathers of the Jewish state required heroic tales to help create a new secular Jewish national and personal identity: an identity for a modern Jew who felt connected to his or her physical homeland and to the nation's ancestors and who internalized the mystical connection between Jewish fearless warriors of times past and present. The development of a heroic myth in the early 1940s received strong additional back wind from the obvious threat posed by Field Marshal Erwin Rommel's Nazi Afrika Korps advancements in north Africa in 1941–1943. Developing and believing in a Jewish heroic "last stand" at that time was more than understandable. Accordingly, Yadin subtitled the 1966 English version of his book on Masada *Herod's Fortress and the Zealots' Last Stand.*

For secular Zionism, which preached that Jews should return to their homeland of Zion, creating this symbolically powerful and mystical connection to bridge the gap between "heroic Jews then" and "heroic Jews now" was essential. The political and ideological statement was that Jews have always lived in Zion, have always fought for it, and, if necessary, have died for it. The Masada mythical narrative was a vibrant element in promulgating that statement. In the early 1940s, of course, the threat of a Nazi invasion of Palestine was very real when Rommel's Afrika Korps advanced on northern Africa toward Egypt. The existence of that threat called for a model cognitive tale of what was to be done. Masada played a major role in that historical era. When the excavations of Masada took place, therefore, the Masada mythical narrative was very well established. It was embraced by the state of Israel as one of its representative mythologies, as thousands of youth were made to climb the rock of Masada and study the myth. The Masada mythical narrative became a cornerstone in the shaping of national and personal identities for millions of (mostly secular) Israeli Jews in modern Israel.

The Josephus Narrative

Josephus provides the only source about the fateful events in Masada.[2] Two views are prevalent regarding the reading of Josephus: one calls for a liberal reading, giving rather thick interpretations, and the other prefers to add only a minimal amount of interpretation. I adhere to the second version. The main reason is that a liberal reading of Josephus simply gives rise to some rather fantastic interpretations, a few of them even contradicting what he wrote.

The story of Masada is not a discrete and isolated historical sequence. It was part of the AD 66–73 Jewish revolt against the Roman Empire. This revolt was a majestic failure on the part of the Jews. They suffered a bitter and humiliating military and political defeat, and the Roman army burned the second Jewish temple to the ground. Masada was the last chapter in the suppression of the revolt by the imperial Roman army. Josephus's account includes strong criticism of the decision to rebel. The Roman Empire in the first century AD was at its peak of military power, controlling vast areas from today's Britain to Mesopotamia. Deciding to revolt against such military might certainly demanded some serious military, as well as political, strategy. There is no evidence for either.

During the revolt a few Jewish ideological groups existed. Two are most relevant for Masada and the myth: the Sicarii and the Zealots (Ben-Yehuda 1995). The Zealots probably carried the main burden of the revolt, but the connection between them and the Sicarii is not entirely clear. When Josephus provides us with the story of Masada, he is quite consistent; he leaves no doubt of the fact that the people of Masada were Sicarii.

The name Sicarii comes from the name of a small dagger, sica, that these people used to hide beneath their robes. They used the daggers to assassinate their opponents and to create unrest. The Sicarii were the first known group of Jews who preached and practiced political assassinations (Ben-Yehuda 1993). That Josephus was not a supporter of these assassins is also obvious. In Jerusalem the Sicarii were involved in so many acts of violence and killings against other Jews that they were persecuted and their leader, Menachem Ben-Yehuda, was caught and tortured to death. They were forced to flee the city. Headed by their Sicarii leader, Elazar Ben-Yair, they escaped to Masada.[3] All this took place long before the Roman army put a siege on Jerusalem and decimated the city. The Sicarii were to remain on Masada to their end. Josephus does mention an unrest involving the Sicarii in Alexandria in Egypt after the fall of Masada, but it is unclear from where, exactly, these specific Sicarii came to Egypt. Josephus states only that they came from Judea, fleeing the war there.

While in Masada, the Sicarii raided villages. One of their raids was on the nearby Jewish settlement of Ein Geddi. According to Josephus, the Sicarii raided Ein Geddi during Passover. They chased the men out and killed seven hundred of the women, the children, and the weak and took the victims' food supplies to Masada. Moreover, the Sicarii refused to leave Masada and go to Jerusalem to help the besieged Jews there fight the Romans.

Following the destruction of Jerusalem in AD 70, there were three fortresses left with rebels: Herodion, Macherus, and Masada. The first two were conquered, and then after an intermission (caused by the sudden death of the Roman governor of Judea and the appointment of a new governor, Flavius Silva), the Roman army laid siege to Masada, the last rebel-held fortress. The siege may have begun late in the winter of 72 and may have lasted till the spring of 73. It was a standard Roman siege system (Shatzman 1993, 1995) that probably lasted no more than five to twelve weeks (Roth 1995). It was not accompanied by any major or significant resistance by the Sicarii. When the Sicarii realized that there was no escape for them, they decided, probably influenced by Ben-Yair's two persuasive speeches and possibly some coercion, to commit collective suicide rather than become slaves to the Romans.

The Masada story, as told by Josephus, is definitely not a heroic tale. It is a tale of a doomed revolt, about a group of Jewish assassins who did not fight the Romans but chose suicide instead (rather than, say, a Samsonite end). As I have indicated elsewhere (1995) and above, in the early decades of the twentieth century, secular Zionism transformed this sad and tragic story into a heroic myth.

The Excavations of Masada and the Construction of Knowledge

The excavations of Masada were clearly meant to give support to the myth. Yadin's many interviews with the media, as well as his writings, leave very little doubt that he was interested in providing scientific credence to the mythical version.

In order to examine in detail exactly how Yadin was able to use the archaeological excavations to give support to the mythical version of the events on Masada, one needs to go to the various elements of the story as given by Josephus and compare them with the way the archaeologists presented them. Because up to 1989 Yadin was the only person to write about the results of the excavations, it is easy to perform this examination. Obviously, the Masada mythical narrative consists of many elements and it is virtually impossible to detail them all in the space of this chapter. I have therefore chosen only a few illustrative cases.

An important and instructive research process consists of examining the way the excavators of Masada were formulating and constructing knowledge. They had real, physical and tangible findings, of course. But how could one interpret these findings? The way to do it is obvious if one has some idea what to expect, a conceptualization of what the original site was like, what it was all about, who was there and why. In the case of Masada, the archaeologists were extremely lucky. They had the textual account from Josephus Flavius, providing a historical conceptualization not only of what happened on Masada, but also of the site's physical description. Thus, Yadin and his staff had a relatively powerful and detailed historical base that supplied the interpretative backbone and framework for the findings. The excavators had something much more powerful than Josephus Flavius, though. They had the Masada myth. That myth, as we saw earlier, was based on an interesting interpretation of Josephus Flavius. Clearly, the excavators set out to find archaeological evidence for the myth, not for Josephus's narrative.

It is very plausible to assume that Yadin's interest in Masada was originally ignited and fueled by his hope to find there some significant scrolls, perhaps something equivalent to the famous Dead Sea scrolls. However, when no significant scrolls were found, he was captured by the ambience, magic, and mystery of Masada, and his interest was transformed and focused on the myth.

Providing scientific credibility for a myth is not an act; it is a process. In such a process, myth-favoring interpretations are given to physical evidence. How is that accomplished? The process we have in mind here, clearly, is the social construction of scientific knowledge.[4] Since a process is what we are interested in, we need to examine how it unfolds. What we find is that the Masada myth was created from a series of discoveries, debates, and publications.

During the two periods of the 1963–1965 archaeological excavations of Masada, the staff had an almost daily meeting, usually at 19:15. These meetings were where all the available professional staff members met to exchange views, discuss findings, plan the work, and tell each other what happened during the day. Luckily for us (and as a result of Yadin's keen sense of history), most of the daily sessions were taped and later transcribed (transcripts are available in the Institute of Archaeology, Hebrew University).

Examples

Sicarii versus Zealots

One of the most important and obvious elements of the myth involved who was actually on Masada. Yadin deliberately and systematically avoided using the term *Sicarii* to describe the Masada rebels and used the term *Zealots* instead. This is completely inconsistent with Josephus Flavius. According to Josephus, these two groups were distinctly different. Yadin did not explain why it was that he preferred the term *Zealots* over *Sicarii*. But it is quite obvious that while the term *Sicarii* describes an unpleasant group of robbers and assassins, the term *Zealots* is positively associated with freedom fighters. That Yadin prefers *Zealots* to *Sicarii* is politically and ideologically understandable and is consistent with his views. However, it is scientifically wrong and misleading.

Josephus consistently claims that the Masada rebels were Sicarii. With one exception, he acknowledges no other types of people in Masada. The one exception was Simon (son of Giora) and his forces. Simon escaped to Masada, but the Masada rebels "suspected him, and only permitted him to come with the women he brought with him to the lower part of the fortress, while they dwelt in the upper part of it themselves" (*Wars of the Jews*, 4.9.3, in Josephus 1981: 541). Later some of the mistrust disappeared and Simon and his forces joined the Sicarii of Masada in raiding the countryside.

One of the early tactics Yadin used to neutralize the fact that the rebels on Masada were Sicarii was to argue that there were many groups of people in Masada. If this line of argumentation can be established, then one need not explicitly state that there were Sicarii there, as Josephus does. Here is what Yadin said in the daily meeting of November 25, 1963 (p. 2): "It seems to me that the most natural interpretation is that part of the Qumran people, factions from them, in fact escaped to Masada. . . . We know that different and new groups convened together every time in Masada. One time Bar-Giora [Simon]. One time this [person] came with his group, and that with his group." To begin with, there is absolutely no indication in Josephus of this type of "different groups" convening in Masada. Yadin may refer here to a small scroll fragment found in one of the casemates in Masada that Yadin identified as having an Essene origin. The transcripts of the December 2, 1963, evening meeting (p. 1) identify the text as identical to the texts of the Essenes in Qumran. Indeed, there were Essenes in Qumran (not too far from Masada), and Yadin may have been tempted to conclude that the presence of the aforementioned scroll in Masada could be taken as an indication that there were Essenes at Masada. In fact, Yadin wrote that "a minority of scholars have long suggested that the Qumran sect should be identified with the Sicarii Zealots, the very Zealots that occupied Masada" (1966a: 173). He also stated: "It seems to me that the discovery of this scroll serves as proof indeed that the Essenes also participated in the great revolt against the Romans. . . . It is . . . likely that a considerable number of Essenes also joined the rebellion. And after the country had been destroyed and Masada remained the sole stronghold and outpost in the war against the Romans, it is likely that all who had fought together and survived found shelter there, among them also the Essene participants. This, it seems to me, explains the presence of the Qumranic sectarian scroll in Masada" (1966a: 174). This is an interesting speculation, but one that receives absolutely no substantiation from Josephus, who makes a clear distinction between the Zealots and the Sicarii in the Masada context and does not associate any of them with the Essenes. Of course, there is another, much easier and more plausible and logical explanation for the presence of an Essene scroll on Masada, and that is that the Sicarii of Masada raided Qumran, or some other unknown Essene settlement, just as they raided Ein Gedi (which may have had Essene dwellers), and part of the spoils of their robbery was the scroll. This interpretation, however, does not accord with the general line of argument Yadin wanted to develop. Another telling example relates to the "Battle of Masada."

The Battle of Masada

Josephus does not describe any "battle" of Masada. This is a significant omission. Josephus had a clear "interest" to represent the Jewish opposition in a manner that would demonstrate the strength of the Roman army that conquered them. For example, his descriptions of the Roman conquest of Jerusalem, Gamla, Yodfat, and Macherus provide vivid details about the heroics of the Jewish rebels and their desperate (but unsuccessful) struggles and raids against the Roman imperial army. His failure to mention any active fights, resistance, or raids by Masada's defenders against the Romans is not insignificant. Thus, while the impression one typically gets is that there was a war around Jerusalem with fights, battles, and struggles, no such impression is projected about the Roman siege of Masada. In other words, there really was no "battle" around Masada, and the Sicarii, so capable of committing assassinations and raiding nearby villages, were not genuine warriors who had the motivation and willingness to fight the Roman army. However, the mythical version that viewed those Sicarii as heroes required and therefore emphasized a "battle" because such a battle is an essential ingredient of a heroic "last stand" narrative. To understand the extent to which the assumption about a "battle" tinted Yadin's view, let us look at the transcript of the November 5, 1963 session. There has been a puzzling find of "sand stones" there. The excavators try to explain the find, and Yadin explains that Shmaria Guttman found many such stones and warns against a premature interpretation of the find. And yet, out of all the likely possible interpretations of the find, Yadin mentions only one. He states that during the battles, parts of Masada walls were destroyed; in order to commence repairs, the Masada rebels (he never mentions "Sicarii") took materials from nearby buildings. This created the "sand stones." One must pay attention to the fact that this "early" interpretation hinges entirely on the assumption that there were indeed battles. A similarly fantastic interpretation of the evidence involves the three skeletons discovered at locus 8.

Skeletons at Locus 8

The discovery itself was first mentioned in the transcripts of November 14, 1963 (p. 3), where Amnon (probably Ben-Tor) reports that in locus 8 (on the lower terrace of the Northern Palace) the bones of a child or a baby and those of an adult were found. The report states that the archaeologists also found in the site a large number of scales of armor and arrows, all in good condition. This discovery, according to the transcripts, did not cause any debate and was just reported without any significant discussion. The next time the discovery was discussed was on November 26, 1963. It is apparent that at the daily evening meeting the archaeologists were discussing the remains of three skeletons found in the northeastern part of the lower terrace of the Northern Palace, the place the archaeologists marked as "locus 8." This locus is part of a small

Figure 8.3. The three levels of Masada's Northern Palace, viewed from the north. Locus 8 is on the extreme left side of the square-shaped lower level of the palace. It looks like a lying *L*.

structural complex to the east of that level of the villa-palace identified by Netzer as "Frigidarium 8" (Aviram, Goerster, and Netzer 1991: 167). Below is the translation from Hebrew of the protocol of the meeting of the archaeologists on that day, discussing the find:

> *Dr. Haas:* Three skeletons were found in locus 8. . . . One of a woman. . . . This is a woman aged 17–18, and there is also a skeleton of a child aged 11–12 . . . the third skeleton . . . he is first of all a man and his age is between 20–22, quite young too.
>
> *Yadin:* . . . It is obvious that the child and woman can not be a mother and a son because of the age difference, so if there really was a family here, the man—could possibly be the father of the child. . . . In those periods YA HABIBI! there is a plus-minus of a year . . . here you make it 23 and there 10 and everything is OK. . . .
>
> The man and the woman can certainly be a pair! But the son is not from this woman. . . . Could be her or his brother.

The next time we meet this discovery is two months later, on January 17, 1964, when it is reported, again by Amnon, that he found an almost complete skeleton while excavating locus 8, as well as hair, armor scales, a sandal, and an adult skull, and he reported about continuing the excavation in locus 9. No discussion followed the dry report. It is important to add that no more discussions of the discovery in locus 8 can be found in the transcripts.

The discovery in locus 8 is an interesting and intriguing one. So is the November 26 discussion. There is nothing in the discussion, or the find, that could prepare one for what was about to unfold with this discovery over the next ten years. Yadin, we must remember, like others, was looking for some empirical support for the Masada mythical narrative, some tangible "proof" that would disperse all doubts about the supposedly heroic acts that took place in Masada. So let us follow Yadin's statements about the dramatic find of the remains of the three skeletons in locus 8. As we move ahead from 1963, let us remember the discussion that took place on November 26.

Our next stop is 1965. In that year Yadin published the interim summary for the first season of the excavations of Masada. The Israeli Exploration Society published the document in Hebrew. There, on page 22, he writes: "It can not be stated with certainty, that these skeletons are those of the family of that last warrior who remained the last [alive], killed his family and set the palace on fire . . . but, seemingly, there is no doubt that these skeletons are those of the people of the Great Revolt" (Yadin 1965). In the English version of the report, the section treating the findings in locus 8 does not even mention the skeletons.

What does Yadin say in the Hebrew version quoted above? First, he seems to be absolutely certain that those skeletons are of the people of the Great Revolt. Maybe so. But what is the justification for this strong statement? None is provided. Look at the more interesting first part of the statement. There, Yadin states that these remains may be those of the last rebel alive (he actually prefers the word "warrior") who killed his family, set the palace on fire, and then killed himself. Yadin carefully phrases this statement, but the factual basis for this wild speculation is simply not provided. By making this speculation, Yadin must also assume that the palace that Josephus mentions in the context of the collective suicide is the Northern Palace. What if this collective suicide occurred elsewhere, such as near the Western Palace, not mentioned by Josephus (see Ben-Yehuda 1998)? If so, then Yadin's claim has no support. By the time the uninformed reader finishes reading this, the qualifier "It can not be stated with certainty" that precedes the account seems to have evaporated as an incredible tale is laid out by the man who has become the authority on Masada. Because Yadin solidifies and repeats this particular speculation until its astonishing climax in 1973, let us return for a minute to Josephus Flavius and see what he has to say about that last person alive on Masada. Josephus describes how the people on Masada killed their families, how they "laid all they had in a heap, set fire to it," and

> then chose ten men by lot, to slay the rest; every one of whom laid himself down by his wife and children on the ground, and threw his arms about them, and they offered their necks to the stroke of those who by lot executed that melancholy office; and when these ten had, without fear, slain them all, they made the same rule for casting lots for themselves, that he whose lot it was should first kill the other nine, and after all, should kill himself . . . so, for a conclusion, the nine offered their necks to the executioner, and he who was the last of all, took a view of all the other bodies, lest perchance some or other among so many who were slain should want his assistance to be quite dispatched; and when he perceived that they were all slain, he set fire to the palace, and with the great force of his hand ran his sword entirely through himself, and fell down dead near to his own relations. (*Wars of the Jews*, 7.9, in Josephus 1981: 603)

Obviously, Yadin's speculative interpretation is not consistent with the original version provided by Josephus Flavius. To begin with, the last person alive did not kill his family and then himself. He killed the other nine survivors and then himself. Second, chances that this mass death scene took place in the lower level of the Northern Palace-villa are very slim. While we do not know exactly where the rebels killed themselves, the lower level of the Northern Palace-villa seems hardly the place. The rebels did not live there; it was distant and difficult to access, and it would have been difficult to convene 960 people there. The size of the central square is only 18 × 18 meters. Even if we add the two wings—eastern (10 × 6 meters) and western (8 × 3 meters)—we are still left with a rather small area that, together with the central area, has maybe 408 square meters. In fact, the first team that excavated Masada had already noted that the area of the Northern Palace is such that "it is difficult to assume that close to a thousand people got there together" (Avigad et al. 1957: 64). Third, the "family" Yadin mentions is not so convincing, when the age differences are taken into account. Fourth, no shred of hard evidence exists to suggest that the bones that were found in locus 8 are of the Jewish rebels of Masada.

Our next stop is 1966. In that year the Hebrew and English versions of Yadin's popular book on Masada were published. Both books refer to the discovery of the three skeletons in locus 8. There are, however, some differences between the two versions of the book. In the Hebrew version Yadin wrote that they found "the remains of three skeletons. One skeleton was that of a man in his twenties who was perhaps one of the commanders of Masada. . . . Nearby, on the stairs, the skeletal remains of a young woman were discovered. . . . The third skeleton was that of a child. . . . Could it be that we had discovered the bones of . . . [the last] fighter [on Masada] and of his family?" (1966b: 54). The English version offers the following text:

> We were arrested by a find which is difficult to consider in archaeological terms, for such an experience is not normal in archaeological excavations. Even the veterans and the more cynical among us stood frozen, gazing in awe at what had been uncovered; for as we gazed, we relived the final and most tragic moments of the drama of Masada. Upon the steps leading to the cold-water pool and on the ground nearby were the remains of three skeletons. One was that of a man of about twenty—perhaps one of the commanders of Masada. . . . not far off, also on the steps, was the skeleton of a young woman. . . . The third skeleton was that of a child. There could be no doubt that what our eyes beheld were the remains of some of the defenders of Masada. (1966a: 54)

Yadin quotes from Josephus the passage about the last person alive on Masada and then adds, "Could it be that we had discovered the bones of that very fighter and of his kin? This, of course, we can never know for certain" (58). Now the speculation gets thicker. It is not just the last rebel, but "one of the commanders" of Masada. Mind you, the November 23,

1963, transcript reveals nothing of the excitement and awe Yadin refers to above. On the contrary, reading Yadin's words at that session reveals a healthy amount of humor. Moreover, finding skeletons or bones in an archaeological excavations is certainly not "unusual." What makes this particular find unusual is the ad hoc and later interpretation Yadin made of it. But this is not the end. The next time Yadin discussed the discovery in locus 8 was in 1970.

In 1970 Yadin wrote that the skeletal remnants found in locus 8 "are probably the remnants of one of the important commanders of the revolt and his family members" (382). In the *Encyclopedia Judaica* Yadin describes the very same remnants: "The skeletons undoubtedly represent the remains of an important commander of Masada and his family" (1971: 11:1007). Note how the doubts and uncertainty are gone, how Yadin moves from "probably" to "undoubtedly" and how the "important commander" and "his family" slip in. Nothing we know of in the physical evidence justifies this change. And yet one must also note the careful phrasing of "his family," which could be interpreted in a few ways. In a few years, even this will disappear.

However, the most intriguing interpretation of the discovery in locus 8 was presented on April 11, 1973. On that date, Yadin gave a speech at the top of Masada to members of two professional associations—the Society for the Study of Eretz Israel and Its Antiquities, and the Society for the Protection of Nature: "I shall mention the remains of the three fighters that we found in the northern palace: a very important commander, his wife and their child, just like in the description of Josephus Flavius" (Yadin 1973). An immense gap is evident between the April 11, 1973, statement and the November 26, 1963, factual report; the departure from Josephus Flavius is obvious as well. Suffice it to say that if until 1973 Yadin was careful to report the finding of three skeletons and to add his interpretation of the find, the 1973 account differs qualitatively. The three skeletons became those of a family (father, mother and child) of "warriors," headed by a very important commander. The 1973 text fits much better and can be easily interpreted within the Masada mythical narrative.

In 1991 volume 3 of the Final Reports of the 1963–1965 excavations was published. This volume was written by Professor Ehud Netzer. There Netzer describes locus 8 and states that "near the bottom of the pool, in the southwestern corner, were found the remains of a boy aged about 10; beneath him was a large stone covering the skull of a woman aged about 18. Another concentration of human remains was revealed in the southeastern corner, also near the bottom" (Aviram, Foerster, and Netzer

1991: 167). To Netzer's scientific credit, we must note how careful and factual he is. And Netzer did participate in the excavations. He does not mention an "important commander" or his "family" or the "last warrior," nor does he even state that these skeletal remains had anything to do with the rebels on Masada. There is also no mention of the "awe" Yadin described (for more on this issue, see Ben-Yehuda 2002: 124–125).

Clearly, the discovery in locus 8, according to Yadin's 1966 version, left the excavators mesmerized. As we could already see, that is not what was reflected in the transcripts. So it must be asked, How was this stunning discovery processed by the media? In the November 24, 1963, issue of *Ma'ariv,* a daily Jewish secular Hebrew newspaper, toward the end of a long report written by Yadin himself, eight of ninety-two lines are devoted to this discovery: "Here we found some evidence of their [the zealots] tragic end. Inside more than 400 armor plates, 30 arrows and parts of a dress, we discovered two human skeletons. One of an adult, perhaps a woman, the second of a child. Nearby we found the bones of a woman" (p. 15). *Yediot Aharonot,* another daily Jewish secular Hebrew newspaper, on the same date (and again on December 1, 1963) also has a long report about the findings on Masada. That daily paper, too, reports on both dates about finding two skeletal remains of a woman and a child, but without any interpretation. Searching for more references to this discovery in *Ma'ariv* yielded some later mention of it in 1965, when the excavations were coming close to their end and some summaries were made. In *Ha'aretz,* also a daily Jewish secular Hebrew newspaper, of March 28, 1965 (p. 7), the skeletons found in locus 8 are mentioned as such with absolutely no interpretation. However, on page 3 of *Ma'ariv* of the same date, a report about the missing bodies can be found. The reporter, Tzvi Lavie, states: "On one of the stairs of the northern palace three [skeletons] were found, of a man, woman and child, that were probably among the last of those committing suicide, and who went down to set the palace on fire, as described in Yoseph Ben-Matityahu's book." Lavie's source must have been Yadin. *Hamodea,* a daily Jewish ultra-orthodox Hebrew newspaper, in its November 25, 1963, issue (p. 3) reported on the finds from Masada. Among the many discoveries the report mentions, it is also noted that in the Northern Palace the excavators found "a skeleton of a child and of an adult . . . and 300 armor plates . . . which probably belonged to a high ranking Roman officer." *Hatzophe,* a daily Jewish orthodox Hebrew newspaper, mentions nothing. So it is clearly the case that when the discovery in locus 8 was actually made, it most certainly did not create the impact attributed to it by Yadin in 1966 and later. That later addition was obviously a dramatic

Figure 8.4. The three levels of the majestic Northern Palace, viewed from the top and toward the south. The photograph was taken while the excavations were taking place and before reconstruction. The huge supporting walls for the lower level of the palace are seen, as well as the enigmatic circular middle level. In the upper part of the picture, the storerooms and the large bathhouse are clearly visible. Locus 8, on the left side of the lower level of the palace, is open. Photograph courtesy of the 1963–1964 Archaeological Excavation Expedition to Masada, the Institute of Archaeology, Hebrew University, and the Israel Exploration Society.

social construction created by Yadin, aimed to give a nice support to the mythical narrative.

The Siege Ramp

As a final example, I investigate how the archaeological interpretation of the western ascent to Masada became a formative part of the Masada myth. The way in which the Romans handled the siege of Masada is an important issue. Was it a particularly difficult task? A long or a short siege? What was the structure of the siege system? These questions are difficult to answer from an archaeological point of view. Other information is easier to obtain: for example, the number of Roman military camps around Masada, the circumvallation wall around Masada, and the nature of the physical defense of Masada. One of the thorny issues here concerns the western ascent to Masada, or, as it is better known, the siege ramp.

Tactically speaking, Masada's apparent Achilles' heel is to be found on its western side. On that side there is a huge natural spur leading from the bottom of the mountain to its top. This spur was probably used by the builders of Masada as the main entry road to Masada, and it was this natural spur on which the Roman army built its ramp. Even today, climbing to Masada from the west side on this natural spur takes only a few minutes and requires very little effort.

The Romans chose to focus their main military effort to penetrate and conquer Masada on the west side, precisely because of that natural spur. Here is what Josephus Flavius tells us about it:

> The Roman commander Silva . . . undertook the siege itself, though he found but one single place that would admit the banks he was to raise; for behind that tower which secured the road that led to the palace, and to the top of the hill from the west, there was a certain eminency of the rock, very broad and very prominent, but three hundred cubits beneath the highest part of Masada; it was called the White Promontory. Accordingly, he got upon that part of the rock, and ordered the army to bring earth; and when they fell to that work with alacrity, and abundance of them together, the bank was raised, and became solid for two hundred cubits in height. Yet this bank was not thought sufficiently high for the use of the engines that were to be set upon it; but still another elevated work of great stones compacted together was raised upon that bank. (*Wars of the Jews*, 7.8.5, in Josephus 1981: 600)

Josephus's words here are clear. While the Romans chose the western ascent via the natural spur to Masada, even that natural spur was not high enough for their war machines, for example, a battering-ram, so

Figure 8.5. The siege ramp as viewed from the western side of Masada looking from north to south. Photograph by Nachman Ben-Yehuda, January 1997.

they had to build a structure on top of that spur. One can assume that building the additional structure could not have been an easy or fast task even under normal circumstances, and it must have been more difficult under siege conditions. In any event, what is important to notice here is that the Roman army did not build the western ascent to Masada from the bottom of the mountain. Most of that massive ascent, still visible today, was there before the Roman siege began. The Romans only added to it. This means that the Roman army's engineering effort in building an elevated platform for its attack on Masada was not a very major one.

Alas, almost all texts about Masada fail to make this point clear or explicit. The impression one gets from reading the many different sources, and from the explanations given by most tour guides, is that the Roman army built the entire western ascent to Masada. This interpretation implies that the engineering effort of the Roman army involved in conquering Masada was a very strenuous one. Indeed, archaeologist Ben-Dov (1993), quoting other anonymous archaeologists, claims that the siege ramp is an artificial structure.

The issue of the siege ramp came into an interesting focus in two separate affairs in 1993 and 1995. In 1993 Israeli geologist Dan Gill published a paper in the prestigious journal *Nature*. The major point of that paper was that "Contrary to the prevailing opinion that the Roman assault ramp at Masada in Israel was entirely man-made, geological observations reveal that it consists mostly of natural bedrock" (569). Based on his geological observations, Gill added that "these geological observations . . . reveal that the bulk of the ramp consists of natural bedrock which was adapted by the Romans. . . . The triangular prism probably represents the remnants of an artificially raised earthwork. Thus, some earthwork was piled up on top of the spur, but based on a reasonable reconstruction of the slope required to haul up the wall-battering siege machines, they would have had no need to raise the spur much higher along most of its length" (570). Gill continues to argue that in the passage quoted earlier from Josephus Flavius, his "description is highly exaggerated" because he was not near Masada during the siege and the measurements given by Josephus are grossly inaccurate. Basically, Gill argues that the effort invested by the Roman army in building the siege ramp was genuinely minimal and that the task was not as hard or impressive as the myth stipulates. According to Gill, building the siege ramp could be accomplished in a relatively short period of time.

The fact remains that Josephus does mention a natural spur and in no place does he mention a major engineering effort. Archaeologists were aware of this. Livne's 1986 book about Masada states explicitly that the Roman siege ramp "was built on a natural spur that rose . . . to Masada" (82). Even Yadin's book (1966a: 220) quotes directly from Josephus the passage I quoted earlier indicating that there was a natural spur there. However, Yadin's (as well as Livne's 1986) rhetoric gives the impression that the natural spur was insignificant and that the Roman effort was very strenuous and significant, contrary to Gill's conclusions. The purpose of this rhetoric is obvious. It is meant to persuade the unsuspecting reader that the effort made by the Roman army in building the siege ramp was unusual and unprecedented. Here is what Yadin says about the siege ramp: "The ramp . . . is undoubtedly one of the most remarkable siege structures of the Roman army which exists in the world today. It is in a good state of preservation" (220). By presenting the effort of building that siege ramp as so unusual, Yadin and Livne imply that there must have been something very valuable and extremely important on Masada to justify such a titanic effort. If we keep this in mind, the next puzzle becomes more easily explainable.

The paper by Gill is to some extent puzzling. Josephus Flavius can be read as stating that there was a spur, or what he called an "eminency," on the western side of Masada, on which the Roman tenth legion built the siege ramp. Why does Gill seem to assume that it is not mentioned there? My guess is that Gill was, perhaps more than anything else, influenced by Yadin's book. While it is not stated very explicitly, the impression one gets from Yadin's book (1966a: 220–221) is that the Romans built the whole structure on the western side of Masada. In no place does Yadin state explicitly that there was a natural, very large spur on the western side of Masada, leading to the top of the mountain. Of course, building that siege ramp was quite an impressive effort, but surely not as impressive as building the whole thing by themselves.

The much more puzzling question concerns Yadin. His quotation of Josephus Flavius cannot but be taken as evidence that he was fully aware that Josephus can be very easily understood to say exactly what Gill does. Why does he not state this explicitly in his text? Why cloud this issue in such a way as to let the average reader and visitor assume that when it is stated that the Romans built the western siege ramp, they actually built the whole structure on the western side of Masada? Why not state, in a clear and unambiguous voice, that the Roman army utilized a natural geologic spur, upon which it built the siege ramp? The reason seems evident. By not telling the reader or visitor explicitly about the natural spur, he gives the impression that indeed the Romans built the whole structure. In this way, the effort of the Roman army is magnified tremendously, and the historical construction that emerges is one that attributes to the Roman army a gigantic effort.

In 1994 the siege ramp received more publicity when archaeologist Ehud Netzer published a long piece in *Ha'aretz* about it. In response to a letter by one of the volunteers who participated in the Masada excavations, Netzer states very clearly: "No one has claimed that the entire ramp was man-made. . . . It is also clear that the engineers of the Roman army, in seeking to erect the siege ramp under particularly difficult circumstances, chose the place where it would be easiest" (1994: 7). Netzer states that he does not disagree with Gill "in principle," but that they do seem to have different opinions about the amount of effort exerted by the Roman army. Netzer feels that Gill's conclusions about the size of the natural spur are exaggerated and that "it is thus possible that the bedrock is smaller than Gill imagines it to be."

The interesting point is that there seems to be agreement between Josephus, Gill, and Netzer about the principle. That is, they all agree that there was a natural spur leading to Masada on its western side. Their basic argument is about the size of that natural spur and the implications of that size. A small spur means a big effort on the part of the Roman army. A large spur means a small effort on the part of the Roman army. Having studied the Masada mythical narrative (Ben-Yehuda 1995), I have no question that the mythical tale most certainly conveys the impression

Figure 8.6. Members of the Israeli Archaeological Exploration Society making their ascent over the siege ramp to the Masada plateau. The photograph is dated October 13, 1976. Courtesy of the Israeli Government's Press Office.

that the entire slope leading to Masada from the western side was constructed by the Roman army. The mythical narrative makes the point that the Roman army's effort to conquer Masada was gigantic. It is virtually impossible to find a text written, or given orally by most tour guides, that states simply and explicitly that there was a natural spur leading to Masada from its western side and that the Roman army built its siege ramp on that natural spur. Because no one really knows for sure the size of the natural spur, it is difficult to assess accurately the effort expended by the Roman army in building its siege ramp. However, it is obvious that the Romans did not build the entire slope on the western side.

Conclusion

The 1963–1965 excavations of Masada provide us with a natural laboratory to examine how archaeology and politics interacted. The main conclusion is this: there can be very little doubt that Yadin, followed by others, constructed interpretations for Masada that supported the Masada mythical narrative, which is a political ideological narrative. This was accomplished not by falsifying any of the factual finds or artifacts, but rather by contextualizing these findings within the mythical narrative. Doing so involved ignoring competing explanations and interpretations, as well as providing some very creative explanations about findings.

Notes

This chapter is based partially on my 1995 and 2002 books.
Translations from non-English sources are my own unless otherwise indicated.

1. Aviram, Foerster, and Netzer edited the volumes, the first two of which were published in 1989 and the third in 1991. The first volume is focused on chapters about the ostraca and inscriptions (written by Yigael Yadin and Joseph Naveh) and about the coins (written by Ya'acov Meshorer) found in the excavations. The second volume (written by Hannah M. Cotton and Joseph Geiger) examines the Latin and Greek documents found in Masada. Volume 3, the largest volume, deals with the buildings, the stratigraphy, and the architecture of Masada (it was written by Ehud Netzer). In the summer of 1994, volume 4 (consisting of about four hundred pages) was published. Its topics were the oil lanterns, the fabrics, the wood products, the catapult stones, and the skeletons found in Masada. Volume five (possibly the last), which was published in 1995, focused on the architecture and art found in Masada. As is becoming clearer and clearer, the scientific importance of Masada lies not so much with the Sicarii, but with important discoveries in other areas, such as coins, scriptures, collections of fabric materials, Herodian architecture, and Roman army siege tactics.
2. Throughout the text, references to Josephus Flavius are based on Josephus 1981.
3. It is not entirely clear from the text whether the first to conquer and occupy Masada were Sicarii and whether, following the escape from Jerusalem, they had to reconquer it. Josephus does not provide dates or details for these events (see Cotton and Preiss 1990).
4. The basic issues here relate to questions about social influences on the choice of research and the role of those influences in the crystallization of interpretations, or on constructing and contextualizing the facts. For some basic references, see Cole 1992; Fuchs 1992; Knorr-Cetina 1981; Latour and Woolgar 1979; Pickering 1992; Zuckerman 1988.

References

Avigad, Nachman, Michael Avi Yonah, Yochanan Aharony, Shmaria Guttman, and Emanuel Dunayevski. 1957. *Masada: An Archaeological Survey during*

1955–1956 [in Hebrew]. Jerusalem: Ministry of Education/Hebrew University/Israeli Exploration Society.

Aviram, Joseph, Gideon Foerster, and Ehud Netzer, eds. 1989a. *Masada: The Yigael Yadin Excavations, 1963–1965: Final Report.* Vol. 1, by Yigael Yadin, Joseph Naveh, and Ya'acov Meshorer. Jerusalem: Israel Exploration Society/Hebrew University.

Aviram, Joseph, Gideon Foerster, and Ehud Netzer, eds. 1989b. *Masada: The Yigael Yadin Excavations, 1963–1965: Final Report.* Vol. 2, by Hannah M. Cotton and Joseph Geiger. Jerusalem: Israel Exploration Society/Hebrew University.

Aviram, Joseph, Gideon Foerster, and Ehud Netzer, eds. 1991. *Masada: The Yigael Yadin Excavations, 1963–1965: Final Report.* Vol. 3, *The Buildings, Stratigraphy, and Architecture,* by Ehud Netzer. Jerusalem: Israel Exploration Society/Hebrew University.

Aviram, Joseph, Gideon Foerster, and Ehud Netzer, eds. 1994. *Masada: The Yigael Yadin Excavations, 1963–1965: Final Report.* Vol. 4. Jerusalem: Israel Exploration Society/Hebrew University.

Aviram, Joseph, Gideon Foerster, and Ehud Netzer, eds. 1995. *Masada: The Yigael Yadin Excavations, 1963–1965: Final Report.* Vol. 5, *Art and Architecture,* by Gideon Foerster with a contribution by Naomi Porat. Jerusalem: Israel Exploration Society/Hebrew University.

Ayalon, Amos. 1972. *The Israelis: Founders and Sons* [in Hebrew]. Jerusalem: Schocken Books.

Ben-Dov, Meir. 1993. "In Contradiction to the Claim Made by Geologist Dan Gill, Archaeologists Claim: The Masada Siege Ramp Is Man Made" [in Hebrew]. *Ha'aretz,* Aug. 13, p. 6.

Ben-Yehuda, Nachman. 1993. *Political Assassinations by Jews: A Rhetorical Device for Justice.* Albany: State University of New York Press.

Ben-Yehuda, Nachman. 1995. *The Masada Myth: Collective Memory and Mythmaking in Israel.* Madison: University of Wisconsin Press.

Ben-Yehuda, Nachman. 1998. "Where Masada's Defenders Fell." *Biblical Archaeology Review* 24, no. 6 (Nov.–Dec.): 32–39.

Ben-Yehuda, Nachman. 2002. *Sacrificing Truth: Archaeology and the Myth of Masada.* New York: Prometheus Press/Humanity Books.

Cole, Stephen. 1992. *Making Science: Between Nature and Society.* Cambridge, MA: Harvard University Press.

Cotton, Hanna M., and Yehonatan Preiss. 1990. "Who Conquered Masada in 66 A.D. and Who Occupied It until It Fell?" [in Hebrew]. *Zion* 55:449–54.

Dayan, Moshe, ed. 1983. *Masada.* Paris: Armand and Georges Israel.

Feldman, Louis H. 1975. "Masada: A Critique of Recent Scholarship." *Commentary* 53:218–248; also in *Christianity, Judaism, and Other Greco-Roman Cults: Studies for Morton Smith at Sixty,* ed. Jacob Neusner, pt. 3 (Leiden: Brill, 1975).

Finley, M. I. 1966. "Josephus and the Bandits." *New Statesman,* Dec. 2, pp. 832–833.

Fuchs, Stephan. 1992. *The Professional Quest for Truth: A Social Theory of Science and Knowledge*. Albany: State University of New York Press.

Gill, Dan. 1993. "A Natural Spur at Masada." *Nature* 364 (6438): 569–570.

Josephus Flavius. 1981. *The Complete Works of Josephus*. Trans. William Whiston. Grand Rapids, MI: Kregel Publications.

Knorr-Cetina, Karin. 1981. *The Manufacture of Knowledge*. New York: Pergamon Press.

Kohl, Philip L., and Clare Fawcett, eds. 1995. *Nationalism, Politics, and the Practice of Archaeology*. Cambridge: Cambridge University Press, 1995.

Latour, Bruno, and Steve Woolgar. 1979. *Laboratory Life: The Social Construction of Scientific Fact*. Beverly Hills, CA: Sage.

Livne, Micha. 1986. *Last Fortress: The Story of Masada and Its People* [in Hebrew]. Tel Aviv: Ministry of Defense.

Magness, Jodi. 1992. "Masada—Arms and the Men." *Biblical Archaeology Review* 18 (4): 58–67.

Narkis, Uzi. 1983. "Judea Capta." In Dayan 1983: 24–27.

Netzer, Ehud. 1994. "Masada Ramp Thesis Is Still as Firm as Bedrock." *Jerusalem Post*, Dec. 21, p. 7.

Pickering, Andrew. 1992. *Science as Practice and Culture*. Chicago: University of Chicago Press.

Rabinowitz, Abraham. 1990. "Lots of Controversy: Six Years after the Death of Yigael Yadin, His Colleagues Have Begun Publishing the Fruits of His Fabulous Archaeological Career." *Jerusalem Post*, Weekend Magazine, Mar. 16, pp. 6–9.

Roth, Jonathan. 1995. "The Length of the Siege of Masada." *Scripta Classica Israelica* 14:87–110.

Shapira, Anita. 1992. *Land and Power (The Sword of the Dove)* [in Hebrew]. Tel Aviv: Am Oved.

Shargel, Baila R. 1979. "The Evolution of the Masada Myth." *Judaism* 28:357–371.

Shatzman, Israel. 1993. "The Roman Siege on Masada" [in Hebrew]. In *The Story of Masada: Discoveries from the Excavations*, ed. Gila Hurvitz, 105–120. Jerusalem: Hebrew University/Society for Studying Eretz Israel and Its Antiquities.

Shatzman, Israel. 1995. "Panel Talk on the Roman Siege of Masada" [in Hebrew]. In *Masada: Transcripts of Discussions about the New Reconstruction of the Site Ma'ale Hachamisha*, 40–41. Tel Aviv: National Parks Authority/Ministry of Tourism/Authority for the Development of the Negev.

Shavit, Ya'acov. 1986. "Truth Will Rise from the Land: Points to the Development of Public Jewish Interest in Archaeology (till the 1930s)" [in Hebrew]. *Katedra* 44:27–54.

Silberman, Neil Asher. 1989. *Between Past and Present*. New York: Anchor Books/Doubleday.

Silberman, Neil Asher. 1993. *A Prophet from amongst You: The Life of Yigael Yadin: Soldier, Scholar, and Mythmaker of Modern Israel*. Reading, MA: Addison-Wesley.

Yadin, Yigael. 1965. *Masada: First Season of Excavations, 1963–1964* [in Hebrew]. Preliminary Report. Jerusalem: Israel Exploration Society. Also available in English.

Yadin, Yigael. 1966a. *Masada: Herod's Fortress and the Zealots' Last Stand*. London: Weidenfeld and Nicolson.

Yadin, Yigael. 1966b. *Masada: In Those Days—At This Time* [in Hebrew]. Haifa: Shikmona Ma'ariv Library.

Yadin, Yigael. 1970. "Metzada" [in Hebrew]. In *Encyclopaedia for Archaeological Excavations in Eretz Israel*, 2:374–390. Jerusalem: Society for the Investigation of Eretz Israel and Its Antiquity/Masada.

Yadin, Yigael. 1971. "Masada." In *Encyclopaedia Judaica*, 11:1078–1091. Jerusalem: Keter; New York: Macmillan.

Yadin, Yigael. 1973. "1900 Years to the Fall of Masada" [in Hebrew]. *Ma'ariv*, Apr. 16, pp. 15, 33.

Zerubavel, Yael. 1995. *Recovered Roots: Collective Memory and the Making of Israeli National Tradition*. Chicago: University of Chicago Press.

Zuckerman, Harriet. 1988. "The Sociology of Science." In *Handbook of Sociology*, ed. Neil Smelser, 511–574. Newbury Park, CA: Sage.

NINE

Recovering Authenticity

West-Bank Settlers and the Second Stage of National Archaeology

MICHAEL FEIGE

During the 1950s and 1960s, biblical archaeology was considered to be a central part of Israel's "civil religion" (Liebman and Don-Yehiya 1983) and was even hailed as "the national pastime" of the newly established state. The excavations of Hatzor, Masada, and the Judean desert caves were headline news. Professional archaeologists, most notably Yigael Yadin, became popular heroes. Academic conferences of the Israel Exploration Society attracted audiences of thousands, among them top political leaders. Coins, stamps, and other national symbols expressed the country's interest in the field.[1] By the 1970s, though, the popular enthusiasm for archaeology had dwindled, and today few nonarchaeologists follow developments in the field with interest.

As the popularity of archaeology waned, one group, not to be found among the many enchanted by the digs of the early years after independence, developed its own interest in biblical archaeology. The religious Gush Emunim movement and those affiliated with it who had settled in the communities established in the Israeli-occupied West Bank became enthusiastic about the subject. Some of its members went to study archaeology; many took field trips around their homes, looking for remnants of the ancient past; a few tried to create small archaeological collections in their settlements. Lectures, conferences, and books organized the rapidly accumulating body of knowledge. Perhaps most importantly, experts in the field among the settlers included some of the movement's best-known political leaders and ideologues.

In this chapter I explore some of the questions raised by the interest in archaeology on the part of key members of an ultranationalistic, fundamentalist religious movement. My starting point is the theoretical literature on the uneasy intersection between archaeology and nationalism. Nationalist movements use archaeology as a basis for truth-claims about the ancient origins of the nation, its past grandeur, and its presence on the national territory since time immemorial. Scholars have found that both colonial powers and nationalist movements have developed archaeology and presented its findings as proof of ancient national roots.[2] Although the Israeli case may be exceptional in the intensity of popular interest in archaeology, it conforms to the general pattern. Here I trace the social location of national archaeology after the decline of the national passion and after archaeology acquired professional autonomy. My chapter takes a critical view of the nationalizing project.

Gush Emunim has attempted to reawaken a postideological society–in which archaeology retreated many years ago to academia, museums, and salvage excavations–to an interest in digging for national roots. The settlers' interest in archaeology is more limited and controversial than the earlier avatar of national archaeology. I address the goals of such a "second awakening" and discuss how it differs from the first.

A further set of issues has to do with the conflict situations that inevitably occur when a particularistic and sectarian group uses scientific practices and knowledge in pursuit of its political goals. Gush Emunim is a fundamentalist religious group that believes that God gave the land of Israel to the Israelites and their descendants. This view brings up the age-old question of how "true believers" reconcile science with their religious beliefs. A complementary question involves the relationship between professional archaeologists, who declare that they distinguish nationalist engagement from professional obligation, and the enthusiastic newcomers to the field, who want to redefine the profession along more nationalistic lines.

In other words, instead of concentrating on the "golden age" of cooperation, I want to shift the focus of research to the period after the creation of the link between archaeology and the national effort. Research on national archaeology has dealt mainly with dominant national movements (Zionism, in the Israeli case). When we explore the second phase, the focus naturally moves to the use of archaeology by other actors in a new context. The politics of archaeology during the latter stages of nationalistic archaeology raises important new issues. On the one hand, the professional archaeologists are no longer committed to the national project; on the other hand, those who want to reconnect nationalism and archaeology find themselves opposed by strong institutions, both state and professional. What happens to national archaeology after the national movement slows its momentum has not yet been studied. Here I explore how national archaeology tends to reappear as a subversive practice in postideological societies.[3]

Gush Emunim and the Appropriation of Land: Contested Authenticity

Gush Emunim is a messianic religious movement that holds that Israel should annex the territories occupied in the 1967 Six-Day War and settle Jews there. For its adherents, the West Bank is Judea and Samaria, the cradle of the nation and part of the land promised by God to the Israelites and their descendants. Since its founding in 1974, Gush Emunim's main political strategy has involved the establishment of Jewish settlements on contested land, which is heavily populated by Palestinian Arabs. Some of these settlements had prior approval from the Israeli government; others have been the result of prolonged political struggles. The many dramatic events in the movement's history include its campaign to stop the Israeli withdrawal from Sinai in the context of the peace agreement with Egypt; the activities and capture of the "Jewish Underground," a terrorist group that consisted of members of the movement; and, in the past decade and a half, the crisis that followed the Oslo accords and the establishment of the Palestinian Authority. Currently, some two hundred thousand Jews live in 120 settlements in the occupied territories. Fewer than half are connected to Gush Emunim. As a formal organization, Gush Emunim ceased to exist in the mid-1980s, but other organizations with a similar ideology have emerged to contest recurrent threats to the settlement project.[4]

Almost from the outset, Gush Emunim settlers found themselves pitted in a bitter conflict against the Palestinian Arab residents of the occupied territories, as well as against left-wing Israelis who denied their right to establish a presence there. The basic cognitive problem with their political discourse was that their adversaries and neighbors, the Palestinian Arabs, had resided in these districts for decades or centuries, thereby enjoying, in the eyes of many Israeli and overseas observers, a firm status of authentic natives with irrefutable rights to the land. Gush Emunim began its settlement efforts at a time when the very notion of Western and modern peoples moving to live among Orientals and natives was discredited as immoral, the cardinal sin of the postcolonial world. The settlers' problem was and remains achieving native status and persuading others of their authenticity, despite the facts that they are overwhelmingly Western and modern, they work in middle-class occupations, and they prefer suburban-style dwellings. To these one might add the striking similarity between Palestinian villages and popular images of ancient biblical life, a resemblance that was not overlooked by the settlers, who claim to be returning to and reviving the land of the Bible. Redefining *native* and *authentic*, a process that is one of the foremost challenges of the late-modern age of blurred boundaries and hybridity, is thus also a prime cultural challenge that confronts the settlers.[5]

Gush Emunim settlers have no doubts that they are the true natives and have a right to the land. In their religious and national worldview, the land is theirs; no other ethnic or national group can share their territorial rights. The Palestinian Arabs, in their eyes, are no more than temporary trespassers. Individual Arabs may have certain rights under the law, but their national collective cannot. This concept of exclusivity is manifestly and unapologetically nonhistorical and metahistorical: Jewish rights stem from the divine promise, found in the Bible, regardless of actual historical precedence or contingent sociodemographic realities.

But the metahistorical concept of divine right enjoys little understanding and scant support outside the settlers' camp. Most Israeli Jews are secular or hold some sympathy for religion. Among those who do not adhere to religious precepts, the idea that the occupied territories are God-given finds little acceptance. Gush Emunim has to use other strategies to influence wider audiences. For example, the settlers stress the importance of the territories for national security reasons and promote positions and beliefs about the untrustworthiness of the Palestinian Arabs and of non-Jews in general. These claims are not the core of Gush Emunim's theological position, but they find attentive ears among many secular Israelis.

Another way to endear the Gush Emunim settlement endeavor to Israeli sensibilities is to uncover the Jewish history of the disputed territories. Zionism, like other nationalist movements, based itself on the people's ancient historical and mythical bonds to the land.[6] Gush Emunim settlers want to capitalize on a well-established discursive pattern that pays large dividends, thanks to its association with the consecrated national narrative. Many, perhaps most, secular Israeli Jews are almost as apathetic about Jewish history as they are about Jewish theology; Israel has been diagnosed as being in a postideological, and perhaps post-Zionist, stage (Ram 1999; Silberstein 1999; Nimni 2003). In comparison to claims of divine promise, though, historical arguments are considered to have a better chance of constructing the settlers as the authentic owners of the land and as the native population of Judea and Samaria. This is why the first sites chosen by the settlers for settlement were the historical cities of Hebron and Shechem (Nablus), which they believed would encounter less resistance from the Israeli public.[7] Their use of archaeology can also be seen as an attempt to restore the connection between the Jewish people and the ancient homeland.

Biblical Archaeology and the Reproduction of the Ancient Map

Gush Emunim's interest in archaeology is limited to "scriptural fundamentalism," namely, proving the truth of the Bible, finding the precise spots on the map that are mentioned in the holy text, and understanding phenomena in their geographical context. Its members' "science" is contextual and pragmatic, looking for specific answers to questions raised by their religious worldview. The settler-scholars are not professionally trained archaeologists and, according to Israeli law, are not permitted to conduct excavations. But they follow the professional publications of Israeli archaeologists with much interest and do some limited research near their own homes. The fruits of their research and their interpretative efforts are presented mostly to their own public through books and lectures.[8]

Gush Emunim uses archaeology to substantiate its claims regarding Jewish ownership of and rights to live in territories populated by others who propagate similar claims. The similarity to the older Zionist and Israeli use of biblical archaeology is striking. The problem faced by the Zionist movement and the Israeli state was how to (re)connect a diverse population of immigrants to a land populated with a group of different nationalities. Archaeology was recruited to serve the claim that the Jewish people, who left the land nearly two thousand years before and were dispersed among the nations, were now returning to their ancient homeland. With its aura of a neutral scientific discipline, archaeology was given the task of providing irrefutable proof of the truth of the Zionist narrative.

This is the main function of settler archaeology–proving the Jews' rights of primacy on the land, especially vis-à-vis the Arab villagers' claims to centuries of authenticity. A settler in Hebron told me why, in his mind, there is no basis for Palestinian archaeology: whenever an Arab lifts a stone, there is a "Jewish stone" laughing at him from underneath it.

Basically, Gush Emunim's project can be understood as the "normalization" of the occupied territories within the boundaries of Israel, as part of a nonproblematic and homogeneous whole, through the establishment of a common Jewish past. The basic claim, if we may draw on archaeology as a metaphor, is that the mythic unity of the Jewish people and Jewish land can be found and recovered underneath the ground and that geopolitical divisions and boundaries are only "surface deep." This logic is best exemplified in the annual conferences at the College of Judea and Samaria in Ariel, where the research is presented before an audience of academics and laypersons, under the rubric of "regional studies." The conferences are part of a discourse that reproduces the basic assumption that Judea and Samaria are neutral regions that can be studied in isolation from the political context. These events pretend to a spurious banality as regional conferences inside Israel, at which experts discuss questions of purely academic nature and offer suggestions for further regional development. But as Meron Benvenisti caustically noted, "these 'innovations in research' do not address the issue of the million and more Palestinians among whom the scientific researchers have settled. The demography, economics, society, and political views of the Palestinians are irrelevant" (1992).

Archaeology is meant to counter the hostile semiotics of the territories, consisting of Arab villages, cities, and refugee camps, as well as army camps and recently established Jewish towns. The problem was not so acute for Israelis right after the establishment of the state; most local Arabs fled or were evicted during or in the wake of the 1948 war (Morris 1987). But there was a large Arab population in the territories occupied in the 1967 war, visible to anyone traveling there. Archaeology is a means to teach Israelis how to see beneath the surface and through the Arab populations, rendering them irrelevant, if not totally invisible.

For Jewish settlers, supporters of the Gush Emunim worldview, the surface hides a deeper truth, clues of which can be found by looking around or digging underground. Their research is semiotic, in the sense that they decipher present objects as signs and remnants of the past. For example, they ask whether the proximity of an Israelite town or village named in the Bible can be inferred from a contemporary Arab settlement with a similar name. The modern Arab town is not their subject of research; its presence symbolizes the absence of a deeper and more important entity. It is from the semiotic network spread across the area, some of it always apparent and some of it revealed by excavation, that the settler-scholars assemble what they consider to be the real map of Judea and Samaria.

Such discovery and recovery are closely linked to other strategies of "Judaizing" the land. Settlers tend to give their settlements names taken from the Bible, such as Ofra, Tekoa, Beit El, and Elon Moreh. These places are built approximately on the sites of the ancient settlements described in the Bible. The "right place" can be ascertained from the Bible (though never exactly), and archaeological findings strengthen the case. For example, the settlement of Shiloh is adjacent to the excavations of the ancient city of the same name.

Looking at the entire project from a broad perspective, the settlers define themselves as symbolically reproducing the experiences of the biblical patriarchs when they first arrived in the land. The Judea and Samaria of Gush Emunim is a "born-again landscape" (see Jackson 1980); its new residents regard themselves as resetting the geographic context to its original form. Space undergoes a process of redemption or conversion, transformed from a non-Jewish landscape into a Jewish landscape. With some reservations, the settlement enterprise of Gush Emunim can be seen as an attempt to duplicate an ancient and imaginary geography that never actually existed in the same way (see Aran 1993).

Giving ancient names to new Jewish settlements ipso facto defines them as older than the surrounding Palestinian villages and towns. Beit El is defined as a continuation of the ancient biblical city on roughly the same spot; this supposedly makes it more authentic than the nearby Palestinian city of Ramallah, let alone Jilazoun, the refugee camp across the main road, and allows Beit El's residents to define themselves as the true natives of the region.

The Gush Emunim settlement enterprise is accompanied by cultural and educational elements that make the Jewish past central to shaping the Israeli present. This in effect constitutes a cultural critique of modern secular Zionism, which, the settlers contend, tends to forget the origins of its own identity. The importance of creating a new or renewed map that reflects a tentative return to the biblical one is demonstrated by Rabbi Yoel Elitzur's complaint about the alleged oversights of the Zionist settlement enterprise, which

> neglected ancient names and preferred names denoting a memorial or monument to some deceased Zionist leader (with all due respect to their memory, these names are often meaningless to later generations). There is no need to give examples of this "burial" of the historical Land of Israel; all one needs to do is to travel the Sharon road or the Judean Coastal Plain, the Jezreel Valley, or the Zevulun Valley, and look at the signs pointing to places with names like Sirkin, Citrin, Warburg, and Vitkin, who were doubtless men of great renown in their own generation, yet whose commemoration has turned entire districts of an ancient yet living land into a modern cemetery. (Elitzur 1980a: 12–13)

Ze'ev (Zhabo) Ehrlich, Elitzur's neighbor in the settlement of Ofra and a fellow warrior in the name-renewal struggle, seconds the argument, noting the historical responsibility borne by the settlers: "The Land of Israel preserved the ancient names throughout all the vicissitudes of its history and through all the changes of language and population it experienced. It is fitting that we, too, should take care to preserve the names. Thus, with God's help, we will maintain the identity of the land and our ancestors' footprints on it" (Ehrlich 1980: 16).

Elitzur and his colleagues found themselves struggling in two opposite directions. On the one hand, their cultural project was meant to assist Gush Emunim in its goal of strengthening the Jewish hold on the occupied territories. On the other hand, they were also critical of the hastiness of their own associates, the leaders of Gush Emunim, when they gave their settlements "improper" names. They felt that some settlements, like Efrat, the largest in Gush Etzion, were established in the wrong place: "Its correct location should be found, so as not to confuse coming generations with two versions of the Land of Israel" (Elitzur 1980a: 10).

In a similar vein, the Government Names Committee insisted on the name Halamish for the site its residents called Neve Tsuf; even the High Court of Justice, which they petitioned, would not allow them to create the identity they desired. With the support of the local council, the residents continue to refer to Neve Tsuf. Elitzur concurred with their claim: "In fact, 'Halamish' is a historical name in its own right. In Talmudic times, there was a city by that name in Bashan . . . some twenty kilometers east of Ramat Magshimim. It's a shame to resurrect it in the wrong place" (Elitzur 1980a: 22). Here, incidentally, is evidence of the radical potential of reproducing the biblical map. Elitzur referred to a site located in what is today Syrian territory. The "true" map of Israel, which can be discovered through scientific archaeology, is not congruent with the current boundaries of the political entity of Israel, which, from the settlers' perspective, are inherently arbitrary and temporary.

The Consumption of Biblical Archaeology

Archaeological research has further uses for the settlers. Its findings supply sites for hikes on the contested ground. Settler children take many hikes, some under the aegis of their school or youth movement, others as recreational activity with friends. Hiking is a political statement of the right to visit and be present on any spot on the sacred map. Young people are expected to see and feel close to the world of their biblical ancestors through the remnants of the past, while disregarding the Arab villages they see in front of them. One guide was surprised at my question, "Ramallah wasn't there in the time of the Patriarchs, so why should it be part of a hike that is meant to follow in the footsteps of the Patriarchs?"

Archaeology also provides a substructure of scientific knowledge and credibility to political claims. Local experts have accumulated extensive knowledge about the areas of political conflict and apply it when an opportunity comes. For example, when the then education minister Shulamit Aloni, a prominent leftist, claimed that the Tomb of Joseph in Nablus was in fact the grave of a relatively recent sheikh, the settlers had a ready answer. Benny Katzover, the head of the Council of Judea and Samaria, sent her a letter that began, "I have more than a reasonable basis to believe that you have been misled by the archaeologists with regard to the following facts . . . " The facts in question, which detailed proofs of the antiquity of the site, were provided by the experts around him (Ehrlich 1987). Whether the claims were persuasive is beside the point. Katzover and his fellow settlers want to present themselves as "rational men of science," whose claims are based on logic well understood by their secular opponents.

The settlers with a penchant for biblical archaeology have an emotional affinity with explorers of the past and identify most profoundly with the Protestant clerics and laypersons who traveled through the country, Bible in hand, seeking to identify biblical sites (on this historical phenomenon, see Silberman 1982). For those Christians, as for the settlers, archaeology was a mystical experience of great emotional intensity. Living in the land of the Bible, together with an awareness of ancient Jewish life that once existed in the very same place, with artifacts from antiquity right there in arm's reach, generates excitement and even exhilaration. The researchers "live" their field of research and "sense" whether their claims are correct. In an anecdote recounted at a conference in 1993, Elitzur took the importance of the experiential component to its extreme. If one does not burst into tears, it is a sign that a site has been misidentified:

> Here's a personal story. . . . A few years ago I guided a group of hikers at Ein Giv, that is, Givon. I stood above the very deep excavation there and explained to the group what it was that I saw there. . . . One girl sat alone, looking at me. . . . When I went over to her she said, "You must know, I'm very disappointed. When your father was our guide here we all cried." Why can't I make people cry? . . . I've done that at Beit-El, at Ha'ei, in all kinds of places, but I have a hard time with Givon. Why? It has always been very difficult for me to be absolutely certain that I am actually standing next to the Pool of Givon.[10]

Discovering the inner truth of the territories is part and parcel of the existential project of Gush Emunim and its supporters. They see themselves as transferring their residence onto holy ground, in opposition to the Arab population and their supporters in Israeli society. Their true and perhaps only lasting coalition is with their ancestors who walked the land in biblical times and left some traces of their passage under the surface. Thus the practice and metaphor of archaeology connects and disconnects the settlers from various real and imaginary groups. It creates a double link, one with the patriarchs and kings of ancient days, the other with fellow Jews inside and outside Israel. Digging deep, in a literal or metaphorical sense, is a political statement of radical disengagement from the neighboring Palestinians, whose social landscape is thereby defined as invalid and out of touch with the true nature of the sacred space.

Religion, Scientific Archaeology, and the Nature of Fundamentalism

Another function of archaeology, relevant only for the settlers, touches upon the crucial issue of religion and science. The settlers need to know whether they can define their settlements as direct continuations of ancient towns for religious reasons. Different rules apply to cities that existed in biblical times than to newer ones. Specifically, a town that was fortified in the time of Joshua celebrates the holiday of Purim the day after the rest of the world (what is called Purim demukafin [Purim of walled cities]). In contemporary Israel, only Jerusalem is a direct continuation, since there is no doubt that it stands on approximately its ancient site. The Jewish settlers in Hebron, confident that they are returning to the ancient city of the patriarchs, began celebrating Purim demukafin as well. But the residents of other new settlements were not sure whether they were entitled to do so. Elitzur has endeavored to define some of them as the direct continuation of the ancient biblical town and change the date on which they celebrate the holiday (more precisely, to get them to celebrate both days because of the doubt) (Elitzur 1983, 1988). At stake here is another aspect of the construction of a native and authentic identity. If it is taken seriously by the settlers, it also implies a change of religious practice.

Not all settlers accept Elitzur's project. In Israel, archaeologists are not in favor with religious Jews, because of the long and bitter struggle connected with the excavation of ancient graves and bones (Aronoff 1986; Weingrod 1995; Hallote and Joffe 2002). Hence there is a radical and even revolutionary element in the settlers' idea of studying the Bible in its historical context, given that their camp has long since accepted the view that the Bible grants historical ownership rights.[11] For example, Rabbi Zalman Melamed rejected Elitzur's idea of a two-day Purim in his settlement of Beit El (Elitzur 1980b). Evidently Rabbi Melamed considers that such a symbolic declaration that modern Beit El is a direct continuation of the biblical Beit El is too radical, because of the slippery slope of the implication that secular humanistic science can contribute to *halakhic* decisions. This reaction would indicate that the rabbinical system of *halakhah*, which feels threatened by scientific discoveries, continues to exist alongside the innovative combination of holy studies with secular science.

Rabbi Ya'akov Ariel's two-volume atlas of the biblical borders of the land of Israel demonstrates the differences between the two types of knowledge. Rabbi Ariel defines his work as research and links it to the "fervent desire" of Rabbi A. I. Kook, whose writings are accorded almost sacred status by the core of Gush Emunim, to see science studied at the yet-to-be-established Central World Yeshiva. Rabbi Ariel criticizes secular scholars for de-emphasizing land-of-Israel studies and claims that "Land of Israel studies in general demand a new and thorough examination, from the geographic, Biblical, historical, archaeological, and other angles." He defines his sources as "tradition and Kabbalah, as they have been handed down from generation to generation" (Ariel 1988: 12). Rabbi Ariel dismisses the accepted method of using Arabic village names to identify biblical sites as "medieval alchemy"; he does not reject archaeological findings as such, but he "uses" them only to corroborate tradition, as well as a source of illustrations in the margins of his text.

Researchers such as Elitzur and Ehrlich proceed on totally different assumptions. They use a combination of Jewish sources, archaeological findings, and the names of Arab villages to identify various sites. They quote both *halakhic* and scientific sources and adopt the accepted academic pattern of substantiation and references. Rabbi Ariel, however, works within the confines of traditional Judaism and refuses to allow secular scientific disciplines to penetrate his studies in any significant way. The new researchers do not reject his methodology out of hand but supplement it with insights from various scientific fields, some of which may seem quite sacrilegious. Rabbi Ariel and traditional rabbis rely on the divine promise and *halakhah* as the basis of the Jewish people's right to the land of Israel. The new researchers wholeheartedly accept the *halakhic* explanation but also focus on proof of the ancient history of the Jewish people in its land.

This difference has major significance for potential dialogue with those outside the camp. Whereas the rabbinical apparatus is closed to secular Israeli Jews, even arousing animosity and alienation among them, the scholars use explanatory strategies that resonate more with the secular public and are linked to well-established Zionist methods of land acquisition. These researchers' links to secular science make them more sensitive to changes in the normative patterns of discourse in contemporary Israel and give them some say in the state educational system, particularly with regard to Bible studies. Using the findings of modern Western science to base claims of ownership of the land is an expression of the perceptual revolution that produced the Gush Emunim movement, a revolution that is directed just as much at traditional *halakhic* Judaism as it is at secular Israelis.

The logic underpinning these studies, like the logic of the entire settlement enterprise, stems from a perception of the Bible not only as a sacred text but also as a history book. What is written in the Bible is considered to be true in the moral sense as well as an accurate account of historical events. The settlers aspire to establish settlements on the "land of the Bible" and at the same time attempt to determine the locations of the biblical settlements themselves. From this point of view, settlement and scholarship are two sides of the same coin, both of them aiming to create a tangible manifestation of the holy text in the daily life of the present.

According to Gush Emunim's followers, the Bible describes the ancient Israeli "Golden Age," which is their model of reference and identification. Gideon Aran (1993) shows how Gush Emunim interprets the Bible through the mediation of secular Zionism. For traditional Judaism, and for Ultraorthodox Jews today, the important texts, in the scholastic and practical sense, were the Talmud and other rabbinic writings. It was secular Zionism that propagated the Bible's privileged status at the expense of other sacred writings, which it dismissed as "exilic." Gush Emunim adopted this view of the Bible (while holding onto the importance of the Talmud) with the same idea of using it to reappropriate national territory. Just as it is for secular Zionism, the Bible for Gush Emunim is a political text. It legitimates action aimed at changing the national, legal, and demographic reality in the areas it describes.

But the synthesis of the sacred with the profane, of myth with scientific history and archaeology, does not mean that the settlers compromise their religious belief to accommodate scientific principles. In a conference held in the Ariel, Yoel Bin-Nun sharply attacked Yigael Yadin's assertion that whenever he encountered a contradiction between archaeological findings and the Bible, the former took precedence. Bin-Nun claimed that there are two types of discourse that reflect historical truth and that a correlation, on the simple factual level, must be found between them. If it is written in the Bible that a settlement existed in a particular place, then that is where it must be found. On this point the settlers find themselves in conflict with the Israeli archaeological establishment.

Comparing First- and Second-Stage National Archaeology

The settlers' interest in biblical archaeology bloomed decades after the waning of Israelis' mass interest in the subject. One can see their interest as mimicry, perhaps as taking a successful nation-building practice and reapplying it on new terrain. One way to understand the reappearance of archaeology as a nationalist practice is through the similarity of situations. Whenever a new community attempts to establish itself in a land already populated by others, issues of legitimacy arise, and archaeology can help construct a useful and defensible past.

But the similarities are misleading. Zionism in earlier times was the Jews' return to the land of Israel in general, not to any specific place within it. Zionist settlement efforts focused on areas and sites that were not occupied by Arabs. Sacred places like Hebron and Shechem (Nablus) were neglected by the prestate Zionist settlement enterprise. Gush Emunim, in contrast, seeks to return the people of Israel to the core territory of Judea and Samaria that was the scene of its earliest history. This purpose leads to a difference between how the Zionist movement and Gush Emunim use archaeology. The former was interested in biblical archaeology, or Jewish archaeology, as such. The sites it studied were not necessarily connected to the cradle of the nation, although Jewish themes were usually preferred. The Gush Emunim settlers are interested in biblical archaeology in the strict sense of the word. They desire to uncover the truth of the Bible itself, in the places where the most dramatic events took place, and where confrontation with the Palestinian Arabs is most bitter and direct.

Before and during the early years of the state, archaeology was viewed as being, in a sense, a substitute for religion. The people's historical roots in the land, uncovered by a scientific discipline, would replace divine promise as the legitimation of the Zionist project. For today's religious settlers, archaeology has a radically different use–enhancing religious beliefs rather than replacing them. They adopt a secular scientific practice to combat the process of secularization, not to integrate within it.

The national archaeology of a half century ago can be seen as an uneasy alliance between a scientific discipline and a national movement. Archaeologists rarely compromised their professional ethics, nor were they asked to do so (Elon 1994). There was a fragile and limited affinity between the interests of the profession and those of political figures, reflected chiefly in how archaeological findings were presented to the public. In other words, while national leaders such as David Ben-Gurion (the first prime minister) and Yitzhak Ben-Zvi (the second president of Israel) eagerly asserted that archaeology proves the truth of the Zionist claims, they did not intervene in the profession's ongoing research programs. For Gush Emunim, nationalism and archaeology are tightly connected; the national role of digging up the relevant past in order to strengthen the present identity is much more pronounced. Hence the settlers have little interest in nonbiblical archaeology or in the archaeology of other regions, ethnic groups, and religions.

The Zionist movement, and later the state of Israel, had much to gain from autonomous archaeologists who enjoyed high esteem in the world academic community. So that archaeology could play a national role, it had to be presented as impartial and professional. This is not the case with the settlers' research. They do not belong to an international network of practitioners; they pursue a much more limited scope of research. True, they hope to impress Israel's professional archaeologists with their case, but the academic world is only a sideshow. Their real clients are the Israeli general public and the settler community itself.

The Newcomers and Professional Archaeology

"The association between the development of archaeology and nation-building was so obvious as to remain largely unquestioned throughout the nineteenth century and most of the twentieth century," writes Philip Kohl (1998: 228). The situation is very different in Israel today, as it is in other modern states. The political meaning of appearing late on the scene is that Gush Emunim finds itself playing on a multiorganizational field, where nationalism is contested and no longer enjoys hegemonic status. Professional archaeology in Israel has developed an autonomous agenda; furthermore, criticism of alleged compromises made during the nationalist period of the early years of the state has emerged within the discipline itself.

Professional archaeology in Israel is in the process of constructing a historical narrative that is different from that of the Zionist movement and radically alien to that of the Gush Emunim settlers. The historical narrative advocated by Zionism, that the Israelite tribes conquered the land of Canaan and eventually established a unified kingdom that later split in two, was uncritically taken from the Bible. Israeli schools taught this narrative not only in Bible classes, but also in history classes, as indisputable truth. Gush Emunim, being a religious and nationalistic movement, takes this historical narrative as self-evident.

But professional biblical archaeologists in Israel and abroad were quick to notice that the evidence of excavations does not coincide with the biblical story in many points.[2] In fact, even the so-called national archaeologists, like Yigael Yadin and Yochanan Aharoni, had their doubts about the biblical narrative. Today, there is hardly a single professional archaeologist who accepts the biblical narrative as reflecting actual historical occurrences. Archaeology was expected to prove the truth of the biblical stories but in fact undermined them. As a result, professional archaeologists gradually retreated from their nationalist pretenses and national leaders no longer had use for their services.

In addition, starting in the late 1970s, Israeli scholars in the humanities and social sciences developed a critical view of the national endeavor. The so-called new historians questioned the validity of other parts of the Zionist narrative, as did critical sociologists (Pappe 1995; Ram 1995; Silberstein 1999; Nimni 2003). An integral part of their criticism of the Zionist narrative was the claim that the sciences were applied for nationalist purposes, thereby compromising and even betraying their social role and moral calling. By the time Gush Emunim appeared on the scene, Israeli scholars were unwilling to be dragged uncritically into national projects, and certainly not by an ultranationalist religious group.

Gush Emunim researchers, therefore, found themselves in clear opposition to the Israeli archaeological establishment. Most Israeli archaeologists wanted nothing to do with the newcomers and criticized their conferences and publications harshly. In their view, the settlers' "science" was no more than ideological statements thinly veiled by academic lingo. Settler researchers, for their part, claimed that professional archaeologists avoided digging in Judea and Samaria for political reasons and thus missed out on their national calling and on the opportunity to make major discoveries. While the settlers did not wish to appropriate the archaeological discourse from its established practitioners, they suggested a re-Zionization of archaeology. They demanded that the archaeologists return to their historical role of assisting the Zionist project in developing the bond between the people and the land.

The conflict focused in part on the altar on Mount Ebal near Shechem (Nablus), especially because here the settlers enjoyed the rare collaboration of a professional archaeologist. Adam Zertal of the University of Haifa claims to have unearthed there an altar from the period of Joshua. Many archaeologists have sharply criticized his interpretation (see Kempinski 1986 versus Zertal 1986); the settlers enthusiastically and uncritically took Zertal's side. The fact that most professional archaeologists do not merely reject his interpretation, but actually ridicule it, only shows, in the settlers' minds, how tilted the establishment is against their worldview.

Yoel Bin-Nun accepts Zertal's claims and explains in detail why, according to biblical sources, the structure found on Mount Ebal is indeed a Hebrew altar from the time of Joshua. As a result, he must contend with other findings of the excavations, primarily the presence of the bones of animals that the Torah does not prescribe as sacrificial offerings. Zertal claims that this indicates a link between the religion of Israel and the earlier Canaanite religions, thus challenging the religious dictum that the Torah is God-given. Bin-Nun explains these findings in another way: "There is insufficient basis here for such a far-reaching interpretation that fallow-deer and roebucks were sacrificed at any time" (Bin-Nun, 1985: 142).

Zertal's excavation site occupies a central place in the settlers' suggested tour of the area and is shown to visitors as proof of the ancient Jewish presence there and the truth of the biblical narrative. It is described in a guidebook published by the Samaria Seminary, which recounts the discovery of the ancient altar in terms of epic adventure and religious revelation: "On October 13, 1983, most of the doubts in the logical mind of archaeologist Adam Zertal fell away. . . . It is not completely clear what it was in the huge area that lit up his imagination . . . but his experienced eye picked up the fine, consistent note that made all the difference. . . . Zertal: 'I remember it as if it was only yesterday. . . . Suddenly the light burst forth. . . . I immediately opened to the book of Leviticus, where the altar was described'" (Maudlinger 1987: 12–15).

The author goes on to discuss the significance of the discovery and expresses his disappointment with its critical reception and the mistaken impression it made in Israel and throughout the world: "The features of the altar correspond exactly to the biblical passage's unique and specific description! The discovery of America and man's first step on the moon are nothing in comparison" (Maudlinger 1987: 15).

Discussion: The Double Irony of Second-Stage National Archaeology

Gush Emunim's interest in archaeology shows the importance for nationalist movements of digging the land and recovering the past; it also proves, however, that the shifting social, political, and historical context must not be overlooked. The Jewish settlers in the West Bank found themselves in a conflict situation, not only vis-à-vis their Palestinian neighbors but also vis-à-vis large sections of the Israeli public and most of Israeli academia. Their brand of biblical archaeology was a latecomer; tied to religious practices, it was not accepted by most Israelis. The established Israeli archaeology that encountered Gush Emunim has fostered a critical perspective on its own past participation in the nation-building project and has undergone a process of professionalization that has detached it from some, if not all, of its national functions. Professional archaeology has retreated into its specialized institutions and concentrated on the demands of its academic field. The archaeologists of today see themselves in terms of a rigorous profession and have developed mechanisms of seclusion through a state-sponsored accreditation system. They are zealous of their disciplinary boundaries and unwilling to accept what they dismiss as the pseudoscience of a religious group. Gush Emunim settlers, by contrast, want to de-professionalize Israeli archaeology, detach it from its universalist pretenses, and reconnect it to the nation-building process. In their mind, this is in full accordance with the rules of science, because it will move the discipline closer to fulfilling its "true vocation" of uncovering the historical roots hidden beneath the surface of the land.

This situation is ironic. The settlers initially wanted to use archaeology in order to achieve legitimacy for their political claims through participation in the well-established national discourse. But their very strategy has instead earned them the label of irrational fanatics. Even as they seek to join their voice to the chorus of the national discourse, they discover that they are further excluded and marginalized by the voice of scientific rationality. One should remember that this is only part of the picture, since archaeology is an important part of the inner Gush Emunim discourse and executes identity-forming functions that are not affected by the degree of acceptance by the outside world.

But there is another irony here associated with the appropriation of national archaeology. The idea of seeking national roots through excavation was suggested by the national movement, in the belief that the deeper the archaeologist's spade reaches, the more authentic the national identity becomes. This practice never stated how deep is enough, thereby permitting others to make their own claims using the same strategy. The archaeological stopping point seems arbitrary; the Gush Emunim settlers are quick to notice the shaky moral grounds on which the archaeological institutions stand when they ask why digging for national roots was legitimate and scientifically sound at one point in recent history but is so no longer. Gush Emunim is actually attempting to use biblical archaeology, a national practice, against those who initiated it and will not allow the newcomers to join in.

Gush Emunim's use of biblical archaeology shows how, in a postnational age, national archaeology can become a subversive practice aimed at those who used it in the past. This point has general importance for the future study of the intersection between nationalism and archaeology. Research on national archaeology has concentrated on its role in the establishment of the national ethos, but it seems that the practice has surprising new roles when others adopt it. Future research should concentrate on the new role of national archaeology in the postnational world.

Notes

1. On Israeli archaeology and nationalism, see Abu el-Haj 1998, 2002; Ben-Yehuda 1995; Elon 1994; Feige 2001a; Hallote and Joffe 2002; Shavit 1997; Silberman 1993; Zerubavel 1995.
2. On archaeology and nationalism, see Anderson 1992; Diaz-Andreu and Champion 1996; Kohl 1998; Kohl and Fawcett 1995; Meskell 1998; Smith 1986; Trigger 1984.
3. This chapter utilizes data collected in 1992–1996 for my PhD dissertation. It is based on interviews with settlers and professional Israeli archaeologists, a review of the literature published by the settlers, and attendance at conferences in the College of Judea and Samaria and at other semiacademic events.

   Translations from non-English sources are my own unless otherwise noted.

4. On Gush Emunim, see Newman 1985; Lustick 1991; Aran 1991; Sprinzak 1991; Feige 2002.
5. The concept of the authentic has received much attention in sociological and anthropological literature lately. See MacCannell 1973; Bruner 1994; Waitt 2000.
6. On Zionist memory, see Zerubavel 1995; Wistrich and Ohana 1995.
7. The Jewish return to Hebron in 1968 preceded the establishment of Gush Emunim. See Feige 2001b.
8. These publications appear in Hebrew. Most impressive among them are the series of edited proceedings of the annual conferences at the College of Judea and Samaria and other series dedicated to specific regions such as Hebron, Samaria, and Judea.
9. On Zionism as Diaspora nationalism, see Smith 1995.
10. From the 1993 Judea and Samaria conference at the Samaria college Ariel.
11. On the general question of fundamentalism and science today, see Mendelsohn 1993.
12. See, for example, Finkelstein and Silberman 2001; for much more radical statements, not accepted by Israeli archaeologists, see Whitelam 1996.

References

Abu el-Haj, Nadia. 1998. "Translating Truths: Nationalism, the Practice of Archaeology, and the Remaking of Past and Present in Contemporary Jerusalem." *American Ethnologist* 25 (2): 166–188.

Abu el-Haj, Nadia. 2002. *Facts on the Ground: Archaeological Practice and Territorial Self-Fashioning in Israeli Society*. Chicago: University of Chicago Press.

Anderson, Benedict. 1992. *Imagined Communities: Reflections on the Spread of Nationalism*. 2nd ed. London: Verso.

Aran, Gideon. 1991. "Jewish Zionist Fundamentalism: The Bloc of the Faithful in Israel." In *Fundamentalism Observed*, ed. Martin E. Marty and R. Scott Appleby, 265–344. Chicago: University of Chicago Press.

Aran, Gideon. 1993. "Return to the Scripture in Modern Israel." *Sciences Religieuses* 69:101–131.

Ariel, Ya'akov. 1988. *The Land of Israel Border Atlas according to Halakhic Sources* [in Hebrew]. Jerusalem: Cana Publication.

Aronoff, Miron J. 1986. "Establishing Authority: The Memorialization of Jabotinsky and the Burial of the Bar Kokhba Bones in Israel under the Likud." In *The Frailty of Authority*, ed. M. J. Aronoff. New Brunswick, NJ: Transaction.

Benvenisti, Meron. 1992. "The Wretchedness of Academia" [in Hebrew]. *Ha'aretz*, Apr. 10.

Ben-Yehuda, Nachman. 1995. *The Masada Myth: Collective Memory and Mythmaking in Israel*. Madison: University of Wisconsin Press.

Bin-Nun, Yoel. 1985. "The Altar on Mt. Ebal" [in Hebrew]. In *Before Efraim, Binyamin, and Menashe*, ed. Ze'ev Ehrlich, 137–163. Ofra: Ofra Field School and Land of Benjamin College.

Bruner, Eduard M. 1994. "Abraham Lincoln as an Authentic Reproduction: A Critique of Post-Modernism." *American Anthropologist* 96 (2): 397–415.

Diaz-Andreu, M., and T. Champion, eds. 1996. *Nationalism and Archaeology in Europe*. Boulder, CO: Westview.

Ehrlich, Ze'ev. 1980. "Beit Lavan and Not Levonah" [in Hebrew]. *Nekuda* 3:16.

Ehrlich, Ze'ev. 1987. "The Tomb of Joseph" [in Hebrew]. *Judea and Samaria* 1:153–162.

Elitzur, Yoel. 1980a. "Those Are the Names" [in Hebrew]. *Nekuda* 10:3–12.

Elitzur, Yoel. 1980b. "When Should Purim Be Celebrated in Beit-El and the Army Camps around It?" [in Hebrew]. *Tehumin* 1:109–119.

Elitzur, Yoel. 1983. "Purim: One Day of Two" [in Hebrew]. *Nekuda* 55:10–11, 34.

Elitzur, Yoel. 1988. "The Time of Purim in the City of Lod" [in Hebrew]. *T'humin* 9:367–380.

Elon, Amos. 1994. "Politics and Archaeology." *New York Review of Books*, Sept. 22, 14–18.

Feige, Michael. 2001a. "Identity, Ritual, and Pilgrimage: The Meetings of the Israeli Exploration Society." In *Divergent Jewish Cultures*, ed. Deborah Dash Moore and Ilan Troen, 87–106. New Haven, CT: Yale University Press.

Feige, Michael. 2001b. "Jewish Settlement of Hebron: The Place and the Other." *GeoJournal* 53:323–333.

Feige, Michael. 2002. *One Space, Two Places: Gush Emunim, Peace Now, and the Construction of Israeli Space* [in Hebrew]. Jerusalem: Magnes Press.

Finkelstein, Israel, and Neil Asher Silberman. 2001. *The Bible Unearthed: Archaeology's New Vision of Ancient Israel and the Origin of Its Sacred Texts*. New York: Free Press.

Hallote, Rachel S., and Alexander H. Joffe. 2002. "The Politics of Israeli Archaeology: Between 'Nationalism' and 'Science' in the Age of the Second Republic." *Israel Studies* 7 (3): 83–116.

Jackson, J. B. 1980. *The Necessity for Ruins*. Amherst: University of Massachusetts Press.

Kempinski, Aharon. 1986. "Joshua's Altar–an Iron Age I Watchtower." *Biblical Archaeological Review* 12 (1): 42, 44–49.

Kohl, Philip L. 1998. "Nationalism and Archaeology: On the Construction of Nations and the Reconstruction of the Remote Past." *Annual Review of Anthropology* 27: 223–246.

Kohl, Philip L., and Clare Fawcett, eds. 1995. *Nationalism, Politics, and the Practice of Archaeology*. Cambridge: Cambridge University Press.

Liebman, Charles S., and Eliezer Don-Yehiya. 1983. *Civil Religion in Israel*. Berkeley: University of California Press.

Lustick, Ian. 1991. *For the Land and the Lord: Jewish Fundamentalism in Israel*. New York: Council on Foreign Relations.

MacCannell, Dean. 1973. "Staged Authenticity: Arrangements of Social Space in Tourist Settings." *American Journal of Sociology* 79 (3): 589–603.

Maudlinger, M. 1987. *The Land of Shekhem* [in Hebrew]. Alon Moreh: Itzuv Shalem and Midreshet Shomron.

Mendelsohn, E. 1993. "Religious Fundamentalism and the Sciences." In *Fundamentalism and Society*, ed. Martin E.. Marty and R. Scott Appleby, 23–41. Chicago: University of Chicago Press.

Meskell, Lynn, ed. 1998. *Archaeology under Fire: Nationalism, Politics, and Heritage in the Eastern Mediterranean and Middle East*. London: Routledge.

Morris, Benny. 1987. *The Birth of the Palestinian Refugee Problem, 1947–1949*. Cambridge: Cambridge University Press.

Newman, David, ed. 1985. *The Impact of Gush Emunim*. London: Croom Helm.

Nimni, Ephraim, ed. 2003. *The Challenge of Post-Zionism: Alternatives to Israeli Fundamentalist Politics*. London: Zed Books.

Pappe, Ilan. 1995. "Critique and Agenda: The Post-Zionist Scholars in Israel." *History and Memory* 7:66–90.

Ram, Uri. 1995. *The Changing Agenda of Israeli Sociology: Theory, Ideology, Identity*. New York: SUNY Press.

Ram, Uri. 1999. "The State and the Nation: Contemporary Challenges to Zionism in Israel." *Constellations* 6 (3): 325–338.

Shavit, Ya'akov. 1997. "Archaeology, Political Culture, and Culture in Israel." In *The Archaeology of Israel*, ed. Neil Asher Silberman and David Small, 48–62. Supplement of *Journal for the Study of the Old Testament*. Sheffield, England: Sheffield Academic Press.

Silberman, Neil Asher. 1982. *Digging for God and Country*. New York: Knopf.

Silberman, Neil Asher. 1993. *A Prophet from amongst You: The Life of Yigael Yadin, Soldier, Scholar, and Mythmaker of Modern Israel*. Reading, MA: Addison-Wesley.

Silberstein, Laurence J. 1999. *The PostZionism Debates: Knowledge and Power in Israeli Culture*. New York: Routledge.

Smith, Anthony D. 1986. *The Ethnic Origins of Nations*. Oxford: Blackwell.

Smith, Anthony D. 1995. "Zionism and Diaspora Nationalism." *Israel Affairs* 2 (2): 1–19.

Sprinzak, Ehud. 1991. *The Ascendance of Israel's Radical Right*. New York: Oxford University Press.

Trigger, B. G. 1984. "Alternative Archaeologies: Nationalist, Colonialist, Imperialist." *Man* 19:355–370.

Waitt G. 2000. "Consuming Heritage–Perceived Historical Authenticity." *Annals of Tourism Research* 27 (4): 835–862.

Weingrod, Alex. 1995. "Dry Bones: Nationalism and Symbolism in Contemporary Israel." *Anthropology Today* 11 (6): 7–12.

Whitelam, Keith W. 1996. *The Invention of Ancient Israel*. London: Routledge.

Wistrich, Robert, and David Ohana, eds. 1995. *The Shaping of Israeli Identity: Myth, Memory, and Trauma*. London: Frank Cass.

Zertal, Adam. 1986. "How Can Kempinski Be So Wrong?" *Biblical Archaeological Review* 12 (1): 43, 49–53.

Zerubavel, Yael. 1995. *Recovered Roots: Collective Memory and the Making of Israeli National Tradition*. Chicago: University of Chicago Press.

TEN

Appropriating the Past

Heritage, Tourism, and Archaeology in Israel

UZI BARAM

I. Preface

Amos Oz wrote, "archaeological digs have little to say to me, even though roots in the past are important." That formulation is jarring. Israeli ideology and discourse, and thus Israeli identity, are connected to archaeology, to the tactile connection to the past in a particular place. Yet for this important Israeli novelist and political analyst, a frequently quoted public intellectual, archaeological artifacts do not inspire an appreciation for the past. For Oz, the stories from and about the past are more significant than material excavations into the past. Nevertheless, he maintains that "we must fight for the rights of archaeologists to conduct their diggings in the face of ultra-Orthodox opposition, unrelated to the subjective experiential weight of pottery shards" (1987: 215–216). Oz illustrates a contradiction between lack of interest in archaeological excavations and a belief that archaeological excavations in Israel must receive support; although he remains unimpressed with the endeavor, he recognizes that it is an important and contested project for Israel.

Zionism, particularly via the political projects initiated at the end of the nineteenth century, ties Jews as a socially historically constituted group of people to the land of the state of Israel. The construction and rationalization of the connections between that people and that territory necessitated grounding history in the land, a task facilitated by archaeology. For Israelis the relationship between themselves and the land has shifted as the country has changed. One significant entry point for exploring the transition is the transformation of the presentation of the archaeological past to external audiences. As the target tourist has changed, so has the metanarrative of archaeology, with implications for how Israelis understand themselves and their state. In this chapter I explore some of the changes in the use of archaeology in Israel. A large corpus of publications critiques, analyzes, and discusses the use of archaeology in Israel for nationalist purposes (e.g., Trigger 1984; Silberman 1989; Glock 1994, and many others). Some of the critiques foreshadow the recent interest in the relationship between archaeology and nationalism (Kohl and Fawcett 1995; Diaz-Andreu and Champion 1996). But over the past decade, a new concern, a postnationalist agenda, has been added to the critique of archaeology. The impact of tourism seems to have overtaken nationalism as a factor that guides the discourse of archaeology. Just as exposing nationalism propelled a critical understanding of the archaeological endeavor in the twentieth century, there are important implications to archaeology's embrace of tourism in the twenty-first century. The twin components of archaeo-tourism on one hand and profits and access on the other are paradoxical pressures for contemporary archaeology, challenging interpretations and presentations in manners that might benefit the public but might not always work to the benefit of archaeology (Silberman 1995; Killebrew 1999; Baram and Rowan 2004).

II. Archaeology in Israel

Over the past two decades, archaeology in Israel has recovered important finds at places associated with the biblical narratives (e.g., the House of David inscription from Tel Dan in the north of Israel and the Ekron inscription from Tel Miqne near the coast). Archaeologists have been revising understanding of the Iron Age (e.g., Finkelstein and Silberman 2001) and the early Islamic period (e.g., Magness 2003), adding complexities to the historical narrative and its social implications. And excavations have exposed extensive views of the classical-period landscapes for cities like Sepphoris, Caesarea, and Beit She'an. Israel is one of the most intensively excavated places in the Middle East, if not the planet, and has a long tradition of archaeological investigations. The search for the past has been propelled, and complicated, by literary and historical records, particularly the Bible. Archaeological investigations, more than any other avenue for exploring the past in that land, have captured the imagination of Western audiences, providing an impetus for people to visit Israel. Archaeology, with its diverse theoretical and methodological approaches, has provided a tremendous amount of materials for the present to consider the past and of tactile things for people to see, contemplate, and photograph.

Nationalism was an essential aspect of the development of the mainstream of Israeli archaeology, as its critics have shown. Evidence of nationalism comes from excavations at such ancient places as Masada (Ben-Yehuda 1995; Zerubavel 1995) and the Old City of Jerusalem (e.g. Johns 1988; Abu el-Haj 2001) and through the discoveries of the Dead Sea Scrolls (Silberman 1993). Yet the vast majority of the excavations are salvage operations as Israel undergoes the urbanization common throughout the region. When scholars criticize the nationalism of Israeli archaeology, they tend to overlook the salvage operations, Western financial support of archaeological excavations, and community development programs. There is a gap between the majority of archaeological excavations and the examples typically subject to criticism that creates a distorted picture of the larger complexities driving Israeli archeology. Archaeology has an instrumentalist function, but nationalism is no longer the prime mover in the discourse and agenda of archaeology in Israel.

The appropriation of the past has shifted, as illustrated by the types of projects and the marketing of the past. The critiques of Israeli archaeology have shown the impacts of nationalism, but in the continuing critical endeavor of understanding the influences on archaeology and archaeological representations, new factors need to be included. After considering the intersection of nationalism and archaeology in Israel, I will discuss the appropriation of the archaeological past for tourism.

III. Representing the Nation through Archaeology

Archaeology, as the study of the past, has been haunted by attempts of varied nations to "resurrect their greatness in the past" (Kohl and Fawcett 1995; Diaz-Andreu and Champion 1996) by picking and choosing certain places and times to emphasize nationalist themes. For Israel, that attempt requires building temporal bridges between the present (with the triumphs of Zionism and military strength) to antiquity (with examples of successful and even failed polities, military endeavors, and famous people). The selective treatment of excavations and a focus on golden ages, specifically the concentrated efforts on the Late Bronze and Iron Ages, led scholars like Bar Yosef and Mazar (1982), Trigger (1984), Silberman (1989), and Abu el-Haj (2001) to highlight Israeli archaeology as contributing to a political agenda that constructs nationalist narratives.

The majority of archaeological excavations in Israel focus on sites associated with the Bronze and Iron Ages, with the classical period (Hellenistic, Roman, and Byzantine) lagging behind (for the archaeological chronology, see table 10.1). The prehistoric periods are outside the main thrusts of that research, except as laying the groundwork for the later periods. The Islamic eras (after 660 CE, with the exception of Crusader rule from 1099 to 1299 CE) receive the least systematic archaeological attention of any period in the Middle East. And within the Islamic period, the Ottoman centuries—until recently—were ignored, avoided, or bulldozed (Baram 2002). The result is a gap in time, a separation between present and past in the land and in history. Archaeology in Israel, according to this line of interpretation, fails to account for the history of the territory during 1900 years of exile (Zerubavel 1995).

Israel is a nation-state that has used archaeology to ground its claims to a land, to construct a common heritage for a diverse grouping of people, and to tie nationalism and archaeology together (though it is hardly unique in doing so). The unity of a dispersed and diverse people emerges from the "origins" stories from antiquity. Trigger (1984) pigeonholed this type of archaeology as colonialist. Scholars have documented and explained that many twentieth-century states employed archaeology to foster national identity, both in terms of a positive portrayal of the nation and in terms of obscuring other histories existing within the state boundaries (see Kohl and Fawcett 1995; Diaz-Andreu and Champion 1996); Israel fits the pattern. But due to the extensive amount of archaeological investigations and the weight given to their findings (in museum exhibits, publications, and films), archaeology and Israeli nationalism seem deeply intertwined. The institutions of the state and Israelis themselves seem to have successfully used archaeology to ground their present in the past. There are some ironies in that dynamic, a dynamic that can be traced through a brief consideration of Zionism.

Modern political Zionism began a century ago, under Theodor Herzl's leadership, as a modernist endeavor that valued technology and notions of progress. In his utopian novel, *Altneuland* (*Old New Land*) Herzl (1987) presented his dream for a modernist society in Palestine, one that reconstructed European culture in the land of Israel. His focus fell upon Haifa, a port city on the Mediterranean, rather than on the ancient and religious city of Jerusalem, as he envisioned a new society for a secularized

Table 10.1 Chronology for Israel

Paleolithic	1,500,000–18,500 BP
Epipaleolithic	18,500–12,300 BP
Natufian	10,300–8500 BCE
Neolithic	8500–4500
Chalcolithic	4500–3300
Bronze Age	
Early	3330–2000
Middle	2000–1500
Late	1500–1200
Iron Age	
I	1200–926
II	926–586
Babylonian and Persian	586–332
Classical Ages	
Early Hellenistic	332–198
Late Hellenistic	198–63
Herodian/Early Roman	65 BCE–70 CE
Late Roman	70–324
Byzantine	324–640
Islamic Periods	
Early Islamic Period	
Umayyad Caliphate	661–750
Abbasid Caliphate	750–1258
Fatimid Caliphate	910–1171
Crusaders	1099–1299
Late Islamic Period	
Ayyubid Dynasty	1169–1252
Mamlük Empire	1258–1517
Ottoman Empire	1517–1917

and cultured Jewish people. The first waves of Zionist settlers in Palestine had little interest in looking to the past for support of their endeavor. As socialists, building a new type of society was the goal. Yet by the 1920s archaeology began to play a role in linking these settlers to the land. During those years Jewish nationalists in Palestine sought to label the land and the features of the landscape as a means of legitimating Jewish claims to Palestine (Berkowitz 1997: 134–135; Benvenisti 2000); a similar gaze occurred for archaeological sites representing the Jewish past. Elon (1994) tells the story of Kibbutz Beit Alpha and ancient ruins to explain how the past became important to Zionism. In the 1920s, while digging a foundation for a building, kibbutz members uncovered the mosaics of an ancient synagogue. At first, these secular settlers considered avoiding the archaeological find, but when a link between themselves and the find was made (between ancient Jews living in that area and their settlement), the mosaic at Beit Alpha entered Zionist history as a modern Jewish excavation revealing a hidden ancient Jewish presence in the land. The imagery in the synagogue mosaic did not fit assumptions about Jewish practices, but the tactile evidence of an ancient synagogue made the find meaningful to the kibbutz members and to the state-building endeavor. The coupling of archaeological finds and Zionism grew in significance with the creation of the state of Israel in 1948. As the embodiment of Jewish national identity, the state took on excavations and presentations of the past to solidify its legitimacy among the Jewish people both in Israel and in the Diaspora. The leaders of the state turned toward the past rather than continuing the orientation toward the future (as in Herzl's utopian vision). Myron Aronoff argues that in Israel's early years, "as a conspicuously new construct, creating the impression of constituting a natural community has been a monumental challenge for the new state. Perhaps the primary goal of Israeli political culture has been to make the continuity of the ancient past with the contemporary context a taken-for-granted reality" (1991: 175). That naturalization of the past succeeded for Israelis. The endeavor of archaeology, as a link between people and the land, was seen as an achievement in its own right and helped to construct the notion that all Jews have a common ancestry. The actual finds illustrated for Israelis the antiquity of Jews in the land. Images from Jewish antiquity, both real and imagined, allowed Israelis to see a transformation of the landscape of Palestine into the landscape of Israel.

For example, near the Jaffa Gate of the Old City of Jerusalem, a building with a minaret is readily called the Tower of David (Migdal Da'vid). The Tower of David, in the early twentieth century, became one of the most visible symbols for Zionism. That image faded when Jordan controlled the Old City of Jerusalem (1948–1967) but returned as the structure became a major museum for Israeli Jerusalem after the 1967 Six-Day War. The noticeable Islamic nature of the tower, and an Ottoman-period construction date for the walls around the Old City of Jerusalem, continue to be disregarded in perceptions of the place. Benvenisti (2000: 44) explains that considerable efforts were expended on cartography and that a new geography was drawn for Palestine. Archaeology undermined the extant Palestinian landscape; an Israeli past became visible throughout the rereading of extant landscape (Benvenisti 2000). Katz (1985) discusses how teacher-guides would point out the Jewish landscape of Palestine to youth groups and organized hikes around the country. The notion of knowing the land (in Hebrew: *yediat ha'aretz*) (Benvenisti 2000: 57) allowed the creation of a new landscape for Israelis and for Israel.

In the early days of the state, such figures as Yigael Yadin and Moshe Dayan became associated both with the leadership of the country and with archaeology. The fact that both Dayan and Yadin served in the same government in the late 1970s might explain how, though they took different pathways and had different relationships to the past (Dayan as a collector; Yadin as an excavator), both used their relationships with the past as foundations for their political aspirations.

Moshe Dayan, Israeli war hero, held high-ranking ministerial positions in the Israeli governments of the 1950s through the 1970s. Dayan, with an eye patch, was a public face of Israel. He was also a passionate collector of antiquities. Never an archaeologist, he looted sites and purchased artifacts from antiquity dealers for private display. In *Living with the Bible*, Dayan wrote: "I was not content only with the Israel I could see and touch. I also longed for the Israel of the 'timeless verses' and the 'biblical names,' and I wanted to give tangibility to that too" (1978: 6). The impulse for recovering the past was not just ideological. Dayan, an Israeli general, concludes his telling of the biblical landscape by noting that if "indeed permanent borders for Israel are to be determined, she will be confronted with the same problem that faced the kingdom of Israel in David's time" (225–226). After his death, the Israel Museum in Jerusalem exhibited a portion of Dayan's extensive antiquities collection (which the museum purchased despite public outcry over buying what belonged to the nation).

Silberman (1993) has explored the intersection of past and present for Israeli politics and archaeology through the figure of Yigael Yadin. Yadin, the son of an archaeologist, led parallel careers in archaeology and in politics. Yadin's excavations at Masada focused a global spotlight on that plateau in the desert; it became one of the most recognizable archaeological symbols for the state of Israel. Yadin uncovered fortifications, weapons, and potsherds; he gave public lectures on the excavations and published a popular volume *Masada: Herod's Fortress and the Zealot's Last Stand* (Yadin 1966) that focused attention on the famous heroic moment when the Jewish revolt against Rome came to an end. Yadin made Masada, as well as the excavation at Hazor and the finds from the Dead Sea caves, into larger-than-life myths in the period of nation-building in Israel. Skeletons found by Yadin received state burials in the late 1970s because they were associated with the Jewish uprisings against Roman rule and were seen as direct ancestors of the Israeli army. Bowersock (1985: 52) asserts that Yadin misrepresented the past (specifically the history of the Bar Kokha Revolt of 135 CE) by presenting the revolt in a positive light and not presenting other finds from that time period. A more even-handed account of Yadin's role notes that he was invested in the discourse that privileged nationalist interpretations of the past even while engaging in public debates against the overtly political uses of archaeological finds (Aronoff 1991: 183–184).

The implications of Yadin's stories of the past and his engagement in Israeli politics seem to parallel each other. Yadin's splinter party helped bring the Likud to power in 1977, ending the Labor Party rule that started with the founding of the state, and he assumed the post of deputy prime minister. Silberman concludes that, like his political fortunes, which ended in disappointment, even Yadin's archaeological stories escaped his control and were used by others for their own political purposes (Silberman 1993: 366).

As should be evident, the link between archaeology and nationalism, in all its complexities, is well established for the Israeli case. Archaeology in Israel has a long genealogy of outside concerns. The Grand Tour, the convention of Western European travel and education, included the biblical sites of the Holy Land. Westerners came from Europe and North America to see the landscapes of antiquity, and many wrote up their accounts of travel. The founders of archaeology in nineteenth-century Palestine include Edward Robinson, an American who identified tells and ruins in terms of a biblical geography, and Sir William Matthew Flinders Petrie, a Briton who brought with him stratigraphic techniques and a ceramic typology. Glock (1994) situated the archaeology as a Western construct with a Western agenda. But today more than biblical scholars, archaeologists, and nationalism drive excavations and the study of the past in Israel. As Israel and other small countries become deeply embedded in the global economy, one source of income is tourism; and one of the resources for tourism is the archaeological past. Silberman (1995) argues that a strong connection exists between archaeology, nationalism, and tourism. This suggestion adds another factor for understanding the social context of archaeology in Israel. Most discussions of archaeology and nationalism in Israel have assumed a primary significance for the ideological needs of the state, ignoring its material applications. In today's global economy, Israel needs tourists. Over the 1990s, the Israeli Ministry of Tourism geared up for an expected major increase in tourism for the first year of the millennium. One particularly important aspect of the campaign, as it relates to the advertising of Israel, focuses on Israel's archaeological history. The archaeological past, as seen in excavations, artifacts, and the cultural landscape, is a major draw for Western tourists. The need for tourists is outweighing the ideological needs of the state, and the pressures on Israeli archaeology have come to be understood more clearly in terms of tourism than of nationalism. This dynamic is part of a larger shift in Israeli society; the use of archaeology illustrates the stresses on Israeli society. As Silberstein (1999) notes, the fiftieth anniversary of the state of Israel correlated with a rethinking of the nationalist discourse and the nature of Zionism. Israeli archaeology is no longer focused on nationalist themes. Whether this is a result of shifting priorities or of a loss of nationalist concerns might be visible after a consideration of the divisions in Israeli society.

IV. Divisions in Israel

Israeli identity, as well as Jewish identity, is marked by diversity, but there is an "underlying belief in unity, despite an awareness of the existence of considerable ethnographic diversity" (Webber 1992: 246). Archaeology has contributed to a revival of traditions that help to maintain the belief in unity and to mask divisions. The tensions between the diversity and the unity can be found in the attempts to commemorate a heritage for the many peoples of Israel.

In 1998 Israel celebrated a half century of statehood. The fifty-year mark provides a respectable benchmark for dividing the history of the state: its first twenty-five years were much different from the second twenty-five. The first period saw the War of Independence, the 1956 War, the Six-Day War, the War of Attrition, and the Yom Kippur War; the second saw peace treaties with Israel signed by the Egyptian president Anwar Sadat, the Palestine Liberation Organization chairman Yasir Arafat, and the Jordanian king Hussein. Now, with nearly 6 million people living within the boundaries of the state, Israel is one of the economic powers of the region, owing both to massive American support and to the underdevelopment of the Palestinians. Whereas the ideology once emphasized settling the territory, draining the swamps, irrigating the deserts, and building the land, and the communalism of the kibbutz and the moshav was taken as a national ideal, now Israelis build malls, use cellular telephones, watch CNN, and eat at MacDonald's. The role of the past and the uncovering of the past have changed as well.

Who lives in the state of Israel? The essential division is assumed to be between Palestinians and Israelis. Their conflict over the land and national territorial integrity involve the past as much as the present. Israel uses the biblical events of the Late Bronze Age and the Israelites of the Iron Age to ground its claims to the land. The Palestinians invoke the Canaanites, of the Middle Bronze Age, to supersede Israeli claims.

But there is complexity in both national groupings. For Israelis, the Palestinians are the Other: rivals in a nationalist contest for territory. Palestinian identity, as Khalidi (1997) shows, is historically contingent, changing with the dynamics of Ottoman, British, and Israeli control over Palestine. The lack of a state apparatus that determines identity has left open the question of which markers are used to determine peoplehood. For Khalidi (207), the variables in the indeterminateness of Palestinian identity include the Palestinian territories' borders with Israel; the educational system in Israel and Gaza and the West Bank; identity cards used by Palestinians in Israel; the Palestinian Authority, domestic and abroad; and the management of antiquities for national identity. For Israelis, the state determines identity. Yet there are multiple, competing groupings; the divisions and tensions cross religious-secular, class, ethnic, and gender lines. Beinin argues that the formation of the Israeli state "prepared the way for the national chauvinism, regressive gender policy, and demagogic appeal to Oriental Jews" by the right wing, which opposed the Labor Party–based formation of Israel (1991: 123). This divide in Israeli society revolves around Jewish ethnicity and class and impacts the construction of the archaeological past. The founders of political Zionism and the early leaders of the state (and still the majority of the political leadership) were Jews of eastern European descent (the Ashkenazi). Today, the majority of the Jewish population of Israel is from the Middle East or descended from Middle Eastern families. These Sephardic (more properly called Mizrachi—*Sephardic* refers to ancestry in Iberia, while *Mizrachi* means easterner) Jews gained a measure of political power with the rise of Likud governments starting in 1977, though they remain the majority of the underclass in Israel (Cohen-Almagor 1995:

478–479). The Likud and the National Unity governments that followed the 1977 elections changed the cultural definition of the state, allowing Mizrachi traditions to gain official support even as they remained culturally marginalized.

In addition to the ethnic divide, the religious-secular divide in Israel is very deep. It impacts transportation, travel, time, and education. Thus, for example, certain streets close for the Sabbath, and restaurants and shops close on religious holidays. In terms of archaeology, the religious parties in the Knesset (the Israeli parliament) have enacted restrictions on the excavation of any burials less than five thousand years old to prevent disturbing the ancient Jewish dead. The peace process, the revolution in information technology, and the growth of Israel's market economy are forces working to further the divide between religious and secular Jews in Israel. The assassination of Prime Minister Yitzhak Rabin in 1995 illustrated the depth of the divide within the Jewish communities of Israel.

The notion of "them against us" works to keep Israelis together (the story of the Masada excavation provided an ancient validation for that notion). While nationalist archaeology aided in tolerating separation from neighbors and encouraging unity among Israelis, the external as well as internal needs of the state are supplanting that purpose for archaeology. There is a marketing of new representations of the past in Israel and its heritage. The surplus meaning of heritage is marketed for those who have resources: Western tourists.

V. Archaeology and Post-Zionism

The Israeli victory in the 1967 war opened up the highlands of the West Bank, the Golan Heights, and Sinai. Research and salvage operations allowed archaeologists to survey and excavate a wealth of artifacts and information on ancient settlement patterns from areas associated with the Jewish national past. For example, Sinai contained the potential for verifying the Exodus narrative, the central story of freedom from Egyptian bondage and conquest of Canaan, retold each year at Passover. Excavations and surveys brought forward a tremendous amount of archaeological information from the territory. After the Camp David Peace Accords, Israel returned Sinai to Egypt. That agreement included Israel's promise to hand over artifacts excavated from Sinai. In 1994 Israel returned the artifacts to Egypt (Einhorn 1996: 135).

The artifacts of Sinai are a component of heritage for Israel. Yet they were given to Egypt. As the Israeli Antiquities Authority returned those items to Egypt, its director made clear that if Israel returned the Golan Heights to Syria, the artifacts recovered from that territory, including the materials relating to Jewish heritage, would be returned with the land (Balter 2000). If archaeology is closely tied with nationalism, why are material remains of Jewish heritage given up?

In the Sinai case, there were twenty thousand artifacts, dating from Islamic, classical, and Pharaonic periods. On one level, the Hague Convention for the Protection of Cultural Property in Areas of Armed Conflict required repatriation. But there are many cases around the world in which repatriation is required but does not occur, and Israel has had its share of disagreements with international organizations and conventions. Repatriation, most famously with the Parthenon/Elgin Marbles, is contested using competing nationalist politics. In the case of the Sinai artifacts, Einhorn (1996) argues that the Hague convention is vague on the question of artifacts excavated from occupied territories, indicating that the issue was not uncomplicated when Israel chose to return the Sinai artifacts. The implications of the restitution are important for archaeology in Israel. For example, since some of the Dead Sea Scrolls are contested under the same convention (the Qumran Caves are in the occupied West Bank), the decision-makers in the Israeli negotiation team must have been concerned over the precedent set by its action.

The implications of the decision to proceed with restoration despite the danger of setting precedence may include a simple point. By the 1990s, archaeological artifacts had lost some of their meaning for the state. Israel fulfilled its obligations under the Hague convention without any noticeable public debate. For the majority of the twentieth century, Zionist ideology required tactile connections between Jewish heritage and the land of Israel. Today, after the state of Israel has passed the half-century mark, that line of argument for legitimacy is less pressing because nationalist needs are being subsumed by diplomatic and economic needs.

Recently the notion of post-Zionism has entered Israeli cultural and intellectual thought (Silberstein 1999). There are two pathways within post-Zionism. One is a return to the non-Zionist and anti-Zionist positions of many Jews that existed before the Holocaust. This line maintained that Zionism required too great a sacrifice of individuals who were Jewish, that establishing a Jewish state would risk alienating friends and supporters of Jews, and that Palestinians would be wronged by Israel. The other strand of post-Zionism is favorable to the Zionist enterprise as established a century ago in Basel under Theodor Herzl. Its view is that Zionism has reached its goal of settling the Jewish people in a Jewish state and therefore has nothing left to accomplish. The next steps, according to this post-Zionism, are to continue to normalize Israelis, to raise their sense of security (physical and metaphysical) and economic well-being (see, e.g., Arad 1996).

One can debate—and Israelis do—whether the country has entered a post-Zionist phase (Silberstein 1999). Yet the integration of Israel and Israelis into globalization and Americanization has greatly impacted people's sense of identity, culture, and heritage. The recent influx of more cultures into the narrative of the Israeli past, the uncovering of "forgotten periods" and minorities within the dominant archaeological epochs, and the presentation of other peoples' histories are creating an abundance of histories that is changing the meaning of archaeology for the state. The result may well be fewer excavations, fewer grand stories about the past, and an archaeological understanding of the land that is less relevant for its dominant society.

That change can be seen in the archaeology of Masada. Masada is the often-used example through which critics of Israeli archaeology illustrate the nationalist uses of the past. And from the Israeli Defense Forces' use of the site for inductions to the state's minting of commemorative coins with the slogan "Masada Shall Not Fall Again," this Roman-period archaeological site became a rallying point for nationalist identity. Yet the Israeli Defense Forces no longer use the plateau for induction ceremonies. Youth groups no longer hike up the hill before dawn with the same fervor as they did in the 1950s and 1960s. As Ben-Yehuda (1995; also this volume, chapter 8) discusses, the Masada myth is no longer needed for Israeli national consciousness.

Ben-Yehuda (1995) lays out the Roman historian Josephus's version of the fall of the Zealots at Masada and the discontinuities between that history and the myth constructed in the 1930s and 1940s about Masada. Yadin's 1960s excavations at Masada were an exciting endeavor, one foreshadowed by the energy of youth leaders and culture-makers in the early days of the state of Israel. Ben-Yehuda emphasizes that Yadin did not create the Masada myth. Rather, his writings on Masada carefully focused on the excavations and its finds. It was in the telling of stories that the narrative of Masada was created; as an oral tradition, Masada took on mythical status (see also Elon 1994).

The peak of association between the state and the story at Masada occurred during the time that Golda Meir was prime minister. During the early 1970s, the notion of a "Masada Complex" for the state became an image both negative and positive for Israel. Masada, as a place and a story, became intertwined with Israel and the modern state became associated with the history of the site.

Though Masada is still on the standard list of must-see tourist sites for visitors to Israel, it no longer plays a significant role for indoctrinating soldiers into the Israeli Defense Forces, for new immigrants, or for official visitors to the state. The story and myth of Masada no longer resonate for Israelis, Ben-Yehuda (1995) explains. But international audiences still seek it out. Part of the experience of visiting Masada used to be the challenging climb to the top of the plateau. But today tourists need not climb the difficult snake path to the top of Masada; a cable car makes the ascent easy. Postcards and soft drinks at the base of Masada, along with the numerous tour buses, give the place the look of a tourist destination rather than a historic site. It has been transformed from the locus of Israeli identity to the focus of international tourism.

No longer is Masada a key to Israeli identity, though it continues as a stage for celebrations. Neither are Israeli political leaders associated with archaeology. This transition (also noted by Elon 1994; Zerubavel 1995; and others) reflects new divisions and tensions within Israeli society. Nationalist discourse on the past has not disappeared; rather, archaeology is contested by more than monolithic ideological concerns. Both internal divisions and external economic pressures are impacting the symbolic aspects of archaeological excavations and finds even as new techniques and methodologies are improving the fieldwork and analysis of archaeology. As Upton notes for tourism in general, "Capitalism no longer seeks raw materials and markets for its industrial goods alone, but cultural raw materials that can be transformed into hard cash through the conservation, restoration, and outright fabrication of indigenous landscapes and traditional cultural practices for the amusement of metropolitan consumers. In this light, the rise of heritage and cultural tourism stands as another episode in the two-century history of modernity, though perhaps one given particularly urgency in the face of the increased, and increasingly global, scale of tourism and the transformation of local cultures and societies that it has seemed to engender." The interest in heritage tourism seems related to the local as antique, an experience to visit and consume. Upton goes on to state that even invented antiquity can serve these consuming habits, that authenticity is not a requirement or even a necessity (2001: 298). The tourist industry tries to sell to tourists by fashioning an imagined society, one that redefines the country's reality (Cohen-Hattab 2004: 64); the shift in presentation of places like Masada is a component of the transformations of Israeli society.

VI. Tourism in Israel Today: Disconnected Landscapes

Just before the new millennium began, Israel presented itself for Western consumption (according to Israeli Ministry of Tourism advertising) as a "country blessed with historical, archaeological, and religious treasures," as containing many places and many landscapes. Different audiences were encouraged to see the country from different perspectives; that is still the approach taken (Baram and Rowan 2004). In magazines and newspapers (such as the general readership of the *New York Times* as well as the more specific audience of, for example, the *Biblical Archaeology Review* and *Archaeology* magazine), Israel is presented with the line: "No one belongs here more than you." That quite remarkable slogan is then split into three different presentations of Israel.

One intended audience for the slogan is the general tourist. The earlier concerns for bridging the divides within Israeli society, the concerns for building the nation, seem to dissipate, replaced by a call for tourists, whoever they are, to come to Israel.

The images in the advertising use a general proclamation of Israel as a place where "the horizons you'll see will expand the ones you've got." The Ministry of Tourism uses dramatic full-color pictures of significant places of antiquity—Jerusalem's Tower of David, Masada, and Old Jaffa at sunset—to raise expectations for tourists that, as the advertising states, "the closer you get to it, the deeper it will move you." An association is created between those places and consuming general spiritual experiences for a wide target audience.

A different set of imagery and presentation is used to encourage specifically Jewish tourists to travel to Israel. Again Jerusalem is invoked, but this time with the explanation: "Being Jewish, you are heir to a unique history, heritage, and culture. Perhaps you feel it sometimes more than other times. Perhaps, at times, you barely feel it at all. But it's there—inside a part of your heart, within a place in your soul. And that's why you owe it to yourself to visit the one place on earth where you will learn about so much—but nothing more than about yourself." The invocation of Jewish pride to attract tourists to Israel is not an innovation of the 1990s. Zionism early on recognized the possibilities of attracting Jews to Israel by invoking Jewish pride (Berkowitz 1997: 125–146). Yet this particular configuration for attracting those alienated from their Judaism illustrates a sophisticated approach to luring visitors.

A third representation of Israel attracts a Christian audience. From this perspective, tourist campaigns depict Israel as the Holy Land, a term that is not found in the other two representations. That descriptor, in a subtle fashion, separates the two Israels: the Jewish state and the Christian Holy Land. For Christian tourists, the footsteps of Jesus are stressed. Jerusalem is represented by the Church of the Nativity; the horizon is no longer that of Masada but of the Sea of Galilee. The advertising states clearly that by going to Israel, "you'll grow closer to the spirit of the man who once taught—and walked here."

Taken together, such advertisements provide an interesting inducement for people wanting to visit Israel. Each group can see a different place with different connections to their history. During their time in Israel, most will face a segmented past, focused on a history they want, or are encouraged, to see.

These advertising campaigns reflect tours available in Israel. For example, for Jewish tourists from the West, a guide will select case after case to provide concrete evidence—buildings, tombs, and artifacts—of people who were symbolic if not genetic ancestors. A tour of this Israel will attest to two unmistakable lines: one is an unbroken link between the Jewish past and the Jewish present in Eretz Yisrael (Hebrew for the Land of Israel), and the other links all Jews in the Diaspora to the state of Israel. And the message is so powerful, even though it is never explicitly spoken, that it serves to frame the historical questions that are asked by tourists. Tourists' questions relate to the dominant or hegemonic discourse of the nation, which is to say the landscape as traversed by Jews, though often contested or intersected by the activities of Romans or Arabs or Crusaders at various points in the past. In this tour, historical interrogations take on a Zionist hue, connecting the Jewish past to the Jewish present in Israel.

A Christian tour group will likely see a different Israel, a different landscape, and a different heritage in the land advertised as Holy. The places of the New Testament are introduced: the tour will follow the "footsteps of Jesus" through Nazareth, Jerusalem, and the Sea of Galilee. Since Bethlehem is now in the Palestinian National Authority, Israel has constructed a tourist Bethlehem on the outskirts of that city and within the boundaries of the greater Jerusalem metropolitan area, so that Christian visitors can see (and more importantly, consume) that aspect of Jesus's life story.

The most striking part of these different tours is not their success in allowing tourists to see very different heritages, but rather their ability to carve a small country into these separate landscapes. Two tour groups might return to the West with two very separate images of Israel. The collective goal for all tourism is the same: economic resources for the state. To facilitate access to those different landscapes for different interest groups, the Ministry of Tourism's Web page (www.goisrael.com) has contact links for Jewish, Protestant, Catholic, Muslim, and ecological tourists (Baram and Rowan 2004: 12). Advances in tourism technology have allowed for fragmentation of the landscape of Israel; for an archaeotourism that fragmentation encourages tellings of the past for particular audiences. The impact of the transformation in presentations of the past is not just representational. The state supports archaeology by encouraging visitation and by encouraging excavations. Three examples are provided below.

VII. Archaeology in Israel Today: Consuming the Past

For centuries, Armageddon has meant end-times battle of horrific proportions. As the end of this millennium approaches, it also means tourists for Israel.

KANSAS CITY STAR, FEBRUARY 22, 1997

By exposing the material layers of the past, archaeologists work in the service of the state, looking to present the past for international tourists. Three ongoing archaeological projects illustrate some of the issues involved with the intersection of heritage marketing and archaeological excavations. The Israeli Ministry of Tourism planned an acceleration of tourism for the millennial year, marketing the past in Israel for a broad audience. Yet events overtook the planning and the violence of the al-Aqsa Intifada depressed tourism. The impact of designing attractions for tourism was not diminished by the downturn in tourism, however. The archaeological work, started in preparation for the projected massive tourism, illustrates the paradoxes of heritage tourism.

A. Beit She'an—Excavating Employment

Beit She'an is located south of the Sea of Galilee, near the Jordanian border. A poor development town, marked as Mizrachi, it has high unemployment, a position on the periphery of the state, and a weak industrial base. Nevertheless, it did produce a political leader, David Levy, who was a significant figure in Israeli politics for three decades, serving as mayor of Beit She'an and in numerous posts in Likud governments.

In the 1980s the Israeli government, the National Park Authority, and the national tourist board joined with the Antiquities Authority and the local town council in setting up excavations in the shadow of Tel Beit She'an. The politics of the town and the place of local officials in national politics encouraged the massive excavations. As Hershel Shanks, the editor of *Biblical Archaeology Review* and a U.S.-based promoter of Israeli archaeology, notes: "Out of poverty came riches. Or perhaps more accurately, from Beit She'an's economic troubles came archaeological treasures—a surprisingly rich and well-preserved city," the Greco-Roman city of Scythopolis (1990: 18).

Tel Beit She'an contains evidence from the Neolithic to the Assyrian conquest of 732 BCE. The Beit She'an valley is fertile and the site is situated at the crossroads between ancient Canaan and its northeastern neighbors. There are biblical accounts for the site, including mention of it during Solomon's reign. But the tourists visit the site in the shadow of the tell; the later city is the focus of the massive excavations by the Israeli Antiquities Authority (see fig. 10.1). The city was founded during the Hellenistic period; eventually Nysa-Scythopolis, as it was known during the Roman era, became the largest city in the Decapolis. During the Jewish revolt against Rome (66–70 CE), the Jewish inhabitants were massacred. In the second century, the city contained active markets, lofty temples, bathhouses, and a great theater. At the start of the fifth century, Scythopolis became the capital of *Palestina Secunda*. It covered four hundred acres and had an estimated forty thousand inhabitants. Under Persian rule and then the Muslim rule of Palestine, it continued as a great city. In 749 an earthquake devastated Beisan, as the city had become known. Sugarcane production overtook linen as the primary industry. The people of Beisan fled during the 1948 war that created the state of Israel, and a new city was created, mostly for North African immigrants (David Levy is Moroccan). Massive archaeological excavations started in 1989 to uncover the classical-period city.

On one level, the excavations provide employment for people in an economically depressed town (such towns are called development towns in the Israeli discourse). But the significance of the excavations for economics goes far beyond that. As Silberman (1995: 259–260) notes, this is archaeology for the sake of tourism. The excavation of Beit She'an has little in common with Masada or with the aims of an archaeology that supports nationalism and the state. The Greco-Roman city has little to offer the state in terms of ideology, but it attracts tourists to the present-day Beit She'an, serving a significant component of the Likud government's electoral coalition. Tourist attractions tend to have little meaning for the locals; the attractions are a commodity for tourists to consume, and it is hoped that their spending will filter into the local community.

The excavations of this late Roman–early Islamic city have become one of the central projects for the Israeli Antiquities Authority. While

Figure 10.1. Tourists at Beit She'an

small-scale excavations across the country have moved into private hands, government-supported digging goes on in Beit She'an.

B. Optimism for Armageddon: The End Battle for Tourism

Megiddo is a classical tell having layers associated with religious structures, historic figures (e.g., the biblical King Solomon), and rich material culture. Megiddo is also associated with war. Eric Cline (2000) lists thirty-four battles known from archival sources to have taken place at Megiddo. Those battles include Thutmose III's conquest at Megiddo in 1479 BCE; Josiah, king of Judah, falling in battle against Egyptian forces; Saladin fighting the Crusaders in 1187 CE; and the 1918 British defeat of the Ottoman army during the First World War. Because of the many wars at Megiddo, it is not surprising that the place became the New Testament's site for the ultimate battle between good and evil—*Har Megiddo* (Hebrew for "the hill of Megiddo") became corrupted into Armageddon. The site was inhabited continuously for six millennia (ca. 7000–500 BCE). It has abundant water supplies, fertile agricultural hinterlands, and close contact with neighboring peoples. It sits on a strategic location on the Via Maris, which was the major international military and trade route of antiquity linking Egypt in the south with Syria, Anatolia, and Mesopotamia

Figure 10.2. Megiddo Bronze Age Gate

in the north and east. Megiddo controls a bottleneck along this road where it emerges from the narrow ʻAruna pass into the fertile Jezreel Valley.

The archaeology has its own rich history. Tell el-Mutesellim was identified by Edward Robinson in 1838. At the start of the twentieth century, Gottlieb Schumacher excavated for Germany. The University of Chicago undertook massive excavations in the 1930s; Yigael Yadin searched for evidence of Solomon's empire in the 1960s. The most famous result is the structure known as Solomon's Stables. Since the 1990s, Tel Aviv University's excavations have focused upon clarifying the stratigraphy and chronology of the tell. The excavations have encouraged Israel Finkelstein to propose a new ceramic typology and with it, a new biblical history, published as *The Bible Unearthed* (Finkelstein and Silberman 2001). The excavations brought renewed attention to Megiddo. Although they focus on the Bronze and Iron Ages, a flood of tourists was expected to visit the site for the year 2000. They did not come, and the tourists that visited the site saw very little that connected with the New Testament (see fig. 10.2). Continuing plans for presenting Megiddo emphasize its Iron Age history; the Christian aspects of the place are left to the imaginations of the tourists.

Figure 10.3. Model of Jerusalem at the Holyland Hotel

C. A Miniature Jerusalem: Seeing the City without Being in the City

With the encouragement of advertising, some people are attracted to Israel, or the Holy Land, in order to seek out the past, usually their own past. While the act of discovering and recovering the past does draw some tourists, only a small minority engage in excavating (whether as volunteers on expeditions or for the "Dig for a Day" program) or even encounter ongoing excavations. The majority of tourists see the remains from the past in the form of foundations and other components of the archaeological record, reconstructions of the past landscapes, or artifacts in museums. The images of archaeo-tourism depict a depopulated landscape, an ancient place without the contemporary peoples and their conflicts. The only people are the tourists and those people positioned to host the tourism, or to be photographed for tourists' consumption.

Authenticity is a significant feature of visiting the place where "Jesus walked" or where Jews can feel that they belong in a spiritual and historical sense. The representations of the past can be linked rather than derived from archaeology. For instance, at the Holyland Hotel in Jerusalem, tourists can see a miniature version of Jerusalem at the time of Jesus (fig. 10.3). This small-scale model of the ancient city (the ratio is one to fifty) provides both photographic opportunities and the chance to gaze upon the entire city without having to walk its actual streets and be distracted by the continual urban growth and modern-day tensions. The owner of the Holyland Hotel had the model built in the 1960s, with the assistance of archaeologists, and the model has been updated with new finds from excavations in Jerusalem. The miniature city reflects scholarship on Jerusalem's physical layout around 66 CE, just before the Jewish revolt against Rome that led to the destruction of the city. The city model, in which the presentation of the past is close to but separated from its archaeological grounding, might represent the future for tourism in Israel.

Israeli newspapers in April 2004 noted that the model would be moved to the Israel Museum because its popularity resulted in the presence of tourist buses that interfered with the residential neighborhood. The model is displayed at the Israel Museum next to the Shrine of the Book, an exhibit dedicated to the Dead Sea Scrolls. The location is prestigious and not surprising. Models of Jerusalem have been and are popular means to represent and see Jerusalem. They have a long history in the United States; Rowan (2004) discussed the Jerusalem at Chautauqua, New York, which was created in the late nineteenth century. In addition, Jerusalem was prominently displayed at the 1904 St. Louis World's Fair (with twenty-two streets and three hundred buildings) and in the Holy Land Experience in Orlando, Florida. Rowan notes that building Jerusalem in Orlando allowed "control over what is represented and how it is presented" and that the presentation made pilgrimage possible without "costly travel, inconvenient political realities, and face-to-face encounters with people of differing cultural backgrounds" (261, 264). A similar approach has now been taken in Jerusalem itself. Near the southern wall of the Temple Mount/the Haram es-Sherif, Israeli archaeologists excavated Roman and Byzantine, Umayyad and other layers and turned the area into an archaeological park. As al-Natsheh relates, a museum was opened in 2001 in the park. Employing a wide array of technology, including a sophisticated simulation of Roman Jerusalem, the Davidson Centre museum conveys the history of the Temple Mount from Roman to Islamic times. Al-Natshe critiques the presentation, arguing against its political agenda: "It is difficult for the general public, and particularly Western Jewish and Christian tourists, to leave this museum without being convinced of what they have seen, and without being filled with nostalgia. Rebutting the statements made in the exhibitions is a very complicated task, and requires combining numerous sincere, patient and scientific efforts in order to attain the same technical and academic heights seen in this museum" (2003: 58). The task is made greater by the tropes of representing Jerusalem; depictions are meant to engage and entice tourists to see the particular past of the city that interests them. After all, the tourist advertising insists: *No one belongs here more than you.*

VIII. Conclusions

Heritage and identity are interlocked by contemporary states to construct notions for nationhood. One of the effective tools to construct national or ethnic identity has been archaeology. As many scholars have noted, archaeology provides the spatial and tactile "proof" for primordial ethnicity. Israel has used archaeology to construct a simple and effective narrative about a people coming to a place (the Israelites of the Late Bronze Age to Iron Age) and resisting the might of great empires (the cultural survival during the ages of Mesopotamian empires and the classical period)—material histories that were unearthed when that people constructed a state in the twentieth century. The archaeology provided an influential narrative for nationalism. But just as the ideology of Israel changed over the decades since the state's founding in 1948, so have the uses of archaeology. Though nationalism continues to be significant in Israel, particularly for unifying a diverse group of people within the national identity, the positioning of the country within the global economy has encouraged the development of tourism in Israel focused in part on archaeology. Archaeology is a resource for tourism. Yet archaeo-tourism creates contradictions for Israeli understandings of history and heritage.

If the past is seen as an economic resource to be harvested, one can expect more marketing of archaeological materials and archaeological sites by the state and transnational organizations and more disconnections within sites and among the archaeological sites of Israel. Bauman (2004) describes the crisis in historical representations for Israel, the post-Zionism, and its impact on archaeology in national parks. The struggles and divides in Israeli society (Silberstein 1999) are reflected in the presentation of the past (Bauman 2004: 224), and the presentation of a particular past impacts tourists' and local residents' understandings of their own identity. As Cohen-Hattab (2004) notes, tourism is political, and there is a long history of its use by Israelis and Palestinians to emphasize certain themes in the conflict over the land between the Mediterranean Sea and the Jordan River.

The experience of walking near or on past landscapes, the experience of seeing remains of the past, and the tourist use of photographs as authentic reminders of visits to sites may be overtaking the history from the archaeological record. As the past is marketed for tourists, as the past is made into a commodity, the marketing for heritage tourism requires a multiplicity of themes to accommodate the largest possible audience for the past as a resource. Archaeological sites are being marketed for tourists to entice them to spend, not necessarily to promote nationalist themes among the citizens of the country.

Consequently, the state must negotiate the changing social context of archaeology as it rethinks how to represent itself to its citizens and to external audiences.

In the Tel Aviv metropolitan area, in the city of Rishon LeZion, a small excavated site by the side of a major road is nearly invisible to tourists going from Tel Aviv to Jerusalem. It is a minor archaeological site; the highway department surrounded the Roman-era farmstead foundation with a fence and put up a small interpretive sign. For the people of Rishon LeZion, it is a useful illustration of the connections that are inscribed in the national ideology. But will such "unprofitable" presentations continue? A similar concern exists for the excavations that are recovering evidence for epochs that are not part of the tourist imagination. Archaeologists now regularly study the top layers of excavations; in other words, they include the Late Islamic periods such as the centuries when the Ottoman Empire ruled Palestine. While their results are appearing in the scholarship, the Ottoman-period structures in such places as Sepphoris/Zippori are used to house information kiosks rather than being integrated into the presentation of the past.

Furthermore, when Amos Oz calls for supporting excavations in the face of Ultraorthodox opposition and economic development, he writes in terms of the previous era's conceptualization of archaeology as telling the story of the nation; that support might shift when the heritage is marketed toward consumers rather than toward nationalism. In a sense, the state is caught between two of its self-created pressures: archaeology for ideology versus archaeology for profits. The dynamic tensions among archaeology as the uncovering of remains, archaeology as analysis and interpretation of the past, and archaeology for nationalism and/or archaeo-tourism are haunting the representation of the past even after the mass tourism for the turn of the millennium failed to appear.

Acknowledgments

I want to offer thanks to Phil Kohl for inviting me to participate in this volume and for comments on my argument. Mara Kozelsky and Lois

Crum provided editorial suggestions that improved the manuscript; Art Keene sparked my interest in this topic; Yorke Rowan, Joel Bauman, and Rachel Ben-Dov offered insights and feedback on Israeli archaeology; and Amy Reid's help and support was essential. Responsibility for the chapter rests with its author, however.

References

Abu el-Haj, Nadia. 2001. *Facts on the Ground: Archaeological Practice and Territorial Self-Fashioning in Israeli Society*. Chicago: University of Chicago Press.

Arad, Gulie Ne'eman, ed. 1996. Israeli Historiography Revisited. Special issue, *History and Memory* 7 (1).

Aronoff, Myron J. 1991. Myths, Symbols, and Rituals of the Emerging State. In *New Perspectives on Israeli History: The Early Years of the State*, ed. L. J. Silberstein, 175–192. New York: New York University Press.

Balter, Michael. 2000. Artifacts Prompt Tug-of-War. *Science* 287 (5450): 33.

Baram, Uzi. 2002. The Development of Historical Archaeology in Israel: An Overview and Prospects. *Historical Archaeology* 36 (4): 12–29.

Baram, Uzi, and Yorke Rowan. 2004. Archaeology after Nationalism: Globalization and the Consumption of the Past. In *Marketing Heritage: Archaeology and the Consumption of the Past*, ed. Y. Rowan and U. Baram, 3–23. Walnut Creek, CA: AltaMira.

Bar-Yosef, Ofer, and Amihai Mazar. 1982. Israeli Archaeology. *World Archaeology* 13 (3): 310–325.

Bauman, Joel. 2004. Tourism, the Ideology of Design, and the Nationalized Past in Zippori/Sepphoris, an Israeli National Park. In *Marketing Heritage: Archaeology and the Consumption of the Past*, ed. Y. Rowan and U. Baram, 205–228. Walnut Creek, CA: AltaMira.

Beinin, Joel. 1991. Class, Ethnicity, Gender, National Conflict, and the Formation of Israeli Society. *Radical History Review* 51:114–123.

Benvenisti, Meron. 2000. *Sacred Landscape: The Buried History of the Holy Land since 1948*. Berkeley: University of California Press.

Ben-Yehuda, Nachman. 1995. *The Masada Myth: Collective Memory and Mythmaking in Israel*. Madison: University of Wisconsin Press.

Berkowitz, Michael. 1997. *Western Jewry and the Zionist Project, 1914–1933*. Cambridge: Cambridge University Press.

Bowersock, G. W. 1985. Palestine: History and Modern Politics. *Journal of Palestine Studies* 14 (4): 49–57.

Cline, Eric H. 2000. *The Battles of Armageddon: Megiddo and the Jezreel Valley from the Bronze Age to the Nuclear Age*. Ann Arbor: University of Michigan Press.

Cohen-Almagor, Raphael. 1995. Cultural Pluralism and Israeli Nation-Building Ideology. *International Journal of Middle East Studies* 27:461–484.

Cohen-Hattab, Kobi. 2004. Zionism, Tourism, and the Battle for Palestine: Tourism as a Political-Propaganda Tool. *Israel Studies* 9 (1): 61–85

Dayan, Moshe. 1978. *Living with the Bible*. New York: William Morrow.

Diaz-Andreu, Marguerita, and Timothy Champion, eds. 1996. *Nationalism and Archaeology in Europe*. Boulder, CO: Westview Press.

Einhorn, Talia. 1996. Restitution of Archaeological Artifacts: The Arab-Israeli Case. *International Journal of Cultural Property* 5 (1): 133–153.

Elon, Amos. 1994. Politics and Archaeology. *New York Review of Books*, Sept. 22, pp. 14–18.

Finkelstein, Israel, and Neil Asher Silberman. 2001. *The Bible Unearthed: Archaeology's New Vision of Ancient Israel and the Origin of Its Sacred Texts*. New York: Free Press.

Glock, Albert E. 1994. Archaeology as Cultural Survival: The Future of the Palestinian Past. *Journal of Palestinian Studies* 23 (3): 70–94.

Herzl, Theodor. 1987. *Old New Land*. Trans. Lotta Levensohn. New York: Markus Wiener. Originally published in 1902.

Johns, Jeremy. 1988. Mamluk Jerusalem. *Antiquity* 62:527–532.

Katz, Shaul. 1985. The Israeli Teacher-Guide: The Emergence and Perpetuation of a Role. *Annuals of Tourism Research* 12:49–72.

Khalidi, Rashid. 1997. *Palestinian Identity: The Construction of Modern National Consciousness*. New York: Columbia University Press.

Killebrew, Ann E. 1999. From Canaanites to Crusaders: The Presentation of Archaeological Sites in Israel. *Conservation and Management of Archaeological Sites* 3:17–32.

Kohl, Philip L., and Clare Fawcett, eds. 1995. *Nationalism, Politics, and the Practice of Archaeology*. Cambridge: Cambridge University Press.

Magness, Jodi. 2003. *The Archaeology of the Early Islamic Settlement in Palestine*. Winona Lake, IN: Eisenbrauns.

al-Natsheh, Yousef Said. 2003. The Digital Temple Mount. *Jerusalem Quarterly* 19:53–58.

Oz, Amos. 1987. *The Slopes of Lebanon*. San Diego: Helen and Kurt Wolff.

Rowan, Yorke. 2004. Repackaging the Pilgrimage: Visiting the Holy Land in Orlando. In *Marketing Heritage: Archaeology and the Consumption of the Past*, ed. Y. Rowan and U. Baram, 249–266. Walnut Creek, CA: AltaMira.

Shanks, Hershel. 1990. Glorious Beth Shean. *Biblical Archaeology Review* 16 (4): 17–31.

Silberman, Neil A. 1989. *Between Past and Present: Archaeology, Ideology, and Nationalism in the Modern Middle East*. New York: Anchor.

Silberman, Neil A. 1993. *A Prophet from amongst You: The Life of Yigael Yadin: Soldier, Scholar, and Mythmaker of Modern Israel*. Reading, MA: Addison-Wesley.

Silberman, Neil A. 1995. Promised Lands and Chosen Peoples: The Politics and Poetics of Archaeological Narrative. In *Nationalism, Politics, and Archaeology*, ed. P. L. Kohl and C. Fawcett, 249–262. Cambridge: Cambridge University Press.

Silberstein, Laurence J. 1999. The *PostZionism Debates: Knowledge and Power in Israeli Culture*. New York: Routledge.

Trigger, Bruce G. 1984. Alternative Archaeologies: Nationalist, Colonialist, Imperialist. *Man* 19 (3): 355–370.

Upton, Dell. 2001. "Authentic" Anxieties. In *Consuming Tradition, Manufacturing Heritage: Global Norms and Urban Forms in the Age of Tourism*, ed. N. alSayyad, 298–305. New York: Routledge.

Webber, Jonathan. 1992. Modern Jewish Identities: The Ethnographic Complexities. *Journal of Jewish Studies* 34 (2): 246–267.

Yadin, Yigael. 1966. *Masada: Herod's Fortress and the Zealot's Last Stand*. New York: Random House.

Zerubavel, Yael. 1995. *Recovered Roots: Collective Memory and the Making of Israeli National Tradition*. Chicago: University of Chicago Press.

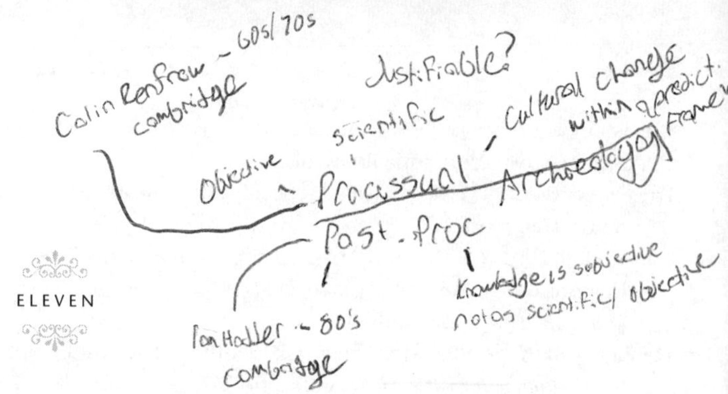

ELEVEN

An Archaeology of Palestine

Mourning a Dream

GHADA ZIADEH-SEELY

Politics and Archaeology

Addressing the topic of politics and archaeology in Palestine has been a difficult and painful task. As one of the first generation of "homegrown" Palestinian archaeologists, I lived under occupation most of my adult life; for me, the subject of nationalism and archaeology goes beyond intellectual discourse. It reflects on personal and professional shortcomings intertwined with political upheavals and turmoil. With professional training in both processual and postprocessual schools of archaeology, I find the postprocessual approach a more effective means to address the multifaceted aspects of my identity as a Palestinian and as a professional archaeologist who has lived under Israeli occupation. Therefore, I will not attempt to sanitize this chapter with a cloak of scientific objectivity devoid of my personal experiences.

In this chapter I reflect on the unsuccessful attempt to create an archaeology that is relevant to the national struggle of Palestinians without compromising professional integrity. The task proved to be unattainable in light of the fierce struggle between Palestinians and Israelis over the same territory, which both nations claim as their homeland. The idea of creating a homegrown Palestinian archaeology with a high level of professional training and vision was the brainchild of Albert Glock. Glock, a biblically trained American archaeologist, was initially drawn to Palestine because of its biblical legacy. However, unlike most biblical archaeologists, and after extended firsthand personal experiences, he changed his views. Glock came to the realization that biblical archaeology in general and its offshoot, Israeli archaeology, had been grossly manipulated to uproot Palestinians from their homeland, transforming them into a people without history. To create some balance with regard to this overwhelming anti-Palestinian archaeological tradition, Glock hoped to establish a different archaeological tradition that would become an essential part of the Palestinian national identity. The course of this short experiment, which began in the 1970s, was radically altered with the assassination of Glock in 1992. As Glock's former student, I consider here the theoretical and political views that characterized the movement in light of the turbulent political events in the region. I also outline the pragmatic steps necessary to create a credible Palestinian archaeology now that Palestinians are one step closer to realizing their dream of national sovereignty.

Living under occupation is not an experience with which most people are familiar; therefore, it might be useful at this juncture to highlight some of the Israeli occupation's practices. Palestinians can be detained indefinitely without being charged or brought to trial. Both individuals and groups are frequently deported despite international condemnation. The escalating restrictions on mobility had turned Palestinians into virtual prisoners within their own towns and homes. Widespread land confiscations and house demolitions are seen from the Palestinians' perspective as the worst practices and the most threatening to their very existence. Those practices and many more martial laws were devised and implemented under the British Mandate. For the past fifty years Israelis have adopted and "improved" upon those martial laws in administering their occupation of the West Bank and Gaza. The indefinite closures of schools and colleges and the curtailing of economic growth have been particularly harmful. Such policies are intended to undermine the potential of building an educated, prosperous Palestinian society.

The Need for Palestinian Archaeology

At a time when the archaic European concept of nationalism and nation-states seems to be giving way to multinationalism and globalization, the struggle for a Palestinian national identity continues. Inevitably, archaeology became central to the creation of a Palestinian national identity, just as it was in the creation of the state of Israel. The desire for a national identity and a national archaeology emerged in response to the threat Palestinians faced from the overpowering Israeli occupation. Israeli generals and archaeologists alike, who in many cases are the same individuals, have not only worked diligently to negate Palestinian history, but also have threatened to physically eliminate Palestinians' presence and material culture from the land. The rise of national sentiments among Palestinians and other Arabs in the Middle East materialized, for the most part, during a colonial era that created new political boundaries and realities in the Middle East. The colonization of Palestine by Britain between 1917 and 1948, however, and especially the establishment of the state of Israel on the larger part (20,735 square kilometers) of what was historically known as Palestine, created a far more complicated reality. In its effort to create a purely Jewish state, Israel forced an estimated 770,000 Palestinians out of their homes and proceeded to destroy 418 villages (Khalidi 1992: 582–585) so that none of the refugees would attempt to return. Although today this practice is referred to as ethnic cleansing, in 1948 the rest of the world stood by and cheered the creation of the Jewish homeland. Even to this day, few are willing to address the issue of these refugees.

The remaining parts of Palestine, which consisted of the West Bank (5,948 square kilometers) and the Gaza Strip (361 square kilometers), were annexed by Jordan and Egypt, respectively. The West Bank and Gaza were occupied by Israel in 1967; thus from then till the present, Israel has been in control of the entire Palestinian territory. Although Israel did not again force the mass exodus of Palestinians witnessed in 1947–1948, its appropriation of the remaining part of Palestine took the form of aggressive land seizures to build Israeli settlements, thus creating new realities on the ground. Settlement-building continues in earnest, despite the lip-service condemnation that comes from the international community. As is evident in this book and many other publications, Israel has used archaeology as an effective weapon not only to appropriate the land, but also to create a historical justification for the appropriation. Israel's Zionist archaeology was not an entirely new phenomenon, since its roots lay in biblical archaeology. The prevalent biblical archaeology motivated many Western nations to invest in, interfere with, and expropriate the past with the pretext that the biblical heritage of Palestine belongs to the nations of Christianity rather than to the Muslim inhabitants of that land (Silberman 1991: 76–84). Interest in the biblical heritage of Palestine, intertwined with imperialist expansions, preceded the emergence of archaeology as a discipline. Early-nineteenth-century explorers, such as Ulrich Seetzen (in 1809), John Lewis Burkhardt (in 1810–1812), Buckingham (in 1816), Robinson (in 1838), and others, who were motivated only in part by religion, visited sites mentioned primarily in the Old and New Testaments. The result was a new kind of pilgrimage, one that furthered the Protestant nations' imperial ambitions (Silberman 1998: 13). With the founding of the Palestine Exploration Fund in 1865, a scientific base for biblical archaeology was established (Abu El-Haj 2001: 22). It was not coincidental that when early Western interests in archaeology began to materialize in Palestine, Tell el-Hesi, a site of great biblical significance, was the first site to be excavated by Sir Flinders Petrie in 1890. Since then the majority of archaeological excavations in Palestine have been focused on sites believed to have some biblical significance.

The question must be asked: is there a need for Palestinian archaeology, given the ongoing struggle between Israelis and Palestinians over the land and its cultural heritage? The answer, undoubtedly, is yes. As Trigger correctly points out, the inseparable nature of nationalism and archaeology is not inherently adverse. He asserts that, especially "when combined with an awareness of the dignity of all human beings, it [archaeology] has helped to provide the basis for resisting colonial and dynastic oppression and for creating a more broadly based popular sovereignty that promotes political freedom as well as social, economic, and intellectual development" (1995: 277). The issue here is what parameters are needed to define an archaeological tradition that is relevant to the Palestinians. There is a consensus among Palestinians that their archaeological tradition is bound to be the antithesis of the Israeli archaeological tradition. However, debate continues over the nature of that antithesis. On the one hand, there are Palestinians who call for an archaeology that is fashioned after Israeli archaeology, with all its blatant political trappings. That means an archaeology that provides a historical right to the land. Such a goal can be achieved by promoting a research agenda that links the Palestinians to the Canaanites. Proof of a Canaanite ancestry, since the Canaanites existed prior to the Israelite conquest, would negate the equally blatant Israeli claim that this land is theirs because they are the descendants of the Israelites. Following in the footsteps of Israeli archaeologists, some Palestinians call for research efforts that overemphasize the Canaanite connection. Since most archaeological sites in Palestine contain levels representing sequential, multiperiod occupations, implementing such an agenda would lead to the physical destruction of the material evidence of cultural periods that stand between the Palestinians and their claim to a historical right to the land, a practice that would mimic the one widely implemented by Israeli archaeologists.

On the other hand, a course that at least for a while was advocated by some Palestinians called for a serious examination of the entire scope of archaeological research in Palestine. Although admittedly nationalistic, with a clear political agenda, this program would examine the issue of reconstructing ethnicity based upon the archaeological record. As Trigger explains, ethnicity "was a subjective concept that archaeologists cannot hope to study to any significant degree in the absence of specifically relevant historical or ethnographic data" (1995: 277). Furthermore, he notes that there are more appropriate problems that archaeologists are better equipped to investigate. From an archaeological and political perspective, it seemed that the only way out of this cyclical trend of exploiting the archaeological record was to recognize the multiethnic nature of Palestine's history. This program also cautioned against the reconstruction of the ethnic identities of historical and prehistorical peoples. To adopt such a research agenda and to try to reconstruct past ethnicities would likely lead to compromising the archaeological data and the scientific integrity of the discipline. This short-lived archaeological discourse ultimately failed to win popular consensus among Palestinians. The rest of this chapter details the course of events leading to and following the downfall of this unsuccessful approach in Palestinian archaeology.

Palestinians and Archaeology: A Background

By contrast to the role it played in Israeli society, archaeology was alien and marginalized in Palestinian society. The alienation could be attributed to several causes, one of which is the distinct perception of history and identity in peasant societies. As in most peasant societies, oral history was the primary means for relating to the past. In general, oral history does not take into account the material culture or embrace the wider nationalistic framework. Oral history is often confined to the local level, where events take place and heroes live and often change identity in each family's history (Rappaport 1989: 92). Such perceptions should not be surprising, since national identity is a relatively new European concept. Oral history, transferred from generation to generation, concentrated on the extended family or the clan. The exception to this rule is elite ruling families who possess written documentation to substantiate their oral heritage relating them to a wider political context. For those exceptional few, most of the written records come from the Mamluk (the thirteenth to sixteenth centuries AD) and Ottoman (1517–1917) periods.

The second factor that contributed to the alienation between Palestinians and archaeology was Islam's disdain for all pre-Islamic cultural relics originating during *"Jahilliya"* or the age of ignorance (Potts 1998: 195–197; Trigger 1989: 44). To avoid embracing premonotheistic religions again, Islam tradition encourages the detachment of Muslims from that distant past. The fear of reverting to idol worship is the likely reason for the Islamic discouragement of the faithful from admiring the material culture, particularly monuments that glorify individuals. This restriction extends even to the material remains of the Islamic era and includes the tombs of important early Islamic figures.

The third factor that has a profound impact on shaping Palestinian attitudes toward archaeology is the antiquity laws devised by the British Mandate authorities in 1928. Those laws are still implemented throughout Palestine/Israel and Jordan today. An example is the Jordanian Provisional Antiquity Law of 1967, number 12, article 5, and the Israeli Antiquities Law of 1978, number 885, chapter 8. Both laws, based on British Mandate regulations, state that "lands that contain archaeological material can be confiscated by the State and the owners will be compensated as the State sees fit." Under Israeli occupation, these laws have been used as tools to increase the pressure on the Palestinian population and to confiscate more land for building Jewish settlements in the occupied territories. The growing Palestinian population's need to build on archaeological sites has been magnified by the loss of 78 percent of Palestine to Israel in 1948. Following the 1948 Arab-Israeli war, the West Bank population increased to several times its former level due to the influx of Palestinian refugees from what is now Israel proper. That was combined with a high population growth following the Second World War.

During the British Mandate, 1920–1948, a handful of Palestinians were employed and trained as archaeologists by the Department of Antiquity. Notably, only two of those Palestinians held college degrees, D. Baramki and S. Husseini. The rest functioned primarily as guardians of archaeological sites. A survey of the *Quarterly of the Department of Antiquity* and the *Journal of the Palestine Oriental Society* shows that, aside from the published work of Baramki at the site of Qasir Hisham, the publications by Palestinians remained on the fringes of folklore and studies of architecture, the social context of village architecture, and Muslim shrines (Glock 1994: 75–76). For almost two decades following the 1948 war, the growth of archaeology within the Palestinian community was stunted. Economic hardship, the displacement of thousands of refugees, and the lack of local educational institutions were principal factors in deterring the growth of what could have been Palestinian archaeology. During this period, a small number of Palestinians managed to get some training by joining excavations run by foreign archaeologists, mostly as laborers or as employees of the Department of Antiquity. A handful of those actually went abroad and acquired graduate degrees in archaeology, history, or ancient languages. Among them are Muawiya Ibrahim and Fauzi Zayadine, both of whom live and work in Jordan. This small group of pioneers remained dispersed and lacked a coherent theoretical or methodological framework. Their work frequently had to do with the excavations they joined and the Western scholars with whom they trained. Unfortunately, their work had a larger impact on Jordanian than on Palestinian archaeology.

At the same time, while the Palestinians were trying to carve an existence for themselves as a dispersed refugee community, archaeology within what is known today as Israel proper was booming. With the massive influx of Jewish emigrants from Europe, interest in physical artifacts and monuments grew rapidly during the early part of the twentieth century. In 1914 the Jewish Palestine Exploration Society was founded, modeled after nationalistic European antiquarian societies. Following the establishment of the state of Israel, archaeology became a national ritual that provided the physical confirmation of the modern Jewish right to the land (Silberman 1990: 105).

The Emergence of a New Tradition

It was not until the 1970s, when several Palestinian universities were established, that a distinctly Palestinian archaeological program began to emerge. Archaeology became for the first time part of the Palestinian university curriculum in 1976 when Albert Glock, ironically not a Palestinian, joined Birzeit University. Glock was one of several young American archaeologists, including, among others, P. Lapp and W. Dever, who had excavated important biblical sites such as Samaria and Ta'anach during the late 1950s and 1960s. This group, in O. Bar-Yosef's words, "was a school in itself, characterized by meticulous stratigraphic work including a detailed analysis of earth layers and pottery from stratified deposits. Furthermore, there was a tendency towards interdisciplinary work, involving scholars from various sciences as staff with the declared aim of reconstructing all possible aspects of ancient life" (1982: 313). In a few years, Glock managed to attract a number of Palestinian students to major in archaeology. The program quickly evolved into a department, offering an interdisciplinary undergraduate degree in archaeology. The archaeology majors were required to get equal training in archaeology and in one other discipline such as anthropology, history, biology, or geology. The department graduated its first class in 1982. At the same time, other Palestinian universities began to offer courses in archaeology, although none actually offered degrees in the subject. Since then, many of the younger generation of Palestinian archaeologists have managed to acquire scholarships to graduate schools in the United States and Europe. Scholarships, mainly provided by Amideast and the British Council, were part of developmental projects in the occupied West Bank and Gaza, intended to create an infrastructure of educated Palestinians. Palestinian graduates had the obligation to return to the Occupied Territories to serve their communities.

At Birzeit University the archaeology program, with its interdisciplinary features, was intended to create a team of skilled researchers whose specialties would complement each other. Part of the strategy included attracting undergraduates in chemistry, biology, and physics to handle the hard-science aspect of the research. Although the program did not have a clear political agenda at first, several factors were shaping the general direction and the framework. The first and most important objective was to create an image that reversed the general antagonistic views toward archaeology within the Palestinian community. An appealing Palestinian archaeology, it was declared, should distance itself from the reigning biblical archaeology, which "totally ignored Palestinian society except, in the best of cases, being depicted as quaint, fossilized illustrations of biblical life" (Glock 1985: 468–469). Secondly, a Palestinian archaeology should help Palestinians by countering the practices of the Zionist Israeli archaeology that had been actively employed by the occupation to dispossess Palestinians of their land and cultural history. Winning the local approval meant winning on only one of the two fronts. The second was gaining international scientific and professional credibility. That was the reason for adopting the tenets of processual archaeology, at the time the most widely recognized archaeological theoretical approach. It is ironic that the archaeology at Birzeit adopted processual archaeology, with its emphasis on hypothesis-testing and ecological reconstruction, despite its apolitical stance regarding archaeological research. The single most explicit theoretical or ideological position taken was creating an interdisciplinary team of archaeologists. By assembling a core of Palestinian archaeologists with diverse expertise to carry out archaeological research from data collection to publication,

Glock hoped to make the department independent of the skills offered by biblical archaeologists and institutions.

Although these political considerations were important in shaping a new Palestinian archaeology at Birzeit, efforts and energy remained focused on the academic training of Palestinian students. The academic training at Birzeit was primarily in Near Eastern archaeology with a special emphasis on Palestine. The basic core courses divided Palestine's archaeology into four respective sections: prehistory, Bronze-Iron Age, the Greco-Roman period, and the Islamic period. In addition, a range of upper-level courses dealt with research methods, ethno-archaeology, Mesopotamia, Egypt, and other special topics. One of the strongest features of the program was the emphasis on fieldwork. Undergraduates at Birzeit needed a minimum of twelve fieldwork credit hours, the equivalent of two summer seasons in the field, to graduate. In reality, most of the undergraduates spent at least three or four summers in the field. It was not the classroom, but the fieldwork, aspect of the program that began to shape the political dimensions of a distinctly Palestinian archaeology. At the time, both ethno-archaeology and the direct historical approach seemed to provide the cultural-historical connection needed to make archaeology relevant for the masses.

Two new and unconventional areas of archaeological research became the trademark of Birzeit's Department of Archaeology. The first was "refugee camp archaeology." Between the late 1970s and the early 1980s, a few studies were conducted at refugee camps, some of which were totally abandoned, such as the Abu-Shukhidem camp; others were only partially abandoned, as Tell al-Sultan, near Jericho, was. Those studies involved undergraduate students of architecture in addition to the archaeology undergraduates. While the architecture students' jobs were to produce accurate and detailed plans of the camps, the archaeology participants were documenting the presence and distribution of surface artifacts. Combining the architectural with the artifactual records was essential for reconstructing spatial activities. The objective of this exercise was to document the adaptation processes and strategies of Palestinian refugees after losing their homes, lands, and livelihoods. One crucial aspect was the comparison of the material evidence from the camps with the material evidence from the ruined villages that the refugees called home. That was a dangerous task because these villages lay within Israel proper, a restricted area for most West Bank Palestinians. Only Glock, being an American, had the opportunity to visit and document those remains. His work, in addition to the work of others, was finally published after his assassination in a book entitled *All That Remains* (Khalidi 1992).

The second area of study that distinguished archaeological research at Birzeit was Ottoman Palestine. The combination of processual archaeology and the direct historical approach was implemented in the long-term research project at the village of Ti'innik. The Ti'innik study evolved out of earlier excavations of the site by the American School of Oriental Research. Although the early excavations were concerned with biblical history, the 1980s work shifted the focus to the present and to the Ottoman villages. The project began with ethno-archaeological research addressing the issue of site-formation processes (Ziadeh 1984). This topic is particularly important in Palestine, where the continuous occupation of the same site for thousands of years is the rule rather than the exception. The ethno-archaeological study of a Palestinian village generated controversy among some Palestinian nationalists who failed to appreciate it within the framework of its cultural continuity. Years of the colonial ideology of the "unchanging Orient" have left Palestinians ashamed of their own culture. That was the reason for the misinterpretation of ethnographic studies.

Subsequently, the research at Ti'innik shifted in favor of the direct cultural-historical approach. That required the systematic tracing of the material culture over time, and thus came the innovative excavations of the Ottoman and Mamluk remains at Ti'innik. The focus of this research was to track change and continuity in the material culture of a Palestinian village over a five-hundred-year span (Ziadeh 1991). These excavations were innovative in two ways. First, other archaeologists have long neglected the Ottoman period, partly because of its irrelevance to the biblical tradition. In fact, the British-devised antiquity laws do not recognize material remains after the seventeenth century as archaeological. Second, these excavations would have represented the first research-oriented program in the occupied West Bank undertaken by a Palestinian institute. Previously most of the projects by the Department of Archaeology at Birzeit were either salvage excavations or surface surveys; both types resulted in minimal disturbance to the material culture. (The legal complications of excavating in occupied territory are addressed below.)

This relatively new focus of archaeological research in Palestine conformed to the widely accepted processual definition of archaeology. If we begin with the definition of archaeology as "the study of the material expression of human thought and action, we are not confined to the past, as an etymological definition of the term would suggest" (Glock 1994: 80). Aside from the academics, the archaeology of Mamluk and Ottoman periods had a political dimension. It provided physical evidence for a history and traditions that are still alive and very much part of the living Palestinians' memory and to which each individual and family can trace their roots. At the time, the archaeology of Ottoman Palestine was alien from mainstream historical archaeology, even though it deals with the same time frame. The rift, as some scholars see it, resulted from the narrow focus of historical archaeology on the colonial expansion of the Western world, not its impact on the indigenous populations (Schmidt and Patterson 1995: 15). Fortunately, the 1990s saw an increased number of archaeologists bridging this arbitrary divide between the past and the present by treating the material remains of the near past with the same interest they treat the remains of the distant past (Baram and Carroll 2000).

Adopting a class-conscious archaeology was another feature that guided the Birzeit research agenda. It emerged, in part, from the younger generation of class-conscious Palestinian archaeologists. The reality was that by the late 1970s most Palestinian students at local universities were sensitive to class issues. Class issues became a staple of political debate in the newly established local higher education institutes. Local universities made higher education accessible to the underprivileged masses. Prior to the 1970s, only the wealthiest of Palestinians would have been able to acquire higher education by studying abroad. The implication for Palestinian archaeology was shifting the archaeological inquiry from monumental sites and centers of power, a feature of antiquarianism, to less lustrous villages. Being less impacted by foreign influences, these villages demonstrated stronger evidence for cultural continuity compared with the monumental sites. As a crossroads between three continents, Palestine has a history of successive invasions of foreign powers, whose impacts and relics are evident in major Palestinian centers, particularly Jerusalem. A general review of Middle East archaeology, including that of Palestine, shows an unbalanced interest in fortified cities, temples, and palaces. This selective research of the upper stratum of ancient society reflects the class background of Middle East archaeologists. Most of them did not come from humble peasant backgrounds. The archaeology of monuments in the Middle East thus became the equivalent of the historical archaeology of Western colonialism.

Finally, and in response to the overwhelming "Western Scholarship and the Silencing of Palestinian History" (Whitelam, 1998), the archaeology program at Birzeit adopted the policy of accepting the multiethnic nature of Palestine's cultural history. The ethnic identity of past cultures could not be totally ignored under the circumstances, although realistically researching it needed to be approached with extreme caution. In reference to the issue of ethnic construction from the archaeological evidence, Glock states: "However, as in all good science, we do not favor one answer or the other. We will test for the multicultural indicators as a hypothesis to determine the probability of its truth" (1994: 83). His statement is particularly important because it stems from his realization that connecting the material culture to a specific ethnic group is an unattainable research goal, though it should not be dismissed in its entirety at this stage. Considering the early Greek functional definition of *ethnos* as "1)—a united people; 2) with a common language; 3) with a defining religion; 4) in possession of a land; and 5) with a common past and future goal" (Thompson, 1998: 30), most archaeologists agree that reading all of these features in the always fragmentary archaeological record is a very difficult, if not impossible, task. I should clarify here that none of the theoretical-political approaches discussed above were charted in a single manifesto. Rather, most of these positions developed gradually over the years and mostly in response to daily challenges forcing archaeologists to define their aims and directions.

Challenges and Difficulties

Teaching archaeology and practicing archaeology in the occupied territories presented two enormous challenges. The first was the Israeli stranglehold on academia in general and archaeology in particular. But probably the most difficult challenge was the second, to convince Palestinians that archaeology, traditionally associated with Western colonialism, could be actively used to their advantage.

From the inception of the archaeology program at Birzeit, the restrictions on excavation activities and even simply teaching in a classroom posed serious problems. With the indefinite university closures, it sometimes took an entire year to finish a three-month course. A bigger challenge was fulfilling the fieldwork requirements of the Birzeit curriculum. The Israeli-run Department of Antiquities, which controlled excavation permits in the West Bank, never recognized Palestinian professionals as qualified and, thus, permitted to conduct excavations. In an interview, the archaeological staff officer in the occupied West Bank, Isaac Magen, categorically denied the presence of qualified Palestinian archaeologists to carry on an excavation (Radford 1993: 64). This statement is rather astounding in light of the fact that many Palestinian archaeologists had earned graduate degrees in archaeology from renowned universities in the United States and Europe and most had extensive field experience. Despite the restrictions, the Department of Archaeology at

Birzeit managed to hold several summer field schools between 1976 and 1987, thanks to the determination and connections of Albert Glock. As former director of the American School of Oriental Research and one of the remaining staff members of the 1960s excavations at Ti'innik, Glock managed to obtain dig permits. With permit in hand, he next needed to get students to the site. Under occupation Palestinian students needed the military governor's permission to take temporary residence near the excavation site. A list of the names and identification card numbers of the participants and residence addresses was submitted so that students would not be arrested on the spot.

Owing to the legal complications of excavating in occupied territories, the early excavations conducted by the Birzeit University Department of Archaeology were limited to salvage operations. An important legal issue concerned ownership of the recovered artifacts. According to the mandate antiquity laws, which remain in effect even now, artifacts are the property of the state, that is, the Israeli occupation. Unquestionably and correctly, the Department of Archaeology had no intention of turning over the artifacts to the Israeli Department of Antiquity. Convinced that the artifacts found on Palestinian soil were part of the Palestinian heritage and conscious that the Israelis could force them to hand over the recovered material remains, archaeologists from Birzeit resorted to stalling as a legitimate tactic. Under the same antiquity laws, archaeologists were permitted to retain the recovered artifacts for the duration of their scientific research. That loophole in the law allowed us to retain the artifacts, while hoping that a future political solution could be reached. This tactic had a drawback, though: it forced us to publish only preliminary reports following the completion of the fieldwork.

The issue of excavating in the occupied territories is controversial and very complicated, to say the least. According to the Hague convention, excavating in occupied territories is banned in order to prevent the occupying power from looting the cultural heritage of the occupied nation. In compliance with the Hague treaty, Palestinians limited their excavations to salvage operations, while Israel conducted extensive excavations throughout the West Bank and Gaza. Israel's justification was that digging in the occupied territories was crucial for preserving the Jewish heritage that would otherwise be destroyed in the process of establishing Israeli settlements. Establishing Jewish settlements on or near biblical sites is core to building Israel's Zionist identity (Feige, chapter 9, this volume). While the salvage excavations in the West Bank and Gaza were necessary for the Jewish settlements, they were conducted very slowly, if at all, in the Arab sector (Yahya n.d.). In fact, delays and the withholding of building permits to accommodate the growing Palestinian population were, and continue to be, part of Israel's policy to make life unbearable for the Palestinians in the occupied territories in the hope that they will relocate elsewhere.

Under these circumstances, Glock and his young Palestinian colleagues decided that engaging in salvage excavations in occupied Palestine was both legal and necessary. Salvage operations in the West Bank would, on the one hand, reduce some of the pressure on the Palestinian population and, on the other, hopefully lessen the Palestinian disenfranchisement with archaeology. Birzeit's archaeologists conducted six salvage excavations at Tell Jenin between 1976 and 1983. Tell Jenin, located in the center of the business district in the town of Jenin, constituted prime real estate; destruction was inevitable. The Department of Antiquity's policy was to hinder, rather than to facilitate, Palestinian growth and expansion. Only when frustrated Palestinians took matters into their own hands and began clearing the site for construction, did the Department of Antiquity step in to stop them from further work. As a result, an enormous part of Tell Jenin's archaeological record was destroyed. In fact, by the time the Birzeit archaeologists became involved, half of Tell Jenin was already bulldozed, and a bus station had been constructed. Unfortunately, it became clear that Birzeit's involvement with the site was a drop-in-the-bucket solution to an acute problem. The real solution requires a formula that delicately balances the need for archaeological preservation and the mounting needs of Palestinians to expand and grow. This task calls for major governmental policy beyond the means and power of an academic department of archaeology.

It was not until 1985 that Birzeit's Department of Archaeology conducted its first research-oriented excavation. The excavation of the Ottoman village at Tell Ti'innik was part of a research design adopting the direct historical paradigm. This bold step was taken in the belief that the Hague convention's ban on excavations in occupied territories applied to the occupier, not the occupied. Although the excavation of the Ottoman remains was conducted within the theoretical framework of the direct historical approach, it had an inevitably political dimension. Looking for continuity and change in the material culture that starts with the present Palestinian village and extends into the deep past provided the Palestinians with a strong sense of cultural continuity. Direct cultural continuity was very significant, considering the heritage-appropriation campaign launched by Israel (Scham n.d.). Research on the Ottoman period focused on the issue of continuity in the material culture, consciously avoiding the Israeli practice of making ethnic links to the past (Ziadeh 1991).

Changing the Palestinian attitudes toward archaeology was a difficult task among both the masses and the intellectuals. These attitudes ranged from the extreme apathy of the majority to the dangerous views of an ultrazealous national minority. The majority's attitude toward archaeology was described eloquently by the editor of the *Birzeit Research Review*:

> On the Arab side . . . we find a benign and lethargic neglect. It is as if the Palestinian intelligentsia having asserted, in the abstract, historical rights to the land, is contented that others authenticate what appears to it as self-evident. But the only self-evident truth to deduce from this assertion is that those who investigate an arena of knowledge tend to bring into their investigation their own ideological preferences and priorities. In the archaeology of the Holy Land it is Biblical archaeology and Israeli-Zionist offshoots that have, so far, reigned supreme. As a result the pluralistic nature of Palestine's past has virtually vanished from public awareness, and with it significant parts of the Arab past, traditions and cultural heritage. (Tamari 1987: 1)

Increasingly, one can see a gradual change in Palestinians' attitudes toward their cultural heritage. Attitudes regarding the remains of the more distant past, however, remain unchanged.

The Birzeit Department of Archaeology's efforts to engage Palestinian intellectuals also failed. The research agenda adopted by the department seemed to many people too neutral and apolitical. Inspired by the Israeli archaeologists, whose goal was to establish a link between the modern state of Israel and the Israelite period (1150 BC), some Palestinian intellectuals wanted to advance an explicitly political agenda. For them, a desirable archaeology would provide a link between the modern Palestinian population and the Philistines (1190 BC). By creating this link, Palestinians would win the argument of historical legitimacy by predating the Israelites' arrival. The adoption of such a dangerous dogma, tempting as it was, was nevertheless rejected on the following grounds:

1. Palestinian archaeologists cannot adopt this position while criticizing Israeli archaeologists for using the same kind of arguments.
2. The war against Zionist prejudices cannot be won using similar tactics. Palestinians need to be creative in choosing the arenas and the battles.
3. Even if the Palestinians decided to engage in such endeavors, they would not have the power and the resources to match Israel's investment in archaeology.

The developments described above preceded the first intifada of 1987, a grassroots movement of rebellion and civil disobedience that had profound impact on the Palestinian dream of achieving a national identity. The events of the 1990s not only changed Palestinian society but also profoundly changed the course of Palestinian archaeology.

Palestinian Archaeology after the Intifada

In December 1987 the first intifada, a national uprising, erupted following decades of oppression under Israeli military rule. The first intifada ended in 1993 with the symbolic establishment of Palestinian authority in the West Bank and Gaza. One of the first measures taken by the occupation in 1987 was to close all the institutions of higher education. The closures had a crippling effect on the infant Palestinian archaeology programs at local universities. Before 1987 Palestinian universities had experienced frequent but shorter closures and over the years had learned to adapt. Palestinian archaeologists, both faculty and students, maneuvered around these closures by working and teaching off campus. The situation beginning in 1987, however, became nearly impossible, not only because of the extended university closure, but also because of the crippling effect of the intifada on daily life in the occupied territories. Archaeological research ground to a halt, as did the enrollment of new archaeology majors. Activities were restricted to offering a few courses mainly to students who were near graduation.

By 1992 anti-Israeli and anti-American sentiments among Palestinians had reached a boiling point, thanks to the pro-Israel American foreign policy. Those sentiments became a polarizing factor in a conflict that took place at the Department of Archaeology, Birzeit University. The conflict between processually and traditionally trained Palestinian archeologists became entangled with the national anti-American sentiments and culminated with the assassination of Albert Glock on January 19, 1992. Thus a new phase of Palestinian archaeology began, or rather ended. The loss of Glock had, and for years to come will have, a devastating impact on the growth, direction, and future of Palestinian archaeology. Following the assassination of Glock, most of the people working in the Department of Archaeology left, myself included, and after a ten-year struggle, the department was finally shut down in 2003 (Yahya n.d.).

Palestinians placed great hopes on the establishment of the Palestinian Authority in the occupied territories. Unfortunately, the Oslo negotiations had failed to address several crucial issues, among them the control of archaeological sites in the Palestinian areas. The eruption in 2000 of the second intifada, which is still continuing, was the loudest testament to the failure of the Oslo negotiations in achieving a just peace. Even the symbolic Palestinian control was shattered with the siege and destruction of Arafat's headquarters in Ramallah. At first glance the discussion of cultural heritage seems almost surreal in light of the tragic loss of life on a daily basis. Nevertheless, the reality is that cultural heritage is a crucial factor in the Palestinian-Israeli conflict. The conflict from the Palestinians' point of view is not only about being written out of history, but also about the negation of their physical presence in their land by a force with a trowel in one hand and a firearm in the other.

The final status of Palestinian archaeology will remain in suspension for as long as Palestinian nationhood remains unrealized. In the meantime, the emerging new realities on the ground are alarming to say the least. The looting and destruction of the archaeological record is escalating on two fronts. The first is intensified Israeli Judaization of archaeological sites in the West Bank and Gaza (Scham n.d.), thus curtailing the Palestinian National Authority's control over sites previously agreed upon in the Oslo treaty. Second is the increased looting of archaeological sites by both Israelis and Palestinians. Operation Scroll, for example, launched on the eve of the handing over of Jericho to the Palestinians in November 1993, was nothing but state-sponsored looting of artifacts (Abu El-Haj 2001: 244–245). The operation consisted of a rampage of Israeli archaeologists into the caves surrounding Jericho in search of another cache of Dead Sea Scrolls. On the Palestinian side, the increased archaeological looting is triggered in part by economic hardship. With unemployment rates exceeding 60 percent and because of the insatiable appetite of the Israeli and international markets for Jewish relics, looting is on the rise (Yahya n.d.). Another motivation for the increased destruction of sites by Palestinians stems from a shortsighted effort to combat Israel's land-grabbing policy. Some Palestinians are resorting to the destruction of the archaeological record as a way to stop Israel from appropriating more land.

Another alarming trend in post-intifada Palestinian archaeology is its nationalistic overtones. Such a trend is being promoted at the expense of scientific integrity. The statement by Arafat citing a passage from the Qur'an in reference to the Canaanites implies the official adoption of the dogma that Palestinians are descendants of the Canaanites and thus have a greater historical right to the land. It seems that the earlier notion of creating a link between the Palestinians and the Philistines, which circulated among intellectuals in the 1980s, was dismissed probably because the Philistines' influence was limited to the southern coast of Palestine. The most disturbing aspect of the new direction of Palestinian archaeology concerns the individuals who are shaping the new policies. Many of these so-called archaeologists, who serve as advisers to the Palestinian Authorities (Abu El-Haj 2001: 245), are politicians with little archaeological training. Sadly, that means that Palestinian archaeology is going to be held hostage by nationalism, which will curtail independent academic inquiry, at least for the time being. I am hoping that this phase of ultranationalism will pass with the establishment of a Palestinian state. When a Palestinian state becomes a reality, the threat to Palestinian identity will decrease to make room for an archaeology with less national overtones.

Conclusion

It is evident that even with the establishment of a Palestinian state, the problems of archaeology in Palestine will not be solved automatically. Archaeology seems to be the least pressing issue on the agenda of the Palestinian authorities. What the Palestinian authorities need to do is to adopt an antiquities policy that will allow the growth and development of Palestinian society and at the same time preserve its subterranean cultural resources (Glock 1994: 79). Undoubtedly, there is a growing appreciation among Palestinians toward their ethnographic heritage. This tendency is demonstrated in the increased number of small private museums, the renovations of traditional architecture, and the growing interest in traditional crafts and garments. However, Palestinians also need practical policy measures that will make archaeology a feasible economic endeavor. Increasing the number of state-sponsored archaeological activities will benefit Palestinian society in more ways than one. First, it will provide much-needed employment opportunities. Such opportunities will certainly curb the site-looting activities. Second, in an area with few natural resources, site preservation will boost tourism in Palestine, potentially generating a significant portion of the Palestinian economy. As I. Hodder correctly noted while digging at Catal Hüyük in Turkey, attitudes toward archaeology quickly change, even in a conservative Islamic context, once people realize its economic potential (1998: 128–130).

Finally, to shift the blame from the Israeli and Palestinian sides, the international community, particularly its archaeologists, has been grossly reluctant to take a stand. While reading Arnold and Hassmann's article (1995) on the archaeology of Nazi Germany, I could not help but think that none of this is shocking compared with the practices of Israeli archaeologists. Yet, I had to ask myself why the criticism of Nazi archaeology has made it into mainstream archaeology, whereas Israel's Zionist archaeology is cited as a great example for the powerful role of archaeology in generating national aspirations. In reality, the only critics of Israel's archaeological practices are either Israeli or non-Israeli Jewish scholars (see chapters of this volume; Silberman 1982, 1989). I strongly believe that the criticism of Israel's archaeological practices among politically correct Western scholars is long overdue. Imposing sanctions by the international community on Israel for its involvement in the illegal trafficking of antiquities is also essential. Such measures are important not only for the preservation of the cultural heritage of Palestine, but also for restoring Palestinian faith in a world that stands by watching while they are being wiped out of the present and effaced from history.

References

Abu El-Haj, Nadia. 2001. *Facts on the Ground.* Chicago: University of Chicago Press.

Arnold, Bettina, and Henning Hassmann. 1995. "Archaeology in Nazi Germany: The Legacy of the Faustian Bargain." In *Nationalism, Politics, and the Practice of Archaeology*, ed. Philip Kohl and Clare Fawcett, 70–81. Cambridge: Cambridge University Press.

Baram, Uzi, and Linda Carroll, eds. 2000. *A Historical Archaeology of the Ottoman Empire: Breaking New Ground.* New York: Kluwer Academic/Plenum Publishers.

Bar-Yosef, O., and Amihai Mazar. 1982. "Israeli Archaeology." *World Archaeology* 13 (3): 310–325.

Glock, A. 1985. "Tradition and Change in Two Archaeologies." *American Antiquity* 50:464–477.

Glock, A. 1994. "Archaeology as Cultural Survival: The Future of the Palestinian Past." *Journal of Palestine Studies* 23 (3): 70–84.

Hodder, I. 1998. "The Past as Passion and Play." In *Archaeology under Fire*, ed. L. Meskell, 124–139. Routledge.

Khalidi, Walid, ed. 1992. *All That Remains: The Palestinian Villages Occupied and Depopulated by Israel in 1948.* Washington DC: Institute for Palestine Studies.

Potts, D. T. 1998. "The Gulf Arab States and Their Archaeology." In *Archaeology under Fire*, ed. Lynn Meskell, 189–199. London: Routledge.

Radford, Dave. 1993. "The Politics of Israeli Archaeology." Master's thesis, Sheffield University.

Rappaport Joanne. 1989. "Geography and Historical Understanding in Indigenous Colombia." In *Who Needs the Past: Indigenous Values and Archaeology*, ed. R. Layton, 84–94. London: U. Hyman.

Scham. S. n.d. "The Future of Arab and Jewish Pasts in Israel/Palestine." In *Filtering the Past, Building the Future: Archaeology, Tradition, and Politics in the Middle*

East, ed. R. Boynter, L. S. Dodd, and B. Parker. Tucson: University of Arizona Press, in preparation.

Schmidt, P., and Thomas Patterson. 1995. Introduction to *Making Alternative Histories: The Practice of Archaeology and History in Non-Western Settings*, ed. P. Schmidt and Thomas Patterson, 1–24. Santa Fe, NM: School of American Research Press.

Silberman, Neil. 1982. *Digging for God and Country*. New York: Alfred A. Knopf.

Silberman, Neil. 1989. *Between the Present and the Past*. New York: Henry Holt.

Silberman, Neil. 1990. "The Politics of the Past: Archaeology and Nationalism in the Eastern Mediterranean." *Mediterranean Quarterly* 1 (1): 99–110.

Silberman, Neil. 1991. "Desolation and Restoration: The Impact of a Biblical Concept on Near Eastern Archaeology." *Biblical Archaeologist*, June, 76–87.

Silberman, Neil. 1998. "Power, Politics, and the Past: The Social Construction of Antiquity in the Holy Land." In *The Archaeology of Society in the Holy Land*, ed. T. E. Levy, 9–23. London: Leicester University Press.

Tamari, Salim. 1987. "A Weak Spot" [editor's preface]. *Birzeit Research Review* 4: 1–2.

Thompson, Thomas. 1998. "Hidden Histories and the Problem of Ethnicity." In *Palestine in Western Scholarship and the History of Palestine*, ed. Michael Prior, 23–40. London: Melisende.

Trigger, Bruce. 1989. *A History of Archaeological Thought*. Cambridge: Cambridge University Press.

Trigger, Bruce. 1995. "Romanticism, Nationalism, and Archaeology." In *Nationalism, Politics, and the Practice of Archaeology*, ed. Philip Kohl and Clare Fawcett, 263–279. Cambridge: Cambridge University Press.

Whitelam, Keith. 1998. "Western Scholarship and the Silencing of Palestinian History." In *Western Scholarship and the History of Palestine*, ed. Michael Prior, 9–22. London: Melisende.

Yahya, A. n.d. "Archaeology and Nationalism in the Holy Land." In *Filtering the Past, Building the Future: Archaeology, Tradition and Politics in the Middle East*, ed. R. Boynter, L. S. Dodd, and B. Parker. Tucson: University of Arizona Press, in preparation.

Ziadeh, M. Ghada. 1984. "Site Formation in Context." Master's thesis, Washington University.

Ziadeh, M. Ghada. 1991. "Change and Continuity in a Palestinian Village." PhD diss., University of Cambridge.

4

South and Southeast Asia

TWELVE

The Aryan Homeland Debate in India

SHEREEN RATNAGAR

The nation is a modern phenomenon, and nations, India included, have constructed themselves and their images in the modern period. It is in this context that I attempt an explanation of how an Aryan identity came to be inscribed into the construction of ancient Indian civilization. In the ancient Indian texts, the Aryan identity was associated with a certain culture and ritual. Aryan culture was imbued with high status, and Aryan rituals were believed to be particularly efficacious, though accessible to only a few. In modern India the concept of Aryan identity is not shunned, in spite of associations with the horror of Nazi history in Germany. This concept is current even though the category did come to be smudged by connotations of physical type in the colonial period, given British interest in racial categories as explanations of cultural difference. The reason is that in Sanskrit *arya* carried only the connotations of status and culture.

As I discuss the nation as a modern construct and explain what Indians mean by the label "Aryan," I shall outline what historical linguistics tells us about the Indo-European homeland and about the Indo-Iranian language(s) (in the period 5000 to 2000 BC). Indo-Iranian, a branch of Indo-European, is the parent of the Indo-Aryan languages, including Sanskrit, the classical language of ancient India. In spite of the difficulties of matching the evidence in the early texts of the

Indo-Iranian branch with available archaeological evidence, it is reasonable to infer that the early Aryans were immigrants in South Asia after 2000 BC during the last days of the Harappa civilization (2600–1800 BC) or after its demise. When the Harappa civilization was discovered, it was interpreted unequivocally as Dravidian (rather than Aryan) by John Marshall, whose excavation report on Mohenjo-daro is in many ways the founding text of Harappan studies. It was only later that scholars began to challenge this identity, for reasons explained below.

Archaeologists as members of society are influenced by social movements of their own times. Nowhere is this more evident than in the cases of Somnath and Ayodhya. The authorities demolished an ancient ruined temple at Somnath in 1951, in the early days of the Indian republic, in spite of protests from citizens. The home minister at the time went along with the popular clamor to obliterate the "shame" that had been perpetrated by the desecration of this temple by a medieval Muslim invader (as the public understood it) and overruled the objections of the Archaeological Survey of India (ASI, a body created, inter alia, for the preservation of ancient monuments). Thus, after a token excavation, the Somnath temple was demolished. In the late 1980s and 1990s, swept along by street clamor for the righting of the "wrongs" perpetrated by medieval Muslim invaders, an ex-director general of ASI actually became part of a movement for the demolition of Babur's mosque at Ayodhya and helped create the fiction that temple ruins existed under the foundations of the mosque.

Even though the constitution of India grants all religious minorities full rights, political and cultural, current majoritarian movements insist that the religious majority is entitled, in some ludicrous way, to superior rights. There is a spurious distinction between "sons of the soil" (Hindus, Buddhists, and Jains) and "aliens," whose ancestors and religions originated elsewhere (Muslims and Christians). For the archaeologist to search for ancient groups who may have referred to themselves as Aryan is fraught with difficulty; but worse, a preoccupation with the ancient Aryans—who were in any case only one section of ancient Indian society—as either indigenous or foreign feeds the politics of exclusion and of upper-caste dominance.

Following Hobsbawm and Gellner, my first point is that there is nothing primordial about the Indian (or any other) nation, however ancient its civilization or individual culture elements. It has been said by Anderson that the nation is an imagined political community. Nations are essentially political entities, constituted as states. They are "imagined" because their boundaries are arbitrarily drawn, and because their members are too numerous to be actually known to one another; they are "communities" because nations are never purely political phenomena: they are believed to have common interests or collective consciences and are often conceived as immortal, worthy of the sacrifice of lives. Nations emerged in Europe in the late eighteenth century in tandem with the decline of divine kingships, the development of countrywide markets, and the birth of modern bureaucracies.

Gellner has insisted that nations are inventions of modern times, times when the old bonds of religion, kinship, and locality were decaying with industrialization, society was becoming impersonal, and the means of speedy communications across countries appeared. Often a language was imposed as the medium of education and administration in districts where it was not the currency of daily life. Similarly, cultural constructs such as the "typical Dutch meal" created and emphasized a national mainstream.[1] For Anderson (1983: 40) the extension of literacy and the advent of the printed newspaper with mass circulation in Europe meant that thousands read the same message each day, which affected the interactions among members in "profoundly new ways."

In addition to communications, administration, language, and state-directed education, the past plays an important role in the construction of a nation. Like other cultural constructs, the pasts of nations were invariably selective and patchy.[2] A common past invokes a kind of substitute for a blood relationship between people. Nations "create and preserve . . . images of themselves as continuously existing." A society's experiences are underwritten by its understanding of its past, and simultaneously, the content of the remembered past influences how society views the present. By constructing "a canon of historical research," intellectuals and professional historians "participate in the formation of a political identity and give shape to the memory of a particular culture" (Connerton 1993: 13–16). In a book on ancient India, Romesh Chunder Dutt (1888: x–xi) wrote about the pioneering work of those Western Indologists who had brought new sources, the texts of ancient times, to light. He emphasized the importance of knowing about the "Hindu period." Significantly, he then said, "No study has so potent an influence in forming a nation's mind and a nation's character as a critical and careful study of its past history."

According to Hobsbawm and Gellner, ideas of national mainstreams and national cultures were constructed by intellectuals, and these became incorporated into modern education systems. So it was in modern times that the great traditions (or "high cultures") of civilizations could be accessed by the masses. Later, the "folk" came to be included in, and compendia of folklore were made as part of nationalist projects celebrating the primitive stages of a nation, but the high culture as included in public education was what came to define the newly created nation. Here, then, is one way in which nations were the conscious creations of modern elites. In India, people of different provinces and social groups were brought together in a national movement to free the country from British rule and by the institutions of the freedom struggle. As they cast their assertions of Indianness, they were inevitably influenced by ideas of India and its past then current in the West.

The articulations of Indian nationalists such as Jawaharlal Nehru on their conceptions of Indianness and Indian civilization drew on centuries of Indological scholarship. The British as the dominant imperial culture, and with reference to Brahmanic tracts and worldviews, produced Indological knowledge. Compilations and classifications of traditions, traditional law, religious beliefs, and customs provided data for use in colonial administration. Breckenridge and van der Veer (1993) point out that as colonial administration became routinized, the production of Orientalist Indology was systematized, and many of its ideas—some still current—were absorbed by Indian nationalists.

In the Indologist-to-nationalist scholarship, certain elements were said to give Indian civilization its uniqueness. The soul of the land lay in its villages; Indian civilization was imbued with spirituality and tradition in contradistinction to technology, rationality, and modernity; caste was the characteristic—almost the defining framework—of Indian society; and ancient religion was structured on two distinct cultural streams: "Aryan" and "Dravidian."

Aryan India

Let us explore the inscription of Aryanness onto Indianness. It was in 1786 that William Jones delivered the lecture in which he made his famous statement on the affinity between Sanskrit, Greek, and Latin—an affinity so strong that there must have been, he said, a common ancestral language. With Franz Bopp there began, in 1816, an era of comparative philology, exploring the parallels between Sanskrit and the European languages. The early Indologists were taught by Brahmans that all extant Indian languages were offshoots of Sanskrit and that there were also foreign and local words in these languages. As Robert Caldwell's comparative grammar of Dravidian languages was published in the 1850s, however, and as it began to be known that the Munda languages constituted a third group, there emerged the notion of a pre-Aryan "substratum" (Trautmann 2004: 136–157). Small wonder, then, that H. H. Risley, organizer of the great Indian census of 1901, which classified communities into dozens of races and hundreds of castes, thought that it was the Aryan "invasion" that made caste the organizing principle of Indian society: the fair Aryans conquered the dark Dravidians and took wives from the subjugated population (so that half-breeds came into existence) but would not allow Dravidian men into their fold. Castes were thus groups with varying degrees of Aryan blood. The idea took root that "Indian civilization was formed by a big bang, caused by the conquest of . . . Aryan . . . invaders over . . . savage aboriginal Indians" (Trautmann 1999: 287). Dravidian languages, it may be noted, were spoken in northern India before they were replaced by Indo-Aryan.

R. C. Dutt thus wrote in his history of ancient India (1888: 4–5) that "the Hindu Aryans as conquerors and settlers on the banks of the Indus" were a robust race who appropriated lands from the "aborigines of the soil," who "struggled to maintain their own against the conquerors."[3] Dutt sees the ancient period as a series of Aryan conquests that spread civilization further across India so that the "zone of unreclaimed barbarism . . . receded."[4] Another instance—selected at random from library shelves—is provided by Havell's two-volume tome on architecture, with a subtitle significant for us: *A Study of Indo-Aryan Civilization*. In his introduction to this foundational text, Havell writes, "The history of India is the history of Aryan institutions, traditions, and culture. . . . The Aryan tradition of building is still a living art in India"; the British must understand this ancient civilization, akin to their own, in order to rule India successfully; and "Great Britain could grant to India no greater boon than the restoration or reconstruction of her ancient Aryan constitution" (1915: xxvii, xxviii, vii).

For his part, Nehru, in *The Discovery of India*, suggests, apropos to the cultural transformation that followed the Indus civilization, not conquest but a great cultural synthesis between immigrant Aryans and the Dravidians of the Indus cities: "Out of this synthesis and fusion grew the Indian races and the basic Indian culture, which had distinctive elements of both" (1946: 73). Following the Indological tradition, Nehru suggests (84–85) that Aryan conquest and interaction with Dravidian speakers gave rise to the caste system but that instead of annihilating the indigenous communities, the Aryans assimilated them. As for professional archaeology, Marshall's long founding statement on religion[5] in the Mohenjo-daro excavation report (1931) conceives of the latter as Dravidian and claims that Mohenjo-daro proves that there is nothing inherently primitive about Dravidian culture.[6]

Much of the importance of the Aryan identity in India accrues from its place in the earliest extant religious text of the Hindus,[7] the *RgVeda*. Orthodox Hindus accord a prime place to the Vedas. Ancient treatises often claimed to be written on the authority of the Vedas, because these were believed to be the source of all knowledge and infallible (Gonda 1965: 7–8). Gonda points out (9–10) that in ancient times people ceased to understand these tracts but still believed in their authority, as a way of "clinging to continuity" and in a search for certainty. In the *RgVeda* the *Āryaḫ* were those who worshipped certain deities with characteristic rituals and in a particular language. Such worship was the mark of a righteous person or *Ārya* (Nandi 2001: x).[8] "Aryan" was what the authors of our earliest texts, Indian and Iranian, called themselves.[9] Among the Buddhists of later times, *arya* meant "worthy" or "honorable." Later it was an honorific: for instance, a daughter-in-law in a classical Sanskrit play addressed her father-in-law as *arya*.

A line of thought from the later nineteenth century to the 1950s saw Hindu religion as first expressed in its purest form in the *RgVeda* but conceded that with its emphasis on mantra and sacrifice, nature deities, the Soma cult, and the beginnings of caste hierarchy, it did not comprise the sum total; *puja, bhakti,* the theism of Vaishnavism and Saivism, propitiations of village goddesses, and protection from demons of all kinds were as much part of Hinduism as was Vedic ritual. Many of these latter phenomena derived from a Dravidian "substratum." Whereas the Vedic Aryans were thought to be male-dominated and worshippers of male gods because they were pastoralists, the Dravidians as agriculturists were thought to believe in the principles of fertility and in mother goddesses. "Aryan" vis-à-vis "Dravidian" became a device for mapping numerous beliefs and rituals.[10]

Aryanism became increasingly identified with Hinduism in the nineteenth century with the birth of a reform and modernizing movement within Hinduism, the Arya Samaj. Founded in 1875, the Arya Samaj advocated a return to the pure religion of the Vedas, devoid of idol worship and the rituals of popular cults. For the founder of the Arya Samaj, Dayanand Saraswati, *Aryan* should replace the term *Hindu,* because the latter was not the original name of the Indian people and was used by foreigners in a derogatory sense (Pashaura Singh 1999). He urged his audiences to call themselves Aryan. Regeneration would come with the restoration of Vedic fire rituals and the study of the texts. Dayanand claimed that the Aryans came from Tibet to Aryavarta, the motherland (the northern Indian plains) and lived there in glory until a period of decadence set in (Banga 2004). Dayanand supported an anti-cow-slaughter movement then current and stressed that Aryans were different from Christians and Muslims. Here, then, are early assertions of "Hindu" nationalism. Later, other leaders claimed Hindu spiritual superiority, especially in the face of British policies seen to favor the Muslims. It was in the Punjab, the homeland of the Arya Samaj, that the Hindu Sabha was founded in the early twentieth century and Lala Lajpat Rai stated that Hindus were a nation because they represented a type of civilization that was uniquely theirs (Jaffrelot 1996: 18–19).

In 1933 the Hindu Mahasabha issued a statement recognizing the "fundamental unity of ancient Aryan culture of India." Three years later followed a statement that the public needed to become aware that Hindusthan was primarily for the Hindus, and that Hindus lived for the preservation of the Aryan culture and the Hindu religion. Hindi should become the national language, and foreign tongues and words should be eliminated. Programs for the "reconversion" of Muslims, Christians, and Sikhs were suggested (see Baird 1998).[11] As Hinduism increasingly became associated, in some spheres, with being Indian, so did the Aryan identity. Moreover, being Aryan had also acquired racist overtones.

Race

In the nineteenth and early twentieth centuries, the term *race* was often used to refer to a group of people with certain characteristic sociocultural attributes. The speakers of the early Indo-Aryan language constituted a "race," it was thought. With its hierarchy and division into endogamous groups, caste endogamy was necessary to maintain the racial purity of the Aryans: castes were conceived as races. Today racism is condemned: cultural attributes are not essential to, or inherent in, a group, and neither language nor culture is biologically or genetically transmitted, to say nothing of claims to genetic superiority on the part of this or that group. Yet in late Victorian England, perhaps because it was important to explain differences between peoples and to understand "savages," a pseudoscience developed that incorporated information not only about the evolution of species, about ethnography and linguistics, but also about human skulls and fossils (Robb 1994: 22). Nineteenth-century anthropologists thought that the migrations of groups explained diversity, that hunters or gatherers were physiologically closer to the apes than were the tall blond Europeans, and there came about "a certain obsession for acquiring and measuring skulls of various 'races', which were in fact more ethnic or tribal groups" (Shipman 1994: 75).[12] In the United States, racialist science was used to justify slavery and to prove that the enslaved, with smaller skull cavities, were inherently less intelligent (Bates 1994: 225).

Such ideas inevitably came to India. The British administration assumed that criminality was biologically inherited, and it classified certain landless and marauding groups as "criminal tribes." Officials who led campaigns against highway robbers initiated programs of craniometry. Even a modernizing reformist such as Ram Mohan Roy sent "Hindu" skulls to Edinburgh in 1822 for analysis (Bates 1994: 232). It was sincerely believed that there was a correlation between criminals and skull shapes and between the finest noses and the highest castes (243). Embedded in the discourse was the primary distinction between Aryans and non-Aryans (see Bayly 1994: 168–172). Many scholars and officials assumed that Aryan skulls were dolichocephalic, or "long-headed," as opposed to the brachycephalic, or "broad-headed," skulls of the "lower," autochthonous groups, even though many north-Indian Brahmans were found not to have long heads (Kennedy 1995: 46–48). Such thinking had been fueled by readings of certain RgVedic references to the Dasas and the Dasyus as expressing racial differences, when in fact it was in language and religion that these ancient groups were seen to differ from their enemies, the RgVedic poets (Trautmann 2004: 206–212).

What is unfortunate is that even today, although craniometry is on the wane, such racism (by which I mean seeking an inherent connection between culture and physiology) survives, sometimes with reference to genetics or blood groups. Physical anthropology in India continued to be preoccupied with skull types until a surprisingly late date. The middle class, even if it knows nothing about genetics or is incapable of giving a working definition of "Aryan," insists on the "genetic superiority" of the upper castes over the outcastes. In 1995 the physical anthropologist K. A. R. Kennedy, admitting that the identification of Aryans is not within the competence of the physical anthropologist, reported (49–54) that there was a biological affinity between the skulls at Harappan sites and those of Gandhara (cultures of the latter have been interpreted as vestiges of Aryan immigrants). He did not acknowledge that those who spoke a particular language in the past may not necessarily have constituted an internally breeding group. Kennedy stated (correctly) that a new language cannot be proof of an invasion (56), but he added the observation that the *RgVeda* "does not claim a *foreign* home for the Aryans" (emphasis mine), thereby confusing ancient geography with present-day national boundaries.

There is other work by American physical anthropologists that argues in the same vein, utilizing skull and dental morphology with reference to Aryans and Dravidians, to posit the absence of a biological interruption after the Harappan period. The issue is not that a very small collection of skulls, bones, and teeth today represents the residents of Mohenjodaro and Harappa. What is at issue is that, by implication, this argument challenges the theory of Aryan "invasion," even though invasions in history do not generally result in total population replacement and even though the external origins of a language mean immigration and not necessarily an invasion. I challenged the relevance and integrity of such physical anthropology (Ratnagar 1998), asking whether nineteenth-century preoccupations were still with us and questioning the relevance of bones to language groups and the use of particular physical features to demonstrate population continuities. There was a defense by Kennedy, Hemphill, and Lukacs (2000), who do not seem to have understood the absence of a link between culture and physical type, and by Walimbe (2000) and Joglekar (2000), with a final rejoinder from me (Ratnagar 2000).

Language

Thus far we have seen that Aryanness became a crucial issue in certain perceptions of Indian civilization and Hinduism and that even today tendencies persist to view it as a matter of biological inheritance. I now will attempt to explain why we should identify the homeland of the Indo-Europeans with the steppe country in Eurasia: my reasoning comes from historical linguistics and the concept of bilingualism and language replacement. It will become clear that archaeology does not neatly prove or disprove the theory of migrations but that it does indicate the possibility of the immigration of small and disparate groups, at various times (during the second millennium BC) and over different routes, into South Asia. After we have viewed the theory of Aryan migration in all its strengths and weaknesses, when it is established that this is a reasonable hypothesis, we can explore the social and political background of why it has generated controversy. Let us thus move to "Aryan" as a linguistic label.

Sanskrit, and the later northern Indian languages that derived from it, belongs to the Indo-Aryan group. Vedic Sanskrit has strong affinities

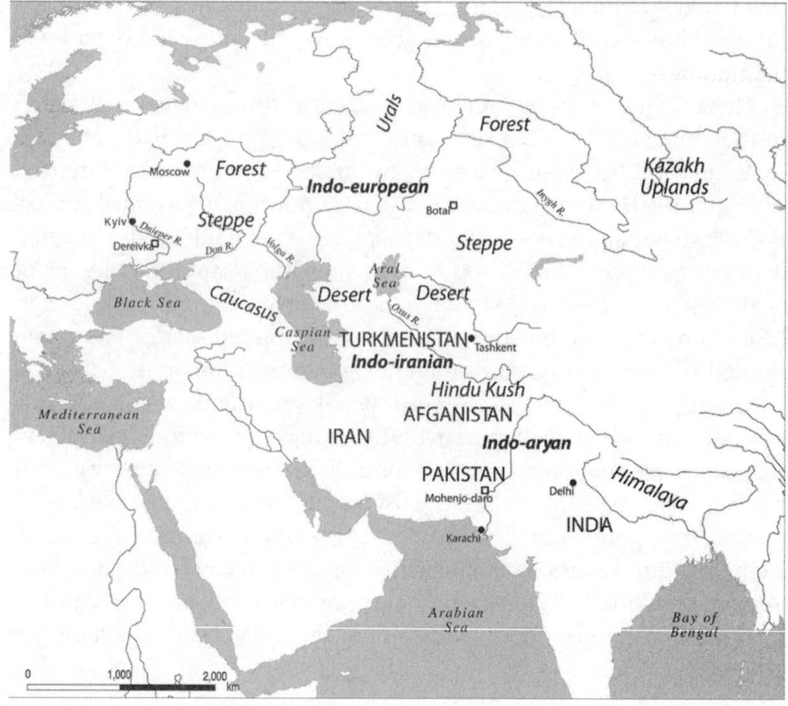

Figure 12.1. Eastern Indo-European language areas

with Avestan, and they belong to the Indo-Iranian language group. Indo-Iranian is in turn part of the huge Indo-European family of languages. Vocabulary and language structure are what justify these inferences about affinity. Indo-Aryan (of the *RgVeda*) and Avestan made the same innovations in the parent language. They are in fact so similar that, with reference to phonetic correspondences, one can translate entire Avestan sentences, word by word, into Vedic Sanskrit (Harmatta 1992: 357–358). Moreover, the cultural affinity (especially in cult, ritual, and mythology) between the two bodies of text is marked (Shrimali 2002: 32). Therefore no one contests the common origin of the two languages: a period of unity, perhaps in a northern Iranian or central Asian homeland, before they diverged into two sets of languages, is a reasonable inference. The only way branches of this Indo-Iranian parent language would have reached their later speech areas would have been through migration.

Let us briefly review the evidence for the Eurasian homeland of the progenitor of the Indo-European languages, and for the projected migrations of the Indo-Iranian speakers—in short, the reasons why we say that the language of the *RgVeda* came into India with migrants in the later second millennium BC.[13]

Among the earliest known languages of the Indo-Iranian family are the languages of the *RgVeda*, that of the *Gathas* of the Zoroastrians (composed in the early second millennium BC a few centuries after the schism of the Iranian-language speakers),[14] and linguistic remnants used by the Mitannians in Syria and by chariot-horse trainers in Anatolia. The *RgVeda* and the *Gathas* went through centuries of oral transmission before they were collated into written texts, whereas the material in Syria and Anatolia was inscribed on clay tablets between about 1600 and 1380 BC. Meanwhile, the languages of the Kafiri-Nuristani and Dardic language families, spoken in northeastern Afghanistan and northern Pakistan, have forms of Indo-Aryan that are considered earlier than their counterparts in Avestan and the *RgVeda* (Witzel 1995a: 110; 1995b: 322–323), and we can take these to be a fourth early Indo-Iranian branch.

It is significant, besides, that the language remnants that the Mitannians, a chariot-warrior aristocracy (who ruled a Hurrian-speaking populace), brought into Syria are closer to Indo-Aryan than to Avestan. The Mitannians were charioteers and horse-breeders, and the Hittite archives contain a manual of horse training said to have been authored by one Kikkuli the Mitannian. The words for numbers, for the horse, and for the chariot (and the names of deities in other texts, viz. treaties with the Hittite rulers) are strikingly similar to the language of the *RgVeda*. Mehendale (1993: 46) argues that Mitannian belongs to a stage older than the language of the *RgVeda,* a stage "before the forefathers of the Indo-Aryans came to India." For instance, Mitannian preserves the diphthongs (*aika* for "one") of Proto-Indo-European that Vedic transformed into simple vowels (*eka* for "one"). The secure dating of the Mitannian texts indicates that the separation from the parent group of Indo-Iranians would have occurred before 1600 BC, perhaps around 2000 BC. This in turn gives us an indication that the earliest poetry of the *RgVeda* was composed around 1600 BC. The period of composition may have lasted until 1200 or 1000 BC (Gonda 1975: 20–23; Deshpande 1979).

That the migration could not have occurred westward out of India is indicated by numerous bits of evidence.

In early Sanskrit literature (not necessarily in the *RgVeda* itself), the words for the elephant, the tiger, and the monkey are either coined terms or loan words from Dravidian or Munda.[15] These animals are all characteristic of South Asia. Instead, Indo-European languages have common words for the horse, cow, sheep, goat, and deer. Moreover, the *RgVeda* contains dozens of non-Indo-European words.

Although all stages of the agricultural cycle are well documented in that text (Nandi 2001: 39–41), Shrimali avers (2002: 29) that these occur mainly in the interpolations and that most of the terms used are either coined or are non-Indo-European in origin. As for the Old Avestan texts, there are references to the chariot, the horse, the camel, the house, the clan, and so forth, but none to agriculture (Skjaervo 1995: 167–168). (Indian river names, to be sure, are Sanskrit—a fact that Bryant [1999] considers strange. It is held by Kochhar [2000], however, that the immigrants transferred existing names into the new country.)

In addition, Hittite was an Indo-European language current in Anatolia between 1400 and 1200 BC, intrusive into that country (whose earliest, non-Indo-European, language is known as Hattic). Hittite is the most archaic of the known Indo-European languages, the closest to Proto-Indo-European.

The horse is an animal of the Eurasian grassland (the Pontic-Caspian steppe) and could not have been taken from India to Iran and Syria. Horse sacrifice, it needs to be noted, was an important and prestigious ritual in the *RgVeda* (Shrimali 2002: 39) and is generally believed to be an Indo-European feature. One could add that where the early Avestan material is concerned, personal names contain elements that mean "horse" (*-aspa*, thus Vishtaspa, etc.) as well as "camel" (*-ushtra*, thus Zarathushtra, Frashaoshtra) (Skjaervo 1995: 168).

There is a group of languages known as Finno-Ugric (Hungarian, Estonian, Finnish, Sami, etc.) that have a prehistoric homeland in the forest zone north of the Pontic-Caspian steppe, and about two hundred words are common to these languages. These languages received many loan words, in different periods, from Proto-Indo-European, and the archaeological evidence supports this in the sense that the forest zone saw agriculture and animal domestication much later than did the steppe. The loan words are for things like "to drive," "hunt," "sickle," "goat," "milk," and so forth.

Not so well known is that Proto-Indo-European also had contact with Proto-Kartvelian, spoken in the southern Caucasus (Anthony 2001: 17–18).

If the authors of the *RgVeda* had been indigenous to India, we would expect some aspects of central India and the Deccan peninsula to be mentioned at least in passing in the text. In addition, early Indo-Aryan languages, with the exception of Sinhalese, remained mostly north of the Vindhyas.

There is also the problem of retroflexion. Sanskrit is the only Indo-European language to have retroflex forms of *t, th, d, n,* and so forth. All South Asian languages have these retroflex forms, so that retroflexion in the extant *RgVeda* is explained only by "Dravidianization of the Aryan language" (Deshpande 1979: 257). For centuries, the *RgVeda* was transmitted orally, so that it is safe to infer that the poetry, when compiled and edited as a text, incorporated spoken forms. Furthermore, in the case of this poetry, it was of prime importance to enunciate the verses correctly so that they would have their intended efficacy at the sacrifice and so that the text would be very well preserved (Gonda 1975: 15–16; Deshpande 1979: 242–247). So it is not impossible that some degree of retroflexion was present at the outset. Deshpande concludes that early Sanskrit was sometimes handed down by men for whom it was in fact a second language (1979: 297; 1995: 75–8), their mother-tongue being Dravidian. Bryant (1999) thinks that there are flaws in the Dravidian substratum theory and that linguistic convergence is not necessarily the outcome of bilingualism. However, if India had been the Indo-European homeland, surely other, if not all, Indo-European languages—Avestan in particular—would have had retroflexion.

Dispersal

Why did the Indo-European languages, of all the language families of the world, have such a wide dispersal? A language can be dispersed only with the movement of speakers of that language. It appears that the extensive dispersal was connected with the domestication of the horse, which is unique to the Indo-European homeland and its ecology. The words for the horse in the various Indo-European languages come from the same origin. The wild progenitor of the horse was native to the Eurasian grasslands east of the Volga, and it thrives in stretches where the grass grows knee-high. It also appears that it was in the homeland, at an early date, that the wheeled vehicle was introduced.

Harmatta (1992: 367–368) makes the stimulating suggestion that where the Indo-Iranian branch is concerned, there may first have been slow, short-distance, movements of cattle breeders, but that later, with the domestication of the horse (around 3500 BC) and the introduction of the war chariot, it was possible for the Indo-Iranians to make raids into distant lands to the south (into Babylonia, as the Kassites) and the southeast (toward India). It was with the subsequent advent of horse-riding that groups who remained in the homeland could keep huge herds and develop a cavalry, so that their migrations (in the later first millennium BC) became massive. This appears to be more valid than my suggestion in 1999 (Ratnagar 1999: 228–231) that horse-mounted pastoralism explains migrations into India in the second millennium BC. Kohl (commenting on Lamberg-Karlovsky 2002) too warns against assumptions that there were huge sheep and horse herds in the Bronze Age. Besides, South Asia does not have vast stretches of natural grassland and is not horse-breeding country.

The horse-riding chief and his retinue *has* perhaps left traces in South Asia, but in a relatively late period, in and after the seventh century

BC, in megalithic burials of central and peninsular India (all Iron Age). Individuals were buried with a horse or horse trappings, pottery, ornaments, and various iron artifacts, and there is a striking correlation of burials with a horse on the one hand and exceptionally long iron lances (sometimes called "javelins" or "spikes") on the other. The lance was a new weapon of the Iron Age, presumably for the horseback rider, usually only about 2.5 centimeters thick but 1 to 2.1 meters (usually 1.5 meters) long. It appears that the position of the lance in these burials carried symbolic significance. Little has been written about this strange cooccurrence of the horse, evidence for horse-riding, and the iron lance at about a dozen peninsular sites. Thus there is little we can say about the movements of seemingly horse-mounted chiefs and their retinues and their dispersals across the peninsula, let alone address the question of the language they may have spoken. All we know is that these bits of evidence were relatively late.

However, in the second millennium BC, as in northern Syria and Iran, so too in northwestern South Asia, we have literary evidence for horse-drawn chariot warfare,[16] in which the charioteer was armed with bow and arrows and perhaps a mace, rather than warfare using cavalry. (It was considered déclassé for a Vedic chief to mount a horse.) Chariot horses are stall-fed, thus bred in fewer numbers than if free-grazing.

What, then, can be the explanation for the early dispersal of the Indo-Iranian branches? Perhaps it is basically ecology: given the low carrying capacity of the steppe, its severe winters, and periodic failures of rainfall, herds can swell and dwindle rapidly and minor fluctuations may trigger out-migration. Connected with the fragile ecosystem are the slow increments in wealth and status that a family can expect from success in animal breeding over the long term.[17] Wealth and status come more easily from leadership in looting or raiding one's neighbors. This in turn gives scope for the rise of warrior aristocracies, but more importantly for us, periodic warfare causes the repeated displacement of families and clans, if not entire tribes.

Archaeology

Before we survey the archaeology, let us clarify just what kind of archaeological evidence we would be looking for. We would look for intrusive cultures of the second millennium BC in the northwestern border regions of South Asia, and for Central Asian or Iranian materials in them. But we can hardly search for the archaeological correlates of the *RgVeda*.

The *Rgveda* is a collection of poetry composed between 1500 and 1200 (or 1000) BC, often to accompany various stages of the sacrificial ritual. Transmitted orally, the hymns were arranged in a written corpus around 700 to 500 BC. The extant text comprises ten books: the second to the seventh include the poetry of six separate clans, dedicated mainly to the deities Agni and Indra and the deified Soma. (An invigorating drink was pressed from the *soma* plant and offered to the gods during the sacrifice.) The hymns of the *RgVeda* were set in the regions of present-day Afghanistan, northern and central Pakistan, and present-day northern India up to the Jumna river. Sharma points out (1999: 87) that there would have been some overlap in the lands of the Vedic and Avestan poets. Kochhar (2000: 94–140) explores the habitat of the ephedra plant, with which the RgVedic Soma has been identified, and finds that the region known to the poets was confined to the Hindu Kush and surrounding terrain and not, for instance, the Indo-Gangetic divide in which flows a river that some believe to be the Vedic Sarasvati. In Book 8 there are references to camels, to the best horses, to mountains, and to snow (Witzel 1995b: 317). There are references to the crossing of rivers, the Indus included: in Book 2 the Bharata clan wages successful battles against the enemy Dasas in their hill forts and hence moves down the passes that give entry into South Asia (322). (For the variety of habitats and land use, see Nandi 2001: 39–41.) The *RgVeda* does not refer to the Vindhya mountains of central India (Gonda 1975: 24).

The subject of the poetry of the *RgVeda* is "almost exclusively ritual" (Witzel 1995a: 93). Most hymns invite the gods to the sacrifice. The language is elaborate and would have been appreciated only by the upper crust (92). Situations are not explained from first principles, as much of the background would have been known to the sacrificer or audience. This and many internal features of the language contribute to the obscurity of much of the text. The meanings of entire verses remain doubtful, and even in the ancient commentary texts, we find that verses of the *RgVeda* have been misunderstood (Winternitz 1927: 68–69).

Even though agriculture is mentioned in the later interpolations, there are indications that the poets belonged to mobile groups. The word *grama*, which means "village" in later Sanskrit, in the *RgVeda* meant basically a "group" of people. It was a mobile group, with cattle, carts, horses, and chariots. *Grama* came to connote the temporary camp of such a group. It appears, besides, that populations were small. Nandi, for instance, finds on internal evidence that the fighting groups could have comprised no more than about 150 men; in one instance it is just 21 warriors of two localities who are vanquished (Nandi 2001: 13). Thus, we cannot expect that mounds would mark the habitations of those who followed the RgVedic rituals.

Furthermore, the text reveals the interactions of the *aryas* with local people, some of whom were subjugated. Aside from acculturation and the assimilation of various culture elements between migrant and autochthon, there was intertribal rivalry among the Aryans (Sharma 1983: 36–38; see also Hock 1999: 160–161). Not all Aryans who migrated into India followed the religion of the *RgVeda*. Thus, at the most, archaeologists may ask what kind of techno-complex (in the sense used by David Clarke) could logically match the setting of the RgVedic hymns.

Concerning archaeological correlates of the initial stage of Proto-Indo-European unity, some scholars (Mallory 1989: 198–215; Parpola 1993; Anthony 2001: 17–19, 25–26) have pointed to the late fifth or early fourth millennium BC Sredni Stog and related cultures of the Pontic-Caspian steppe that in their later development saw the emergence of a mobile herding economy with, possibly, the domesticated horse. The date of horse domestication continues to be debated primarily because the skeleton of the horse is not visibly transformed with the onset of domestication and because the stratigraphic context of a tooth with bit abrasion is open to doubt (Levine, Renfrew, and Boyle 2003). After 3500 BC, a large part of this steppe had cemeteries of more mobile stockbreeders, perhaps horse-mounted, who knew the wheeled vehicle, metallurgy, and agriculture (this was the Yamnaya or "pit-grave" horizon). Eastward, in Kazakhstan, sites such as Botai (after 3500 BC) have yielded thousands of horse bones, though it is not clear whether the horses were ridden or just hunted at the site. In this eastern region there gradually appeared around 2200 BC a new culture with metallurgy, large-scale cattle and sheep herding, elaborate animal sacrifices, and chariot burials in the graves, and also, paradoxically, fortified settlements. The main sites are Sintashta and Arkaim. After 2000 BC, the Andronovo culture flourished east of the Urals. People raised crops and rode the horse and the Bactrian camel. Full horse-mounted nomadism and warfare did not develop until a millennium later, but it cannot be doubted that horse-riding itself was mastered around 2000 BC.

Andronovo pottery is found in limited contexts at some sites of the Bactria-Margiana Archaeological Complex (BMAC) in, say, 2200–1600 BC. And this is where correlations with the literary evidence on Indo-Iranians usually begin: Carpelan and Parpola (2001: 132–134), for instance, see the Proto-Iranians remaining west of the Urals at this stage; they see the remains of the Proto-Indo-Aryans in the Andronovo culture.

It has been suggested that although the prosperity of the BMAC culture was based on agriculture, and although it was a local development, it was Aryans from the northern steppes who imposed their rule over its fortified settlements (137) in the same kind of coup as in Mitanni. Significantly, the fortified settlements are small, and the sites are generally "single-period . . . with less than a meter of cultural deposit" (Kohl 1984: 146). Perhaps a clan occupied each settlement. The massive fortification walls and towers are almost out of proportion with the sizes of the settlements.

The attention scholars have paid to the BMAC in the context of the Aryan identity accrues from the following factors: (1) Horse bones were found in Margiana (Kelleli 1 and Tapi Depe), as also in Namazga VI contexts in the Turkmenistan piedmont (Kohl 1984: 141), together with steppe ceramic elements and steppe burial forms (141, 146–147). (2) The remains of the ephedra plant, identified as Vedic *soma,*[18] were found at Togolok-21 in Margiana, in vessels lying in the ruins of a fortified ritual building (Parpola 1995). (3) The concentric circular walls around the small settlement at Dashly 3 in Bactria prompted Parpola (1995: 368) to identify this and similar settlements as forts of the Dasa people against whom the RgVedic Aryans often fought. (4) Several artifactual similarities link Margiana with the western fringes of South Asia: BMAC artifacts that have parallels elsewhere include flat violin-shaped figurines (also seen in Swat); rare kidney-shaped chlorite vessels (seen also at Mehrgarh South Cemetery); "columns" and disks of white stone (also at Shahdad east of Kerman in Iran and at Mehrgarh Cemetery and Sibri); some seal types (Kohl 1984: 147–149) with counterparts at Shahdad, Harappa, and Mohenjo-daro; bronze mirrors with parallels at Shahdad, Mehi, Mohenjo-daro, and Harappa; bronze cosmetic flagons reported from Mehrgarh South Cemetery and from Chanhu-daro; bronze shaft-hole axes or adze-axes also known at Shahdad, Khinaman, Sibri and Mohenjo-daro, Harappa, and Chanhu-daro; and bronze animal-headed pins also seen at Harappa and Mehrgarh South Cemetery. In addition, horse and Bactrian-camel bones occur at the site of Pirak, which, like Mehrgarh and Sibri, is located near the foot of the Bolan Pass.

Is the artifact trail adequate evidence for migrations? No geographic pattern is discernible. Most of the artifacts probably belong to the ritual sphere, yet we do not find references to anything like them (except perhaps the imagery on a few seals) in the *RgVeda* or the Avestan texts. Likewise, many of them are artifacts of bronze, which receives scant mention in the *RgVeda*. While Mallory states (1989: 227–231) that the Indo-Iranian identity of the Andronovo culture is hard to disprove, Lamberg-Karlovsky (2002) points to its long time-span and wide geographic reach and to the fact that the BMAC, with a very different material culture, is also identified as Indo-Iranian. While it has been argued that the imagery on BMAC seals, including snakes and mythical animals and birds, could represent struggles between good and evil as known in the Avestan texts (Kohl 1984: 149, quoting Sarianidi), Francfort (2001) rejects the Iranian identity of the BMAC, suggesting that the "Iranization" of Bactria occurred later, and finds in the iconography of the BMAC seals no correlates in the texts. I would add that one does not expect seals and advanced agriculture and metallurgy as remains of the people of the *RgVeda*. Let us, however, consider the archaeological evidence in some northwestern regions of South Asia.

Some scholars claim that after 1800 BC, Indo-Aryans entered the narrow Swat valley in the mountain region of northernmost Pakistan, where Dardic languages have been spoken. After 2500 BC there appeared in this and surrounding regions an entirely new cultural horizon, and it has reasonably been inferred that the authors of this "Gandhara Grave culture" were immigrants (see Stacul 1989). For Kochhar (2000: 186, 222) "non-RgVedic Aryans" (presumably he means speakers of Dardic or Kafiri languages) arrived around 2000 (or 1700) BC, to be followed by the "actual RgVedic people" in around 1400 BC. In the period 2000 to 1400 BC, which is represented mainly by inhumation and cremation burials, stone houses were built, ground stone tools were used with a range of bone tools, and there was some metal. A grey pottery has strong similarities in fabric and shape (e.g., cups on high pedestals) with pottery from sites in northeastern Iran, and there is also a painted red ware. A range of crops was grown,[19] including the grape, and sheep, cattle, and pigs were kept; there is also evidence of the horse. Horses were buried with people in two graves at Katelai in the lower Swat valley. At the settlement of Birkot Ghundai, too, horse bones were found. Around or after 1500 BC, the settlement of Aligrama saw a violent destruction. Horse burials with pieces of horse harness occur in the cemeteries of Dir and Chitral in "warrior graves" after about 500 BC, when stone fortifications also came up around some settlements.

There are intrusive cultures on the Indus plains too, after about 1800 BC. Among the first of these to be reported was the posturban Cemetery H culture at Harappa (Vats 1940: 203–245). Here two kinds of burial occurred in succession, inhumation and then fractional burials. The burial urns were of a pottery finer than those of the Harappan period, with pictures of the sun, stars, peacocks, and the like painted on them. Vats was convinced they expressed the people's ideas about life after death, and he found resonances with the poetry of the *RgVeda*: the hounds of Yama, the offering of a goat to Agni at the funeral, and so forth. Yet in his honesty, Vats stated that one could not carry the match of text and pot paintings too far, since this was not the residue of the cremation rituals mentioned in the text. As for the "Gomal Grave culture" not far away, it is little known and bears testimony of a complex ritual of disposal of the dead.

Dikshit (1969: 51) notes that whereas some authorities have identified the Painted Grey Ware (PGW) culture of the Ganga-Jumna interfluve with early Aryans, others make the equation with the Ahar or the Banas culture; some even suggest that the latter represents the first, and the PGW culture the second, influx of Aryans. One cannot proceed very far on this reasoning, because what is meant by "culture" is largely pottery types. Ghosh (1994) in fact pointed out that the PGW does not occur in northwestern Pakistan or Afghanistan, the region of the *RgVeda*. For Sharma (1983) the PGW culture is to be correlated with the world of the *later* Vedic texts, as these sites are located in the zone where certain flora, which are mentioned in the texts, are known and as rice, iron, and glass were excavated.

Other archaeologists have characterized the Chalcolithic Banas/Ahar culture as Aryan, because of an absence of burials and certain shapes in black-and-red pottery; recently, at Gilund, a characteristically BMAC terra-cotta in the shape of a stepped cross has also been found (Possehl, Shinde, and Ameri 2004: fig. 15).

Horse bones have occurred in the sites of the BMAC; the Gandhara Grave culture; at Pirak at the foot of the Bolan pass (where there are other stray Central Asian elements as the sequence moves from copper or bronze to iron); the Late Harappan–PGW overlap at Bhagwanpura; and at PGW Hastinapur, in contexts with or without fortifications, metallurgy, or seals. They also occur in the warrior graves in central and southern India mentioned above. Can we say, then, that horse remains mark the routes of Aryan immigration? Certainly the horse is an exotic element in South Asia and was very much a part of the Indo-Iranian culture. Yet it would surely be dangerous to conclude that the horse necessarily means the presence of those who spoke Vedic Sanskrit. A cooccurrence of the horse *and* the Bactrian two-humped camel (as at Pirak but, to my knowledge, not in the Gandhara Grave culture of Swat) would be a more convincing indicator of migrants from Afghanistan, northern Iran, or Bactria.[20]

Language Replacement

There are many second-millennium regional cultures in the northwestern borderlands of South Asia, thus, that bear traces of immigrant groups. It could be said that this evidence shows that it was not by force of numbers, or by overpowering the local people, that Indo-Aryan speech came to prevail in large parts of northern India. Language replacement could have occurred by way of bilingualism. Perhaps local communities took to speaking Indo-Aryan not because they were outnumbered, but because Indo-Aryan was the language of people with skills in horse-breeding and chariot-building, groups who had achieved military or political ascendancy, whose complex rituals (sacrifice on a large scale) were viewed with awe as highly efficacious, and whose wealth in animals was a matter of envy.

After a period of bilingualism, indigenous communities could have begun to use Indo-Aryan terms and phrases among themselves, so that ultimately they began to converse between themselves in Indo-Aryan. Language replacement has occurred in many parts of the world and is not necessarily a result of the migration of hordes of people. And where it has occurred (in ancient Mesopotamia, in medieval Turkey, and in Ireland, for instance) anthropologists have not begun searches for contrasting skull types or trails of destruction.

Arguments for an Indigenous Origin

Shnirelman says in this volume (chapter 1) that it is in popular perception and not academia that latter-day Russians have begun to insist on an Aryan identity. In India, however, it is a section of scholars, professional archaeologists included, who view the Aryans as indigenous, in keeping with current political trends. Let us take a look at a conference volume published a little more than a decade ago (Deo and Kamath 1993).[21] The Mythic Society in Bangalore organized the conference. The volume is not the work of a lunatic fringe: its senior editor was director of a major center for archaeological study (and my respected teacher), and several professors as well as an ex–director general of the Archaeological Survey of India are among the contributors. There are two papers that accept the idea of Central Asian origins, one of them by a specialist in the Kushan period of the first centuries of the Christian era (B. N. Mukherjee), and the other by a linguist-Sanskritist (M. A. Mehendale). The latter is one of only two papers that refer to Mitanni. As for Finno-Ugric contacts, these are mentioned in only one paper, by V. S. Pathak (Deo and Kamath 1993: 92). There is the inevitable paper on bones, by S. R. Walimbe, which, disconnecting language and race, nevertheless refers to the absence of marked change in skull morphology as an argument against "invasion"—which in any case is not the same thing as immigration and is not the essence of the external-origins theory. S. P. Gupta argues the fallacy of race, the fallacy of the theory of invasion (there are no broken walls or ruined cities, etc.), and says there is no clear division between Aryan and Dravidian, linguistically. Yet he is constrained to make a case that the *absence of* the use of iron, the alleged occurrence of the horse,[22] and the coexistence of city and village in the Harappa culture make the latter equivalent to Vedic culture. Having painstakingly tried to draw up a match of culture elements, Gupta concludes by saying the two were different manifestations of the same culture complex.

In the same volume, S. R. Rao, the excavator of the Harappan site of Lothal, claims to have found evidence of fire altars used in Vedic sacrifice and Vedic deities and myths in the images on the seals; he reverts to his old theory that the language of the Harappan seal inscriptions is a variety of Sanskrit.[23] As regards the "fire altars," the argument is strained. If we are to interpret certain fixtures as a ritual element, we need to establish that they have recurrent and regular features. Nowhere does Rao state which attributes would distinguish a ritual fire "altar" from an ordinary hearth or industrial kiln, except for observations that one or two are exceptionally large (brick-lined) pits. In any case, oval cooking pits with central columns of clay, on which were fixed baking pans, have been found in other cultures (Dhavalikar 1995: 96) where they are not ritual fixtures. Further, does the occurrence in a Lothal pit of a single jawbone indicate animal sacrifice? A gold pendant (a sphere of gold leaf) found in one of these is said to be a gift to a Vedic priest, but what exactly establishes this connection remains a mystery.

Instead of continuing with a point-by-point refutation, let me refer the reader to the general tone of this conference volume. In his keynote address, the president of the Mythic Society states (Deo and Kamath 1993: xvii): "We should remove the distorted impression that the forefathers of the present-day Indians were the invaders of India and foreigners to India." There is more than one reference to foreign conspiracy and the Christian hand. European notions of superiority, it is said, received a blow with the discovery of Sanskrit and the "most advanced, refined and cultured race of the world" (52). Missionaries had discovered that the intellectual and moral authority of the Brahmans would be a major obstacle to their evangelization. "Missionary scholars . . . had already perceived the potential of the science of comparative philology in uprooting the hold of the Brahmins, Sanskrit language and Vedic tradition over the minds of the Indian masses" (32). One participant asks how the Vedic Aryans could have been "agro-pastoralists" since these are "two different levels of technology," two different ways of life, he thinks (104). Yet another participant thinks that to say the early Aryans were pastoralists is to say that they were "barbarians" (157).

We have seen the importance given to being Aryan in modern India and the key place given to the Vedas as the fount of Hinduism. When Indian nationalism first expressed itself, it was a liberating, modernizing force and a move toward unity. Consider, for instance, the sober assessment of Dutt, whose early history is mentioned above. In 1888 (23n1) he wrote of the early home of the Aryans that it was probably somewhere in Central Asia, even though patriotic Indians would not admit that their first home could be anywhere outside India. Dutt also stated that speaking the same language did not amount to belonging to one race. He lived in an age before the perversion of nationalist ideas had begun.

Where latter-day reconstructions (as embodied in the conference volume discussed above) are concerned, however, we are not dealing with a matter of innocent patriotism. Let the Western reader not imagine, either, that all this is because Indian society is in some way more "religious" than other societies. In many of the newer nations of the world, religion is not confined to the private sphere. As the political class seeks its following, religion is co-opted. In India, temple leaders (called "seers" and "godmen" by the media) become fixers for administrators seeking promotions or transfers and for political aspirants; candidates for elections are chosen according to the predominant religion or caste of the constituency in question; preachers at mosques tell their congregations to vote for this or that party. "Hindutva," politically embedded, is not at all the same thing as Hinduism. Hindutva is, as Patnaik and Chalam (1996) explain, the articulation of the projected interests of certain sections of society (those labeled "Hindus"), interests viewed as conflicting with those of other sections (other faiths). The nation, far from being the liberating force it once was, has in the hands of the Hindutva movement become something that excludes.

Scholars taking the Hindutva position give minimal attention to philology and even less to language-replacement theory. Indian archaeology, too, has not developed its analytic tools with due rigor. It conflates concepts such as "culture" with distinctive kinds of pottery, in many cases. There is also the painful reality of the low standard of Sanskrit studies in India, with no fresh translations or editions of the *RgVeda* in recent times. Scholars with a nationalist bent have, almost inevitably, read the early Sanskrit literature (the "greatest," "oldest," "best" in the world) with the remains of the "glorious" Harappa civilization, even though the latter is incontestably urban, seafaring, and internationally mercantile, as well as preoccupied with animals like the monkey—all of these are features absent from the *RgVeda*. Given this agenda, it has become imperative for these archaeologists to highlight "identifications" of fire altars and of the horse on Harappan seals and to read the hitherto undeciphered script as expressing an Indo-Aryan language. The excavator of the Harappan town of Dholavira, instead of systematically publishing the finds as they have been unearthed, interprets the site as a Vedic town (whatever that may mean), even though the *RgVeda* has nothing to do with the Rann or the Kutch mainland. There was a project on "Sarasvati" valley archaeology, generously funded by the Hindu nationalist government in power until 2004, aiming to correct the "error" in the naming of the Harappa civilization. (It was named after the Indus instead of the Sarasvati, the latter being a river, said [quite incorrectly, it appears to me—see Kochhar 2000] to be of central importance in the poetry.) Inevitably, some scholars have sought to argue for cultural continuity from the Harappan civilization to that of the Ganga, even though the latter lies in a totally different location and begins its development at least eight hundred years after the demise of the former. State examinations for college-teacher eligibility included questions, to be answered in eight lines, about the similarities between the Indus and Ganges civilizations. Popular lectures sought to arouse anger by stating that "Marxist" scholars actually describe the RgVedic Aryans as "nomads"—how insulting!

Reading the *Aryan Problem*, I felt twinges of embarrassment and a small degree of compassion for the narrow-mindedness and low self-esteem behind this kind of writing. But there is also the question of expediency, as was pointed out when I presented the material in this chapter as a paper at the University of Delhi in February 2005. It cannot be a coincidence, for example, that the volume came out in 1993, after the "heroic" demolition of the medieval mosque at Ayodhya.

It is probably in the context of opportunism that another, more recent volume (Tripathi 2005) was produced. Here too we are told that the *RgVeda* is much older than 1500 BC, that the Aryans are indigenous to India (and many more archaeological cultures are said to be Indo-Aryan), and that Sanskrit is nothing but Proto-Indo-European (13).[24] There are strange statements. The editor says, "Vedic civilization is either identical with Harappan and Indus civilization as Saraswati civilization, or continuous with them as a developmental stage" (13); V. N. Misra asserts that because many RgVedic hymns were written on the banks of the Sarasvati and this river flows in India, we can conclude that the Indian subcontinent was the original homeland of the Indo-Aryans (177–178); S. Singh finds that Arya is "the Supreme Being in His capacity of the nearest reference point in the context of the management of the support cycle of life in phenomenal realm" (123); M. K. Dhavalikar states that it is the text of the *RgVeda* that gives evidence of "a heavy concentration of settlements in the Sarasvati and Drishadvati basins" (203). He says (208) that besides Indian names such as Somasena and Arisena occurring in Mesopotamian tablets, "there are two more names: Al Alli Asrani and Ila Brabani," and for the latter cites Parpola 1995. I can find no such mention in Parpola 1995. There is only one reference, by A. M. Shastri (103), to Iranian identification with Aryanness, and that is with reference to the tradition of origins further east. Some contributors to the volume, including archaeologists with claims to academic distinction, appear to have become interested in Aryans only recently. Is their rush to conform to the majority a symptom of the insecurities that prevail among the middle classes, or did the scholars succumb to the temptations of political patronage and rush to discover the indigenous origins of the Aryans?

There are other modern nations that identify their ancient past (and glory) with the Aryans. *Ariyana*, the "land of the Aryas,"[25] denotes both Iran and Afghanistan to the peoples of these two countries. The Achaemenid emperor Darius claimed Aryan ancestry and the initiation of writing in the Aryan (Old Persian) language. The Pahlavi kings of the twentieth century pretended to be the legitimate successors of the Achaemenids and emphasized Persianness over Islam, exhorting the world to call their land "Iran." Even so, official Iranian thinking in the days of the shah and after the revolution grants that the Aryans were immigrants into Iran and acknowledges the existence of a pre-Aryan period of Iranian history. There has been *no* attempt, political, administrative, or scholarly, to doctor the historical sequence to claim indigenous origins.

Why is it, then, that so many Indians should find the thought of external Aryan origins to be threatening? This question put to university students elicited the glib answer that Iran had a homogeneous culture and religion, which is false. For the main part, the answer lies in twentieth-century majoritarianism and the politics of exclusion pursued in India. On the one hand, Muslims are projected in some schoolbooks and in popular discourse as alien invaders, the destroyers of temples, and the violators of Hindu women. On the other hand, citizens who have for centuries been treated as outcaste or untouchable claim that the Harappa civilization was *their* creation, that they are the autochthonous population. In such a scenario it would not do to acknowledge that the ancestors of the upper-caste leaders of the Hindu chauvinism were themselves of foreign origin.

At an international conference, "India and Iran: The Confluence of Musical Cultures," at the National Centre of Performing Arts in January 2005, Ashok Ranade stressed that we must think of a "culture zone" that incorporated both Iran and India, one in which there were constant exchanges between the two countries even as Arab, Turkish, and Afghan elements were being absorbed by either or both of them. Another scholar found that rather than the "tree" or "wave" models of cultural interaction, it is the "spaghetti" model that best represents the give-and-take in music that went on for centuries. How ironic that those Indian intellectuals who are so preoccupied with their Aryan ancestry have not yet realized that "few people have been more closely related in origin and throughout history than the people of India and the people of Iran" (Nehru 1946: 148).

Notes

1. This does not mean that the nation is a falsehood (Anderson 1983: 15). Instead, Gellner (1983: 54) was insisting that the boundaries of nation-states could not possibly coincide with those of specific culture traditions.
2. Jawaharlal Nehru, a romantic nationalist, admits that of our Indian nation we "make and preserve the pictures of our choice" (1946: 63).
3. Even a modern scholar like Gonda sees Dravidian culture as a "substratum" from which Aryans repeatedly borrowed and adapted (1965: 15).
4. See Bayly 1994 for exceptions among the colonial administrators who did not think in this way.
5. His framework and assumptions have been used in a large number of subsequent passages or tracts on the Harappan religion.
6. Aside from these two language groups, of course, there are also in India speakers of Munda languages and languages related to those of Tibet and Burma.
7. *Hinduism* was a term coined in the 1820s in the view—often contested—of a religion that was all-embracing.

8. *Arya,* was used in contradistinction to *dasa; arya* could thus mean those who, under the leadership of the god Indra, defeated the Dasas (Monier-Williams 1899: s.v. "arya"). Apte (1965) gives the word the connotations of "worthy, high, honorable," etc. For *Arya*, see also Macdonell and Keith 1912.
9. Avestan, the ancient language closest to RgVedic Sanskrit, also uses this term. The later Persian emperor Darius the Achaemenid claimed not only his Persian ancestry but also that he was "an Aryan of Aryan seed."
10. Colonial Indology was built on knowledge gleaned from Brahman scholars and ignored many non-Brahmanic strands and protest movements (see Hardy 1995; Dalmia and von Stietencron 1995; Sontheimer and Kulke 1997). Hinduism was incorrectly understood as an all-embracing whole. Modern Hinduism is in fact a "form of corporate and organized and syndicated religion" (Frykenberg 1997: 89) defined by the upper castes and classes and by colonial codifications of law and government controls of temple treasuries. Brahman supremacy has in any case, since the nineteenth century, been contested by the downtrodden (Omvedt 1995), who see the caste system as oppression and the ancient Brahmans as foreign invaders who destroyed the glorious civilization of Mohenjo-daro.
11. Reconversion was a policy of the Arya Samaj. The Hindu Mahasabha was dissolved in the 1960s, but its ideas persisted, e.g., in the thinking of the Rashtriya Swayamsevak Sangh (RSS), a crypto-cultural organization that enjoyed great political power between about 1998 and 2003. Its ideology appealed to the upper castes and their middle-class frustrations about jobs and life in overcrowded cities.
12. Shipman (1994: 87–99) writes about Rudolf Virchow's survey of 6 million German schoolchildren in order to dispel the myth of Christian Germans being blue-eyed and blond Aryans (he was aware of the potential for political abuse). He could not, however, shake the faith of Christian Germans that they constituted a race.
13. The paragraphs that follow draw from Mallory 1989; Deshpande 1979, 1995; Witzel 1995a, 1995b; Harmatta 1992; Anthony 2001; Mehendale 1993; and Skjaervo 1995.
14. Later languages of the Iranian group include Persian, Baluch, Pashto, and Tadjik.
15. Baluchistan is the western frontier of the distribution of the monkey in Asia.
16. In an important review of the evidence, Sparreboom (1985) asks what use the RgVedic cattle herders could have made of the chariot. He finds that chariot racing is more frequent than chariot warfare. But racing was not for sport in a kind of folk festivity. Chariot races were connected with contests between individuals vying for supremacy and prestige.
17. Sharma (1983: 159) comes to the same point in the context of the RgVedic textual evidence.
18. Needless to say, such an identification can never be proved.
19. In the RgVeda, only *yava,* probably barley, occurs as the crop.

20. We must not forget, either, that the Dravidian language speakers themselves may have entered South Asia from the northwest.
21. Note that it was in December 1992 that the mosque at Ayodhya was demolished by a frenzied mob. Movements in academia along the lines of Hindu nationalism were most confident during the period 1990 to 2004.
22. Surkotada is perhaps the only Harappan site whose animal remains have been subjected to detailed study by more than one scholar—see Bokonyi 1997 for identification as horse bones, and Meadow and Patel 1997 for the refutation of this identification.
23. There has been no conclusive decipherment of the script. Needless to say, in Hindutva circles it has become important to project it as encoding a variety of Sanskrit.
24. Also, the Vedic language is "the original language" and "the real Indo-European" (Tripathi 2005: 114–116).
25. From the ancient *Airyānām vaējō* was derived *Erān Vēz*, and thus "Iran."

References

Anderson, B. 1983. *Imagined Communities: Reflections on the Origin and Spread of Nationalism.* London: Verso.

Anthony, D. 2001. Persistent identity and Indo-European archaeology in the western steppe. In *Early Contacts between Uralic and Indo-European: Linguistic and Archaeological Considerations*, ed. C. Carpelan, A. Parpola, and P. Koskikallio, 11–35. Helsinki: Suomalais-Ugrilainen Seura.

Apte, V. S. 1965. *The Practical Sanskrit-English Dictionary.* 3rd ed. Delhi: Motilal Banarsidass.

Baird, R. D. 1998. *Religion in Modern India.* Delhi: Manohar.

Banga, I. 2004. Swami Dayanand's Aryavarta. In *India—Studies in the History of an Idea*, ed. I. Habib, 195–203. Delhi: Munshiram Manoharlal.

Bates, C. 1994. Race, caste, and tribe in central India. In *The Concept of Race in South Asia*, ed. P. Robb, 219–259. Delhi: Oxford University Press.

Bayly, S. 1994. Caste and "race" in colonial ethnography. In *The Concept of Race in South Asia*, ed. P. Robb, 165–218. Delhi: Oxford University Press.

Bokonyi, S. 1997. Horse remains from the prehistoric site of Surkotada. *South Asian Studies* 13:297–307.

Breckenridge, C., and P. van Der Veer. 1993. Orientalism and the postcolonial predicament. In *Orientalism and the Postcolonial Predicament*, ed. C. Breckenridge and P. van der Veer, 1–19. Philadelphia: University of Pennsylvania.

Bryant, E. 1999. Linguistic substrata and the indigenous Aryan debate. In *Aryan and Non-Aryan in South Asia*, ed. J. Bronkhorst and M. M. Deshpande, 59–83. Cambridge, MA: Harvard University Press.

Carpelan, C., and A. Parpola. 2001. Proto-Indo-European, Proto-Uralic, and Proto-Aryan in archaeological perspective. In *Early Contacts between Uralic and*

Indo-European: Linguistic and Archaeological Considerations, ed. C. Carpelan, A. Parpola, and P. Koskikallio, 55–150. Helsinki: Suomalais-Ugrilainen Seura.

Connerton, P. 1993. *How Societies Remember*. Cambridge: Cambridge University Press.

Dalmia, V., and H. von Stietencron, eds. 1995. *Representing Hinduism*. Delhi: Sage.

Deo, S. B., and S. Kamath, eds. 1993. *The Aryan Problem*. Pune: Bharatiya Itihasa Sankalana Samiti.

Deshpande, M. M. 1979. Genesis of Rgvedic retroflexion, In *Aryan and Non-Aryan in India*, ed. M. M. Deshpande and P. E. Hook, 235–315. Ann Arbor: University of Michigan Press.

Deshpande, M. M. 1995. Vedic Aryans, non-Vedic Aryans, and non-Aryans. In *The Indo-Aryans of Ancient South Asia*, ed. G. Erdosy, 67–84. Berlin: W. de Gruyter.

Dhavalikar, M. K. 1995. The living past: The first farmers of Maharashtra. In *Folk Culture, Folk Religion, and Oral Traditions in Maharashtrian Culture*, ed. G.-D. Sontheimer, 87–105. Delhi: Manohar.

Dikshit, K. N. 1969. A note on the problem of the plain black and red ware in northern India. In *Potteries in Ancient India*, ed. B. P. Sinha, 48–55. Patna: Patna University Press.

Dutt, R. C. 1888. *The Early Hindu Civilization, 2000–320 BC*. London. Reprint, Calcutta: Punthi Pustak, 1963.

Francfort, H.-P. 2001. The archaeology of protohistoric Central Asia and the problems of identifying Indo-European and Uralic populations. In *Early Contacts between Uralic and Indo-European*, ed. C. Carpelan, A. Parpola, and P. Koskikallio, 151–165. Helsinki: Suomalais-Ugrilainen Seura.

Frykenburg, R. E. 1997. The emergence of modern "Hinduism" as a concept and as an institution. In Sontheimer and Kulke 1997, 82–107.

Gellner, E. 1983. *Nations and Nationalism*. Oxford: Blackwell.

Ghosh, A. 1994. A note on the homeland of the painted grey ware. In *Painted Grey Ware*, ed. R. C. Gaur, 25–28. Jaipur: Publication Scheme.

Gonda, J. 1965. *Change and Continuity in Indian Religion*. Delhi: Munshiram Manoharlal. Reprint, 1985.

Gonda, J. 1975. *Vedic Literature*. Wiesbaden: O. Harrassowitz.

Hardy, F. 1995. A radical re-assessment of the Vedic heritage. In Dalmia and Stietencron 1995, 35–50.

Harmatta, J. 1992. The emergence of the Indo-Iranians. In *History of Civilizations of Central Asia*, ed. A. H. Dani and V. M. Masson, 1:357–378. N.p: UNESCO.

Havell, E. B. 1915. *The Ancient and Medieval Architecture of India: A Study of Indo-Aryan Civilization*. Reprint, Delhi: S. Chand, 1972.

Hobsbawm, E. 1990. *Nations and Nationalism since 1780*. Cambridge: Cambridge University Press.

Hock, H. H. 1999. Through a glass darkly. In *Aryan and Non-Aryan in South Asia*, ed. J. Bronkhorst and M. M. Deshpande, 145–174. Cambridge, MA: Harvard University Press.

Jaffrelot, C. 1996. The Hindu Nationalist Movement and Indian Politics, 1925 to the 1990s. Delhi: Penguin Viking.

Joglekar, P. P. 2000. Back to bones? A rejoinder. *Man and Environment* 25 (1): 117–118.

Kennedy, K. A. R. 1995. Have Aryans been identified in the prehistoric skeletal record of South Asia? In *The Indo-Aryans of Ancient South Asia*, ed. G. Erdosy, 32–66. Berlin: W. de Gruyter.

Kennedy, K. A. R., B. E. Hemphill, and J. R. Lukacs. 2000. Bring back the bones. *Man and Environment* 25 (1): 105–109.

Kochhar, R. 2000. *The Vedic People*. Delhi: Orient Longman.

Kohl, P. L. 1984. *Central Asia: Palaeolithic Beginnings to the Iron Age*. Paris: Editions Recherches sur les Civilisations.

Lamberg-Karlovsky, C. C. 2002. Archaeology and language: The Indo-Iranians. *Current Anthropology* 43 (1): 63–88.

Levine, M. A., C. Renfrew, and K. Boyle, eds. 2003. *Prehistoric Steppe Adaptation and the Horse*. Cambridge, U.K.: McDonald Institute.

Macdonell, A. A., and A. B. Keith. 1912. *Vedic Index of Names and Subjects*. London: John Murray.

Mallory, J. P. 1989. *The Indo-Europeans*. London: Thames and Hudson.

Marshall, J. 1931. *Mohenjo-daro and the Indus Civilization*. London: Arthur Probsthain.

Meadow, R. H., and A. Patel 1997. A comment on "Horse Remains from Surkotada" by S. Bokonyi. *South Asian Studies* 13:308–314.

Mehendale, M. A. 1993. The Indo-Aryans, the Indo-Iranians, and the Indo-Europeans. In Deo and Kamath 1993, 43–50.

Monier-Williams, M. 1899. *A Sanskrit-English Dictionary*. Delhi: Motilal Banarsidass. Reprint, 2002.

Nandi, R. N. 2001. *Aryans Revisited*. Delhi: Munshiram Manoharlal.

Nehru, Jawaharlal. 1946. *The Discovery of India*. Delhi: Jawaharlal Nehru Memorial Fund and Oxford University Press. Reprint, 2002. Page references are to the 2002 edition.

Omvedt, G. 1995. *Dalit Visions*. Delhi: Orient Longman.

Parpola, A. 1993. Margiana and the Aryan problem. *International Association for the Study of the Cultures of Central Asia Bulletin* 19:41–62.

Parpola, A. 1995. The problem of the Aryans and the Soma. In *The Indo-Aryans of Ancient South Asia*, ed. G. Erdosy, 353–380. Berlin: W. de Gruyter.

Pashaura Singh. 1999. Revisiting the Arya-Samaj movement. In *Aryan and Non-Aryan in South Asia*, ed. J. Bronkhorst and M. M. Deshpande, 261–276. Cambridge, MA: Harvard University Press.

Patnaik, A., and K. S. R. V. S. Chalam. 1996. The ideology and politics of Hindutva. In *Region, Religion, Caste, Gender, and Culture in Contemporary India*, ed. T. V. Satyamurthy, 252–280. Delhi: Oxford University Press.

Possehl, G., V. Shinde, and M. Ameri. 2004. The Ahar-Banas complex and the BMAC. *Man and Environment* 29 (2): 18–29.

Ratnagar, S. 1998. Back to the bones? *Man and Environment* 23 (2): 101–105.

Ratnagar, S. 1999. Does archaeology hold the answers? In *Aryan and Non-Aryan in South Asia*, ed. J. Bronkhorst and M. M. Deshpande, 207–238. Cambridge, MA: Harvard University Press.

Ratnagar, S. 2000. Reply. *Man and Environment* 25 (1): 119–120.

Robb, P. 1994. South Asia and the concept of race. In *The Concept of Race in South Asia*, ed. P. Robb, 1–76. Delhi: Oxford University Press.

Sharma, R. S. 1983. *Material Culture and Social Formations in Ancient India*. Delhi: Macmillan.

Sharma, R. S. 1999. *Advent of the Aryans in India*. Delhi: Manohar.

Shipman, P. 1994. *The Evolution of Racism: Human Differences and the Use and Abuse of Science*. New York: Simon and Schuster.

Shrimali, K. M. 2002. The Rgveda and the Avesta. In *The Growth of Civilizations in India and Iran*, ed. I. Habib, 23–57. Delhi: Tulika.

Skjaervo, P. K. 1995. The Avesta as a source for the early history of the Iranians. In *The Indo-Aryans of Ancient South Asia*, ed. G. Erdosy, 155–176. Berlin: W. de Gruyter.

Sontheimer, G.-D., and H. Kulke, eds. 1997. *Hinduism Reconsidered*. Delhi: Manohar.

Sparreboom, M. 1985. *Chariots in the Veda*. Leiden: E. J. Brill.

Stacul, G. 1989. Continuity and change in the Swat Valley. In *Old Problems and New Perspectives in the Archaeology of South Asia*, ed. J. M. Kenoyer, 249–251. Madison: Wisconsin Archaeological Reports.

Trautmann, T. 1999. Constructing the racial theory of Indian civilization. In *Aryan and Non-Aryan in South Asia*, ed. J. Bronkhorst and M. M. Deshpande, 277–293. Cambridge, MA: Harvard University Press.

Trautmann, T. 2004. *Aryans and British India*. 2nd rev. ed. Delhi: YODA.

Tripathi, D. N., ed. 2005. *A Discourse on Indo European Languages and Culture*. Delhi: Manak and ICHR.

Vats, M. S. 1940. *Excavations at Harappa*. Delhi: Government of India.

Walimbe, S. R. 2000. Tumults in skeletal biology. *Man and Environment* 25 (1): 111–116.

Winternitz, M. 1927. *A History of Indian Literature*. Vol. 1. Trans. S. Ketkar. Calcutta: University of Calcutta. Reprint, Delhi: Oriental Books, 1972.

Witzel, M. 1995a. Early Indian history: Linguistic and textual parameters. In *The Indo-Aryans of Ancient South Asia*, ed. G. Erdosy, 85–125. Berlin: W. de Gruyter.

Witzel, M. 1995b. Rgvedic history: Poets, chieftains, and polities. In *The Indo-Aryans of Ancient South Asia*, ed. G. Erdosy, 307–352. Berlin: W. de Gruyter.

THIRTEEN

The Impact of Colonialism and Nationalism in the Archaeology of Thailand

RASMI SHOOCONGDEJ

Introduction

Over the past few years, archaeologists throughout the world have become increasingly interested in issues of colonialism and nationalism in archaeological interpretation (e.g., Bray and Glover 1987; Layton 1989; Murray 1993; Spriggs 1991, 1992; Stone and MacKenzie 1990; Trigger 1984; Trigger and Glover 1981, 1982). In both contexts, the past has been interpreted by the dominant power in a way that serves the present (Gosden 2004; Trigger 1989; Kohl and Fawcett 1995). Clearly, such interpretation assumes that there is a close relationship between the political environment and the structure of archaeological research. Often, elites and political leaders have sought legitimacy for their own power through the evidence of the past. Colonial self-representations have commonly been regenerated in nationalism. These observations are not new; they have been extensively discussed in anthropology and history (e.g., Chatterjee 1993; Dirks 1992). Nevertheless, little is known about the impact of nationalism in response to colonialism and the study of archaeology within individual countries. In developing countries, archaeology is closely tied to the formation of nation-states (Mangi 1989; Trigger 1984; Winitchakul 1988). However, it is no longer valid to assume that "the core state archaeologists totally dominated the archaeology of peripheral states" (McGuire 1994). For example, in numerous Asian countries with long and complex histories, the investigation of the past through material remains developed in the premodern era, long before the introduction of scientific archaeology (Bleed 1988; Chang 1981; Chakrabarti 1982; Ikawa-Smith 1982). The archaeological tradition, therefore, developed differently than in the West. Furthermore, the native views of the past differ from those of the West. Undoubtedly, Western contributions to archaeology in developing countries entered an already complex intellectual arena. It is important for archaeologists who conduct their research in such countries to make an effort to understand the native concept of the past and how it has been studied.

In this chapter I examine how the dynamics of nationalism affect the nature of archaeological research in Southeast Asia (e.g., Glover and Glover 1990; Higham 1989; Peterson 1982–1983; Smith and Watson 1979). Specifically, I focus on Thailand, asking the following questions: (1) Who controls the past? (2) How did that control develop? and (3) How has archaeology been utilized? Thailand provides an excellent illustration of the complex ties between colonialism, nationalism, and archaeology. Thailand comprises various ethnic groups and peoples with multicultural backgrounds, of which the Thai make up the largest community. The most distinctive characteristic that identifies Thai as a separate ethnicity is the Thai language. One of only a few developing countries that escaped colonial domination, Thailand is the only Southeast Asian constitutional monarchy (see fig. 13.1). Although it has never been colonized, the nation has been highly dependent on Western powers. Through resistance to Western colonialism, the ruling Thai elites–political leaders exercised their own power through a strong colonialist ideology integrating other ethnic groups under official nationalism. It should be emphasized that Thai nationalism incorporated ancient traditions, Buddhism, and Western ideas in a search for self-identity and for ideological weapons against external powers (colonial dominance) and internal political instability. The nature of archaeological research, therefore, was oriented toward the promotion of Thai cultural heritage and was less concerned with the past of other ethnic groups. Little attention has been paid to non-Thai problems by archaeologists working in Thailand. This lack of attention can partly be explained by the government's control of archaeology under the name of "Thai national heritage." A similar situation exists in many other countries, such as Japan, India, and Mexico.

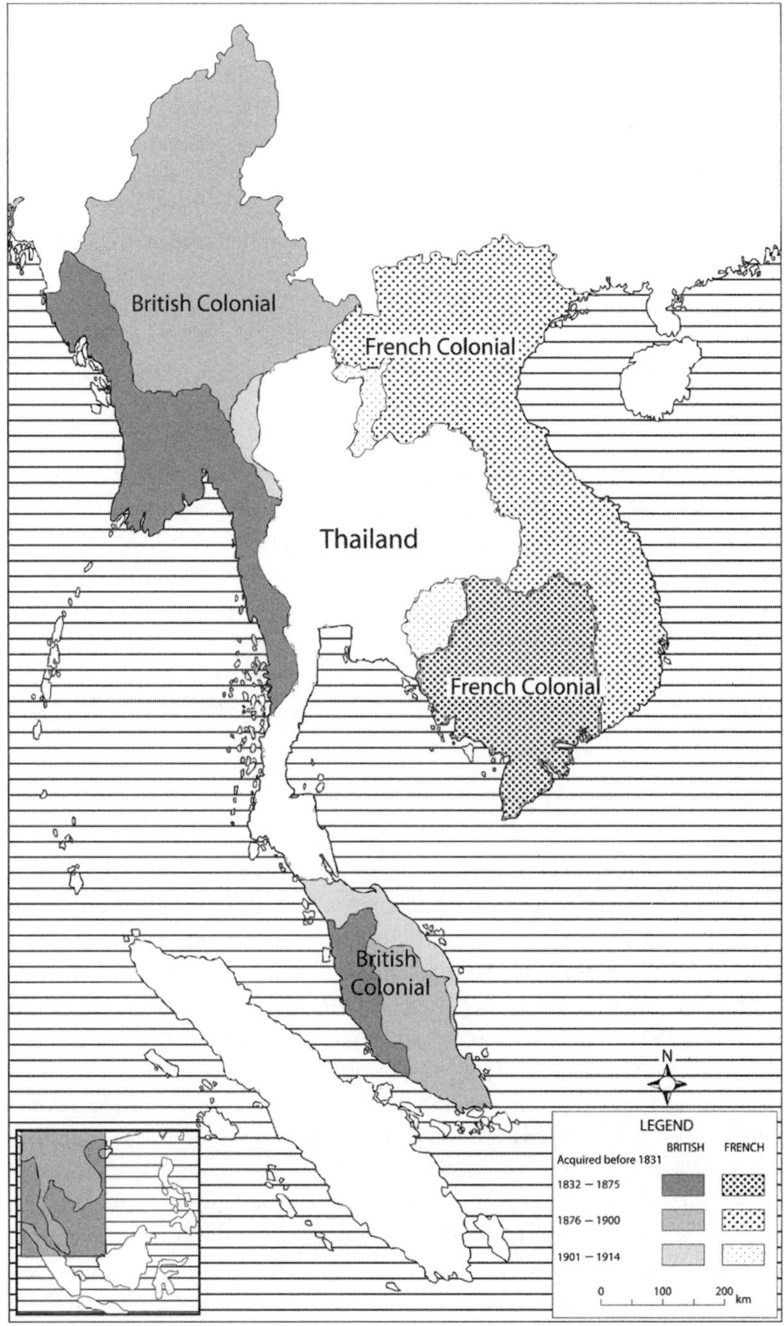

Figure 13.1. Expansion of European control. After Dixon 1993: 70.

This chapter focuses on the period from the second half of the nineteenth century to World War II. There are two reasons for selecting this period. First, the maintenance of Thailand's independence during the late nineteenth and early twentieth centuries entailed many significant social and political changes. Second, the control over the past exerted in this period inevitably continues to have a powerful influence on contemporary archaeology in Thailand. Moreover, the traditional archaeology of Thailand is a part of history; thus, historical approaches are the mainstream of archaeological research in Thailand. Modern Western archaeology is not discussed in the chapter, because it was introduced only after World War II. I also do not consider here the issue of Western colonialism in contemporary archaeology in Thailand, but I have discussed it in Shoocongdej 1992.

The chapter is organized into two major parts. The first part offers a historical perspective on colonial influence and nationalism in Thailand. In the second part, I illustrate the impact of colonialism and nationalism in the archaeology of Thailand through an analysis of excavations linked to the Sukhothai State. As a Thai, I am taking an emic point of view to examine my own past. As a professional archaeologist critically examining the archaeological record, I am taking an etic viewpoint. I believe that archaeologists have a responsibility to eschew nationalist pressures in order to evaluate evidence accurately and credibly.

Perceptions of the Thai Past

A question naturally arises as to how the Thai think about their own past. If one wants to know about Thai perceptions of the past, one must examine the pre-Westernization or premodernization period. There are two traditional types of historiography: the Tamnan and the Phongsawadan, which centered on the Buddhist order and the royal court, respectively (Kasetsiri 1979: 156). Tamnan are stories, legends, and myths concerning the history of Buddhism. They were written in the fifteenth century and declined in the seventeenth century. Phongsawadan are chronological records of major events in each reign, and they focused on the ruling elites or members of a dynasty or kingdom, typically overlooking the history of other states. They began in the seventeenth century and continued to the middle of the nineteenth century (Kasetsiri 1976; Saraya 1982). Tamnan originated in Chiang Mai, northern Thailand, whereas Phongsawadan originated in Ayudhaya, central Thailand, which was believed to be a capital of the Thai people at the time of their writing (Saraya 1982: 82–121).

Both Tamnan and Phongsawadan provide clear concepts of chronological time and geographic space. In particular, Phongsawadan writing reflected ideas that later became the centralist historical ideology, concerning the monarchy, the royal court, and the administrative system. These intellectual traditions affected the historiography and archaeological interpretations of later nationalist periods.

The effort to channel elements of the Tamnan and the Phongsawadan into a national historical tradition received special emphasis in the nineteenth and early twentieth centuries. During this period, most mainland Southeast Asian countries had fallen under the control of Western colonial powers. Burma and the Shan state were under the British; Viet Nam, Laos, and Cambodia were under the French (Steinberg 1987). At the same time Thailand became more open to the Western world, because the country was caught between England and France. The Thai monarch, King Mongkut (Rama IV, 1851–1868), known to Westerners from the Broadway play *The King and I,* decided to modernize the country in order to be accepted as civilized and to escape from colonial rule (Dhiravegin 1974). He communicated with Western diplomats in English. He was also the first king to travel around the country, and in doing so, he encountered various historical monuments. He found the first Thai inscription, which was later called the Ram Khamhaeng inscription, dated to 1292 at Sukhothai (later claimed to be the first capital of the Thai people) (Wan Waithayakon 1965). The Sukhothai inscription number 1 is the oldest evidence of the Thai script: the vocabulary in this inscription contains 83 percent of the Thai language elements (Bradley 1909: 16–18). The inscription commemorated King Ram Khamhaeng, the third king of the Sukhothai kingdom, who succeeded his brother around 1279 and who invented the Thai script. One might say this significant discovery marked the first establishment of archaeology in Thailand and that King Mongkut was a pioneer who tried to combine conventional historical documents with archaeological evidence. Prior to King Mongkut's reign, there was no link between the two fields, even though many historical sources for the Ayutthaya (ca. AD 1357–1767) and early Bangkok (ca. 1767–1851) periods existed.

King Chulalongkorn came to power in 1873 and continued to modernize the country. He also reformed and centralized the administrative system by adopting European administrative organization (Dhiravegin 1974; Wyatt 1984). The consequence of the reforms was the growth of the king's power and control over the bureaucracy. Before his reign, most political entities throughout Southeast Asia were under the control of autonomous lords, for instance, Laos, the Malay states, Sibson Panna, the Shan states, Cambodia, and Lanna (one of the Northern States) (Winitchakul 1988: 389). Various indigenous ethnic groups, such as the Mon, the Khmer (Cambodians called themselves Khmer), the Laotians, the Malays, the Negritos, the hill-tribes, and so on, were integrated under a national framework (Steinberg 1987). Before King Chulalongkorn there was also no definitive boundary map of Thailand; the first modern surveying and mapping occurred during his reign. The production of a map required a reconstruction of the past and a sense of national unity (Winitchakul 1987, 1988). In addition, to counter Western colonial power, Thailand had to demonstrate its own civilization by creating a national history and identity.

Consequently, in the attempt to gain insight into national history and the people, natural resources, and geography of Thailand, several institutions emerged at that time. In 1904 the Royal Thai elites and Westerners who worked in the government or as missionaries in the private sector founded the Siam Society. Although their goal was to conduct research on people, nature, and ancient history, they also concerned themselves with presenting the Siam society in a positive light to show the British and the French that Thailand was as civilized as Western nations and that its cultural traditions had a long history worthy of respect (Davis 1989). In 1907 the Antiquarian Society (or Boran Kadi Samosorn) was founded by the king. King Chulalongkorn made a statement at its first meeting that the origin of Thailand should be dated back a thousand years (Winitchakul 1988: 404).

During this time the French School of the Far East (Ecole Française d'Extrême-Orient) was founded in Hanoi, Viet Nam, in 1901. This organization served as a training institution for French Orientalists and later for indigenous scholars. It remains even now a center of knowledge about Indochinese civilization. During French colonization, many studies were conducted on epigraphy and ancient history, history of art, museology, and archaeology (Forest 1990: 70–96; Janse 1941). French archaeological research was closely tied to history in general and the history of art, oriented toward monumental architecture (in particular, that of palaces and temples) and epigraphic research (Audouze and Leroi-Gourhan 1982: 170–183). The French successfully established a general history of Indochina, focused largely on a cultural chronology of Cambodia (Coedès 1983a). These works, no doubt, had tremendous impact on the development of archaeology in Thailand, especially on the establishment of a cultural chronology before the Sukhothai period.

The Ruling Elite versus Military Nationalism in the Twentieth Century

It is undeniable that a Western perspective on studying the past had been adopted, perhaps consciously, by the ruling elite. During the twentieth century, two strains of nationalism emerged: elite and military nationalism. The era of elite nationalism can be said to have started around 1912, with King Chulalongkorn's son and heir King Vajiravudh. While King Chulalongkorn faced the Western powers, his son was concerned more with internal political stability. His idea of nationalism was different from his father's, because he was educated in Great Britain and faced new problems created by the establishment of a modern bureaucracy. The king therefore defined a new national ideology in order to influence the middle-strata officers, so that they would place their loyalty in him more than in the elite bureaucrats (Kesboonchoo 1987: 107–120). He created the idea of the Thai nation and introduced the slogan "nation, religion, and king" (this slogan is still used [Chumchantra 1987]). Here he tried to link the monarchy symbolically with nation and religion. Another major element in the development of nationalism was the large-scale immigration of Chinese into Thailand (Dixon 1993: 109–114). This contributed to an increased anti-Chinese feeling among the Western-educated Thai upper class. The king tried to assimilate the Chinese through a law proclaiming that all children born in Thailand were Thai citizens. Thus, in order to unite the diverse elements of his state, the king attempted to bridge ethnic diversity with a carefully constructed narrative of the past. Nationalism inevitably affected historical writing and archaeology, which became oriented toward the king, his family, and ancient Thai civilization (Chumchantra 1987).

About the same time, another version of Thai national identity cropped up in response to the world wars. In the era of military nationalism, 1910–1941, Thailand had a large number of students studying overseas. They returned home to take up high-level positions in government service, their status legitimated by education. Furthermore, they brought ideas of democracy and of a constitution with them. As a result Thailand's political system was changed into a constitutional monarchy. During World War II, the military had ultimate power in the country. After

World War II, the Chinese controlled the Thai economy, and there was a growth of Chinese nationalism in Thailand. The military government then promoted the political ideology of "Thailand for the Thai." One of the government's strategies was to call all inhabitants Thai without regard to their regional and ethnic backgrounds; to be Thai was to speak the Thai language and to be Buddhist (Wyatt 1984: 252–260). In any event, the government still regarded nation, religion, and king as the most important components of Thai identity (Winitchakul 1988: 417). But neither military nor ethnic nationalism was constructed on an explicitly ethnic basis.

Case Study: Sukhothai State

Archaeology played a crucial role in the articulation of Thai national identity. The most salient example of how nationalist agendas have appropriated archaeological interpretations of the past is the ancient state of Sukhothai. Sukhothai was a Buddhist state in the central region of Thailand that was surrounded by the states of Lanna and Phayao in northern Thailand, Lopburi in central Thailand, Nakhon Si Thammarat in southern Thailand, and Khmer in Cambodia. It dated between the mid-thirteenth and fifteenth centuries (See fig. 13.2).

According to the Sukhothai inscriptions, Chinese documents, and archaeological evidence, Sukhothai's territories extended to northern, central, and southern Thailand through the extension of trade routes and as the result of marriage and religious relations. It was a hierarchically organized society, including evidence of state ritual, bureaucratic organization, craft specialization, external trade, ancient reservoirs, and so on. Theravada Buddhism was also used as a political ideology to express the political unity of the state. Nine kings of the Phra Ruang dynasty ruled Sukhothai from AD 1219 to 1438. In particular, King Ram Khamhaeng's inscription clearly represented Sukhothai politics and economy:

> In the life-time of King Ram Khamhaeng, this Muang Sukhothai is good. In the water there are fish, in the fields there is rice. The ruler does not levy a tax on the people who travel along the road together, leading their oxen on the way to trade and riding their horses on the way to sell. Whoever wants to trade in elephants, so trades. Whoever wants to trade in horses, so trades. Whoever wants to trade in silver and gold, so trades. When a commoner, noble or prince is dead and deceased, let his ancestral home, his clothes, his elephants, his family, his rice granaries, his servants and his

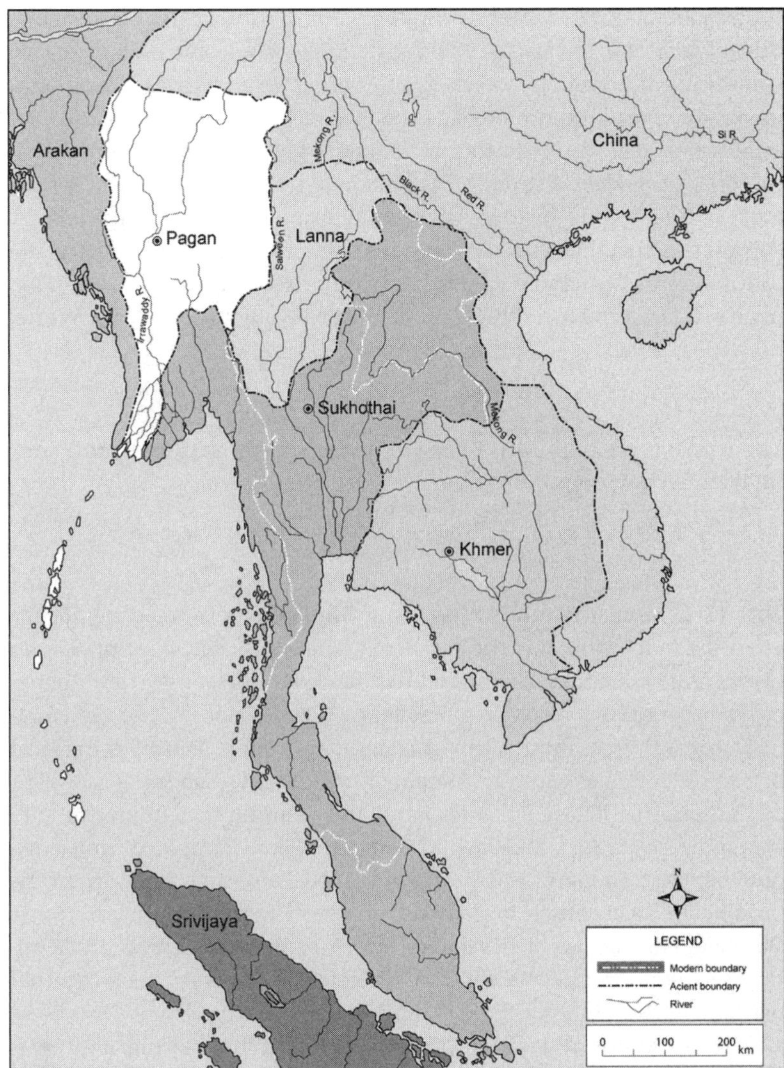

Figure 13.2. Major states in the late thirteenth century. After Senanarong and Ngamnisai 1987: 21.

ancestral groves of areca-nut and betel all devolve on his children. . . . At the gateway there is a bell hung up. If anyone of the public has a complaint or grievance of body or of mind to place before the King, it is not difficult. He goes to sound the bell that is hung up. King Ram Khamhaeng hears him call and, on questioning him, makes an upright investigation for him. (Wan Waithayakon 1965: 9–10)

Archaeological excavations conducted in the city walls and moats yielded evidence of the palace, Buddhist temples, stone and metal artifacts, coins, sculptures, and skeletal remains. Approximately two hundred monuments have been found. Outside the city walls, temples and glazed ceramic kilns have also been found. The glazed ceramic called Sangkhalok ceramic was widely distributed as a trade item in Southeast Asia, Japan, and Madagascar. In the fifteenth century, Sukhothai was completely incorporated into the centralization of the Ayutthaya kingdom from the south, and a city named Sukhothai was the second capital of the Thai (Fine Arts Department 1988; Moore et al. 1996; Vallibhotama 1989; Wongthes 1983, 1986).

The Impact of Colonialism versus the Impact of Nationalism in Thai Archaeology

Did nationality become a burden preventing us from reading the past in another light?
T. WINITCHAKUL, "SIAM MAPPED"

Both King Mongkut and his son, King Chulalongkorn, paid significant attention to investigating the past during the era of centralization. Under the absolute monarchy, the past was entirely controlled by the ruling elites, partly because they were the most literate members of society; therefore, historiography was limited to a small group of people. During the critical period of French expansion in mainland Southeast Asia, King Mongkut put his efforts into studying Thailand and defining the country in relation to neighboring states such as Cambodia. For example, during a dispute between Thailand and France over the control of Cambodian territory, he used a chronicle of Cambodian history to support the claim that Cambodia had been part of Thai territory for a long time (Kasetsiri 1976). This incident directly affected Thai historical writings on the Sukhothai period and the Khmer.

The inscription discovered by King Mongkut in 1833 (fig. 13.3) was accurately translated by the early twentieth century. Dating to the mid-thirteenth century, this inscription is key to the history of Sukhothai and Thailand since it is the oldest known writing in the Thai language. The kings used this inscription and historical documents, as well as ancient ruins, to promote Thai unity and resistance against the dominant French power that had already colonized much of Indochina by that time. They incorporated the centralist historical ideology Phongsawadan (or the traditional record of the Thai royal court) with the Western influence of centralized administration. Consequently, Sukhothai was treated as the

Figure 13.3. The Sukhothai inscription discovered by King Mongkut in 1833

source of national identity. It came to be regarded by the Thai ruling elite as the first independent state of Thai people in the central region. Before this discovery, Thai history dated back only to the Ayutthaya period (ca. AD 1351–1767). The new Thai cultural historical chronology listed Sukhothai as the first national capital, predating Ayutthaya and Bangkok.

This interpretation of Sukhothai, however, contradicts the factual archaeological record. First, from an archaeologist's perspective, the first Thai inscription is only a single archaeological artifact among many. But it is evident that the kings relied more heavily on this inscription than on any other evidence to establish a Thai historical chronology. They made little mention of the other ethnic groups and ancient states that existed earlier than Sukhothai or were contemporary with it. The existence of these other groups and states was excluded from the Thai historic chronology, even though earlier historical monuments had been reported by local and provincial administrators, as well as by Europeans. Not only were earlier ruins found in Sukhothai and its surrounding areas, but also earlier historical monuments were discovered throughout the modern area of Thailand (Fine Arts Department 1960, 1987; Vallibhotama et al. 1992). There was little effort to study the history of ancient monuments of these states, with the exception of Ayutthaya, considered to be the second Thai capital.

Second, the Thai ruling elites tried to deny the dominance of Khmer influence in the past. Owing to racial and linguistic variations in Thailand at that time, it was legitimate for them to oppose themselves to the Khmer. For instance, King Mongkut authorized his position as the king of the Thai nation ruling over Laos, Cambodia, and the Northern States (Saraya 1982: 88–89). This was the starting point of the idea of national unity with the king at the center as a symbol of unity. Nevertheless, clear evidence of Khmer influence existed among the archaeological remains, including a fragment of a Khmer-like sculpture of Jaya Buddha Mahanatha and early Khmer architectural styles in the Phra Phai Luang temple. Regarding the stone epigraphs, in fact, King Mongkut discovered not only the first Thai inscription but also a Khmer inscription believed to be of the same date (Bradley 1909). It should also be noted that the Thai alphabet was adapted from the Mon and Khmer scripts, as well as from Bali and Sanskrit (Coedès 1983b: 1–28). All of this indicates that before the Sukhothai period, various ethnic groups who used Khmer scripts already occupied the area encompassing Sukhothai territory. Recent archaeological research, in fact, shows that Sukhothai was not suddenly occupied by people of Thai ethnicity who claimed their independence from the Khmer empire, but rather Sukhothai developed through marriage-alliance relations (Fine Arts Department 1987, 1988; Kabuanseang 1976; Saraya 1991; Vallibhotama 1989; Vallibhotama et al. 1992; Wongthes 1983, 1986). There was no conclusive evidence that Khmer political elites ruled over Sukhothai.

Third, during King Chulalongkorn's administrative reformation, Sukhothai was used as an example of a centrally controlled state whose territory covered north, central, and southern Thailand. However, Southeast Asia states in the past did not have the same concept of boundaries as modern states do. It was believed that Sukhothai had ruled over most of the present territory of Thailand, whereas other early states had not (Winitchakul 1987). Sukhothai therefore provided the king with a legitimate example to support the establishment of a new territorial integration based on a modern map of Thailand.

Twentieth-Century Nationalism and Western Influence

Now let us turn to twentieth-century nationalism and Western influence in relation to interpretations of the past. Even though many Sukhothai inscriptions were discovered in archaeological sites, the first inscription has still received the most attention (Na Nagara and Griswold 1992). Its translation was completed in the nationalist period. It is a symbol of the Thai nation, its culture and history, and the royal institution. Therefore three preliminary points may be made.

First, the past was still under the control of a Western-educated monarchy. During the era of elite nationalism, when King Vajiravudh tried to limit the authority of the bureaucrats, his administration promoted a new political ideology that the nation and the monarchy were united. The king symbolized unity, and Bangkok was the center of Thailand. Following the concept of "nation, religion, and king," most historical writing and archaeological research strongly emphasized the Sukhothai city and the Thai kings. King Vajiravudh, who was known for his writing ability, wrote an article that expressed his own interpretation of Sukhothai ruins relating to the first Thai inscription. He specifically focused on the reign of King Ram Kamhaeng, the third king of the Phra Ruang dynasty of Sukhothai, who invented the Thai alphabet in 1283 and recorded state activities on the stone inscription in 1292 (Fine Arts Department 1935: 37–68). Sukhothai was viewed as the center of the kingdom that flourished under his rule. However, this narrative also contradicts archaeological data. The epigraphic data from the Srichum temple and the first Thai inscription (Na Nagara and Griswold 1992), together with archaeological evidence (Vallibhotama 1989), indicate that Sukhothai was a small city when it was first established and not the only important city. There were three other important cities: Srisatchanalai, Sraluang, and Songkwae.

Furthermore, it was not until the reign of King Lithai, the sixth king of Sukhothai, in the first half of the fourteenth century, that the Sukhothai state reached its highest point as a Buddhist center of the region.

Second, the ideology of conquest gradually came to play an important role in the process of nationalism. Militarism became an important implement for the political movement under the king's leadership. Using Sukhothai as an example, his propaganda claimed the nation and the Thai language for the Thai ethnic group, establishing a firm basis for the assertion that they had fought for independence from their hostile neighbors, such as the Khmer and the Burmese (Kesboonchoo 1987: 115). Since the French had conducted extensive studies on the epigraphy (Coedès 1968) and the art history of the Khmer empire, the contact in particular with French scholars, no doubt, impacted the way those scholars interpreted the Sukhothai past. Archaeological research in Thailand proceeded in the same direction as French archaeology; in particular, similar art styles were viewed as evidence of migration by outsiders who brought new ideology, techniques, and innovations. This methodology was a new tool that helped to support Thai historiography.

Third, there were also attempts to search for origins of the Thai people. Following the conquest ideology, concerns relating to racial identity led to another type of nationalist ideology in the military era (Wongthes 1986). Strong nationalism was promoted by wartime experiences and greatly influenced by Nazi ideology. Research on the Thai "race" was encouraged by military leaders, in response to growing Chinese economic control and Chinese nationalism in Thailand (Wongthes 1983; Wyatt 1984: 252–260). Moreover, the historical name of the country, Siam, was changed to Thailand in 1939. Many theories on Thai origins have been proposed by both Thai and Western scholars (e.g., Sangvichein et al. 1969; Terwiel et al. 1990) that I will not address in this chapter. The main hypothesis, which is still considered in textbooks today, is that the Thai originally lived in northern China; when the Chinese invaded their land, they migrated to the south and settled in the present Thai territory. Currently, there is an agreement among scholars that the Thai generally originated in South China (e.g., Wongthes 1983). Finally, they defeated the Khmer and claimed their independence by establishing the Sukhothai kingdom.

The study of past and present Thai culture has been under the Fine Arts Department of the Ministry of Education since 1933. Thus, archaeology is under government control. During the period of military nationalism, a director of this department, Luang Wichitwathakan, played an important role in promoting the idea of the great Thai race (Kasetsiri 1979: 166–167). His notion of Sukhothai did not focus on the kings, the capital cities, or the royal dynasties but rather on the Thai people, the Chinese invasion, and the Thai conquest of indigenous peoples before forming the first Thai state. However, archaeological evidence (Fine Arts Department 1987, 1988) indicates that peoples from different races, cultures, and religions have inhabited the region within present Thai boundaries since prehistoric times (e.g., Anderson 1990; Charoenwongsa and Bronson 1988; Fine Arts Department 1987; Glover et al. 1992; Gorman 1970; Gorman and Charoenwongsa 1976; Silpakorn University 1993; Smith and Watson 1979; You-Di 1986). Before Sukhothai, other states existed (e.g., Fine Arts Department 1987; Saraya 1991; Vallibhotama et al. 1992). Therefore, it is clear that Sukhothai, a kingdom of the Thai, did not develop simply by conquering other indigenous states. Rather, people of diverse ethnic groups and cultural traditions have assimilated for many centuries. My point is that modern Thai culture emerged as a product of the interaction among Thai, Khmer, Laotian, Malay, Mon, and immigrant Chinese communities over many hundreds of years. Most importantly, the concept of the Thai identity, which in modern Thai refers to language, culture, and so on, was all created under the development of the Thai nation-state during the colonial period.

Conclusion

Having synthesized and examined the relationships between politics and archaeological interpretation, I conclude that Thai nationalism emerged in response to Western colonialism by incorporating its own perceptions of the past with Western ideas. The Sukhothai case clearly shows us that the past was one of the most important tools used by the ruling elites and political leaders to legitimate their political power over the Thai, other indigenous peoples, and the Chinese. Thai nationalism demonstrates that colonialism and nationalism can be interdependent processes and not exhibit a clear-cut dichotomy. Moreover, perceptions of the past might be interpreted differently by different levels of society, as well as by different ethnic groups within the same nation. This issue needs to be pursued in the future.

Final Remark

Unfortunately, from an archaeological perspective, several questions regarding the Sukhothai state still remain unanswered, such as how Sukhothai emerged, why people settled there, what its relationships were with other states, and so on. Moreover, the first Thai inscription still plays an important role in directing Thai history and archaeology. It remains a symbol of the Thai nation, independence, and monarchy (Peleggi 2002). In 1978 the government designated Sukhothai as the first historical park in Thailand (fig. 13.4), and major archaeological excavations, restoration, and conservation have been conducted primarily in the old city of Sukhothai and nearby ancient cities, using the descriptions in the first Thai inscription as a guide. In 1988 the park was officially opened in honor of the king's sixtieth birthday. Yet, very little active archaeological research since 1980 has been directed toward unanswered questions regarding the Sukhothai state. The entire state is a popular tourist site in Thailand, and in 1991 Sukhothai was included in the World Heritage List. Although recent archaeological investigations at prehistoric and historic sites in various regions of the country have provided us with more information regarding cultural developments in different parts of Thailand, Sukhothai is still known by most of the Thai people as the first capital of Thailand!

I would like to end with a classic statement of His Majesty the King of Thailand on his visit to the Ayutthaya historical site in 1963.

> A new building is the pride of its builder, but an ancient structure is the pride of the nation. One single ancient brick is valuable and should be preserved. Without Sukhothai, Ayutthaya and Bangkok, Thailand would be meaningless. (Charoenwongsa n.d.)

Acknowledgments

An earlier version of this chapter was presented at the fifty-ninth annual meeting of the Society for American Archaeology, Anaheim, California, April 20–24, 1994. However, I am aware that there are current debates whether the inscription is authentic. Since this debate is still going on, I do not address it in my discussion. My special thanks are extended to Prof. Philip Kohl and Dr. Nandini Rao, who encouraged me to publish this chapter. I also thank Dr. Mara Kozelsky for editing this final version in 2004. I thank Frances Hayashida, Carla Sinopoli, and Tristine Smart for their insightful comments on an earlier version. I would like to extend my sincere gratitude to my friend Tristine Smart, who has discussed the issues of indigenous peoples versus archaeologists with me over the years. I am grateful to Wanni Wibunsawadi Anderson, Wiyada Akarawut, and Elisabeth Bacus for their suggestions along the way. In addition, I thank

Figure 13.4. Sukhothai Historical Park, a World Heritage site

Thongchai Winitchakul, who provided the initial inspiration for this discussion. My special appreciation goes to Carla Sinopoli and Larry Zimmerman, who encouraged and supported my efforts throughout. Finally, I thank Pipad Krajaejun, my research assistant, for preparing the maps.

References

Anderson, D. 1990. *Lang Rongrien Rockshelter: Pleistocene–Early Holocene Archaeological Site from Krabi, South-Western Thailand*. Philadelphia: University of Pennsylvania Press.

Audouze, F., and A. Leroi-Gourahan. 1982. France: A continental insularity. *World Archaeology* 13 (2): 170–189.

Bleed, P. 1986. Almost archaeology: Early archaeological interest in Japan. In *Windows of the Japanese Past: Studies in Archaeology and Prehistory*, edited by R. J. Pearson, G. Barne, and K. L. Hutterer, 57–70. Ann Arbor: University of Michigan Press.

Bradley, C. B. 1909. The oldest known writing in Siamese. *Journal of Siam Society* 6 (1): 1–64.

Bray, W., and I. C. Glover. 1987. Scientific investigation or cultural imperialism: British archaeology in the Third World. *Institute of Archaeology Bulletin* 24:109–125.

Chakrabarti, D. K. 1982. The development of archaeology in the Indian subcontinent. *World Archaeology* 13 (3): 326–344.

Chang, K. C. 1981. Archaeology and Chinese historiography. World Archaeology 13 (2): 156–169.

Charoenwongsa, P. n.d. Implementation of Cultural Policy on Cultural Heritage. In author's file.

Charoenwongsa, P., and B. Bronson, eds. 1988. *Prehistoric Studies: The Stone and Metal Ages in Thailand*. Bangkok: Thai Studies Working Group.

Chatterjee, P. 1993. *Nationalist Thought and the Colonial World*. Minneapolis: University of Minnesota Press.

Chumchantra, Y. 1987. Thai historiography, 1932–1973 [in Thai]. Master's thesis, Chulalongkorn University, Bangkok.

Coedès, G. 1968. *The Indianized States of Southeast Asia*, edited by W. F. Vella, translated by S. B. Brown. Honolulu: University of Hawaii Press.

Coedès, G. 1983a. *The Making of Southeast Asia*, translated by H. M. Wright. Berkeley: University of California Press.

Coedès, G. 1983b. *Tamnan Egsorn Thai, Tamnan Phrapim, Kan Kudkon thi Pong Tuk* [History of Thai letter, Buddha amulet, and excavation at Pong Tuk site]. Bangkok: Suksaphan.

Davis, B. 1989. *The Siam Society under Five Reigns*. Bangkok: Amarin Printing Group.

Dhiravegin, L. 1974. *Siam and Colonialism (1855–1909)*. Bangkok: Thai Watana Panich.

Dirks, N. B. 1992. *Colonialism and Culture*. Ann Arbor: University of Michigan Press.

Dixon, C. 1993. *Southeast Asia in the World-Economy: A Regional Geography*. Cambridge: Cambridge University Press.

Fine Arts Department. 1935. *Pramuan Phraborommarachathibai kieokap phrawatisat Siam* [Compiled works on the history of Siam], by King Vajaraudh. Bangkok: Damrong Tham.

Fine Arts Department, Ministry of Education, Thailand. 1960. *Archaeological Seminar on Sukhothai* [in Thai]. Bangkok: Siwaporn.

Fine Arts Department, Ministry of Education, Thailand. 1987. *Four Regional Archaeology* [in Thai]. Bangkok: Hathasilpa Kanpim.

Fine Arts Department, Ministry of Education, Thailand. 1988. *Sukhothai, the City of Phra Ruang* [in Thai with English summary]. Bangkok: Fine Arts Department.

Forest, A. 1990. State, problems, and perspectives of research concerning Southeast Asia in France: "A Great Tradition and Its Vicissitudes." In *Asian Studies Programs for Japanese Universities*, edited by T. Takefumi and V. Cyril, 1:70–96. Tokyo: Institute of Asian Culture, Sophia University.

Glover, I. C., and E. Glover, eds. 1990. *Southeast Asian Archaeology 1986: Proceedings of the First Conference of the Association of Southeast Asian Archaeologists in Western Europe*. International Series 561. Oxford: British Archaeological Reports (BAR).

Glover, I., P. Suchitta, and J. Villier, eds. 1992. *Early Metallurgy Trade and Urban Centres in Thailand and Southeast Asia*. Bangkok: White Lotus.

Gorman, C. F. 1970. Excavations at Spirit Cave, north Thailand: Some interim interpretations. *Asian Perspectives* 13:79–107.

Gorman, C., and P. Charoenwongsa. 1976. Ban Chiang: A mosaic of impressions from the first two years. *Expedition* 8 (4): 14–26.

Gosden, C. 2004. *Archaeology and Colonialism: Cultural Contact from 5,000 BC to Present*. Cambridge: Cambridge University Press.

Higham, C. F. W. 1989. *The Archaeology of Mainland Southeast Asia from 10,000 BC to the Fall of Angkor*. Cambridge: Cambridge University Press.

Ikawa-Smith, F. 1982. Co-traditions in Japanese archaeology. *World Archaeology* 13 (3): 296–309.

Janse, R. T. 1941. An archaeological expedition to Indo-China and the Philippines: Preliminary report. *Harvard Journal of Asiatic Studies* 6:1–54.

Kabuanseang, S. 1976. *History of Sukhothai* [in Thai]. Bangkok: Pikanesa.

Kasetsiri, C. 1976. *The Rise of Ayutthaya*. Kuala Lumpur: Oxford University Press.

Kasetsiri, C. 1979. Thai historiography from ancient time to the modern period. In *Perceptions of the Past in Southeast Asia*, edited by A. Reid and D. Marr. Singapore: Heinemann Educational Books (Asia).

Kesboonchoo, K. 1987. Official nationalism under King Vajiravudh. In *Proceedings of the International Conference on Thai Studies, Australian National University, Canberra, 3–6 July, 1987*, compiled by A. Buller, vol. 3, part 1, pp. 107–120. Canberra: Australian National University.

Kohl, P., and C. Fawcett, eds. 1995. *Nationalism, Politics, and the Practice of Archaeology*. Cambridge: Cambridge University Press.

Layton, R., ed. 1989. *Conflict in the Archaeology of Living Traditions*. One World Archaeology series, no. 8. London: Unwin Hyman.

Mangi, J. 1989. The role of archaeology in nation building. In *Conflict in the Archaeology of Living Traditions*, edited by R. Layton, 217–226. One World Archaeology series, no. 8. London: Unwin Hyman.

McGuire, R. 1994. Abstract of session "Archaeology as a Colonial Endeavor." 59th annual meeting of the Society for American Archaeology, Anaheim, CA, April 20–24.

Moore, E., P. Stott, and S. Sukhasvasti. 1996. *Ancient Capital of Thailand*. Bangkok: Asia Books.

Murray, T. 1993. Communication and the importance of disciplinary communities: Who owns the past? In *Archaeological Theory: Who Sets the Agenda?* edited by N. Yoffee and A. Sherratt. Cambridge: Cambridge University Press.

Na Nagara, P., and A. B. Griswold. 1992. *Epigraphic and Historical Studies*. Bangkok: Roondsaeng Karnpim.

Peleggi, M. 2002. *The Politics of Ruins and the Business of Nostalgia*. Bangkok: White Lotus.

Peterson, W. 1982–1983. Colonialism, cultural history, and Southeast Asian History. *Asian Perspectives* 15 (1): 123–132.

Sangvichein, S., P. Sirigaroon, J. B. Jongensen, and T. Jacob. 1969. *Archaeological Excavations in Thailand*. Vol. 3, *Ban Kao*. Part 2, The prehistoric skeletons. Copenhagen: Mugaard.

Saraya, D. 1982. *Tamnan and Tamnan—History in the Study of Local-History* [in Thai and English]. Bangkok: Office of the National Cultural Commission.

Saraya, D. 1991. *(Sri) Dvaravati: The Initial Phase of Siam's History* [in Thai with English summary]. Bangkok: Muang Boran.

Senanarong, S., and N. Ngamnisai. 1987. *Thai Atlas* [in Thai]. Bangkok: Aksorncharoenthat.

Shoocongdej, R. 1992. Conversations across the continent. *Southeast Asian Archaeology International Newsletter* 2:2–4.

Silpakorn University. 1993. *Recent Archaeological Research in Thailand: Franco-Thai Symposium, Silpakorn University, 9–11 December 1991*. Bangkok: Amarin Printing Group.

Smith, R., and W. Watson, eds. 1979. *Early Southeast Asia: Essays in Archaeology, History, and Historical Geography*. London: Oxford University Press.

Spriggs, M. 1991. Facing the nation: Archaeologists and Hawaiians in the era of sovereignty. *Contemporary Pacific* 3 (2): 380–392.

Spriggs, M. 1992. Alternative prehistories for Bougainville: Regional, national, or micronational. *Contemporary Pacific* 4 (2): 269–298.

Steinberg, D. J., ed. 1987. *In Search of Southeast Asia: A Modern History*. Rev. ed. Honolulu: University of Hawaii Press.

Stone, P., and R. Mackenzie, eds. 1990. *The Excluded Past: Archaeology in Education*. One World Archaeology series, no. 17. London: Unwin Hyman.

Terwiel, B. J., A. Diller, and C. Satayawattana, eds. 1990. *Ancient Tai Were Not Here* [in Thai]. Bangkok: Muang Boran.

Trigger, B. 1984. Alternative archaeology: Nationalist, colonialist, imperialist. *Man* 19:355–370.

Trigger, B. 1989. *A History of Archaeological Thought*. Cambridge: Cambridge University Press.

Trigger, B., and I. Glover, eds. 1981. Regional Traditions of Archaeological Research I. *World Archaeology* 13 (2): 133–255.

Trigger, B., and I. Glover, eds. 1982. Regional Traditions of Archaeological Research II. *World Archaeology* 13 (3): 271–394.

Vallibhotama, S. 1989. *Ancient Settlement of Sukhothai State* [in Thai with English summary]. Bangkok: Thammasart University Press.

Vallibhotama, S., P. Jiajanpongs, and D. Saraya. 1992. Siam before the fourteenth century. In *Essays in Thai History*, edited by V. Snidvongs. Singapore: Southeast Asian Studies Program.

Wan Waithayakon, H. R. H. 1965. *Stone Inscriptions of Sukhothai.* Translation from *L'inscription du roi Rama Gamhen de Sukhodaya* (1292 A.D.) by George Coedès, 1924, 9–10. Bangkok: Siam Society.

Winitchakul, T. 1987. Siam mapped: A history of the geo-body of Siam. In *Proceedings of the International Conference on Thai Studies, Australian National University, Canberra, 3–6 July, 1987*, compiled by A. Buller, 1:155–164. Canberra: Australian National University.

Winitchakul, T. 1988. Siam mapped: A history of the geo-body of Siam. Ph.D. diss., University of Sydney.

Wongthes, S. 1983. *Sukhothai Was Not the First Capital of Thailand* [in Thai]. Bangkok: Chao Phraya Kanpim.

Wongthes, S. 1986. *The Thais Were Always Here: A Social and Cultural History of the Siamese People in Thailand* [in Thai]. Bangkok: Ruankao Kanpim.

Wyatt, D. 1984. *Thailand: A Short History*. New Haven, CT: Yale University Press.

Wyatt, D. 1987. Social change and the emergence of nationalism: Siam. In *In Search of Southeast Asia: A Modern History*, edited by D. J. Steinberg, 324–331. Honolulu: University of Hawaii Press.

Contributors

KAMYAR ABDI was born and raised in Iran and received a BA in archaeology from Tehran University. In 1994 he came to the United States to continue his education. He received his PhD in anthropology from the University of Michigan in 2002. Since then he has been an assistant professor of anthropology at Dartmouth College. He continues to do fieldwork in Iran despite escalating political tensions and increasing bureaucratic obstacles.

UZI BARAM, associate professor of anthropology at New College of Florida, is a historical archaeologist. His principal area of research has been the Middle East, where he has engaged in Ottoman-period archaeology, analyzed Western travel accounts of the region, and studied the intersection of tourism and archaeology. He edited and contributed to *A Historical Archaeology of the Ottoman Empire: Breaking New Ground*; *Marketing Heritage: Archaeology and the Consumption of the Past*; and *Between Art and Artifact: Approaches to Visual Representations in Historical Archaeology*.

NACHMAN BEN-YEHUDA is professor of sociology in the Department of Sociology and Anthropology at Hebrew University in Jerusalem. He has long been interested in studying unconventional social behavior. His written work deals with the European witch craze (1980), deviance and morality (1985), politics and deviance (1990), moral panics (1986), political assassinations (1993), betrayals and treason (2001), and terror and morality (2005). Two of his books that are highly relevant to this collection, *The Masada Myth* (1995) and *Sacrificing Truth* (2002), examined the way archaeologists used the Masada myth in the excavations of Masada. Currently he researches patterns of unconventional and nonconformist social behavior among fundamentalist Jews.

MAGNUS T. BERNHARDSSON teaches Middle Eastern history at Williams College in Massachusetts. He received his PhD from Yale University in 1999 and is the author of *Reclaiming a Plundered Past: Archaeology and Nation Building in Modern Iraq* (Texas, 2005) and a book in Icelandic on Iraq and Iran in the twentieth century. He is currently working on a cultural and political history of 1950s Baghdad.

MICHAEL FEIGE, a sociologist and anthropologist who specializes in Israeli society, collective memory, and political myth, is currently director of the Israeli Studies Program at Ben-Gurion University of the Negev, Israel. He has written numerous books and articles, including most recently *Settling in the Hearts: Fundamentalism, Time, and Space in the Occupied Territories* (Wayne State University Press, forthcoming), and is the coeditor (with Z. Shilony) of *Archeology, Religion, and Nationalism in Israel* (Ben-Gurion Institute, forthcoming).

MURTAZALI S. GADJIEV studied at the Institute of Archaeology in Moscow from 1978 to 1981. He currently is professor at the Institute of History, Archaeology, and Ethnography of the Daghestan Scientific Center of the Russian Academy of Sciences in Makhachkala and directs the Derbent Archaeological Expedition. He is the author of more than 160 scientific works, including the monographs (in Russian) *Between Europe and Asia: Trade Contacts of Daghestan in the Albano-Sarmatian Period* (Makhachkala, 1997) and *Ancient Cities of Daghestan: Experience of Historic-Topographical and Socio-Economic Analysis* (Moscow, 2002) and (with V. A. Kuznetsov and I. M. Chechenov) *History in the Mirror of Para-Science: Critique of the Modern Ethnocentrist Historiography of the Northern Caucasus* (Moscow, 2006).

PHILIP L. KOHL is professor of anthropology and Davis Professor of Slavic Studies at Wellesley College. Articles and books that he has authored or edited number more than 150; one is the collected volume *Nationalism, Politics, and the Practice of Archaeology* (Cambridge University Press, 1995), which he coedited with C. Fawcett. His most recent book is *The Making of Bronze Age Eurasia,* which appeared in the Cambridge World Archaeology Series in 2007. He has conducted extensive archaeological fieldwork in the Near East, Central Asia, and the Caucasus.

MARA KOZELSKY is assistant professor of history at the University of South Alabama and teaches courses in Russian history, nationalism, and religious conflict. Currently she is completing a book about the controversy over religious ruins in Crimea, titled *The Paradox of Holy Places: Crimean Athos in Russian Political Culture.*

GHEORGHE ALEXANDRU NICULESCU is a senior researcher at the Vasile Pârvan Institute of Archaeology in Bucharest, Romania, and teaches archaeological theory in the History Department of Bucharest University.

SHEREEN RATNAGAR was professor of archaeology at Jawaharlal Nehru University until recently. Specializing in the Harappa civilization (*The End of the Great*

Harappan Tradition [Manohar, 2002]; *Trading Encounters between the Euphrates and the Indus* [Oxford University Press, 2004]) and pursuing an interest in pastoral peoples (*The Other Indians: Three Essays* [2004]), she is one of a few scholars who have persistently contested interpretations of the past that are devised to target minorities.

WENDY M. K. SHAW received her PhD from the Department of Art History at the University of California, Los Angeles, in 1999. She has taught at several universities in the United States and in Turkey and currently is employed by the Istanbul Museum of Modern Art. Among her publications are *Possessors and Possessed: Museums, Archaeology, and the Visualization of History in the Late Ottoman Empire* (University of California Press, 2003) and many journal articles.

VICTOR A. SHNIRELMAN, chief researcher at the Institute of Ethnology and Anthropology, Russian Academy of Sciences, Moscow, is the author of about three hundred publications, including several books on archaeology, social anthropology, history, and contemporary ethno-politics. Among his books are *Who Gets the Past? Competition for Ancestors among Non-Russian Intellectuals in Russia* (Woodrow Wilson Press and Johns Hopkins University Press, 1996), *Russian Neo-Pagan Myths and Anti-Semitism* (Hebrew University of Jerusalem, 1998), *The Value of the Past: Myths, Identity, and Politics in Transcaucasia* (National Museum of Ethnology, Osaka, 2001), and *The Myth of the Khazars and Intellectual Antisemitism in Russia, 1970s–1990s* (Hebrew University of Jerusalem, 2002). His interests focus on ethnicity and nationalism in historical perspective, politics of the past, and social memory.

RASMI SHOOCONGDEJ, whose PhD is from the University of Michigan, is assistant professor of Archaeology and a former chair of the Department of Archaeology, Silpakorn University, in Bangkok. Her areas of interest include late-Pleistocene to post-Pleistocene foragers in the tropics, Southeast Asian prehistory, cave archaeology, and archaeology and ethnic education. At present she is the principal investigator of the Highland Archaeological Project in Pang Mapha, Mae Hong Son Province, northwestern Thailand. She is also the cofounder and coeditor (with Elisabeth Bacus) of the *Southeast Asian Archaeology International Newsletter*, which was established in 1992. Besides her professional activities, she has been intensively involved with local communities and the Thai general public on heritage protections and archaeological education.

GHADA ZIADEH-SEELY is adjunct professor of anthropology at Old Dominion University. She initially studied archaeology at Birzeit University under Albert Glock and then earned her MA degree in ethno-archaeology from Washington University, St. Louis, and her PhD in archaeology from the University of Cambridge. Her research focus is Palestinian archaeology and ethnography.

Index

Page numbers in italics indicate illustrations.